Most studies of gender differences in language use have been undertaken from exclusively either a sociocultural or a biological perspective. By contrast, this innovative volume places the analysis of language and gender in the context of a *biocultural* framework, examining both cultural *and* biological sources of gender differences in language, as well as the interaction between them.

The first two parts of the volume focus on cultural variation in gender-differentiated language use, comparing Western English-speaking societies with societies elsewhere in the world. The essays are distinguished by an emphasis on the *syntax*, rather than style or strategy, of gender-differentiated forms of discourse. They show how men and women, and boys and girls, often control different forms of discourse but also often carry out the same forms differently through different choices of language form. These gender differences are shown to be socially organized, although the essays in Part I also raise the possibility that some cross-cultural similarities in the ways males and females differentially use language may be related to sex-based differences in physical and emotional makeup. Part III examines the relationship between language and the brain and shows that although there are differences between the ways males and females process language in the brain, these do not yield any differences in linguistic competence or language use.

Taken as a whole, the essays reveal a great diversity in the cultural construction of gender through language and explicitly show that while there is some evidence of the influence of biologically based sex differences on the language of women and men, the influence of culture is far greater, and gender differences in language use are better accounted for in terms of culture than in terms of biology. The collection will appeal widely to anthropologists, psychologists, linguists, and others concerned with the understanding of gender roles.

Studies in the Social and
Cultural Foundations of Language No. 4

Language, gender, and sex in comparative perspective

Studies in the Social and Cultural Foundations of Language

The aim of this series is to develop theoretical perspectives on the essential social and cultural character of language by methodological and empirical emphasis on the occurrence of language in its communicative and interactional settings, on the socio-culturally grounded "meanings" and "functions" of linguistic forms, and on the social scientific study of language use across cultures. It will thus explicate the essentially ethnographic nature of linguistic data, whether spontaneously occurring or experimentally induced, whether normative or variational, whether synchronic or diachronic. Works appearing in the series will make substantive and theoretical contributions to the debate over the sociocultural–functional and structural–formal nature of language and will represent the concerns of scholars in the sociology and anthropology of language, anthropological linguistics, sociolinguistics, and socioculturally informed psycholinguistics.

1. Charles L. Briggs: *Learning how to ask: a sociolinguistic appraisal of the role of the interview in social science research*
2. Tamar Katriel: *Talking straight: "Dugri" speech in Israeli "sabra" culture*
3. Bambi B. Schieffelin and Elinor Ochs (eds.): *Language socialization across cultures*
4. Susan U. Philips, Susan Steele, and Christine Tanz (eds.): *Language, gender, and sex in comparative perspective*
5. Jeff Siegel: *Language contact in a plantation environment: a sociolinguistic history of Fiji*

Language, gender, and sex in comparative perspective

Edited by

Susan U. Philips, Susan Steele, and Christine Tanz

University of Arizona

The right of the
University of Cambridge
to print and publish
all kinds of books
was granted by law
in 1534.
The University has printed
and published continuously
since 1584.

CAMBRIDGE UNIVERSITY PRESS

Cambridge
New York   New Rochelle
Melbourne   Sydney

Published by the Press Syndicate of the University of Cambridge
The Pitt Building, Trumpington Street, Cambridge CB2 1RP
32 East 57th Street, New York, NY 10022, USA
10 Stamford Road, Oakleigh, Melbourne 3166, Australia

First published 1987
Reprinted 1988

Printed in the United States of America

Library of Congress Cataloging-in-Publication Data
Language, gender, and sex in comparative perspective.
(Studies in the social and cultural foundations of language)
Bibliography: p.
Includes index.
1. Language and languages – Sex difference.
2. Language and languages – Physiological aspects.
3. Children – Language. I. Philips, Susan Urmston.
II. Steele, Susan. III. Tanz, Christine. IV. Series.
P120.S48L35   1987   401'.9   86–17086

British Library Cataloguing in Publication Data
Language, gender, and sex in comparative
perspective – (Studies in the social and
cultural foundations of language; 4)
1. Language and languages – Sex differences
I. Philips, Susan U. II. Steele, Susan
III. Tanz, Christine IV. Series
418   P120.S48

ISBN 0 521 32849 7 hard covers
ISBN 0 521 33807 7 paperback

In memory of Shelly Rosaldo
and her vision of feminist ethnography

Contents

Acknowledgments   *page*   ix
List of contributors   xi

Introduction: The interaction of social and biological
                processes in women's and men's speech   1
Susan U. Philips

Part I   Women's and men's speech in cross-cultural perspective

Introduction   15
Susan U. Philips
  1 The womanly woman: manipulation of stereotypical and
     nonstereotypical features of Japanese female speech   26
     Janet S. Shibamoto
  2 The impact of stratification and socialization on men's
     and women's speech in Western Samoa   50
     Elinor Ochs
  3 The interaction of variable syntax and discourse structure
     in women's and men's speech   71
     Susan U. Philips and Anne Reynolds·
  4 A diversity of voices: men's and women's speech in
     ethnographic perspective   95
     Joel Sherzer
  5 Women's speech in modern Mexicano   121
     Jane H. Hill

Part II   Gender differences in the language of children

Introduction   163
Christine Tanz
  6 Preschool boys' and girls' language use in pretend play   178
     Jacqueline Sachs
  7 Sex differences in parent–child interaction   189
     Jean Berko Gleason
  8 Children's arguing   200
     Marjorie Harness Goodwin and Charles Goodwin
  9 Do different worlds mean different words?: an example
     from Papua New Guinea   249
     Bambi B. Schieffelin

Part III   Sex differences in language and the brain

Introduction   263
Susan Steele
 10 Cerebral organization and sex: interesting but complex   268
     Walter F. McKeever
 11 Sex differences in the patterns of scalp-recorded
     electrophysiological activity in infancy: possible implications
     for language development   278
     David W. Shucard, Janet L. Shucard, and David G. Thomas

References   297
Index   323

Acknowledgments

We express our gratitude and our debt first to Myra Dinnerstein, Director of the Southwest Institute for Research on Women (SIROW) and head of Women's Studies at the University of Arizona. She drew us all into the activities of her two organizations and created and maintained a structure within which this book could come about. We are also grateful to the National Endowment for the Humanities for funding the Conference on Sex Differences in Language held at the University of Arizona in January 1983, where the papers published in this volume were first presented. The conference and the book-editing process were also supported by the University of Arizona Office of Research, under the direction of A. Richard Cassander. The Southwest Institute for Research on Women administered the funds, organized the conference, and provided support during the editing of this book. We should particularly like to acknowledge the help given by Lynn Fleischman and Maureen Roen of SIROW. The authors of contributions to this volume have all agreed to donate their royalties to SIROW, as have the editors. The funds will be used to further study of sex differences and language. We appreciate the contributors' generosity. Finally, a number of students have given valuable assistance to us in various phases of the conference and book editing. We thank, in particular, Barbara Ballou, Betsy Larson, Anne Reynolds, Sirpa Saletta, Peggy Spea, and Miriam Stark.

SUP
SS
CT

ix

Contributors

JEAN BERKO GLEASON is Professor of Psychology at Boston University and chairs the department. She holds a joint degree in linguistics and psychology from Harvard and has been conducting research on language development in children for more than twenty-five years. She began to work on sex differences in language in the early 1970s, and her research has been supported by the National Science Foundation. She published some of the first work on fathers' speech, and she has continued to be active in the field. Currently, she is studying the ways in which mothers and fathers use language to socialize their children.

CHARLES GOODWIN, who received his Ph.D. degree in communication from the University of Pennsylvania, is an Associate Professor of Anthropology at the University of South Carolina. In his research he has been particularly interested in the interactive organization of language. His *Conversational Organization: Interaction Between Speakers and Hearers* provides extensive analysis of how actions of recipients are taken into account by speakers in the production of their talk.

MARJORIE HARNESS GOODWIN, who received her Ph.D. in anthropology from the University of Pennsylvania, is an Associate Professor of Anthropology at the University of South Carolina. She is the author of articles on corrections, directives, stories, play, dispute, and gossip in conversations of black children. A book systematizing her findings, *Language as Social Process: Conversational Practices in a Peer Group of Urban Black Children*, is being prepared for publication.

JANE H. HILL is Professor of Anthropology at the University of Arizona. Her primary interests are in the sociolinguistics of American Indian languages, concentrating on Uto-Aztecan languages. She has done fieldwork on Cupeno, Mexicano, and Tohonno O'odham (Papago). She is an author of *Mulu'wetam: The First People* (with Roscinda Nolasques) and *Speaking Mexicano* (with Kenneth C. Hill), as well as many articles in linguistic and anthropological journals.

WALTER F. MCKEEVER is Professor and Chairman of the Department of Psychology at Northern Arizona University. Previously he was Professor of Psychology at Bowling Green State University. He received his doctorate in clinical psychology from the University of Rochester. Dr. McKeever's research interests are primarily in human experimental neuropsychology, particularly in the areas of hemispheric specialization of function and individual differences in patterns of cerebral organization.

ELINOR OCHS is Professor of Linguistics at the University of Southern California. Her research areas include the study of discourse and the acquisition of language. A major focus in recent years has been the relation of discourse organization to social order and cultural knowledge among groups of speaker-hearers. With her colleague Bambi B. Schieffelin, Ochs has analyzed ways in which young children and other novices acquire knowledge of society and culture through acquiring discourse competence. She is the author of *The Acquisition of Language and Culture: A Samoan Study*, co-author with Schieffelin of *Acquiring Conversational Competence*, and coeditor with Schieffelin of *Developmental Pragmatics* and *Language Socialization Across Cultures*. Ochs has been a Guggenheim fellow and a recipient of several grant awards to carry out research on language use and language acquisition in Malagasy, Western Samoan, and white middle-class American communities.

SUSAN U. PHILIPS is Professor of Anthropology at the University of Arizona, with major research interests in language and gender, language socialization, and language and law. The author of *The Invisible Culture: Communication in Classroom and Community on the Warm Springs Indian Reservation*, she recently began ethnographic research on language use in the Polynesian kingdom of Tonga.

ANNE REYNOLDS is currently a research evaluator with the Chapter I Program of the Tucson Unified School District in Tucson, Arizona. She received her Ph.D. degree in cultural anthropology from the University of Arizona. Her dissertation, *Socialization as an Interactional Process: A Comparison of Two Day Care Centers*, analyzed linguistic and interactional processes in child-care centers serving Hispanic, Anglo, and black populations. In addition to her dissertation, her publications include "The Effect of Ethnicity on the Socialization of Gender Differences in the Day Care Center" and "Child Care Practices in Four African

Societies: A Controlled Comparison." Her research interests include sociocultural variation in the socialization process, patterns of language use in the classroom, bilingual education, and the education of native American groups.

JACQUELINE SACHS is Professor of Communication Sciences, Linguistics, and Psychology at the University of Connecticut in Storrs. She received her Ph.D. in psychology at the University of California, Berkeley. Her research has focused on the child's acquisition of linguistic and communicative competence in the social contexts of adult–child and child–child interaction.

BAMBI B. SCHIEFFELIN is an Assistant Professor of Anthropology at New York University. She has conducted research in the United States and Papua New Guinea on socialization and the communicative development of young children. She coedited *Developmental Pragmatics* and *Language Socialization Across Cultures* and co-authored *Acquiring Conversational Competence* – all with Elinor Ochs. Her most recent work among the Kaluli of Papua New Guinea focuses on language use and social change.

JOEL SHERZER is Professor of Anthropology and Linguistics at the University of Texas at Austin. His research interests are in sociolinguistics, ethnography of speaking, and speech play and verbal art, with a focus on the languages and cultures of native Americans. His book *Kuna Ways of Speaking* is an ethnography of speaking of the Kuna Indians of Panama.

JANET S. SHIBAMOTO, an Associate Professor of Japanese at the University of California, Davis, works on Japanese sociolinguistics and women's language. The author of *Japanese Women's Language*, she recently began work on scientific Japanese.

DAVID W. SHUCARD received a Ph.D. in psychology from the University of Denver. Currently the Director of the Division of Developmental and Behavioral Neurosciences in the Department of Neurology at the SUNY Buffalo School of Medicine, he has been affiliated with the National Jewish Hospital and the University of Colorado School of Medicine in Denver, Colorado. His research has focused on the study of the neurophysiology associated with cognitive processes and intellectual development.

JANET L. SHUCARD received a B.A. in psychology from the University of Denver. She recently began graduate work in the Department of Psychology at SUNY Buffalo. In the interim, she was a researcher in the Human Neurophysiology Laboratory at the National Jewish Hospital in Denver, Colorado.

SUSAN STEELE received her Ph.D. in linguistics from the University of California, San Diego. Currently Professor of Linguistics at the University of Arizona, she has also held positions at the University of New Mexico and Stanford University. Her research has focused on syntactic theory, linguistic universals, and the native languages of North America.

CHRISTINE TANZ is a psycholinguist specializing in children's acquisition of language. She has taught at the University of Illinois and the University of Arizona. She is the author of *Studies in the Acquisition of Deictic Terms*, published by Cambridge University Press in 1980.

DAVID G. THOMAS received his doctoral degree from the developmental psychology program at the University of Denver. He then worked in the Brain Sciences Laboratories at the National Jewish Hospital and Research Center in Denver before joining the Department of Psychology at Oklahoma State University. His research focuses on the physiological bases of perception and cognition, especially during infancy.

Introduction: The interaction of social and biological processes in women's and men's speech

SUSAN U. PHILIPS

An important focus of debate within the research on sex differences and language is the extent to which social and biological processes each contribute to differences in women's and men's speech and language. The disciplines that contribute research to the study of sex differences and language, particularly anthropology, linguistics, and psychology, have in common a view of human behavior as guided and directed by both biological and social processes. Yet within each discipline researchers tend to espouse either biological or social processes as the cause of gender-differentiated language-related behavior.

A major purpose in collecting the papers to be published as chapters in this book was to bring together disparate treatments of gender differentiation in language and language use, in the hope of gaining insight into the nature of the interaction of social and biological processes in this area. Part I, on cross-cultural studies of gender and language, and Part II, on language socialization, argue that there is enormous diversity in the role of language in the social construction of gender and that socialization effects appear at a very early age. Parents speak differently from each other; they speak differently to boys than to girls; and boys and girls speak differently. These two sections offer convincing testimony of human plasticity and of the ways in which biology does *not* constrain the nature of gender in human societies. Part III, on the other hand, is primarily concerned with language-related cognitive differences revealed in experimental tasks, which are taken as evidence of innate biologically based differences in language cognition. Thus, although the two major approaches to language have been brought together in this book, there is still a compartmentalization of causal perspectives here.

Because of that bifurcation, this introduction will focus on the possibility of integrating the two perspectives. The cross-cultural nature of

1

the studies in Parts II and III, which distinguishes this collection of articles, particularly allows us to address what is widespread in societies, and hence possibly influenced by biological processes. Attention will also be given to ways in which future research in both causal camps can facilitate the development of a more integrated perspective. The main issue here is the extent to which human role alternatives are limited or influenced by human biology.

In general, studies of gender view different amounts of sex hormones as the immediate cause of biological differences of diverse sorts between males and females. Several different kinds of biological consequences are distinguished in discussions of the impact of biological differences on gender. Here we shall distinguish among cognitive, emotional, and physical consequences of hormonal differences. Claims of cognitive differences refer to the possibility that women's mental capacities differ from those of men. Claims of emotional differences usually focus on male aggressiveness and female nurturing but may also be based, for example, on the idea that women are more emotional. The most common claim is that physical differences, particularly in that women carry and give birth to babies and that men are physically larger and stronger, influence role differentiation.

The issue to be considered first here, for which all three parts of the book are relevant, is whether or not there are sex-based cognitive differences in language-involved abilities and behaviors. As we shall see, in spite of Maccoby and Jacklin's (1974) claim that language is the only aspect of cognition in which there is evidence of sex differences, such evidence is in fact quite limited at present.

Discussion of cognitive differences will be followed by consideration of the extent to which there is evidence in the chapters of Part I and II of widespread cross-cultural similarities in the gender differentiation of speech of the sort typically related to physical and emotional differences between women and men.

Gender, language, and cognitive processes

The issue that is certainly distinctive in, and perhaps unique to, a focus on language is whether or not there are language-related cognitive differences between females and males that are manifest in language use and language-related behavior.

The disputed claim about cognitive differences is that women have language abilities innately superior to those of men. The other side of this claim is that men's visual–spatial skills are innately superior to women's. This purported difference in spatial abilities has been portrayed as a general mammalian difference related to differences in proportions of hormones, notably testosterone, associated also with the development of primary and secondary sexual characteristics (Buffery and Gray, 1972; Gray, 1971; Gray and Buffery, 1971).

Naturally, this is a politically sensitive issue. Considerable effort (e.g., Maccoby and Jacklin, 1974) has gone into demonstrating that there is no basis for the centuries-old views that men are inherently smarter than women and that gender differences in performance are related to differences in socialization and ideological conceptualization of appropriate gender role. Yet biologically grounded researchers persist in putting forth claims of innate differences, and these claims will not go away by being ignored.

The main kinds of information currently adduced as evidence of inherent sex differences in language-related cognition relate in one way or another to differences in the lateralization, or hemispheric differentiation, of language processing. McGlone (1980) argues that evidence from brain-damaged patients shows that men's and women's speech is impaired differently when there is trauma to the same areas. The differences suggest that women process speech more on the right side of the brain than do men. Women show less impairment of speech than men, overall, when the left side of the brain is traumatized, suggesting greater involvement of both hemispheres in language processing and less hemispheric specialization of cognitive functions than for men. A higher incidence among boys of speech and reading patterns defined as "problems" than for girls has been interpreted in a similar manner.

The findings associated with these so-called pathological circumstances are generally accepted and regarded as consistent and reliable, although, because of the way in which socialization and social context can influence biological processes, many would not accept the view that these differences are strictly biologically determined. Other sorts of evidence, including some presented in Part III, which indirectly measure performance in the decoding of language, are considered more controversial for two reasons. First, although what is being measured may be operationally defined, it is far from clear how what is measured relates to normal uses of language. Thus dichotic listening studies of the sort discussed by McKeever in Part III measure the speed and accuracy of the decoding of words for each ear, but how does this relate to what linguists recognize as linguistic competence in the form of knowledge of grammar and lexicon? The same question arises with respect to studies measuring electrical activity in the two hemispheres in response to music and speech, such as those described by Shucard, Shucard, and Thomas in Part III.

The second concern with methods such as dichotic hearing tests and the measurement of electrical activity in the brain is that the reliability of the methods of measurement is in question, because there has not been consistency in the results obtained in different experiments measuring the same behaviors. In part this has been due to the newness of these methods in application to such problems compared with the long-term use of data from brain-damaged or pathological populations, and to their changing application as these procedures are experimented with and become routinized over time. Regardless of these problems, results from such studies have been taken as evidence of biologically based differences in women's and men's language capacities.

It is important to recognize, however, that, underlying this generalization, different researchers within this general focus on differences in lateralization are saying somewhat different kinds of things, which may vary in their compatibility with arguments for the social origin of gender-differentiated behavior. A comparison of McKeever's chapter with that by Shucard, Shucard, and Thomas is instructive in this respect.

McKeever finds no significant differences between women's and men's performances for either ear on dichotic listening tests, except when sex is treated as interacting with family left-handedness, which, like femaleness, has been associated with a particular pattern of lateralization of hemispheric specialization of language functions. McKeever's results contradict earlier dichotic listening studies, which found women had superior left-ear performance, suggesting more involvement of the right hemisphere in task performance.

Shucard, Shucard, and Thomas find infant boys' and girls' evoked potential responses to outside stimuli to be patterned differently shortly after birth, and to become rapidly more differentiated, with females showing more lateralized responses to language stimuli in the left hemisphere earlier. Note that their study argues for earlier hemispheric specialization for girls. This characterization of early hemispheric specialization may conflict with the view of girls as less lateralized (and hence less subject to the ravages of brain damage) espoused by McGlone and others.

McKeever makes claims about adults, who have had far more time to be influenced by culture than the infants in the Shucard study, but neither study indicates how its results might be manifest in other behavioral domains, such as naturally occurring speech. McKeever believes the sex differences he documents are ultimately related to differences in the amounts of various sex hormones. He ties his work to the earlier tradition that postulates visual–spatial superiority for males and linguistic superiority for females, and the reader is given the sense that such differences are a direct result of the brain's being bathed with these hormones. The Shucard study does not attempt such causal links.

There is, then, considerable diversity among scholars in the biologically oriented tradition regarding how to characterize what are taken as innate sex differences in the processing of language.

The Shucard study raises another issue beyond those of female superiority or male–female differences in language processing, namely, the possibility that the developmental acquisition of language is different for boys and girls, with clearest evidence of language development being earlier for girls than for boys. Such a claim makes no commitment as to whether adult competence will be different, and is compatible with a view of males and females arriving at the same language competence via different developmental routes.

The Shucard study raises the possibility of different routes to the same competence, as do other studies, but there is no clear evidence of such developmental differences from studies that measure children's verbal output. The massive literature on language acquisition does not reveal developmental differences between boys and girls that scholars agree upon. Studies of language socialization such as those in Part II of this volume do not reveal differences in the forms controlled by boys and girls at ages two to five years, only differences in their frequency of use.

These same studies in Part II also make it dramatically clear how early culture makes its systematic impact on children's behavior. For two-year-olds, who are beginning the rapid progression from two-word utterances to full grammar by four years, on up, gender-differentiated speech to children is well documented, as are differences between boys and girls that reflect adult differences.

Nor is there evidence of cognitive differences between women and men in the Part I studies of adult language use in different societies. The possibility that such evidence may be found has been raised in response to the finding repeated in Labovian studies of urban dialect variation in a number of countries that women use fewer stigmatized and more prestige phonological alternates than men, so that their dialect can generally be characterized as more standard, or less nonstandard, than men's.

D. F. Jones and Jones (1975) have interpreted these data as related to women's being more conscious of proper language in their role as primary socializers of children and as transmitters of language and, through language, culture. They suggest that women have undergone a process of selective adaptation to make them better at this job. In other words, the variable difference between women's and men's dialects has been taken as evidence of female linguistic superiority in the form of heightened linguistic sensitivities.

If this view has ever been taken seriously, the studies described in Part I, most of which use methods similar to those of Labov, present evidence that lays it to rest. Most concretely, both Shibamoto for Japanese and Ochs for Samoan found that case markers, grammatical morphemes that indicate the roles nouns have in relation to the verbs in sentences, are deleted more by women than by men. This suggests that men's speech is syntactically more nearly complete or more surface-explicit in these languages, in the way women's speech is said to be in the Labovian studies just discussed. To the Westerner, more deletion is associated with less formality, so we would interpret the speech of Japanese and Samoan women as less formal than that of men in the same cultures. But this inference is not made among Japanese- and Samoan-speakers. Thus neither the behavior of women in Japan and Samoa nor the ideology is what it needs to be in order to be consistent with the earlier proposal that viewed shifts to more elaborate language forms by women as evidence of female linguistic superiority.

More generally, Part I reveals enormous diversity in the gender-differentiated aspects of language form, in their social organization in relation to other dimensions of social life or aspects of social context, and in the presence and nature of ideology about men and women and their speech. In light of that diversity, the Western pattern of women's greater use of preferred variants from standard rather than nonstandard dialectal varieties is revealed not as a dominant and widespread pattern but as one that is quite localized in Western European societies and some of their colonies. Thus dialect is not the most salient code organization affected by gender. Where there are variable code differences, they are not always subject to conscious awareness and evaluation, and where speech differences *are* evaluated, the evaluation is not always in terms of gender, and female speech is considered neither always good nor always bad.

The evidence of female superiority in language-related cognition from this book taken as a whole, then, is quite slim. We do find evidence of biologically based sex differences in the localization of language processing in the brain. But the nature of their relationship to language remains to be determined. There may be developmental differences between boys and girls in the emergence of localization of language functions. Thus far, however, there is no clear behavioral manifestation of such differences in direct measures of language output. There is no evidence of gender difference in control of the grammar and the lexicon of the language for any normal population at any age.

Gender, language, and physical and emotional processes

Thus far we have considered only claims regarding the direct effect of sex hormones on the brain in the form of sex differences in language-related cognition. But there are other, less direct, effects of sex hormones through their influence on physical primary and secondary sexual characteristics and on emotions. These, in turn, are seen as influencing the social roles maintained by women and men. This concern with the extent to which gender roles are influenced by physical and emotional sex differences goes back to Margaret Mead's (1935) arguments that there is great diversity and hence plasticity in male and female roles, so that biology is not as influencing as members of our culture have perceived it to be. Recent discussions of gender (Rosaldo and Lamphere, 1974; Sanday, 1981) have emphasized plasticity and the shaping of individual societies too. But they have also focused on differences in strength and reproductive role and on emotional differences as factors that bring about situations in which women are dominated by men. Cognitive differences are generally not given serious treatment as possible sources of role differences.

Although these physical and emotional influences on role differentiation are not taken up explicitly to any great extent in Parts I and II of this book, the chapters in these sections do reveal widespread patterning in role differentiation. We shall now consider the nature of that patterning and the extent to which physical and emotional makeup influences gender role differentiation.

First and most generally, we find that biological sex regularly undergoes elaboration in the form of gender differentiation in language use, in ways that interact with other social elaborations of basic biological differences, notably *age* and *status*. Thus Japanese, Mexicano, and Samoan men and women are not always different in their speech in the same way; the difference varies contextually. Instead *older* women and men speak differently than do younger women and men. In addition both *age* (older) and *sex* (male) are prerequisites to public political status and power, most clearly among the Mexicano and Samoans but also among the Kuna. Thus regularly we find that it is the *interaction* of gender, age, and status that predicts systematic variation in language use, rather than gender alone.

The way in which age interacts with gender is also evident in Part II, where we find that children's speech is gender-differentiated very early but that the way in which it is gender-differentiated changes over time, so that it must be seen as related to, but not identical with, the gender differentiation in adult speech.

Second, one of the major arguments of the chapters in Part I is that social roles, speaking roles, and the speech genres associated with them are often gender-differentiated, so that gender differences in language use are often a reflection of such differences in activity and are associated with the activity rather than the gender. We see this kind of patterning particularly in Sherzer's discussion of the Kuna, Schieffelin's discussion of the Kaluli (in Part II), Ochs's discussion of Samoans, and Hill's discussion of Mexicano. Thus Schieffelin finds that among the Kaluli one major sentence word order is associated with narratives and another with a mourning genre, and not with men who tell stories and women who mourn.

Although the chapters in Parts I and II give evidence of great diversity in the speaking roles and genres assigned to males and females, some kinds of speech genres are controlled and performed by one gender more often than by the other. Sherzer argues, for example, that across societies it is almost universal that lullabies for children and stylized mourning in the form of tuneful weeping when someone has died are performed by women rather than men. The lullaby is presumably associated with women because of their greater involvement in child rearing, but the association of mourning genres with women is less readily explained, and raises the possibility that biologically based emotional differences, albeit culturally conditioned, may underlie such an association. Another possibility is that the female nurturing role most explicitly associated with child rearing may involve a more nearly lifelong involvement of women in life-sustaining activity, so that death is seen as the counterpart of birth, and hence more as a women's concern.

There is also considerable evidence in the chapters of Part I that men far more often than women realize roles and attendant speech genres in public settings, particularly roles and genres associated with the exercise of legitimized political authority. Sherzer discusses the way in which Kuna men have productive control over speech genres associated with village political meetings that women do not. Hill argues that Mexicano women's exclusion from traditional public-speaking roles associated with political authority contributes to their narrower stylistic range. In the other chapters in Part I, and in Schieffelin's chapter on the Kaluli in Part II, this same pattern of the relative infrequency of female involvement in major public-speaking roles forms part of the background for discussion of other issues. Thus, for example, Ochs's finding of more frequent use of ergative case markers in men's speech is associated with their generally higher frequency in public speech, particularly speech in the political body, the *fono*, where only titled members of the village speak and most of the titles are held by men.

Rosaldo (1974) discusses this pattern of female exclusion from public spheres as an important universal source or manifestation of men's greater legitimized authority and hence greater power. And she links the lack of female participation in public spheres to women's reproductive role, as if they are somehow unable to get out of the house, the private sphere where their influence is far greater. As D. Sapir and Crocker's collection (1977) indicates, public activity often involves the creation, maintenance, and elaboration of ideologies that are widely shared interpretive frameworks, including ideology about the nature of men and women (e.g., Goldman, 1983; Howe, 1977). Sanday (1981) has argued that such ideologies play a major role in the shaping of gender-differentiated behavior.

Scholars responding to Rosaldo's position (e.g., Sanday, 1981; Schlegel, 1977) have discussed whether women are really excluded and, if so, whether they are at such a disadvantage because of it. Far less attention has been focused on whether such lack of participation is related to childbearing, although that too has been studied. The general line in these responses has been to point out that there are different sources and spheres of influence that must be distinguished from one another, and to identify factors that influence the relative power and authority women have in different spheres, and overall in different societies. It has also been argued that it is ethnocentric to equate great power with legitimized authority, because in many societies the power of what Western Europeans recognize as legitimized authority may not be great.

Sherzer in this volume argues along these lines regarding Kuna women's exclusion from public political and religious roles and speech genres. He points out that Kuna women's public involvement in the artistic, symbolic, and economic activities associated with *mola* making give them value and prominence in the society that are at least equal to that of men.

This general line of argument and Sherzer's version of it are important as antidotes to overgeneralization, as evidence of both the diversity in women's circumstances and the factors that contribute to greater or lesser dominance of women by men. But such arguments should not obscure distinctions among what is overwhelmingly dominant, what is more common than not, what is rare, and what is nonexistent. In this book all the societies documented have major political public-speaking roles and speech genres in which women's significant verbal involvement is rare. And there are no examples of public activities in which men rarely participate in major speaking roles and speech genres. To the extent that such roles and forms of speech exert control and influence over men's and women's lives, the men have more power and control than the women.

Thus far we have considered widespread gender differences in speech roles and speech genres of the sort anthropologists have related to physical and emotional differences between women and men. There is also evidence in this collection of widespread differences in male and female *styles* when engaged in the same activities, roles, and speech genres. On this issue most of the evidence comes from the chapters in Part II, on language socialization. Lakoff (1975) and Brown (1980) have both argued that women's speech is more polite than men's, and Lakoff has also said such speech is less powerful in part *because* it is more polite. There is no focused discussion of politeness in Part I, although discussion of related phenomena suggests that what members of societies of Western European background conceptualize as "politeness" is conceptualized quite differently in non-Western societies. Thus Ochs's analysis of sympathy markers relates them to how a person of higher or titled status should behave rather than to gender or to how a polite person should behave.

In contrast, the first three chapters of Part II, on white middle-class and black working-class children, all suggest that young girls use more of what we would call polite directives and styles of arguing than do young boys. Although Schieffelin does not focus attention on this issue in her discussion of Kaluli language socialization, she points out that as children master language, young boys more than young girls are urged and encouraged to be assertive and demanding in their requests to others.

Part II thus offers strong evidence of gender differences in politeness in both black and white American society, and suggests the potential cross-cultural importance of politeness, loosely defined, in the gender differentiation of speech. Such evidence can be viewed as showing greater aggressiveness on the part of males, and hence as supporting a possible biologically based emotional difference between the sexes. But this group of chapters offers particularly strong evidence of the very early age at which socially transmitted gender differentiation is in effect, highlighting the complexity of the interaction of biological and social processes.

Future prospects

As I indicated at the beginning of this introduction, explanations of the differences between men's and women's cognitive, physical, and emotional makeups focus on hormonal differences. The anthropological literature on gender roles usually invokes *physical* differences in strength and reproduction and *emotional* differences as the causes of gender role differences, but it often ignores the possibility of *cognitive* sex differences. But this same literature stresses the ultimate plasticity of human gender roles.

The biologically oriented scholars who argue for cognitive differences view these as interacting with physical and emotional differences, but they usually have little to say about how these processes do or do not influence gender role differentiation.

In future research, scholars who focus on the sociocultural causes of gender differentiation in language should not turn their backs on cognitive causes, which will not die out if ignored, but rather directly and explicitly address whether and how their data are relevant to claims of cognitive differences. There is a corresponding need for scholars who focus on biological causes of gender differences in performance of experimental tasks to address directly the implications of their results for behavior outside the experiments themselves.

Part I

Women's and men's speech in cross-cultural perspective

Introduction

SUSAN U. PHILIPS

The purpose of Part I of this book is to consider the ways in which women's and men's speech are similar and different in different languages and societies. Five languages and societies are treated in the chapters that make up this section: Japanese as spoken in Japan, Samoan as spoken in Western Samoa, English as spoken in the United States, Kuna as spoken by the Kuna Indians of Panama, and Mexicano as spoken by the Nahuatl Indians of Mexico.

Since the mid-1970s the bulk of the many studies of sex differences and language that have appeared in print have focused on sex differences in our own society, particularly on sex differences in language use associated with the possession or lack of power and authority (Lakoff, 1975) in the use of hedges and tag questions. As we shall see in this group of chapters, however, the nature of the society in which biological males and females sustain themselves as social men and women and the structure of the language they speak significantly affect the kinds of gender differences in language function and form that can be discussed and the ways in which they can be discussed.

A comparative view of gender differences in language form has existed within linguistic study since the early part of this century. Sapir's 1915 paper "Abnormal Types of Speech in Nootka" (E. Sapir, 1915) focuses on linguistic devices that imply something about the social identity of the speaker, devices he characterizes as "person implications." While gender is by no means the focus of this paper, Sapir identifies sex and rank as the two dimensions of social identity most likely to be signaled by the aspects of linguistic form that in Nootka signaled "abnormal" speech, such as that of a speaker with a cleft palate. In this paper, as in Sapir's 1929 paper "Male and Female Forms of Speech in Yana" (E. Sapir, 1929), attention focuses on phonological alternates of the same

15

morpheme and on the presence versus absence of particular morphemes, usually affixes, as devices that signal gender or other culturally salient aspects of social identity. Sapir's notion that gender is marked indexically and obligatorily in the morphology of many languages was supported and further documented by other students of North American Indian languages, notably Flannery (1946) and Haas (1944). Thus even the first contemporary cross-linguistic review of sex differences in language, by Bodine (1975), identified this *type* of difference as the major kind of gender difference documented in the linguistic literature. As we shall see, more recent evidence suggests that both the theoretical model of language structure of the time and the areal concentration on North American Indian languages influenced this view.

Jespersen, in his chapter, "The Woman" (1925), took a much broader view of sex differences in language than Sapir. He can be seen as Lakoff's predecessor in claiming that in both English and Japanese women are more polite than men, as well as the source of Labov's (1978) discussion of gender differences in contributions to change and conservatism in language structure. He was also probably the first linguist of this century to assert that lexical differences are the major kind of linguistic differences between women and men. Yet in his description of gender-associated grammatical differences in different languages, it is clear that, like Sapir, Jespersen is talking about phonology and morphology, with no attention to structure above the level of the word – that is, clause and sentence structure, which are the contemporary focus of studies of the syntax of language.

Not until the 1960s did Labov (1972b) and those who use his methods begin to develop a somewhat different set of claims about cross-linguistic similarities in gender differences in language use. On the basis of taped interviews with American English-speakers, Labov found that women use preferred, nonstigmatized phonological variants more than men. In this way they were more like middle-class speakers and less like working-class speakers than men were and spoke more as everyone did in the more "formal" parts of the interview and less as everyone did in the less "formal" parts of the interview. This same finding has been reported for societies in which other Indo-European languages are spoken, including Great Britain, Canada (Montreal), Panama, and Costa Rica (all discussed in Philips, 1980).

There are several major ways in which the Labovian model of gender differences differed from that of the early-twentieth-century structuralists. First of all, he focused primarily on phonology rather than on morphology. Second, he based his analysis on the actual speech of the group he studied rather than on the reports of an informant. Third, he characterized his findings as variable rather than categorical, to use

Labov's own terms. In other words, he made it clear that any given speaker varies her usage and does not use the same phonological variant in the same word every time it is uttered, whereas many earlier claims about gender differences in language form either implied or explicitly asserted that men always speak in one way and women always speak in another. Fourth, Labov's results were quantified, whereas earlier findings not only were not, but could not be because of the method (or lack of it) by which the data were gathered. Finally, all of the phonological variants studied through Labovian methods were subject to conscious evaluation by the speakers who produced them and were thought to be good or bad forms of pronunciation.

While the chapters in this section clearly show the influence of both the earlier structuralist model of gender differences and the more recent variable model of gender differences, all are influenced by yet a third perspective – the ethnography of communication, whose major proponent, Dell Hymes, has for some time advocated the comparative study of language use as it occurs naturally and normally with particular attention to the ways in which the social features of the context in which speech occurs interact with the form of speech (Hymes, 1962). Thus Brown (1979, 1980), Keenan (Ochs) (1974c), and Dauer (1978), whose earlier work is addressed in the chapters that follow, all base their claims about cross-cultural similarities and differences in women's language use on ethnographic fieldwork in non-Western societies.

These chapters are similar to and different from earlier studies of gender differences in language in ways that can be highlighted by comparison with features of the Labovian research. First, these chapters encompass the full range of aspects of linguistic form that can express gender differences – lexical, phonological, morphological, and syntactic. As has been noted, little attention has heretofore been given to *syntactic* features of women's and men's speech, but in this group of chapters the bulk of attention to new properties of language goes to syntactic features, most of which can be characterized in terms of the presence or absence of processes that delete, rearrange, or add linguistic material within a sentence. Thus this section can be seen as attesting to a type of gender difference that has been little documented in languages other than English. Every chapter in this section deals with some aspect of syntax, suggesting that such gender differences are common across languages but also suggesting that the recent theoretical focus on syntax growing out of transformational generative linguistics has shown us new things to look at, and to look for, in men's and women's speech.

Second, while all of the authors base their chapters on empirical research, none relies exclusively on Labovian sociolinguistic interviews as a data base. The data also come from tape recordings of naturally occurring speech activities generated from the normal activities of members of the culture being studied. Moreover, analysis in each of these chapters relies critically on *contextual variation* in language use, taking us well beyond the artificial manipulation of context in the sociolinguistic interview as a source of insight into contextual variation in men's and women's speech. Here we see Hymes's influence.

Third, most of the syntactic differences between men and women that are discussed are *variable* differences, like Labov's phonological difference and unlike Sapir's morphological difference. And like Labov, most of the authors characterize the differences they find in quantitative terms.

Fifth, these chapters as a group deal with gender-differentiated features of language forms of which there are *varying degrees* and sorts of metapragmatic awareness, to use Silverstein's (1975) term, and of stereotyping, to use the term more common in the literature on sex differences and language (e.g., Edelsky, 1979). Considerable attention is given here to how these differing kinds of awareness relate to both linguistic behavior and gender ideology, in the sense in which Ortner and Whitehead (1981) use the term or more broadly.

Finally, whereas both the structuralists and the variationists (e.g., Trudgill, 1972) articulate only an indexical function for gender-varied speech – that is, they both see gender identity as being conveyed or marked by speech differences as if these were a way of saying "I am a woman" – the chapters using this more ethnographic approach offer somewhat more diverse and complex models of gender and language that will be discussed again further on.

The first chapter, "The Womanly Woman: Manipulation of Stereotypical and Nonstereotypical Features of Japanese Female Speech," by Janet S. Shibamoto, examines and offers explanation for differences in Japanese women's speech in two distinct contexts: the *idobatakaigi*, or "well-side conference," equivalent to the American housewives' kaffeeklatsch, and the *hoomu dorama*, Japanese television programs resembling soap operas, in which actors and actresses improvise dialogues from scene outlines. Shibamoto chose to compare these contexts because members of Japanese culture view people in the shows as "more manly" and "more womanly" than in real life, and she wanted to see if this characterization was related to language use.

In both contexts Shibamoto examines the frequency of occurrence of two sets of linguistic variables in the women's speech. The first set are morphological features widely held in Japan to differ in use between men and women. These include the presence of the honorific prefix *o-* attached to nominals, the presence of honorific and humble affixes attached to verbs, and the presence of sentence-final particles thought to be used only by women – all of which are associated with femininity by native speakers of Japanese.

The second set are syntactic features normally not commented on by the Japanese themselves, which earlier research by Shibamoto had shown to occur significantly more often in the speech of women than in the speech of men in conversational interviews. These features included the deletion of subject noun phrases, the postposing of subjects, and the deletion of case-marking particles.

Shibamoto found that while the first set of features occurred more frequently in the TV dramas, the second set did not, consistent with her view that the first set of features are part of a female register, which can be manipulated somewhat deliberately (how deliberately is not clear), while the second set of features cannot be viewed as part of that register. She also found fewer differences between the two settings in the older women's use of the relatively conscious morphological features than in the younger women's usage, which she relates to less femininity's being expected of the older women.

Perhaps her most interesting claim is that socially patterned syntactic differences will generally be less subject to awareness than morphological differences. Close examination of the rest of this section indicates this claim holding up for these chapters. But as we shall see, factors other than the grammatical status of the features also affect awareness.

Chapter 2, "The Impact of Stratification and Socialization on Men's and Women's Speech in Western Samoa," by Elinor Ochs, is concerned, as is Chapter 1, with the nature and explanation of contextual variation in gender-differentiated speech. Like Shibamoto, Ochs looks at language use in several contexts and is concerned with the ways in which different contexts seem to call for different ways of expressing social identity. In contrast to Shibamoto, however, Ochs looks at different variables in different speech activities and focuses on how various aspects of social identity interact, giving particular attention to social rank as it interacts with age and gender differently in different situations.

The linguistic features examined are (1) affect markers through which speakers express sympathy toward what is being discussed, including affective pronouns, determiners, and emphatic particles; (2) variation in the order of subject, object, and verb; and (3) case-particle deletion. Although she examines speech in a variety of settings, including the home and political meetings, Ochs makes a basic distinction between family interactions and nonfamily interactions. She argues that while *gender* affects patterns in word-order choice more than *rank* does, rank has more effect than gender on the other variables examined. Thus high-ranking men and women differ less from each other than both together differ from low-ranking men and women. At the same time, there is evidence of a different pattern of contextual variation for men than for women, which suggests men define more contexts as public than women do.

In contrast to the Japanese, among whom there is conscious awareness of a variety of aspects of social status that affect use of politeness markers, Samoans apparently focus on rank in their cultural ideology about presentation of self, and notions of appropriate behavior for male and female are to some extent derived from this ideology by extension or analogy. Thus Schoeffel (1978) argues that women are expected to act like higher-ranking people in part because sisters are seen as of higher rank than brothers, although they are subordinate to their husbands.

In general, Ochs's data and analysis suggest that the use of affect or sympathy forms is related to this cultural ideology in that untitled younger men use far more affect forms than titled older men. The older women married to titled men, however, show much sympathy as listeners, as do the younger men, but, like the older men, not so much as speakers, a pattern in no way clearly related to such discussions of Samoan gender ideology as Schoeffel's.

For the features other than affect markers that Ochs reports on here, there are not such direct relations to cultural notions of role as for those associated with the affect markers. Instead a general cultural view assumes people will manifest different sides of themselves in different activities that call for different aspects of one's social identity to become salient. It is this aspect of cultural ideology that Ochs presents as motivating the contextual variation she discusses.

In addition, Ochs makes it clear that the sex differentiation for ergative case-marker deletion and word order derive from, or grow out of, cultural notions of sex-differentiated activities that have consequences for language function and secondarily for language form. Thus, while none of the features Ochs documents are subject to conscious awareness, one set is related to cultural ideology about rank, and the others can be related to differences in social activity and thus to differences in language function that are tied to gender role.

Chapter 3, "The Interaction of Variable Syntax and Discourse Structure in Women's and Men's Speech," by Susan U. Philips and Anne Reynolds, also focuses on the nature of contextual variation in gender differences in speech, but here the variation is best characterized as microcontextual. Philips and Reynolds examine the speech of male and female prospective jurors in a courtroom procedure in which they are questioned to determine whether or not they will be fair as trial jurors. They focus on the contraction and deletion of subject pronouns followed by the auxiliary or main verbs "have" and "be," comparing the frequency of contraction and deletion in two parts of the procedure: (1)

dialogic questioning in which jurors give brief responses to questions from the lawyers and the judge and (2) social-background monologues in which the jurors in a set routine provide information about themselves to the judge and the lawyers.

The authors found that while overall more material was deleted in these environments by men, the bulk of the deletion differentiating men and women occurred in the social-background monologues. They suggest that the variationist literature leads one to view this difference as consistent with the notion that men's speech is less formal than women's, yet it is clear that the part of the procedure in which far more deletion occurs is not viewed as less formal. It is, rather, more routinized and repetitious, so that it is easier to retrieve deleted information there than in the rest of the procedure. Thus in these data women's speech is primarily *more redundant* than men's – that is, there is less deletion – and it is only secondarily *more formal*, suggesting routinization and redundancy as primary sources of syntactic deletion, which in its patterning indicates careful monitoring of speech rather than the inattention associated with informality in the Labovian tradition. This chapter also makes the methodological point that analysis of sociolinguistic interview data cannot reveal the actual normal sources of gender-related variability in language form that studies of naturally occurring language use such as this one can and do reveal.

The fourth chapter, "A Diversity of Voices: Men's and Women's Speech in Ethnographic Perspective," by Joel Sherzer, offers a somewhat different approach to intrasocietal variation in gender-differentiated speech from the preceding chapters'. Whereas the previous chapters focused on differences in linguistic form at essentially the sentence level, albeit with attention to differences in speech activities, this chapter is primarily concerned with differences between men and women in whole speech genres. Focusing on the Kuna Indian society of Panama but drawing on information from other societies as well, Sherzer suggests that in small-scale societies in which sexual division of labor is typically clear-cut, the clearest, most pervasive form of gender difference in language use is likely to be a difference in speaking roles and discourse genres associated with those roles.

Thus among the Kuna the speaking roles and speech genres associated with public political meetings and ritualized attempts to cure illness are for the most part restricted to men. The speech genres that occur in these activities are linguistically distinctive in a number of ways, which Sherzer (1974) has described elsewhere, including less elision of vowels, morphemes that frame the speech genres by marking their beginning and end, nominal and verbal prefixes and suffixes that rarely occur in everyday speech, kernel-like sentence structures with little deletion of whole noun phrases and verb phrases, grammatical parallelisms, and lexical items that do not occur in everyday speech (Sherzer, 1974). Major genres performed by women but not by men among the Kuna are lullabies and tuneful weeping during mourning, both of which are performed privately rather than publicly.

Schieffelin's chapter in the next section of the book, on the Kaluli of New Guinea, supports Sherzer's arguments for a genre-based model of gender-differentiated speech. Schieffelin stresses the point that whatever linguistic differences there are between women and men are associated with the *activities* engaged in by women versus men, and not with the gender of the person, so that if a man were to engage in a woman's activity he would use language in much the same way she did.

Sherzer suggests that some gender-associated speech genres may be universal, such as the association of lullabies and tuneful weeping with women. He also points out that although only men are involved in public-speaking roles, women's involvement in the economically and symbolically important making of cloth *molas* gives them as much public visibility as the men have. Nor does it follow from the men's exclusive control over linguistically specialized public-speech genres that women's speech is valued less than men's. Sherzer suggests that women's speech will be disvalued only where women themselves are disvalued.

The final chapter in this section, "Women's Speech in Modern Mexicano," by Jane H. Hill, offers a rather more complex picture of gender-differentiated speech than the preceding papers, in part because the social and linguistic conditions in which the Mexicano-speaking Nahuatl Indians exist are complex. The chapters describing Japanese and American speech deal with language use in large, complex monolingual societies, and the chapters describing Samoa and Kuna speech focus on language use at the village level in still-nonindustrial societies. The Hill chapter, however, focuses on the formerly nonindustrial society of Nahuatl Indians as they have become increasingly drawn into the more complex structures of the modern Mexican nation over the last several hundred years, and on the Spanish–Mexicano bilingualism associated with this process.

In this chapter Hill examines men's and women's use of the Mexicano language in terms of the extent to which the speech of each shows influence from the Spanish language, returning to an examination of the notions raised first by Jespersen and then by Labov that women are more linguistically conservative than men and yet paradoxically more likely to follow a newly established prestige norm than men. Hill distinguishes between two sets of features of Mexicano – one set for which women show less Spanish influence and one set for which they show more Spanish influence. She finds women's Mexicano speech showing less Spanish influence in the lesser use of Spanish loan words, the greater use of Mexicano noun-incorporating verbs, and the lesser use of calques on Spanish relative-clause construction. Women's speech shows more Spanish influence in their use of Spanish final-syllable stress on Spanish loan words rather than Mexicano stress on the next-to-last syllable, and in the use of Spanish possessive constructions. Hill sees these linguistic facts as resulting from a combination of the women's lesser exposure to Spanish, because they are not part of the industrial labor force, and their marginality to male prestige norms for Mexicano use.

For the young men, especially those involved in that labor force, Mexicano ("good" Mexicano) has become highly valued as a marker of ethnic identity, and Hill calls the pure Mexicano they value the "solidarity code." These men have identified the Mexicano stress pattern and Mexicano possessive constructions as features, among others, that mark good Mexicano. Thus even poor speakers and those men who speak Mexicano as a second language attempt to keep their speech Mexicano in these respects. The women, who are less caught up in this norm, are viewed as poorer speakers in terms of it, because they apparently do not monitor and modify their speech to display these particular features. The features for which they *are* more Mexicano are not recognized as such by the males who articulate the norm for good Mexicano, in part because those features occur infrequently.

Nor does it follow from this that women's speech is more valued in terms of the "power code," an older and more covert norm that approves the male use of more Spanish lexical items and other Spanish features in association with public exercise of political power in Nahuatl cultural contexts. For here, the main conscious feature of speech valued is Spanish lexicon, which is used less by women – deliberately, Hill argues, because the power code is associated with male exercise of power. Thus, by conscious male prestige norms, women lose both ways, and men are indeed viewed as the better speakers of Mexicano, even though by a linguist's measures there are many better speakers of Mexicano among the women than among the men.

Hill concludes that women are not adhering more to a national prestige norm, as Labov has argued to explain other data. Nor can they be thought of as simply marginal or scattered in relation to a focused norm reflected in men's speech because they are peripheral in network relations in which men are intensely involved as in Milroy's (1980) British study. Instead they are constrained to a narrow stylistic range within the broader stylistic range of men because they do not have access to the range of use that men do.

From the preceding discussion of the chapters in this section, it should be evident that while there is considerable diversity in the relations among gender roles as they are conceived in the cultural ideology of a society, gender-differentiated behavioral roles, and linguistic behavior, those relations are not limitless, so that we see some cross-cultural similarities in the linguistic variables examined and in the conceptualization of the role of language in the social expression of gender.

First, as noted at the beginning of this introduction, while features examined cross-cut the grammar, the focus is on morphology or syntax, with less attention to phonology or lexicon. Of the morphological features discussed, most are of the sort Sapir (1915) and more recently Silverstein (1975) have characterized as indexical, or deriving part of their meaning from the social context in which they are being uttered. All of Shibamoto's features have this quality, as do Ochs's affect forms. All of the features speakers are consciously aware of are morphological, as Shibamoto would predict. Silverstein (1981) has suggested that segmental sources of meaning are more subject to speaker analysis than nonsegmental sources, which is consistent with Shibamoto's prediction.

Among the syntactic features discussed in these chapters, there is also some commonality across languages and cultures. We see gender differences in the frequency of deletion of subjects in both Japanese and English, and of case particles in both Japanese and Samoan. This is in part a reflection of the commonness of deletion of these particular elements in many languages. And it is important to note that in both Japanese and Samoan, women delete case particles more than men. This finding counters the notion that women's speech always more closely approximates prescriptive grammatical norms because of their innate linguistic superiority.

As a group, these chapters also make it clear that whether or not people are aware of the property of language being studied has important consequences for the kind of social patterning that property will display, as is particularly evident in the Hill and Shibamoto chapters. It is also clear, particularly in the chapters by Ochs, Sherzer, and Hill, that cultural ideology *about* women affects both the kind of speech features that members of the culture will be aware of and the attitudes they will take toward those features.

We see from these chapters that models of the expression of gender identity in speech have gone well beyond the earlier notion of Sapir and the variationists that speech conveys the social information "I am female." Two alternative approaches to that view are offered in these chapters. First we have the notion originally articulated by Garfinkel (1967) that women and men are actively constructing their gender identities with both conscious and unconscious contextual variation in the linguistic expression of gender, a view most evident in the chapters by Shibamoto, Ochs, and Hill. Second, there is the view, clearest in the

Sherzer chapter (and in the Schieffelin chapter in Part II), that gender differences in language form derive from differences in speech roles and speech genres, which in turn are related to gender role differences in activities, with no awareness of those linguistic differences or association of those differences with the activity itself rather than with the gender role. Both these views give rise to a more complex understanding of the multiplicity of factors governing sex differences in speech and enhance awareness that such patterns are not as simple, universal, or unidimensional as much of the literature would suggest.

1. The womanly woman: manipulation of stereotypical and nonstereotypical features of Japanese female speech

JANET S. SHIBAMOTO

This chapter will address the question of how, or whether, a subset of features identified as characteristic of female speech in a single language – Japanese – covaries across situations. Specifically, speech samples taken from situations in which women typically emphasize their femininity and situations in which they typically do not are compared to determine whether frequencies of occurrence of stereotypical morphological features and of nonstereotypical syntactic features vary in the same ways. That is, a first attempt is made to determine whether all the features identified as elements of Japanese women's speech are, in a straightforward way, part of a Japanese female speech register.

Linguistic investigations into the differences between men's and women's language and speech have been pursued with some intensity during the last decade, and many features of language form or patterns of language use exhibiting sex-related variation have been identified, particularly for English. A full elucidation of sex differences in language, however, requires a more systematically cross-cultural approach than has hitherto characterized the field. The reasons for this are twofold. First, although it has been suggested that differences in men's and women's speech are probably universal, the nature of that claim to universality is unclear and hence fails to be an interesting source of explanation for linguistic fact. We wish rather to know if there are universals to be found in the kinds of relationships that may obtain between the feature sex of speaker and specific differences in language form and/or use. Clearly, then, we require information about how languages other than English are marked to denote the sex of the speaker. Is sex-differentiated language found in the same areas of the grammars of all languages – in their phonologies, their lexicons, or their syntax? Are specific forms or rule types the locus of sex differentiation in grammars? Or does the hypothesized universal relationship between sex of speaker and language hold at a deeper level of organization, whose principles may not be immediately apparent upon simple form-by-form comparisons across various languages? In order to make specific statements about the universal properties of the relationship between sex of speaker and language form/ use, a wider variety of language types must be explored in detail. Second, differences in men's and women's language are evaluated by the members of the society in which that language is spoken as symbolic reflections of what men and women are like (Sherzer 1983). Again, the range of possible relations between social identity and language form have only begun to be studied. Clearly, much more ethnographic work in societies of many different sorts will be needed before it will be possible to make interesting statements about the relationship between social structure or organization and type of linguistic form used to express gender differences. In this light, the extensive work that has been done on sex-related differences in Japanese will be of interest, as both Japanese society and the Japanese language differ radically from the American English case.

Women's speech in Japan

The considerable body of research on Japanese female speech that was available in the mid-1970s had identified numerous forms exhibiting sex-related variation. These forms appeared, however, to be found primarily in the phonological and morphological components of the grammar and the lexicon.[1]

Phonology

Sex-related differences in segmental phonology are [i]- and [r]-deletion, as in (1) and (2) below.

(1) a. *Iya*   *da wa* → *Ya da wa*
       disagreeable is SF
       I don't like that.

   b. *Kekkoo de gozaimasu* → *Kekkoo de gozaamasu*[2]
       fine   is
       That's fine.

(2) a. *Wakaranai* → *Wakannai*
       understand-neg
       (I) don't understand.

   b. *Soo iu   no   aru no [o] siranakatta* →
       that call ones be fact DO know-neg-past

       Soo iu no anno [o] siranakatta
       I didn't know there were ones like that.

Deletion of [r] actually involves the deletion of [r] and the following vowel. It occurs before [n], which acquires length. Deletion of [i], on the other hand, is lexically restricted (R. A. Miller 1967; Shibamoto 1980).

Suprasegmental features noted as being characteristic of female speech are high pitch and more extensive use of contrastive pitch–stress patterns relative to male speech. This last feature is in large measure due to the greater proportion of sentences with rising intonation in female speech: 84 percent of female sentences versus 67 percent of male sentences have this intonation contour (*Gengo Seikatsu* 1973).

The lexicon

The most commonly cited lexical characteristics of female Japanese speech are the use of distinct female forms for specific items, the avoidance of Sino-Japanese compound words, special pronominal forms, and sex-differentiated forms of reference and address. Some of the numerous lexical items for which men and women use entirely different forms are listed in (3) below.

(3) | Male forms | Female forms | |
| --- | --- | --- |
| *hara* | *onaka* | stomach |
| *tukemono* | *okookoo* | pickles |
| *mizu* | *ohiya* | water |
| *umai* | *oisii* | delicious |
| *kuu* | *taberu* | eat |
| *kutabaru/sinu* | *nakunaru* | die |

It will be noted that the female forms of the nominals in (3) all are prefixed by the polite/honorific prefix *o-*. As Mashimo (1969), Shibata (1972), and others note, there are many nominals in Japanese to which women either always, or more often than men, attach the polite prefixes *o-*, *go-*, or *omi-*.

(4) | Male forms | Female forms | |
| --- | --- | --- |
| *bentoo* | *obentoo* | box lunch |
| *kane* | *okane* | money |
| *hasi* | *ohasi* | chopsticks |
| *hon* | *gohon* | book |

Although the excessive attachment of *o-* to nominal forms is socially stigmatized, women are said to use the prefix more than men, giving their speech a more refined, or polite, tone.

Kango, or Sino-Japanese compound words, are avoided by female speakers (*Gengo Seikatsu* 1973; Kokugogakkai 1964; Mashimo 1969; Nomoto 1978). In interviews with both male and female speakers, Nomoto reports that female interviewees employed these forms 10.6 percent of the time, as opposed to the male interviewees' rate of 13.7 percent. Larger differences were observed by Tsuchiya (cited in Nomoto 1978:137); in formal conversation, men employed Sino-Japanese forms 22.5 percent of the time and women only 15.5 percent of the time.

Third, there are clear sex-related differences in the use of personal pronouns in Japanese. Exclusively male first-person singular pronouns are *boku, ore, wasi, wagahai*; exclusively female first-person singular pronouns are *atakusi, atasi, atai*. In addition, there are two first-person singular pronouns used by both male and female speakers, *watakusi* and *watasi*; they are adopted particularly in formal contexts, where sex-related differences are purported to disappear.

Although there are second-person pronouns used exclusively by male speakers, *kimi, kisama, temee*, there are none used exclusively by female speakers. *Anata* and *omae* are used by both sexes, albeit somewhat differently. In conversations between husband and wife, for example, the wife will use *anata* to address her spouse, whereas he will use *omae* to address her. *Anata* is a more polite form than *omae*, and this usage is thought to reflect the unequal relationship between spouses. *Anata* is used by men toward persons other than spouses, however, indicating some social distance but not necessarily inequality of status; and *omae* may be used by older women to address children and pets. The latter usage is very restricted.

Finally, men and woman use different address terms. Lee (1976) interviewed Japanese couples residing in the United States to elicit common terms of address and reference for spouses. She reported the following terms of address used between husband and wife, listed in descending order of frequency.

(5) HU → WI
   first name
   kimi, omae
   okaasan 'mother'
   mama

WI → HU
   first name + *san*
   otoosan 'father'
   papa
   anata

Watanabe (1963) also reports a much greater use of *otoosan* or *papa* by women (47 percent) than of *okaasan* or *mama* by men (29 percent).

Thus, although many phonological and lexical features of Japanese female speech have been identified that characterize it as conservative, soft, emotional, polite, and pure (*Gengo Seikatsu* 1957, 1973; Jorden 1974; Kindaichi 1957; Mashimo 1969; Oishi 1957), very little work has been done on sex-related variation in the syntactic component.

Sex-related syntactic variation

Determination of whether the linguistic forms associated with the feature sex of speaker are distributed evenly throughout the grammar or occur only in specific areas within it will give focus to the claim that differences in men's and women's speech are universal. Investigations into syntactic variation, of course, test the claim that although linguistic differences between male and female speech may appear at the syntactic level, they do so less often than at other levels of the grammar (Bodine 1975).[3] In terms of more general sociolinguistic interest, this can be subsumed under a broader claim about the relations between various kinds of "linguistic items" and social factors.

A very tentative hypothesis thus emerges regarding the different types of linguistic items and their relations to society, according to which *syntax* is the marker of cohesion in society, with individuals trying to eliminate alternatives in syntax from their individual language. . . . In contrast, *vocabulary* is a marker of divisions in society, and individuals may actively cultivate alternatives in order to make more subtle social distinctions. *Pronunciation* reflects the permanent social group with which the speaker identifies. (Hudson 1980:48)

This claim fits the majority of the research on Japanese female speech, which heavily emphasizes differences in lexical forms and phonological variation, both segmental and suprasegmental.[4] Very little attention has been given to syntactic variation, however, and those few features presented as evidence of sex-related syntactic variation seem only questionably syntactic.[5] A brief review of the features identified as syntactic variables will illustrate the point.

The literature on sex-related syntactic differences in Japanese focuses on the end of the sentence, where these differences are said to be most apparent (Chikamatsu 1979:2). A suggestion as to why this might be the case is given in Koizumi 1978.

Tookai tihoo ni jisin ga okoru rasii ne.

In this sentence, *jisin ga okoru* is an objective statement. However, the auxiliary verb *rasii* which follows it indicates the speaker's attitude toward the statement, and the final *ne* is a particle expressing the speaker's solidarity with the listener. Now, if we were to devise a structure of "the speaker communicating a message to the listener," it would be the objective statement; the judgment of the speaker toward the message would be the auxiliary, and the attitude of the speaker toward the listener would be expressed by the particle. It appears that particles, which express speaker–hearer relationships, and auxiliaries largely account for the subjective parts of the utterances. This is a grammatical means of reflecting status, solidarity, and in addition to these, sex differences. (p. 48; translation mine)

The first syntactic feature claimed to be variable across sex of speaker in Japanese is that men and women use different kinds of predicates.

Japanese is an SOV language with three major predicate types: verbal (6a), adjectival (6b), and copular (6c).

(6) a. *Zyon wa pan o   taberu*
       John   meat DO eat
       John eats meat.

   b. *Kono keeki wa   oisii*
      This cake TOP delicious
      This cake is delicious.

   c. *Zyon wa   gakusei   da*
      John TOP   student   is
      John is a student.

Hatano (1954) claimed that men tended to produce verbal and women adjectival predicates. This claim was examined in a study of informal male and female speech (Shibamoto 1980), where it was found that both men and women produce verbal predicates most of the time (66.4 percent M; 65.3 percent F). Although some differences in the use of adjectival predicates did appear in the data (Shibamoto 1980, 1981), the proportion of sentences with adjectival predicates per se was not higher for women than for men.

Choice of verb inflections – those affixes that attach to the verb and indicate tense, mode, aspect and, in Japanese, level of formality and politeness – is also said to be constrained by sex of speaker. The claim may be broken down further into the two claims (a) that female speakers produce more predicates morphologically marked for politeness than do male speakers and (b) that speakers exhibit sex-related variability in choice of sentence-final particles.[6]

Verb endings in Japanese are divided into plain (*da-tai*) and polite (*desu-tai*) forms.

(7) a. *Kirei da.*
       pretty is-plain

   b. *Kirei desu.*
          is-polite
      It is pretty.

(8) a. *Hon o   yomu.*
       book DO   read

b. *Hon o yomimasu.*
    read-polite
I read books.

The preponderance of a man's utterances tend to fall into one or other of these categories. In contrast to this, many women's utterances can readily be placed in neither of these two categories. This is believed to be due to the proliferation of honorific expressions and sentence-final particles (Bunkachō 1975:166). Sentence-final particles are those forms in Japanese that follow the verb, adjective, or copular final and signal the speaker's attitude toward what he or she is saying and/or his or her sentiment toward the addressee. One of these is the particle *wa*, which "helps give female speech its characteristically feminine flavor" (Martin 1975:920).

(9) a. *Hon o yomimasu.*

  b. *Hon o yomu wa.*

           SF
   I read books.

Thus, where a male speaker would use the polite form in (9a), the female speaker might choose the plain form of (9b), softening its plainness, however, with the feminine sentence-final particle *wa*, which has the effect of rendering the string more polite.

This use of sentence-final particles, then, is one means by which women blur the distinction between plain and polite forms in their utterances. It appears to be the case, however, in addition to this, that women use more conditional, conjunctival, and other noncompletive verb inflections to end utterances than do men, and this, too, renders it difficult to place the predicate in the plain or polite category.

(10) *Sono tiisai toki wa, ma, sono hiroi   uti   ni sumi,*
    that   little time TOP well that   spacious house in live-and

    dandan-to kawatte itte.
    gradually change go-<u>and</u>
    When (the kids) are little, well, they live in that (kind of) big house, and gradually change, <u>and</u>.

(11) *Nihongo, ne, ohanasi deki<u>tara</u>, nee.*
    Japanese well speak   could-if SF
    <u>If</u> I could, well, speak Japanese.

In a study on honorifics[7] in Okazaki City, Aichi Prefecture, investigators from the National Language Research Institute tested the proposition that women's speech was more polite than men's (Kokuritsu Kokugo Kenkyūjo 1957). Twelve situations were constructed and respondents asked how they would formulate requests, call someone's attention to a forgotten item, and so forth, in each of the given contexts. Responses were divided into three groups and scored on the basis of level of politeness of the predicate: normally polite (0), polite (+1), and rude (−1). Each informant's score was averaged over the twelve situations and the mean scores were averaged across all women and all men. The final scores were significantly different: 0.27 for men; 2.90 for women. This is the strongest support to date available for the claim that women's speech is more polite than men's. It does not address the issue of how much women's speech varies within specific speech contexts, however, nor does it seek support from observational data – a serious flaw, since self-report is not an entirely reliable source of information about what forms would be produced in an actual performance situation (Gumperz 1971).

Turning to sentence-final particles, we see that some sentence-final particles are used exclusively by women and others exclusively by men, and that yet a third set may be used by all speakers.

(12) Particles used by women

wa[8]   (particle implying femininity of speaker)
Sore de   ii   wa.
that with good
That's enough.

Ame ga hutte kita   wa yo.
rain SU fall   come-past
It has started raining.

Hontoo ni yokatta   wa nee.
really   good-past
That was really good.

no   (particle implying femininity/childishness of speaker)[9]
Nani mo itadakitaku nai no.
anything eat-want   neg
I don't want to eat anything.

Sonna ni sinpai sinakute mo   ii   no yo.
so much worry do-neg   even if good
You don't need to worry so much.

Yappari soo   datta   no ne.
after all that way is-past
So, it was like that.

-te   (question)
Tookyoo ni irasita   koto   atte?
Tokyo   to go-past occasion have
Have you ever been to Tokyo?

(command)
Otya o   sasiagete.
tea DO give
Give (them) tea.

(13) Particles used by men

    ze   (emphatic)

              Ore wa moo   iku ze.

              I   TOP already go

              I'm going.

    zo   *(emphatic)*

              Koitu   wa umai zo.

              This one TOP good

              This is good.

    na   *Zuibun atui na.*

              very   hot

              It's really hot, isn't it?

Particles used by both men and women are *yo* and *ne*. Whereas men use these forms directly after plain and polite forms of the copula, adjectives, and verbs, however, women must obey combinatory rules that restrict their use of these forms considerably.

(14) (M) *Iku yo.*

        go

     (F) *Iku wa yo.*

        go

        I'm going.

(15) (M) *Hatizi   da yo.*

        eight o'clock

     (F) *Hatizi   yo.*

        eight o'clock

        It's eight o'clock.

(16) (M) *Ikimasu   ne.*

        go-polite

     (F) *Ikimasu   no ne.*

        go-polite

        I'm going.

(17) (M) *Dame   ne.*

        no good

     (F) *Dame   na no yo ne.*

        no good

        You mustn't do that.

Two points can be made concerning the aspects of form in this section on syntax. First, these features might well be classed with the lexical and morphological features discussed previously; that is, they may not be strictly syntactic. Second, of the numerous features of speech claimed to characterize women's language in Japan, only a few are supported by other than anecdotal data. Shibamoto (1980) was intended as a corrective to this situation; that is, it was a data-based study aimed at identifying what, if any, more unequivocally syntactic phenomena[10] showed sex-related variation.

The site chosen for that study was Mitaka City, an incorporated city of the Tokyo metropolitan area lying on the western boundary of the core 23-ward area of the city. Fifteen male and fifteen female Mitaka residents who were speakers of standard Japanese were interviewed in self-recruited groups of three in informal settings. Each group consisted of friends in the same age groups: 20–9, 30–9, 40–9. The interviews were conducted in the home of one of the interviewees (female subjects) or in the company lunchroom (male subjects). In order to overcome observer effect and the natural stiffness of subjects whose speech is being taped, the duration of the interview was set at an hour and a half to two hours. There were no set topics of discussion, but I was prepared at the outset of each interview with a list of topics of general interest that could be used to start conversation. As the groups became adjusted to the setting, interviewees began to initiate topics and to talk among themselves. At this point, polite verb forms and other markers of formal speech disappeared from the data.

Following the interviews, transcripts were made of the 1st through 150th sentence for each speaker; the first 49 strings, in which the most formal language was found, were discarded and analyses designed to isolate sex-related variation performed on the 50th through 150th strings. The specific focus of the study was on ellipsis and word order.

The results of the study showed that, although at the level of sentence grammar the productions of men and women looked quite similar, there were some differences. First, women were observed to delete subject noun phrases more than did men, although significantly more only in sentences with copular and adjectival predicates (see Table 1.1).

Deletion of subjects, objects, and other elements of sentences occurs more regularly in Japanese than in English, although it is not yet clear precisely when these elements may or may not be deleted. Most researchers claim that whether or not an element may be deleted depends upon how unambiguously it may be understood from context. The patterns of deletion observed in the Mitaka field study, however, indicate that forces other than retrievability operate on deletion. Thus, that sex of speaker can be identified as one such force is of interest, particularly since only subject noun phrases appear to be affected. Very similar patterns of ellipsis for men and women were found for all other nominal categories.

Table 1.1. *Subject-noun-phrase deletion by sentence type and sex*

| | Sentences with subject NP deleted | | | |
| | M | | F | |
Sentence type	No.	%	No.	%
Nominal	231/394	58.6	254/366	69.4[a]
Adjectival	36/110	32.7	80/155	51.6[b]
Verbal	649/996	65.2	636/979	65.0[c]

[a]$p \leq .05$: $t = 2.51$, d.f. $= 28$.
[b]$p \leq .05$: $t = 3.00$, d.f. $= 28$.
[c]$p > .05$: $t = 0.96$, d.f. $= 28$.
Source: Shibamoto (1980).

(18)   *Demo, oerai wa, nee, sonna   site.*
        but   great   that way do
        Dakedo, okao minai   de, ne,okoe dake kiite iru   to
        but   face look-not with   voice only listen prog if
        mattaku   kawaranai wa, ne.
        completely differ-not
        But, (you're) great, doing that. But if (we) just hear your voice without seeing your face, (you) aren't at all different (from us Japanese).

Secondly, when there were subjects present, they tended, in many more cases in female than in male speech, to be postposed. Postverbal shift is the result of application(s) of the Rule of Right Dislocation in (19).

(19)   a. $X \begin{bmatrix} -\text{pro} \\ \left\{ \begin{matrix} \text{NP} \\ \text{ADV} \end{matrix} \right\} \end{bmatrix} Y \rightarrow \quad \begin{matrix} \text{(op)} \ \text{(i)} \ 1 & \emptyset & 3+2 \\ \text{(ii)} \ 1 \begin{bmatrix} +\text{pro} \\ 2 \end{bmatrix} & 3+2 \end{matrix}$

        1   2   3
        Type (ii) does not apply to indefinite NPS

        b. *Ima, moo   tyuugakusei   de, eigo   hazimatta desyo,*
        now already junior high school student is   English began   TQ
        sita   no   ko   ga.
        under GEN child SU-
        Now, he's already a junior high school pupil and English has begun, you know, my younger child.

This is the only rule in Japanese that moves constituents to the right of verbs in sentences (Haraguchi 1973:2). Any kind of nominal or adverbial phrase may undergo rightward dislocation, and the rule may be applied iteratively. There are very few formal constraints on this rule. Two are

Table 1.2. *Sentences with postposed elements by predicate type*

| Predicate type | Strings with postposed elements | | | |
| | M | | F | |
	No.	%	No.	%
Copular	15/394	3.8	46/366	12.6[a]
Adjectival	10/110	9.1	29/155	18.7[b]
Verbal	50/996	5.0	115/979	11.7[c]
Total	75/1,500	5.0	190/1,500	12.7

[a]$p \leq .05$: $t = 4.72$, d.f. $= 28$.
[b]$p \leq .05$: $t = 2.22$, d.f. $= 28$.
[c]$p \leq .05$: $t = 4.40$, d.f. $= 28$.

that relative clauses do not postpose away from head nouns – as one would expect from Ross (1967) – and that interrogative words do not postpose. These are explained by Hinds (1976) in terms of the functions rather than the formal structure of the rule.

Peng (1977) first noted the high frequency with which this rule is applied by female speakers. From formal interviews with eighty female speakers 20–59 years of age residing in two areas of Tokyo, Peng collected 288 samples of postposing, 9.2 percent of all utterances. In a personal communication, he suggested that this phenomenon appeared to be more frequent in the speech of females than in that of males. An examination of 3,000 utterances produced by fifteen female and fifteen male speakers in informal settings shows this to be the case (Shibamoto 1980). In Table 1.2, we see that female speakers produce sentences with postposed elements 2.54 times as often as male speakers over all predicate types. In terms of frequency of rule application, these figures would be somewhat higher, since the rule may be applied iteratively. Two applications of this rule occurred in twenty-three strings among female speakers and in three strings produced by male speakers.

(20) *Soo iu   kankaku wa   nai?*
     that called feeling   TOP have-not
     ima wa, nihonzin ne
     now TOP Japanese
        1   2
     Don't they have that sort of feeling, now, Japanese people?

Finally, I found that subject and direct-object case-marking particles were omitted by female speakers considerably more than by men. Jap-

Table 1.3. *Ellipsis of subject, direct-object, and indirect-object case-marking particles*

	Percentages of particles deleted			
	M		F	
Case	No.	%	No.	%
Subjects	64/584[a]	11.0	127/530	24.0[b]
Direct objects	85/330	25.8	137/339	40.4[c]
Indirect objects	8/122	6.6	5/84	6.0[d]

[a]No. of overt SU NPs with particle ellipted/total no. of SU NPs present.
[b]$p \leq .05$: $t = 4.50$, d.f. $= 28$.
[c]$p \leq .05$: $t = 3.03$, d.f. $= 28$.
[d]$p > .05$ $t = 0.10$, d.f. $= 28$.

anese case particles are often called postpositions and, as that term indicates, follow the nominals whose case relationship to the predicate they indicate. The case particles examined were subject, direct object, and indirect object, exemplified in Exx. (21)–(23), respectively.

(21) a. *Doa   ga   aita.*
         door   SU   open-past

         The door opened.
     b. *Zyon   ga   Meeri   o   butta.*
         John   SU   Mary   DO   hit-past
         John hit Mary.

(22)   *Zyon   ga   Meeri   o   butta.*
         John   SU   Mary   DO   hit-past
         John hit Mary.

(23)   *Zyon   ga   Meeri   ni   hon   o   ageta.*
         John   SU   Mary   IO   book   DO   give-past
         John gave Mary a book.

In informal speech these particles are often not present; rates of ellipsis established in Shibamoto (1980) are given in Table 1.3.

With these findings in hand, I began to consider the relationship of the syntactic variables to the variable features that had been described in the literature. There appeared to be a difference in status between those syntactic variations found in the Mitaka interviews and the lexical or morphological differences, most of which are well known both to linguists and to the general populace, thus approaching the status of stereotypes in the Labovian sense: "marked forms prominently labelled by society" (Labov 1972b:314). Whereas the features identified in Shibamoto (1980) appeared to be below the level of conscious awareness of the speaker, features such as the politeness of female speech as indicated by predicate form, by the attachment of the prefix *o-* to nominals, and by the selection of sentence-final particles have the status of social fact, are part of the general knowledge of the adult members of society, and are referred to freely by members of the speech community.

The various features of female speech

Stereotypes may have a variety of relations to fact, that is, they may be more or less congruent with what occurs in real situations when actual utterances are produced. There may also be a variety of social values associated with the stereotyped features. Some stereotyped features are heavily stigmatized, whereas others are not; some may even have positive prestige value attached. In a thoroughgoing study of one stereotypical female speech marker in Japan, Kitagawa (1977) found that the use of the stereotypical sentence-final particle *wa* was positively valued when used by certain members of the female segment of the speech community (young women) when attempting to convey a specific impression of femininity – coquettishness – and that when used by other speakers or under conditions where the conveyance of a feminine impression was inappropriate, it was not.

If there are a variety of features in different parts of a grammar all of which are associated with female speech, it would be of interest to know if female speakers' behaviors with respect to the features in one segment of the grammar differed from their behaviors with respect to those in another. My preliminary hypothesis in this study was that the lexical and morphological stereotypical markers of female speech would not behave in the same way across situations as would the nonstereotypical syntactic variables and, further, that morphological markings and features that have to do with word formation as opposed to those that have to do with sentence formation will operate at a higher level of conscious awareness and will, therefore, behave in ways similar to lexical rather than syntactic differences despite their treatment within the syntactic component of a generative grammar, the most common treatment of these phenomena in Japanese until very recently.

The situations chosen to examine this hypothesis were casual conversations, where no pressures to appear particularly feminine obtained, and tapes of television "home dramas" (mild soap-opera-like programs), where such pressures, as we shall see, do obtain.

The data

Two sets of data were used in the present study. The first is composed
of tapes of natural conversations among same-sex friendship groups of
standard-Japanese-speaking women. The most natural form of gathering
involving housewives in Japan is the *idobatakaigi* 'well-side conference';
it is the equivalent of the kaffeeklatsch in American surburban neigh-
borhoods. An attempt was made to capture the speech of the *idobatakaigi* by scheduling observations in the home of one of the three
participants gathered for each taping session. All groups consisted of
friends who regularly gathered in this way. Tea and rice crackers or
other snacks, sometimes meals, were served during these sessions; children ran in and out during many; phones rang. Each participant was
asked to fill out a simple biographical questionnaire, after which the
session began. Sessions lasted a minimum of two hours, with the longest
going on for three and a half. This ensured that the subjects would have
time to "forget" the presence of the observer and her tape recorder.
Topics were free and, after a few initial suggestions made by the observer
in order to set conversation going, were raised and pursued, or changed,
by the women themselves.

The second set of tapes were videotapes of Japanese television dramas. These programs, termed *hoomu dorama* in Japanese, are typically
serials eight to thirty weeks in length of a mild soap-opera tone. The
reasons for using televised materials in this study were (a) that many
different situations occur in a short period of time under ideal taping
conditions and (b) that scripts in Japan are not fully written out with
all dialogue set and memorized but are, rather, outlines of scenes that
give the actors and actresses directions as to how the scene is to progress
but leave considerable latitude for personal freedom in terms of specific
utterances. Finally, for the most part – and exceptions may easily be
identified and removed from the sample – men are expected to be "more
manly" and women "more womanly" than they need be in real life.[11]
It seemed, thus, that optimal conditions hold in which to discover what
features women employ in order to convey impressions of womanliness,
and to what degree they do so.

Analysis

All tapes were transcribed in normal orthography. The focus of this
study was sentence rather than discourse structure;[12] accordingly, all
utterances produced by the speakers were lifted out of the full transcript,

in order, but with no indication of which segments form a continuous discourse and which are isolated remarks preceded and followed by tokens produced by other speakers.

The results of these operations were lists of 250 sentences for women 20–35 years of age and 250 sentences for women 35–50 years of age from the conversational groups. These were matched by lists from the recorded television dramas consisting of 259 tokens produced by speakers 20–35 and 147 tokens produced by speakers 35–50.

Each transcript was scored for the presence or absence of the following stereotypical features: (a) honorific prefix o- before candidate nominals, (b) predicates marked for politeness, and (c) "feminine" sentence-final particles. Each transcript was also scored for the nonstereotypical features (a) rate of subject-noun-phrase deletion, (b) rate of subject-noun-phrase postposing, and (c) particle deletion.

Results

O-

Table 1.4 shows the results of scoring for the presence of the honorific prefix o- attached to the nominals produced by women in natural conversation versus those produced by women in the televised dramas. Percentages were obtained by measuring the number of forms with the prefix attached against the total number of candidate nominals produced. It can be seen that there is a consistent, although not, in the older group, significantly large, increase in the percentage of forms with the prefix present across both age groups when the context changes to one where appearing womanly is desired.

Predicate politeness

The proportions of predicates that showed special levels of politeness were calculated for each set of transcripts. The results are displayed in Table 1.5, where it can be seen that a consistent increase in production of these forms occurs in the situation where female speakers are attempting to convey impressions of femininity. Here, too, the increase in production of these forms is not only consistent across the two age groups, but quite large. Further, the nature of the forms produced by each group differed somewhat. For this study, the category of polite predicate included both the honorific and humble forms of verbs.

Table 1.4. *Presence of o-prefix among nominals*

Age of speaker	Conversational tapes		Television tapes	
	Tokens	%	Tokens	%
20–35	11/159	6.9	42/245	17.1[a]
35–50	19/228	8.3	25/133	18.8[b]

[a] $p \leq .05$: $t = 2.74$, d.f. = 6.
[b] $p > .05$: $t = 0.24$, d.f. = 5.

The production of an honorific predicate form is triggered by the subject being someone toward whom the speaker feels a need to show deference.

(24) a. *Yamada-sensei   wa kuruma ni o-nori ni natta.*
               professor TOP car   in   get in-   past
         Professor Yamada got in the car.

   b. *Okusama wa moo   o-kaeri ni natta.*
      wife   TOP already go home-   past
      Your honored wife has already gone home.

Humiliative forms, on the other hand, are produced when the subject is the speaker or a related person/object; the intent is to honor the listener (or some third person) by indicating speaker's own relatively lower status.

(25) a. *Watakusi wa sensei   ni o-hanasi sita.*
      I   TOP professor to   speak- past
      I spoke to the professor.

   b. *Watasi wa siryoo o   o-watasi sita.*
      I   TOP papers DO hand over-   past
      I handed over the papers.

There are also certain suppletive forms, one of which will be discussed below.

A detailed examination of the polite predicates produced by the two sets of speakers in this study showed that there were distinct differences in the strategies used, particularly with regard to the humiliative forms (*kenjō-go*). Both in the dramas and in the naturalistic conversations, slightly under half the polite predicates produced were *kenjō-go* forms. Whereas the television tapes yielded primarily (90.9 percent) forms like those of (24), the *kenjō-go* forms from the conversational tapes were of a somewhat different sort.

Table 1.5. *Predicates marked for politeness*

Age of speaker	Conversational tapes		Television tapes	
	Tokens	%	Tokens	%
20–35	2/250	0.8	15/245	6.1[a]
35–50	10/250	4.0	13/147	8.8[b]

[a] $p \le .05$: $t = 2.17$, d.f. $= 6$.
[b] $p \le .05$: $t = 2.117$, d.f. $= 5$.

(26) a. *Soo, ne, dakara tomodati-doosi de,   ne, si-go-nin   de, ne ano,*
so   uh so   friends   as/with uh 4–5   people with uh well
donata ka (ni) osiete _itadakenai_ nante itte   ta   n   desu yo.
someone by   teach receive   QUOT say prog-past that is
So we were saying couldn't we get someone to teach four or five of us friends.

b. *Zya, obaatyama ka nanka   ni mite   _itadaite_, sensei*
then grandma   or something by look after receive   teacher
site ru   wake   desu ka
do   prog reason is   INT
Then, is it that you have grandma or someone look after (them) and teach?

Here, the *kenjō-go* form is not the main verb, as in Ex. 25, indicating that the speaker is doing something for (or directed toward) the person to whom deference is to be shown. Rather, these tokens use the humble form *itadaku* of the auxiliary verb *morau* 'to receive the favor of (addressee) doing *x*', *x* being the action specified by the main verb. In this sort of sentence, then, the speaker is indicating something done not by speaker for addressee but by addressee or a third person for self. Eighty percent of the humble forms from the conversational tapes were of this sort. The number of tokens was too small to pursue this difference further, but these figures suggest that a finer-grained analysis of the triggers of honorification/humilification, and how they are used by various categories of speakers in different situations, is in order.

Sentence-final particles

Sentences were grouped into three types, depending on the form that occurred in sentence-final position: those that ended in particles commonly associated with female speech (27), those that ended in particles considered neutral (28), and those that had no sentence-final particles present (29).

Table 1.6. *Production of "feminine" sentence-final particles*

Age of speaker	Conversational tapes		Television tapes	
	Tokens	%	Tokens	%
20–35	88/250	38.2	123/257	47.8[a]
35–50	67/250	26.8	45/147	30.6[b]

[a] $p \leq .05$: $t = 1.438$, d.f. $= 7$.
[b] $p > .05$.

(27) *Itiban hayai no da wa nee.*
    most fast   one is
    It's the fastest one, isn't it.

(28) *Kodomo o   nekasete,   yatto   otituku ne.*
    children DO put to bed-and finally relax
    I put the kids to bed, and finally relax, don't I.

(29) *Bakuhatu de mo sitara komaru   Ø.*
    explosion even   do-if be in trouble
    If it exploded, I'd be in trouble.

Again, looking at the figures in Table 1.6, we see a consistent, although by no means dramatic, rise in the use of "feminine" sentence-final particles in the television tapes. That they are used less by the older group of women is neatly explained by Kitagawa (1977), who notes that certain feminine forms are associated with coquettishness and that their use is, hence, less appropriate by older women than by younger women. Accordingly, it is not surprising that there is no significant difference between the samples of older women.

With regard to the relatively small increase in feminine particles among the younger speakers, it should be noted that one character in this group from the television tapes was not of a stereotypically feminine sort, but rather boyish. When her utterances were excluded from consideration, the proportion of feminine sentence-final particles produced for that category of speakers rose to 90.5 percent, which is more in line with what might be expected, and which points clearly to the need to distinguish subgroups of female speakers more finely.

In sum, then, we see that all three of the features identified as stereotypical show the expected effect of increasing in frequency when women attempt to be "womanly." What happens, under the same circumstances, to the nonstereotypical features?

Table 1.7. *Subject-noun-phrase deletion rates*

Age of speaker	Conversational tapes		Television tapes	
	Tokens	%	Tokens	%
20–35	190/250	76.0	173/259	66.8[a]
35–50	182/250	72.8	102/147	69.4[a]

[a]$p > .05$.

Subject-noun-phrase deletion

Rates of subject-noun-phrase deletion were very constant across female speakers of all ages in the conversation tapes. The rate of deletion in the television dramas, however, declines rather than increasing as expected (see Table 1.7). The rate of decline, moreover, is not consistent across groups; the 20–35-year-old group showed a 9.2 percent decline ($t = 1.80$, d.f. $= 7$), whereas the 35–50-year-old group showed a 3.4 percent ($t = 0.22$, d.f. $= 5$) decline only. Although the present analysis of the data is insufficient to support specific claims about potential relationships of this phenomenon, the feature "female speaker," and other linguistic or extralinguistic influences, it is at least possible to speculate that the differences in rates of deletion are tied to a combination of the feature "female speaker" and topic shift. It is true that topics shift more rapidly – as scenes shift – in the televised dramas than is the case in the conversational tapes, and that topic shift impedes subject-noun deletion. Further study, including data gathered from male speakers and controlled for topic shift, will be needed to clarify the relationship between these two factors. We may safely conclude, however, that women do not increase their rates of subject-noun-phrase deletion in any straightforward fashion in order to convey an impression of womanliness or femininity.

Subject-noun-phrase postposing

Rates of subject-noun-phrase postposing also failed to show a simple increase across situation. As shown in Table 1.8, there was a slightly greater than 2 percent increase in postposing among the younger speakers. This was countered, however, by a very slight (0.8 percent) decrease among the older group. No significant differences appeared, and there

Table 1.8. *Postposed subject-noun phrases*

Age of speaker	Conversational tapes		Television tapes	
	Tokens	%	Tokens	%
20–35	9/250	3.6	16/259	6.2
35–50	8/250	3.2	3/147	2.0

were not enough cases of postposing in either corpus to comment upon the changes noted.

Particle deletion

Particle deletion rates show a more interesting pattern (see Table 1.9). For all three major cases, the younger group and the older group exhibit opposing tendencies. Younger women tend to delete more case particles for all cases in the television dramas, whereas the older group tended to delete fewer, although none of these tendencies is significant at $p \leq .05$.

Particle deletion has been related to the degree of informality of speech (Martin 1975). The generally higher rates of deletion seen in older women in the conversational tapes may be related to that only in that they had known one another longer and were more intimate with each other than were women in their twenties or thirties who may only have known one another five or ten years and whose identities as neighborhood housewives were not as firmly fixed. That leaves the opposite pattern, seen in the television tapes, to be explained.

I have at present no data with which to address this problem, but will point out that, in the conversation tapes, the statuses of all the women were crucially similar. They were all middle-class housewives. That is far from the case in the television dramas, where women both young and old had a variety of occupations and statuses. Since it is unlikely that the sort of informality that obtained in the friendship groups would be possible between conversational partners of unequal status (and varying degrees of intimacy), it will be necessary to collect data with more controls for these features before the effect of age on particle deletion can be clarified. It seems clear, however, that more features than overt femininity are at work here.

Table 1.9. *Subject, direct-object, and indirect-object case-particle deletion*

| Age of speaker | Conversational tapes | | | | | | Television tapes | | | | | |
| | SU | | DO | | IO | | SU | | DO | | IO | |
	Token	%	Token	%	Token	%	Token	%	Token	%	Token	%
20–35	14/60	23.3	12/33	36.4	1/12	8.3	34/85	40.0	19/47	40.4	2/18	11.1
35–50	23/67	34.3	24/44	54.6	2/17	11.8	13/40	29.0	15/36	41.7	0/9	0

Conclusions

I have tried to identify parts of a grammar of Japanese where differences
between men and women can be found. I have, further, tried to determine the function of some of these variables, specifically with regard to
the management of the impression of "womanliness" on the part of
female speakers. I have done this in the context of two questions: Do
all kinds of sex-related variation behave in the same fashion? And if
not, how might the differences in behavior be characterized?

I conclude that not all sex-related variations operate in like fashion.
In fact, there seem to be two quite distinct sets of features. The first of
these are the lexical and morphological features, which seem to be
directly related to the impression of femininity. The second is the group
of syntactic variables, the deletion and postposing rules, which do not.

The differences between the two sets might be characterized in a
number of ways, but my suggestion for a preliminary characterization
would be to hypothesize a dichotomy in features of female speech between those that are accessible to stereotyping and those that are not
and, on the basis of my findings in this study, to claim that these features
are found in specific parts of a grammar. That is, that those features of
the syntax that exhibit sex-related variation are not available for stereotyping and that they would thus not constitute, in any straightforward
way, a part of the female speech register. They are not, for example,
the features that are initiated by those adopting female, or feminine,
speech patterns (Shibamoto 1985). Yet they clearly exhibit sex-related
variability, and the task that lies immediately ahead is to determine
more precisely how these features operate in relation to the stereotypical
female features, to other socioculturally influenced linguistic variants,
and, in general, to the Japanese-speaking woman, womanly or
otherwise.

Notes

1   At the level of sentence grammar. Another focus has been on discourse
    features, but these will not be treated here.
2   In the form *gozaimasu*, the preceding [a] is often lengthened after [i]
    deletion.
3   C. F. Wall (personal communication) suggests that frequency, at least fre-
    quency alone, may not be the issue. Salience might be as important.
4   Mashimo (1969), etc.
5   As opposed to morphological.
6   Neither of these claims was, however, examined in Shibamoto (1980).

7   One of the most frequently mentioned features of Japanese is its multiplicity of devices for making utterances polite. The forms referred to as honorifics in this paper, however, are restricted to the various affixes to predicates that indicate politeness or, in Martin's terms, "exaltation" of the subject of an utterance (1975:331) or deference to its addressee. These forms are described in the section on predicate politeness. For fuller discussion of honorifics in Japanese, see Harada (1976); Makino (1970); Martin (1975); Prideaux (1970).

8   Examples taken from Chikamatsu (1979).

9   *No* is used by men in some (informal) situations, but is not as frequent as in the speech of women and children.

10 That is, taking matters of word choice and word-internal formation to be lexical and morphological features, respectively, I intended to look for features involving the shapes of phrasal or clausal constituents and their orders of appearance in sentences.

11 As an anonymous Cambridge University Press reviewer points out, I have implied that the main difference between the housewives' conversations and the speech of the women in the televised dramas is the stereotyping in playacting, whereas it is clear that other aspects of social context (in the dramas) may be affecting my data. Specifically, this reviewer wonders "whether the sexual segregatedness of the conversation compared with the . . . sexual integratedness of the soap operas might not be a factor, so that . . . femininity is partially defined through contrast with males in their presence." This is certainly one additional factor to consider, as are the effects of age or status differences among conversational participants, formality of situation (although the scenes chosen for analysis were all relatively informal), and so forth. I shall note those factors I believe especially likely to be apparent in each part of my analysis, but must reserve a thorough investigation of the interactions of these for future investigation.

12 Although it is clear that discourse structure impinges upon sentential form in significant ways; cf. Shibamoto (1983).

2. The impact of stratification and socialization on men's and women's speech in Western Samoa

ELINOR OCHS

Introduction

This chapter considers gender differences and language use in Samoan society. It will argue that, whereas there are linguistic differences between men's and women's speech, the differences are minor in comparison to what is shared. The similarities in language structure and behavior can be accounted for in part by Gumperz's prediction that sharing of linguistic features will be sensitive to frequency and intimacy of interpersonal contact (1968). More particular to the Samoan case, social rank interacts with gender in complex ways as a social constraint affecting language variation. For certain linguistic features and for certain social settings, relative age and political status are more powerful predictors of usage patterns than gender. Men and women of relatively high rank will speak differently from men and women of lower rank. This appears to be true for expression of sympathy in narratives and for use of case marking in family conversations. Gender joins age and political status as an important social variable in accounting for case marking in conversations outside one's family. It takes precedence over other social variables in accounting for one linguistic behavior – word-order preferences (preferences for ordering of the major constituents – subject, verb, and object).

As suggested by the previous statements, this discussion will focus on the relation between gender of speaker and morphosyntactic features of speech behavior. The speakers are residents of the village of Falefā, located on the island of Upolu, Western Samoa. The speech behavior analyzed here is drawn from a much larger corpus recorded in two periods of field research (1978–79 and spring 1981). The larger corpus includes oratorical speech, but the corpus used in this chapter focuses

Ergative language   *Nominative language*

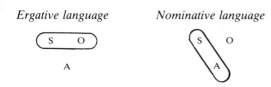

Figure 2.1. Key: s = intransitive subject; A = agent/transitive subject; O = transitive object.

on everyday speech behavior of men and women. The major emphasis is on relatively *informal* speech – discussions, chats, gossip, and story-telling among family and friends. The reader should note that the results of this study are limited to these contexts of use; however, as in all societies, these contexts cover the bulk of language use.

Background

Samoan language

Samoan has been described as an *ergative–absolutive* language (Chung 1978), that is, a language in which subjects of transitive sentences (A) are treated differently from subjects of intransitive sentences (s) and in which subjects of intransitive sentences and direct objects (O) of transitive sentences are treated (at least in some ways) as a single category (Comrie 1978; Dixon 1979). Very commonly, this distinction is expressed through case marking, where transitive subjects (A) are in the so-called ergative case and intransitive subjects (s) and objects (O) of transitive verbs are in the absolutive case.

Such a language contrasts with the more common nominative–accusative language, in which subjects of transitive and intransitive sentences are treated as one category (nominative) and distinguished from direct objects (accusative). The difference between the two language types is represented in Figure 2.1, based on Fillmore (1968) and Dixon (1979).

As in most ergative languages, in Samoan ergative–absolutive distinctions are expressed through nominal case marking. The transitive subject is preceded by the particle *e* when the transitive subject follows the verb (VAO, VOA, OVA). Intransitive subjects following the verb and all direct objects receive no case marking. The difference in marking is presented below.

Transitive sentence

VAO: *'ua   fasi e   le   tama Sina*
      INCPTPERF hit ERG ART boy Sina

VOA: *'ua   fasi Sina e   le   tama*
INCPTPERF hit Sina ERG ART boy
'The boy hit Sina.'

Intransitive sentence

VS: *'olo'o   moe le   tama*
PRES PROG sleep ART boy
'The boy is sleeping.'

This case-marking system is sociolinguistically variable. Its variation is partly but not completely a function of the social distance between language users. Where social relationships are relatively impersonal and distant, there is a greater tendency for Samoans to use the ergative marker. For example, in literacy materials and in radio broadcasts, the ergative marker is always present in the grammatically feasible environments (i.e., when agent NP follows the verb). In face-to-face social interaction, the particle is not always expressed. The social distribution of the use of this particle with respect to gender of speaker will be considered in the body of this paper.

Samoan has a predominantly verb-initial word order. The *verb-initial word-order preference* is related to the fact that most transitive declaratives consist of only one or two constituents, typically verb or verb–object, and most intransitive declaratives have a verb–subject order. Transitive declaratives that contain three constituents may be expressed in a number of word orders, including verb–object–subject, verb–subject–object, subject–verb–object, and, more rarely, object–verb–subject.

In addition to these features, Samoan has a rather elaborate morphological system for expressing affect. There are special affect pronouns (in addition to neutral pronouns) to refer to oneself and special determiners (in addition to neutral determiners) to refer to third persons in a sympathetic manner. These are represented in Tables 2.1 and 2.2. Additionally there are emphatic particles that may modify a range of constituents and convey degrees of intensity and in some cases indicate positive or negative feelings. And of import to this discussion of gender differences is the use of a rich repertoire of respect-vocabulary terms, used across a range of situations.

A final salient feature of Samoan is the fact that it has *two phonological registers* – one called *Good Speech*, or "Samoan in the /t/" and one called *Bad Speech*, or "Samoan in the /k/." As reported by Shore (1977), Good Speech is predominantly associated with Western settings including the school, the church, the radio, and written Samoan (see also Duranti 1981; Ochs in press). Bad Samoan is used in nearly all conversational interactions within the village and in nearly all traditional

Table 2.1. *First-person pronouns*

Category	Neutral form ("I, me, my")	Affect form ("poor I, poor me, poor my")
Full pronoun	a'u	ta ita
Subject clitic pronoun	'ou	ta
Possessive adj., sing., specific, inalienable	lo'u	lota
Possessive adj., sing., specific, alienable	la'u	lata
Possessive adj., sing., nonspecific, inalienable	so'u	sota
Possessive adj., sing., nonspecific, alienable	sa'u	sata
Possessive adj., pl., specific, inalienable	o'u	ota
Possessive adj., pl., specific, alienable	a'u	ata
Possessive adj., pl., nonspecific, inalienable	ni o'u	ni ota
Possessive adj., pl., nonspecific, alienable	ni a'u	ni ata

Table 2.2. *Determiners*

Category	Neutral form ("the, a")	Affect form ("the dear, a dear")
Singular	le, se	si
Plural	—, ni	nai

formal settings, such as village councils, bestowing of chiefly titles, bride-wealth exchanges, and so on. The data on which gender differences in Samoan are assessed consist of this register of Samoan.

Social organization and women's roles

Social stratification. As described by numerous researchers (including Keesing and Keesing 1956; Mead 1928, 1930; Sahlins 1963; Shore 1977, 1982), Samoa is a highly stratified society. There are titled persons (*matai*) and untitled persons and status distinctions within each group.

Those with *matai* titles represent households in political councils and have the right to vote in national elections.

Matai titles fall into two major categories: orator (*tulāfale*) and chief (*ali'i*), each with complementary roles. Particular titles within each village are also ranked, some being more prestigious than others.

Claims to titles may be made through either male or female descent lines (*tamatane/tamafafine*), although the male line is considered the preferable of the two. Women may hold titles, but overwhelmingly the title holders are men. In some villages, only one or two out of a hundred *matai* may be women.

As discussed by Shore (1977, 1982) and Schoeffel (1978), the status of women without titles varies according to several contextual variables. Untitled married women are considered subordinate to their husbands, but have considerable control and authority over the actions of their brothers, including decisions concerning allocation of chiefly titles. In the village at large, untitled married women are evaluated in part in terms of the status of their husbands. Thus wives of *matai* will usually enjoy greater prestige than wives of untitled men. The distinction between spouses of titled and untitled men is codified in Samoan language, which includes special respect-vocabulary terms only for "wife of orator" (*tausi*) and "wife of high chief" (*faletua*).

More generally among untitled persons, age and generation are criteria used to assess relative rank. For day-to-day household activities, these criteria are significant. Of particular interest is the fact that child-rearing is shared by several persons, who have unequal statuses and responsibilities. Sibling caregivers are subordinate to parental caregivers, younger sibling caregivers are subordinate to older sibling caregivers, and so on.

Demeanor and social status. Hierarchical distinctions are associated with particular forms of public conduct and attitude. Within any social setting in which parties are of unequal status, the lower-ranking person will be more active, more accommodating, and attentive to the needs of the other. Untitled to titled person, younger sibling to older sibling, and child to adult will ideally assume this posture. Higher-ranking persons will ideally be more stationary and detached from the activities of those who are not their peers.

Both men and women may assume these demeanors. An untitled woman may act in an accommodating manner in her interactions with a titled man or woman, but she may assume a relatively unaccommodating manner in her interactions with a younger sibling or in-law. If younger caregivers are present, a mother will almost always assume the demeanor of a higher-ranking person with respect to her children, even infants and toddlers.

Socialization and gender identity. When interviewed, adults in the family will note that whereas little boys may sometimes go naked, little girls should always wear at least underpants (see also Shore 1977, 1982). Beyond this, however, there is little to distinguish attitudes toward the early socialization of boys and girls. Mead (1928) reports that traditionally it is young girls who provide caregiving but our observations indicate that currently, although females prevail as caregivers, both male and female older sibs will have this responsibility. All children in the village are expected to attend school; but within a family, school-age children of both sexes will take turns remaining at home for a day to assist in caregiving.

Infants and toddlers are not distinguished by mode of dress. Boys will wear New Zealand imported dresses and girls' underpants, and vice versa. Similarly, hair length will vary, but not necessarily according to gender. Both small girls and small boys may have their hair shaved off, cropped short, or worn long.

Samoans very frequently comment that their children, particularly small children, are cheeky and wild. The first word of Samoan children is reported to be a curse. This view of children covers both sexes. Indeed transcripts of these children indicate that little girls are as verbally assaulting as little boys. It appears, then, that the social status of "little child" (*tamaititi*) overshadows gender identity as social variable affecting behavior.

At the same time, Samoan caregivers feel that much of their task is to get small children to display respect toward others. Respect is indicated by an attentive and accommodating demeanor. Cheekiness is covertly encouraged, but the bulk of explicit socialization is concerned with getting children to know names of others, notice movements of others, greet others, perform for others (sing, etc.), deliver messages for others, report news, and fetch objects. Again, these behaviors are expected of small children of both sexes.

When children reach the age of four, gender identity becomes a more important dimension. At that time, peer groups of the same sex start forming. Members of this peer group come predominantly from the extended family, but children from neighboring household compounds may be included. This group cooperates for both play and work activities. In the afternoons, it is common to see members of these groups together providing care for their younger sibs or running errands or watching some activity taking place. This separation of the sexes is not rigid but continues in many contexts of adult experience and may partially account for certain gender differences in language use.

Men's and women's activities. As in most of the world's societies, women's work differs from that of men in certain respects. As described by Shore (1977, 1982), women are associated more with lighter and cleaner work – European-style cooking versus traditional open oven, gathering sea urchins and other seafood versus tending and gathering materials from the plantations, weaving mats and blinds versus the heavier chores in house construction and maintenance. In practice, other status distinctions (e.g., relative age, rank of spouse or father) may override the gender distinction in determining this division of labor. One often sees *young untitled women* or women who are *wives of untitled men* engaged in the carrying of very heavy loads and unpleasant chores in the back of the compound and in the plantations. Similarly, it is far more likely to find younger untitled men in the village carrying out such heavy work than men with titles, particularly high-ranking titles. This can be represented in terms of a hierarchy of probabilities for carrying out dirty, heavy work:

Untitled male>untitled female>titled male>titled female.

Rosaldo (1974) has pointed out the universal association of women with domestic and men with public spheres of activity. This characterizes Samoan society to an extent. Women who are mothers stay closer to home than do men who are fathers. Fathers have few caregiving responsibilities and tend to spend much of the day engaged in other activities. Having said this, I must point out that women as well as men have a vital public life. As noted earlier, mothers are not the sole caregivers and do not necessarily remain in the household or in the household compound once their infant is a few months old.

This freedom has allowed women to engage in a wide range of activities. A few will take on jobs for which they receive a salary – raising and selling goods at the market in the capital, working in some office in the capital, or teaching at a school. Others will volunteer their services to the hospital in the region or to a variety of women's and church committees. Those women beyond their childbearing years spend much of their day visiting, giving medical assistance (including massages) to a variety of families in the region, and weaving with a group of other women for some economic purpose. Women's committees meet often in the village and in the capital and concern themselves with fund-raising and health and hygiene maintenance and education. Women who have titles participate in village meetings along with titled men (but only one woman did so in the course of our observations [Duranti 1981]). These meetings concern themselves with political issues of interest to the village. They may involve attempts to settle disputes, but there are other forums for this process in the village and in the capital.

These arenas of activity do not easily translate into notions of superior/inferior or authority/power as gender differences have been seen to do in other societies. Rather, Shore's notion of complementarity is more suitable to this division of behavior.

What does seem apparent is that men's and women's activities, both public and private, involve primarily members of the same sex. With the exception of those with salaried jobs outside the village, women spend most of their day with other women and men with other men. As noted, this practice begins with the formation of same-sex peer groups around the age of four.

Men's and women's speech

Theoretical prologue

In 1969–70, I carried out fieldwork in Vakinankaratra, Madagascar, and subsequently analyzed differences between men's and women's speech (Keenan 1974c). In terms of speech behavior, there appeared to be a tidy split between the two sexes. Women were excluded from a major formal genre, oratory; and men shied away from a series of speech activities that women engaged in, for example, gossip and accusations. Women's and men's speech were associated with the features of these genres and activities – women's speech as direct and confrontative, men's speech as indirect and respectful. Both men and women had articulate ideas about one another's speech and there even existed records from the eighteenth century that commented on the differences. Both sexes agreed that men's speech was far superior to women's; the historical documents warned their readers of the potential evil of women's tongues.

Writing on the same topic for Samoa, I find analytic dilemmas that I did not encounter in the Malagasy materials. I shall elaborate on this topic for its potential theoretical and methodological import.

As will be described below, I found that gender differences in Samoan speech were not as clear-cut as in Malagasy. In the Samoan analysis I found myself asking, "*Which* men am I comparing with *which* women?" Where the Malagasy community is egalitarian, the Samoan community is not; rank, as noted earlier, is an important consideration. Nearly all the women in the Samoan community were untitled. The speech of untitled women could thus in some sense be considered representative of women's speech. But considerations of age, generation, marital status, and status of one's spouse and one's father make a difference. The wife or daughter of a powerful chief or the wife or daughter of a pastor will not necessarily conduct herself in the same way as wives or daughters of untitled men, as we have seen in the discussion of light and heavy labor. The men's corpus is more affected by the distinction between titled and untitled, given that roughly one out of three men have a title and that over the age of thirty-five the proportion is even higher (Duranti 1981). As discussed earlier, the distinction between titled and untitled and distinctions among titles have nonverbal behavioral correlates. We would expect speech as well to express and reflect these status distinctions. The speech of an untitled male is not to be taken as representative of men's speech, nor is the speech of a titled male.

Having scratched the surface of the complexities involved in the analysis of men's and women's speech in a Samoan community, I should like to move to more general methodological considerations involved in documenting gender differences in language. The literature is biased toward one important type of comparison, namely, one in which features/strategies characteristic of *most* women are contrasted with features/strategies of *most* men. Even when the study concerns a subset of women in a community, the emphasis is on how *most of these women* speak compared with *most of the men* in the subset.

For example, in certain studies of social dialects such as that carried out by Labov (1966), it has been noticed that women of a particular social class use the prestige variant of a phonological form more in particular contexts than do men of the same social class. While these dialect studies have themselves emphasized that use of the prestige variant is "conditioned" by several sociological variables (e.g., class, ethnicity, gender, formality of situation) and have ranked them as predictors of language use, other discussions have tended to focus exclusively on gender and have not weighed the effects of gender relative to other social features. In the case of the use of prestige variants in social-dialect studies, it is important to weigh the effects of gender as opposed to class. Is the most powerful predictor of use of the prestige variant (in a particular setting) class membership or gender? In the Samoan materials, it is important to relate gender to rank as a social variable affecting speech. As will be discussed in the following sections, gender is a strong predictor of use in certain social contexts but not in others and for certain grammatical and discourse features but not for others.

Making comparisons between men's and women's speech is, then, a complex enterprise. Transcripts have to be located in terms of the status features of the speakers in addition to all the other variables – such as situational role, speaker–hearer–audience relationship, topic, and setting – that have been discussed in the literature on sociolinguistic variation.

The corpus required to make comprehensive comparisons of men's and women's speech is enormous and well beyond that used in the present study. Although the data base includes adult speech of both sexes across a range of statuses, social situations vary tremendously. For any one social situation, there will be a limited set of statuses represented. Generalizations concerning gender differences in speaking will of necessity be tentative, limited to the status represented in the comparison.

Social variation in affect expression

In this section, I discuss the ways in which gender and other social features such as age and title interact as variables affecting the expression of affect. The discussion will focus on one particular dimension of affect, namely, the expression of sympathy/love – what Samoans call *alofa*.

Much has been written about gender differences and affect expression in language. Many have observed that women are more polite generally (Brown 1979; Lakoff 1973a). Brown's analysis of Tzeltal women indicates that women talking in private, in-group situations tend to use what Brown and Levinson (1978) call "positive politeness" and use "negative politeness" in public settings. Men, on the other hand, tend to speak more directly or "bald on record." Positive politeness is approach-based, addressing the face needs of a person to have his values, beliefs, and other facets of his social image appreciated. Much of positive politeness involves showing interest and involvement with another (complimenting, sympathizing, use of relatively friendly address terms, endearments, etc.). This aspect of women's behavior has also been considered as women's tendency to empathize with another or at least to act in a sympathetic manner to a greater extent than do men.

As noted in the description at the beginning of this chapter, Samoan has a rich system of encoding affect. It has a number of affect particles that intensify and sometimes indicate the speaker's mood. Like many languages, it has descriptive terms that indicate the speaker's feelings toward a referent (including love/sympathy, respect, anger). More unusual, Samoan has affect pronouns and determiners that express sympathy toward a referent. The affect pronouns express sympathy toward the speaker and are often used to get a listener to feel sorry for the speaker. The affect determiners express sympathy typically toward a third party but may also be used to express sympathy toward the addressee. Two prevalent situations in which these forms are used are begging and personal narratives. Begging is prevalent in children's speech but is not common in the adult interactions recorded in our study. Personal narratives, on the other hand, are characteristic of adult conversation.

In the context of the narrative, affect forms clue the listener as to how the listener should respond to the narrative. The narrator's use of particular forms constitutes a type of affective first part, to which the listener should supply the appropriate affective second part. If we want to compare men's and women's expressions of affect, and in particular expressions of sympathy, we must do so in terms of this discourse organization. That is, we must look at the extent to which men and women as narrators express and elicit sympathy toward a referent (including themselves) and the extent to which male and female listeners provide sympathetic responses.

Personal narratives were used as a basis for comparing the use of sympathy forms (including pronouns, nouns, determiners, adjectives, verbs, particles, and interjections) across gender and social rank. The narratives were concerned with either loss (including death) or danger and all were told to listeners of the same sex and social rank (i.e., to peers.) The social situations in which the narratives were conveyed were relatively informal; the listeners were not from the narrators' families but were close acquaintances. Because of limitations of the data base, not all statuses could be represented in the comparison. Three different sets of narrator–listeners are represented. The first consists of untitled young men in their early twenties. (Men do not usually hold a title under the age of thirty.) The second consists of men in their mid-forties to mid-fifties who have chiefly titles (*ali'i*). The third set of narrator–listeners is a group of women above the age of fifty who are wives of titled men. Wives of untitled men and young unmarried, untitled women are not represented. Thus, the findings and generalizations associated with the following study should be taken as suggestive and tentative.

The narratives vary in topic. The narratives of untitled men include a speaker's telling of his going to see a film about Dracula and a narrative about a mutual friend in jail. The main narrative in the corpus of titled men's informal conversation concerns how one of the men (the narrator) lost his watch. The titled women's narratives include two narratives in which the narrator is the protagonist, and a third in which another village woman (an intimate of those present) is the major character. The particular narrative data analyzed come from a larger corpus of Samoan adult and child language collected by Elinor Ochs, Alessandro Duranti, and Martha Platt (1978–9, 1981). In our corpus we have more instances

Table 2.3. *Expression of sympathy in narrator's speech*

Affect forms	Corpus 1 (77 clauses)		Corpus 2 (50 clauses)		Corpus 3 (146 clauses)	
Address terms	16	(20.8%)	1	(2%)	0	(0%)
Inclusive we	0	(0%)	1	(2%)	0	(0%)
Sympathy 1st per. pron.	2	(2.6%)	0	(0%)	2	(1.4%)
Sympathy determiner	7	(9.1%)	1	(2%)	4	(2.7%)
Sympathy nominal ref.	8	(10.4%)	1	(2%)	2	(1.4%)
Sympathy adj./verb	7	(9.1%)	1	(2%)	8	(5.4%)
Particles	12	(15.6%)	13	(26%)	31	(21.2%)
Interjections	0	(0%)	0	(0%)	1	(0.7%)
Total	52	(67.5%)	18	(36%)	48	(32.9%)

Note: Corpus 1 = untitled young men; corpus 2 = titled (chief) older men; corpus 3 = untitled older women married to titled men.

of women's narrative, since domestic activities were a major focus of our research.

Narrators' use of affect features. In these three sets of narratives, there are great differences in the narrators' use of affect forms. These differences (in terms of frequencies of occurrence) are codified in Tables 2.3 and 2.4. The differences are tied not so much to gender of speakers as to age and relative rank of the speakers. Women over fifty married to titled men and men of the same age who are chiefs show one pattern, and young untitled men show a different pattern of affect expression. More particularly, the young untitled narrator in the corpus used far more sympathy forms than the other two sets of narrators. This is demonstrated in two ways.

First, in Table 2.3 the number of sympathy forms is compared with the number of clauses in the narratives. If we disregard distinctions of title and age, that is, if we compare only women's speech (corpus 3) with men's speech (corpus 1, corpus 2), we find significant differences in use of affect forms at the .005 level, with men using more affect forms than women. But when we incorporate into our analysis the variables of title and age, we see that the difference is heavily influenced by the frequency of affect forms in the speech of untitled men (corpus 1).

As can be seen in Table 2.3 by examining the percentages in "Total," and again more concisely in Table 2.6, the narrative of the young men (corpus 1) contains such forms almost twice as frequently per clause as do the other two sets of narratives examined. Further, the difference in affect use between untitled and titled men (corpus 1 versus corpus 2) and the difference in affect use between untitled men and older women

Table 2.4. *Sympathy and neutral first-person pronouns*

	Corpus 1		Corpus 2		Corpus 3	
Sympathy	2	(66.7%)	0	(0%)	2	(13.3%)
Neutral	1	(33.3%)	24	(100%)	13	(86.7%)

married to titled men (corpus 1 versus corpus 3) are also significant, whereas the difference in affect use between titled men and older women married to titled men (corpus 2 versus corpus 3) is not.

We can also see the more effusive style of the young untitled narrator by examining the proportion of sympathy-marked to neutral first-person pronouns, as displayed in Table 2.4. Here we can see that, whereas the young untitled male narrator of corpus 1 did not refer to himself often, in two of the three instances he employed the sympathy form. In contrast, the older titled male narrator of corpus 2 referred to himself often but never used the affect-marked form, and the older women of corpus 3 used the affect form only 13.3 percent of the time.

This pattern reflects expectations of Samoans concerning demeanor of relatively high- and low-status persons. One would not expect relatively high-status persons, especially chiefs, to express (and thereby elicit) sympathy for themselves as often as lower-status persons. Relatively high-status persons are expected to conduct themselves in a more restrained and detached manner.

With respect to gender differences, these data tentatively suggest that *title and age overshadow gender* in accounting for affect expression in narration. The women in this corpus used slightly fewer affect features than titled men of the same age, but these two sets of narrators look quite similar when their style is compared with the narrative style of the young untitled male.

Listeners' use of affect features. Let us consider now the use of affect features by those listening to the narratives in the three sets of situations. The comparison here is somewhat flawed by a feature of the data collection. One of the two listeners in corpus 1 (young untitled men) was also the one recording the interaction. Whereas no one else was aware of the recorder, this person was and monitored his speech accordingly. This circumstance may have affected the frequency of sympathy features in listeners' speech in this situation.

Table 2.5 provides a comparison of listener usage patterns across the three contexts examined. We cannot rely on the results of corpus 1, but we can make interesting comparisons between corpus 2 and corpus 3.

Table 2.5. *Expression of sympathy in listeners' speech*

Affect forms	Corpus 1 (33 clauses)		Corpus 2 (43 clauses)		Corpus 3 (59 clauses)	
Address terms	2	(6.1%)	0	(0%)	0	(0%)
Sympathy determiners	1	(3.0%)	0	(0%)	4	(6.8%)
Sympathy nominal ref.	2	(6.1%)	0	(0%)	1	(1.7%)
Sympathy adj./verb	4	(12.1%)	1	(2.3%)	6	(10.2%)
Particles	11	(33.3%)	10	(23.3%)	18	(30.5%)
Interjections	1	((3.0%)	2	(4.7%)	4	(6.8%)
Agreement (yes/right)	3	(9.1%)	1	(2.3%)	3	(5.1%)
Repetition/paraphrase of narration	6	(18.2%)	4	(9.3%)	13	(22.0%)
Total	30	(90.9%)	18	(41.9%)	49	(83.1%)

Table 2.6. *Proportion of sympathy features to number of clauses*

	Corpus 1	Corpus 2	Corpus 3
Narrator	1 : 1.5	1 : 2.8	1 : 3
Listener	1 : 1.1	1 : 2.4	1 : 1.2

The results indicate somewhat different patterns from our earlier analysis of narrator style. As in the earlier analysis, if we compare the "total" row for only men's and women's speech (corpus 1 and corpus 2 versus corpus 3) as listeners, we find a gender difference in affect use that is statistically significant (at .025 level only). But the frequency of affect forms in the speech of older titled male listeners (corpus 2) is significantly lower than that of both the young untitled men (corpus 1) and the older untitled women married to titled men (corpus 3). On the other hand, there are no significant differences in the use of affect forms by young untitled men (corpus 1) and the older titled women.

Narrator–listener affect relations. Combining the results of narrators' and listeners' usage patterns, we can piece together the narrative interactional styles of our different sets of speakers. In Table 2.6 I have indicated the proportion of sympathy features to number of clauses for narrators and listeners in each corpus. This table suggests that untitled younger men use a moderate number of sympathy features as narrators and a large number as listeners, titled older men use very few sympathy features as both narrators and listeners, and untitled older women use few sympathy features as narrators but many as listeners. Although

Table 2.7. *Ergative case marking in two- and three-constituent transitive clauses with postverbal agents (V [x] S [x])*[a]

Situation	Case markers used		Case markers not used		Total
Women to family members	6	(20%)	24	(80%)	30
Men to family members	3	(16.6%)	15	(83.3%)	18
Women to nonfamily, informal	16	(45.7%)	19	(54.3%)	35
Men to nonfamily, informal	12	(75%)	4	(25%)	16

[a]Ergative case markers appear only in these word orders.

speakers across all three corpora used more affect forms as listeners than as narrators, the women in corpus 3 show the greatest increase in affect usage (from 1:3 to 1:1.2), and the titled men in corpus 2 show the least increase (from 1:2.8 to 1:2.4).

In summary, the analyses of affect features in the speech of narrators and listeners indicate that *both gender and rank are important variables, but rank is more important.* Anne Reynolds's statistical analyses indicate that women are more like titled men in the use of affect forms in narration, but they are more like untitled men in the use of affect forms as listeners.

Social variation in ergative case marking

In two earlier studies (Ochs 1982, in press), several linguistic behaviors, including use of ergative case marking, word-order strategies, and deletion, were analyzed across different social contexts.

For ergative case marking, it was found that men use this marking about as often as women do in family interactions but much more often than women in interactions involving nonfamily members. A portion of this comparison is represented in Table 2.7. The data are not broken down into different social statuses of men and women. The women are all untitled. Those in the family interactions are three mothers in their thirties who are either spouses or daughters of titled men. The women interacting informally with nonfamily represent a wide range of ages and social statuses; they are female members of a church congregation, chatting and picking weeds together. The men in the corpus also cover a wide range of ages and social statuses. Those in the family setting are husbands of two of the women recorded; one has a title (orator) and the other does not. The men speaking with nonfamily include the young untitled men and older titled men making up corpus 1 and corpus 2 in the study of affect features above as well as other titled men in other activities.

Unfortunately, it is not possible to break down these categories into their finer groupings. There simply are not enough instances of the behavior we are interested in, namely, ergative case marking (or transitive utterances with postverbal agents). We can only make casual remarks about individual variation and suggest tendencies.

Looking first at the three mothers speaking within the family, I can report that the one married to an untitled man shows the lowest use of ergative case marking (12.5 percent versus 23.8 percent and 36.4 percent for the women married to titled men). Looking at the husbands' speech, I see a similar pattern: The untitled husband had the lower frequency of ergative case marking (10 percent versus 22.2 percent). It looks as if in the household setting husbands and wives parallel one another (12.5 percent to 10 percent and 23.8 percent to 22.2 percent) and the variable of title is influential in accounting for frequency of use of the ergative case marker.

There is such a large group of women talking to nonfamily that no analysis of different statuses of their spouses is feasible. All of the women recorded here, however, were *untitled*. Looking at the men's corpus, we can compare the behavior of untitled to titled men speaking informally outside the family. Here again, rank is a consideration. Untitled men use ergative case marking in 62.5 percent of the possible syntactic environments for this marking, and titled men use it in 87.5 percent of these environments. However, 62.5 percent is still well above the average for women's speech (45.7 percent) in similar social settings. Untitled men in these settings do not behave like untitled women. In these settings gender and title are both relevant in accounting for sociolinguistic variation in ergative case marking.

In summary, in family interactions, title is more important than gender in accounting for variation in the use of ergative case marking. In interactions of a casual nature outside the family, gender and title are both important social variables.

Social variation in word order

The earlier study of sociolinguistic variation in adult Samoan speech indicated that men and women had different word-order preferences.

Table 2.8. *Word-order preferences in three full constituent transitive utterances, by sex of speaker*[a]

Sex	VSO		VOS		SVO		OVS		Total	
Men	17	(44.7%)	14	(36.8%)	3	(7.8%)	4	(10.5%)	38	(99.9%)
Women	9	(24.3%)	13	(35.1%)	12	(32.4%)	3	(8.2%)	37	(99.9%)

[a]This corpus includes speech of men in formal settings.

A summary of these preferences is provided in Table 2.8 and these preferences across social settings in Table 2.9.

These tables indicate several patterns. The first is that women use subject-initial word order far more often than men (four times as much overall). The second is that men use verb–subject–object word order more than women (nearly twice as much overall). The third is that women show a more even use of the different word orders, whereas men seem to show a strong preference for one of these word orders but the particular preference shifts as social conditions shift. Men prefer VOS in talking to their families and VSO in talking to outsiders.

The same corpus used for analyzing case marking is used in this study, and with it come the same problems in assessing the role of other social factors. There are so few instances of three constituent utterances generally that we cannot break down the corpus into finer units. Nonetheless, as in the analysis of case marking, we can make casual comparisons. Unlike in the case-marking study, there do not seem to be important differences in word-order preferences according to whether or not speaker has a title or according to whether or not speaker is spouse of a titled person. Of the three women in the family corpus, one woman married to a titled man had a high frequency of VSO word order (50 percent) and one did not. In fact the second one had a slightly lower frequency of VSO order (7.7 percent) than did the woman married to an untitled man (8.3 percent). Similarly, for SVO orders no consistent pattern was found. The same can be said for these orders for men and for women in speaking to nonfamily. It appears that for this linguistic behavior, gender is the most important speaker-related social variable.

Style shifting across settings

Both men and women alter their patterns of speaking as features of the social context shift (Tables 2.7–9). But men alter their speech to a greater extent than do women. For example, men use between four and five

Table 2.9. *Word-order preferences across settings*[a]

Situation	VSO	VOS	SVO	OVS	Total
Women Family	5 (21.7%)	8 (34.7%)	8 (34.7%)	2 (8.9%)	23 (100%)
Men Family	4 (26.7%)	10 (66.7%)	0 (0%)	1 (6.6%)	15 (100%)
Women Nonfamily, informal	4 (28.6%)	5 (35.7%)	4 (28.6%)	1 (7.1%)	14 (100%)
Men Nonfamily, informal	4 (66.7%)	1 (16.7%)	1 (16.6%)	0 (0%)	6 (100%)
Total	17	24	13	4	50

[a]This corpus is a subset of the corpus in Table 2.8. It does not include formal speech of men.

times as much ergative case marking in speaking outside the family than in speaking among family members. Women use the case marking only twice as much outside the family as inside the family. Similarly, men's word-order preferences shift dramatically from one setting to another, whereas women maintain more or less the same word-order preferences across settings.

These patterns could be partly due to the fact that for men the gender of conversational partner changes from family to nonfamily interaction, whereas for women the gender of the partner is the same across settings. Men talk to men and women and children in the family and to men only in the nonfamily setting; women talk to women and children in the one setting and to women in the other setting recorded. On the other hand, it could reflect additionally a tendency of Samoan women to treat members of their own sex who are of equivalent social status in the village as members of their own families, that is, as intimates, whereas men make a sharper distinction between family and nonfamily relationships. Both of these suggestions are supported by further data analyzed elsewhere (Ochs 1982) that indicate that in formal council meetings titled men have usage patterns of case marking and word order similar to those in their informal speech to nonfamily members. That is, the shift from family (mixed sexes, mixed ages) to nonfamily (same sex, same age group) is sharper than the shift from relatively informal to formal interactions among the latter group. If we look at Rosaldo's suggestion that women's life tends to be more private and domestic and men's more public and social (1974), we can reinterpret it for the Samoan materials as a suggestion that women *treat* life (i.e. relationships) as more private and domestic and men *treat* life as more public and social. Each group provides differing affective frames for the situations in which they participate through verbal and nonverbal behavior.

These patterns are relevant to Chodorow's (1974) hypothesis concerning personality differences across genders. Chodorow and others (Carlson 1971; Gutmann 1965; Mitscherlich 1963, as cited in Chodorow 1974) suggest that women's personalities are less individuated than men, that women have more flexible ego boundaries, that women are more field-dependent. Presumably, in terms of language use this would mean that women shift their speech from situation to situation to a greater extent than do men, that is, that women adapt their speech to different situations more than men. I say that Samoan women are adapting to the situations in which they participate regardless of whether or not they shift their speech patterns. Nonshifting in Samoan women's speech appears to be appropriate to interaction among female peers. On the other hand, I also say that Samoan men are highly adaptive to different social settings. Indeed, the small study of husbands' and wives' speech showing their parallel patterns of language use indicates that both men and women finely tune their speech to the varied social environments of their daily lives.

Chodorow's hypothesis is based on a particular pattern of early socialization in which mothers are the primary caregivers. Children of both sexes initially identify with their mothers, but ultimately sons must distinguish themselves and identify with adult males (usually their fathers). The adult male, however, is usually physically remote during much of the boy's early childhood. The relative availability of the mother and unavailability of the father ultimately affect the personality of female and male children.

This paper suggests that a crucial differentiating experience in male and female development arises out of the fact that women, universally, are largely responsible for early child care and for (at least) later female socialization. (Chodorow 1974:43)

Because her mother is around, and she has had a genuine relationship to her as a person, a girl's gender and gender role identification are mediated by and depend upon real affective relations. Identification with her mother is not positional – the narrow learning of particular role behaviors – but rather a personal identification with her mother's general traits of character and values. (Ibid.:51)

As noted earlier, Samoan patterns of child-rearing differ in important ways from this description. First, children are given care by a wide range of caregivers covering both sexes. This pattern, as reported in Weisner and Gallimore (1977), is the prevailing caregiving pattern across the world's societies. Children of both sexes then have models in their immediate environment, and in this sense boys as well as girls experience a continuous identification with a role model.

Second, whereas mothers are often physically present in the household compound, they are not necessary socially available to interact with a young child. Indeed, if younger caregivers are available the mother will orient the child to these others and involve herself in other activities. This demeanor contrasts with the more accommodating demeanor of Western middle-class caregivers toward their children. The model of "mother" for Samoan children is somewhat different from that for white middle-class children.

Third, what Samoan children do see is a set of older persons of both sexes who are relatively unaccommodating to them but who accommodate to those who are older or otherwise of higher social status. Through these experiences, children develop expectations that people shift their speech and comportment as speaker, addressee, and audience relations shift. Samoans do not have a distinct notion of feminine or masculine personality; indeed, as discussed by Shore (1977), they do not have a concept of personality itself. Instead, persons' attitudes and demeanor are thought to be always shifting, dependent on social conditions at hand.

Fourth and finally, Samoan children of both sexes are socialized into both accommodation and nonaccommodation. As noted earlier, they are encouraged to be both defiant and respectful. Further, starting quite early in their own lives, they are expected to take on caregiving responsibilities. By the age of four, they may be asked to monitor a younger sib and at the same time attend to the wishes of older persons present. In a manner rarely observed in middle-class Western homes, small Samoan children are able regularly to participate successfully in several social activities more or less at the same time, including sib caregiving, the serving of adults, and peer play. These behaviors reflect and socialize young children into the Samoan view of self as many-sided (Shore 1977, 1982) and context-dependent.

These observations confirm Chodorow's notion that gender identity is sensitive to patterns of socialization, but they indicate that socialization itself is variable. In the pattern of socialization described here, gender differences are minimized and other social parameters, primarily age, generation, title, and situational role, take precedence in organizing the language and comportment of men and women.

Note

I am grateful to Sue Philips for her careful reading and helpful comments on an earlier draft of this article. I also thank Anne Reynolds of the University of Arizona for her excellent analyses of the quantitative material in this study. This research was partially sponsored by a fellowship from the Howard Foundation (1982–3).

3. The interaction of variable syntax and discourse structure in women's and men's speech

SUSAN U. PHILIPS AND ANNE REYNOLDS

In the recent literature on gender differences in language use, the results of empirical research have not always formed a consistent or coherent view (Philips 1980). But one area of relative coherence has been the dialectological research in various European languages. In social-dialectological research on American English, gender differences have been evident for some time (Fischer 1958), and research based on La-bovian methods (Labov 1972b) has consistently shown systematic con-textual variation in the differences between men's and women's speech. In his study of New York speech (1972b), Labov found men used higher frequencies of so-called stigmatized phonological variants than women. Both men and women used higher frequencies of stigmatized variants in the parts of the sociological questionnaire Labov viewed as involving less self-monitoring of speech, and hence as less formal (e.g., stories about dangerous situations). And because men used more stigmatized variants in all aspects of the sociolinguistic interview, their speech was accordingly characterized as more informal.[1]

In studies outside the United States that closely followed Labov's method, a similar pattern has been found. Thus in Great Britain (Trudg-ill 1974), Quebec (Sankoff 1974), Panama (Cedergren 1972), and Costa Rica (Berk-Seligson 1978), men use stigmatized phonological variants more frequently than women, and are more like working-class than middle-class speakers in this respect.

These studies of French, Spanish, and English variation all were car-ried out in literate class-stratified societies in Western European coun-tries or their former colonies. There is every reason to think this sociolinguistic pattern is strongly associated with such a social order, and is not universal. Moylan's work in New Guinea (1982), where gender

71

differentiation is reflected in a very different pattern, certainly confirms this view.

In sum, this literature indicates that women more than men use linguistic variants that are used more by members of the higher social strata studied, used more in "formal" (i.e., closely monitored) speech, and viewed as "more correct" by all. However, it is important to keep in mind that this pattern is much better documented for phonological variation than for syntactic variation.

This chapter describes the contraction and deletion of subject pronouns followed by *have* or *be* in the speech of prospective jurors during interviews by judges and lawyers with them in an Arizona state court in a procedure called the voir dire. This data indicates that men delete subject pronoun and auxiliary/main verb more than women in one particular part of this procedure; their style in this part can thus be characterized as more informal, in keeping with the literature just discussed. But this deletion is not prompted by increased informality in the part of the procedure where the greater deletion occurs. Rather it occurs because of a change in the sequential management of topic resulting from a shift from dialogic questioning of jurors to juror monologues.

From this finding it is argued that there is a need to consider how speech activities, genres, or social contexts themselves differ linguistically if we are to explain adequately how and why women's and men's speech is similar and different in the ways that it is. This, in turn, can be done only through the study of naturally occurring speech, and cannot occur if the sole source of data is the sociolinguistic interview. That such studies have not been carried out more and sooner in accounts of language variation is probably due in part to efforts to treat all variation as aspects of style and thus part of the individual's communicative competence, rather than as part of a social system of language activity.

Data base and method of analysis

The data analyzed here is drawn from a study of judges' use of language in the Pima County Superior Court in Tucson, Arizona, carried out in 1978–9. During the course of tape-recording legal procedures in which judges were active participants, four voir dires were tape-recorded and later transcribed. The voir dire is the procedure in which prospective jurors are questioned by both lawyers and the judge in an effort to determine who among them is or is not biased in any way that would affect his or her ability to serve as an impartial juror.

It was evident from observation of the voir dire that it allowed an excellent opportunity to compare the speech of numerous men and women in roughly comparable uses of language, unlike other courtroom procedures, in which women do not appear in sufficient numbers (as plaintiffs, defendants, lawyers, judges) to allow useful comparison.

The four voir dires each lasted a little more or less than an hour, for a total of four and a half hours of taped material. During these four voir dires, a total of thirty-eight male jurors and thirty eight female jurors spoke varying numbers of times. Three of the four cases were civil cases, and the fourth was a criminal case. In the civil voir dires, the judge usually begins the voir dire with general information and instruction to the prospective jurors as a group, then asks them questions that are asked of jurors in all voir dires. The questioning is then turned over to the lawyers, who ask questions related to both the type of case at hand and the factual circumstances of the particular case. In the criminal voir dire, the judge handles most of the questioning and has some leeway and discretion in deciding how to involve the lawyers.

Some judges also require each prospective juror to deliver a brief monologue near the beginning of the procedure in which jurors provide social-background information about themselves and their spouses, guided by a list of the pieces of information they are to deliver. Since the lawyers already have such social-background information on sheets filled out by the jurors when they were first considered for jury duty, this information is redundant. And for this reason, many judges do not require such monologues. Those who do require monologues agree with the lawyers who feel that a comparison of what the jurors say with what they wrote will help them in their selection of jurors. In this data base, two judges requested such monologues, and the third, who presided over the other two voir dires, did not.

Gender is manifest in a variety of ways in this data base. Reference to spouse as husband or wife always identifies the sex of the speaker. In general, one gets the impression that men and women respond differently to the questions posed. Men more often use their jobs as reason for getting off a jury, and women seem more often to use childcare problems as a reason to get off. Women seem to know more of the doctors involved in personal-injury and malpractice cases, presumably because they go to the doctor more. Women more often seem uncertain as to whether they will or will not be biased as a result of a particular experience, and seem to wait for the judge and lawyer to decide this for them more often than men. Women more often seem to feel they will be biased in cases involving harm to children and pictures displaying such harm; men more often seem to feel they will be biased because they have been involved in civil suits similar to the case at hand, or because they feel antagonism toward police, doctors, insurance companies, or whoever and whatever might be central to the case.

In addition, there appear to be grammatical differences between men's and women's speech of a variable nature. The overall initial impression from the transcripts was of more phonological and syntactic deletion by men. It seemed particularly evident from this data base that men were dropping out the beginnings of utterances, particularly utterances that could begin with a personal pronoun immediately followed by a verb and that did so begin when other speakers were speaking in directly comparable environments.

In dealing with the voir-dire data, we decided to look at the contraction and deletion of first- and third-person pronoun subjects followed directly by auxiliary verb or main verb, in order both to determine the nature of the overall pattern of contraction and deletion and to assess the nature of the difference between men's and women's speech in these syntactic environments. First- and third-person singular pronoun subjects–i.e., *I, he,* and *she*–were selected because they appeared far more often than any other subject pronouns in the speech of the prospective jurors. All of the jurors' utterances with these features of form were then coded for the presence of contraction, deletion, or neither. The coding of these data also distinguished between deletions of subject or auxiliary verb alone and both auxiliary verb and subject and, in sentences with no auxiliary verb, made a distinction between deletion of subject alone and both subject and main verb (there were no instances of deletion of main verb but not subject). No utterances immediately following questions were coded, because answers to questions have their own distinct deletion pattern.

It was clear that the bulk of instances of utterances coded involved the verbs *have* and *be,* functioning as either auxiliary verbs or main verbs. It also appeared that there was more deletion during the jurors' social-background monologues than elsewhere in the voir-dire proceedings. For these reasons, tallies were made from the original coding to compare male and female contraction and deletion of subject pronoun and *have* or *be,* functioning both as auxiliary verbs and main verbs. In the tallies we also separated the juror monologues from the dialogic questioning that made up the rest of the voir-dire elicitation of speech from prospective jurors. The focus on *have* and *be* had the additional advantage of their being used as both auxiliary and main verbs, so we could determine whether contraction and deletion worked differently in those two syntactic roles. Finally, from the data coded we excluded negative constructions such as "I have never served on a jury before" and other utterances in which there were words between subject and the auxiliary or main verb, such as "I really am a carpenter, but I drive a school bus."

In the variationist literature on English dialects, considerable attention has been given to the contraction and deletion of *be*. Labov (1969) has argued that deletion of *be* will occur in vernacular black English where contraction of *be* occurs in white English. [2] Wolfram (1974) shows that *be* is also deleted in the speech of white southerners, and he argues that they have assimilated this feature from the black speakers in their area.

Both Labov and Wolfram found much more deletion of *are* than of *is*. Both found more deletion of *be* when it functions as an auxiliary than when it functions as a main verb, though neither makes this distinction as such. Wolfram also indicates that persons of lower socioeconomic status delete more than persons of higher socioeconomic status do, and his tables make it clear that among those who delete *be* most often are more men than women.

Thus far we see that deletion of *be* follows a pattern similar to that of other variationist research in that men's speech is more like that of lower socioeconomic strata than women's speech. But neither Labov nor Wolfram addresses the nature of contextual variation in the frequency of deletion, or speakers' attitudes toward deletion of *be*, so one cannot say that Wolfram's study shows men more often using a variant that is viewed by the speakers as either more informal or more stigmatized.

Both Labov and Wolfram also found that *be* is deleted more often after subject pronouns than after full noun phrases, but it is clear from their examples that *be* is always preceded by some kind of surface subject in the environments they examined, and no mention is made of whether subjects were ever deleted in their data or, if so, how these instances were handled in their analysis.

Indeed, to our knowledge, there has been no variationist analysis of the deletion of subject pronouns. Instead this concern has been given attention primarily by students of discourse analysis. By now, it is generally recognized that whereas in English anaphoric pronouns are used to identify referents already identified in prior discourse by full nouns, in other languages, notably Chinese (Li and Thompson 1976) and Japanese (Clancy 1980; Hinds 1978), deletion of the noun phrase commonly occurs instead. Li and Thompson (1976) refer to such deletion as "zero-pronoun." Thus Clancy (1980) found, in a comparison of English and Japanese pear stories, that where third-person referents had already been previously identified, later reference involved deletion in 73 percent of all instances in Japanese but in only 21 percent of instances in English. All of the English instances of deletion involved subjects, usually where the subject referent is preserved over clauses within the same sentence (Clancy 1980:161). This finding is similar to Li and Thompson's finding that zero-pronouns in Chinese occur most often in a "topic chain" in which the topic is the same through a group of clauses.

As should be evident from the preceding discussion, the "explanation" for pronoun deletion is that the pronoun is recoverable from past discourse. This does not explain why some recoverable referents are deleted and others are not.

The explanations of deletion of *be* and the explanations of deletion of pronouns, both of which are relevant to the data to be analyzed here, are quite different. Neither the variationists nor the discourse analysts have considered the others' variables or the others' explanations. Thus variationists have not considered textual redundancy as a factor in deletion of whole words, and the discourse analysts have not considered formality/conscious monitoring or the socioeconomically determined "lect" of the speaker as a factor in explaining deletion.

Akmajian (1979), however, has examined the contraction and deletion of subject pronouns and the auxiliary verbs *do*, *have*, and *be* together in abbreviated questions. He suggests that in questions such as "Having a good time?" "Are you" can be deleted from the beginning of the sentence, whereas one cannot say, "Are having a good time?" And he argues that the latter cannot occur, because the deletion process is dependent on contraction of the auxiliary verb onto the pronoun, so that if the pronoun is deleted, the contractible verb must also be deleted. Interestingly enough, when Akmajian turns to the analysis of declaratives, he leaves the Labovian assumption that the verb will delete alone intact.

Unlike the others whose work we have discussed thus far, Akmajian explicitly asserts that deletion of subject and contractible verb is characteristic of "informal" American speech style. This is consistent with the characterizations by a number of authors of colloquial everyday or unplanned speech as involving fewer or more attenuated grammatical elements than public, planned, or formal speech (Ferguson 1959; Irvine 1979; Joos 1961; Ochs 1979; Philips 1984; Sherzer 1974). As we shall see in the next section, the analysis of prospective jurors' speech is not consistent with or explainable by this view.

Results of data analysis

In this section, attention will be given first to the ways in which the linguistic context of subject pronoun plus auxiliary verb affects patterns of contraction and deletion, then to the ways in which the type of discourse (dialogic questioning versus juror monologues) the jurors are participating in affects patterns of deletion, and finally to the ways in which social identity, and gender in particular, is related to patterns of deletion in this data base.

Linguistic context

Attention was given to several different aspects of the linguistic context in which sentence-initial subject pronoun and auxiliary verb appeared. First, consideration was given to whether the verb following the pronoun functioned as an auxiliary verb or a main verb. Second, consideration was given to whether the verb was *have* or *be*. Finally, attention was given to whether the preceding pronoun was first-person singular (*I*) or third-person singular (*he* or *she*).

Table 3.1 summarizes the number of deletions and contractions in the data base, and Tables 3.2 and 3.3 display the exact nature of the deletions in the dialogues and monologues, focusing attention on whether the deletion involved both subject and verb or only one, and, of the latter, which.

A chi-square test was carried out to determine whether there was a significant difference in the rates of contraction and deletion when *have* and *be* functioned as auxiliaries as opposed to main verbs. We indicate in Table 3.4 that there is a highly significant difference (X^2 significant at .005 level) between these two syntactic roles, such that there is more deletion and contraction when *have* and *be* function as auxiliaries than when they function as main verbs. This raises the possibility that *have* and *be* carry different sorts of information in these two roles, and that the information carried by auxiliary verbs is either more redundant or less crucial to information processing than the information carried by main verbs.

A chi-square test was also carried out to determine whether the rates of contraction and deletion were significantly different for *have* and *be*. Table 3.5 shows the results of that test, which indicate that this distinction is highly significant in that *be* is far more likely to be contracted than *have* primarily when they function as main verbs (65 percent versus 8 percent), as Table 3.1 indicates. *Have* is more likely to be deleted than *be* primarily when they function as auxiliary verbs (30 percent versus 9 percent), as Table 3.1 indicates.

Finally, although no statistical comparisons were made of the differences between the relation between first- versus third-person singular pronouns preceding *have* and *be* and contraction and deletion, it is clear that deletion occurs far more often with first-person singular pronouns, because all but one of the deletions occur in that environment. There

Table 3.1. *Contraction and deletion of subject pronoun and/or auxiliary/main verb in four voir dires*

	Dialogues			Monologues			Total		
	Contraction % N	Deletion % N	N	Contraction % N	Deletion % N	N	Contraction % N	Deletion % N	N
Subj. + aux.									
Be	54.5 (6)	9.1 (1)	(11)	0 (0)	0 (0)	(0)	54.5 (6)	9.1 (1)	(11)
Have	56.3 (9)	37.5 (6)	(16)	56.8 (21)	27.0 (10)	(37)	56.6 (30)	30.2 (16)	(53)
Subtotal	55.6 (15)	25.9 (7)	(27)	56.8 (21)	27.0 (10)	(37)	56.3 (36)	26.6 (17)	(64)
Subj. + main verb									
Be	87.5 (35)	7.5 (3)	(40)	50.8 (33)	7.7 (5)	(65)	64.8 (68)	7.6 (8)	(105)
Have	0 (0)	0 (0)	(26)	15.4 (4)	19.2 (5)	(26)	7.7 (4)	9.6 (5)	(52)
Subtotal	53.0 (35)	4.5 (3)	(66)	40.7 (37)	11 (10)	(91)	45.9 (72)	8.3 (13)	(157)
Total	53.8 (50)	10.7 (10)	(93)	45.3 (58)	15.6 (20)	(128)	48.9 (108)	13.6 (30)	(221)

Table 3.2. *Single and double deletion in the dialogue data*

	Females		Males	
	Have	*Be*	*Have*	*Be*
Subj. + aux.				
Subj.	0	0	0	0
Aux.	3	0	1	0
Both	1	1	1	0
Subj. + MV				
Subj.	0	0	0	2
Main verb	0	0	0	0
Both	0	1	0	0
Total	4	2	2	2

Table 3.3. *Single and double deletion in the monologue data*

	Females		Males	
	Have	*Be*	*Have*	*Be*
Subj. + aux.				
Subj.	0	0	0	0
Aux.	1	0	0	0
Both	1	0	8	0
Subtotal	2	0	8	0
Sub. + MV				
Subj.	1	0	1	0
Main verb	0	0	0	0
Both	0	0	3	5
Subtotal	1	0	4	5
Total	3	0	12	5

are no instances of *you* as subject in juror's speech, but *you* as subject is frequently deleted in judges' courtroom language use (Philips 1984). Third-person subjects may be deleted less often because the deleted item is less predictable (i.e., it can be *he*, *she*, or *it*) than first- and second- person singular. Greater frequency of use of first- and second-person singular pronouns and hence their routinization may also be a factor in the frequency with which they are deleted.

Table 3.4. Chi-square test of auxiliary–main verb syntactic role

	Dialogue			Monologue			Raw total
	Contraction	Deletion	Neither	Contraction	Deletion	Neither	
Subj. + aux.	f 15	7	5	21	10	6	64
	F 14.47	2.90	9.56	16.80	5.79	14.47	
Subj. + MV	f 35	3	28	37	10	44	157
	F 35.52	7.19	23.44	41.20	14.21	35.52	
Column total	50	10	33	58	20	50	221 = N

f = observed; F = expected.

$$X^2 = \sum \frac{f^2}{F} - N = 245.042 - 221 = 24.042.$$

df = (6−1) (2−1) = 5.

X^2 significant at .005 level (highly significant) (p < .005).

Table 3.5. *Chi-square test of the* be/have *distinction in both dialogue and monologue*

	Contraction	Deletion	Neither	Raw total
Be	f 74 F 56.69	f 9 F 15.75	f 33 F 43.57	116
Have	f 34 F 51.31	f 21 F 14.25	f 50 F 39.42	105
Column total	108	30	83	221 = *N*

$X^2 = 22.61$.
df = 2.
(p < .005)

Discourse context: dialogue versus monologue

The second set of factors considered in their relation to frequency of contraction and deletion of subject pronoun and auxiliary/main verb focused on the difference between the dialogic questioning of jurors in the bulk of all four voir dires and the brief social-background monologue provided by jurors in two of the voir dires.

Chi-square tests were carried out to determine whether there was a significant difference between the monologues and the dialogic questioning in frequency of contraction, frequency of deletion, and both. No significant differences were found between the monologue and dialogue on any of these three measures.

When, however, the kind of deletion was examined (as laid out in Tables 3.2 and 3.3), distinguishing between single deletions in which only the subject pronoun or the verb *have* or *be* was deleted versus double deletions in which both are deleted, clear differences between monologue and dialogue emerge.

Of the thirty deletions in the entire corpus, four involved deletion of subject alone. Interestingly, all of these occur when the verb that follows is a main verb. Five of the deletions involve only the auxiliary verb. The main verb is never deleted by itself. All of these five deletions involve *have* and none involve *be*. The remaining twenty-one of thirty deletions delete both the subject and the auxiliary or main verb.

A chi-square test was carried out to determine whether the proportion of single and double deletions was significantly different in the dialogue and monologue. As Table 3.6 indicates, the proportion was significantly different at the .025 level, in that one element is deleted more often

Table 3.6. *Chi-square test of significance of single versus double deletions in monologues and dialogues*

	Dialogues	Monologues	Raw total
One element deleted	f 6 F 3	f 3 F 6	9
Two elements deleted	f 4 F 7	f 17 F 14	21
Column total	10	20	30 = N

X^2 = 6.43.
df = 1.
(p < .025)

Table 3.7. *Chi-square test of proportion of words deleted in monologues versus dialogues*

	Dialogues	Monologues	Raw total
Words deleted	f 14 F 21.46	f 37 F 29.54	51
Word not deleted	f 172 F 164.54	f 219 F 226.46	391
Column total	186	256	442 = N

X^2 = 5.06.
df = 1.
(p < .025)

than expected in the dialogues and two elements are deleted more often than expected in the monologues.

Relatedly, if we count the proportion of words deleted in the relevant environments, there is a significantly greater proportion of words deleted in the monologues than in the dialogues, because of the greater number of double deletions in the monologues, as shown in Table 3.7.

Why is there more deletion of both elements, and hence deletion of more words, in the juror monologues? In the data base at hand, differences in the discourse context created by the juror monologues, compared with that of the dialogic questioning, help explain these differences in the patterns of deletion for the two types of elicitation from jurors.

In the dialogic questioning, the judge and both lawyers take turns asking the entire group of jurors empanelled for a particular trial whether any of them knows or believes a whole series of things that could cause a juror to be biased. In response to each question, those who would answer yes raise their hands and then the questioner calls on each juror who raised a hand to elaborate or answer one or more additional questions. Usually the questions are very controlling, in that they either call for a yes or a no or for a single-word response. This is because the lawyers and the judge are fearful a prospective juror will blurt out some remark that will bias the other prospective jurors and necessitate dismissing them to call in a new batch. Usually, then, each turn at talk by a juror is short; only infrequently does it go beyond a single sentence. In these data, then, the sentences that begin with a first- or third-person singular pronoun and auxiliary or main verb *have* or *be* are not usually part of a larger turn at talk, but the first or second and last reference to a given subject. Examples of this dialogue are: [3]

(1) DEFENDANT'S LAWYER: D'you feel that in some way that doctor didn't treat ya properly?

JUROR (MALE):   Right.

DEFENDANT'S LAWYER: D'ya feel that because uh that y'might be somewhat more uh inclined for the plaintiff in this case than another doctor who's in the same field as uh doctor you're talkin' about?

JUROR (MALE):   No.

(Tape J, side 2, p. 34)

(2) DEFENDANT'S LAWYER: 'Kay. Was there a lawsuit? Either you were sued or /something/...

JUROR (FEMALE):   /No/ we weren't sued. They...it was the other party but we settled out of court.

DEFENDANT'S LAWYER: I'm sorry. They sued you or you /sued/...

JUROR (FEMALE):   /No/ we sued...we were suing them.

DEFENDANT'S LAWYER: Thank you. – I saw another hand somewhere. (Didn't I?) Yes, ma'am.

JUROR (FEMALE):   Well *I was* in a accident and my daughter was too.

(Tape H, side 2, p. 47)

The monologue differs from the dialogue in the context it provides for the syntactic feature we are examining, in two different respects. First, the monologues involve each juror's producing turns at talk that consist of a number of utterances or sentences, with the same subject's often being sustained over several utterances, so that the same singular personal pronoun appears in subject position several times in a row across sentences in the monologue of each juror who does one. This means that a context is created in which the subject, if deleted, can be retrieved from preceding utterances.

Second, these monologues are routinized, so that each juror provides exactly the same information in the same order, one after another. This repetition of format also creates a redundancy of context, so that if

Table 3.8. *Chi-square test of deletion in first and second halves of voir dire*

	1st half	2nd half	Raw total
Deleted	f 7	f 13	20
	F 11.03	F 8.97	
Not deleted	f 68	f 48	116
	F 63.97	F 52.03	
Column total	75	61	136 = N

$X^2 = 3.85$.
df = 1.
(p < .025)

deletion of subject occurs, it can be retrieved not only from past utterances within the speaker's turn but also from preceding turns by other jurors, not to mention future turns.

(3) JUROR 9:   My name is Sophia K. Jacobs. I'm employed by Krable, Parsons and Dooley. I've been employed there for ten years as a bookkeeper an' junior accountant. My husband is employed by (Amphitheater) school district. He's a teacher. And he's worked there for ten years. I have never been on a trial jury before. I don't have any formal legal training.
(Tape H, side 1, p. 15)

(4) JUROR 10:   Herb R. Beasley, senior. President of Beasley Refrigeration Incorporated. Do commercial refrigeration. And my wife's name is Lillian an' she works in the office. I've never been on a trial jury and no legal training.
(Tape H, side 1, p. 15)

In these examples, there is no deletion in (3) but considerable deletion in (4).

That these contextual redundancies in the monologue do play a role in there being more deletion in monologues is supported by the fact that literally all of the deletions in the monologues occur where the subject is the same as in the two preceding utterances, and by the fact that there are twice as many deletions in the monologues of the last eight jurors as there are in the monologues of the first eight jurors in both of the voir dires in which there are monologues. Thus in the first half of all monologues taken together there are only seven deletions in seventy-five possible, or 9 percent. In the second half of all the monologues taken together, there are thirteen deletions of sixty-one possible, or 21 percent.

Table 3.8 shows that the occurrence of deletion is correlated with whether the subject pronoun plus *have/be* occurs in the first or second half of the voir dire (p<.05). Deletion occurs significantly more often than expected in the second half of the voir dire and significantly less often than expected in the first half.

In sum, more material is deleted in the monologues because of the redundancy created by longer turns at talk in which the subject is sustained over several sentences and by the routinization of the juror monologue, which creates redundancy through repetition of the same speech event.

Gender identity

Finally, we consider whether the gender of the speaker is correlated with patterns of contraction and deletion of subject pronouns followed by *have* or *be* in this data base. Table 3.9 summarizes the rates of contraction and deletion for men and women.

A chi-square test was performed to determine whether the overall rates of contraction and/or deletion were significantly different for men and women. They were not, although the tendency for men to delete more than women (17 percent versus 9 percent) is obvious.

Moreover, when we ask whether men and women differ significantly in their use of single versus double deletions (Table 3.10 summarizes the number of each from Tables 3.2 and 3.3), an analysis of the data in Table 3.11 indicates that women delete one element more often than expected and men delete both elements more often than expected (p<.05). Not surprisingly, this results in a highly significant difference in the proportion of words deleted in the relevant environments by men and women for the corpus as a whole, as indicated in Table 3.12. Thus men delete a significantly greater proportion of words than women.

If we compare men's and women's contraction and deletion in the monologue data and dialogue data separately, it becomes clear that the differences in their patterns of deletion for the corpus as a whole are largely due to men's greater deletion, and double deletion in particular, in the monologue data. Thus, whereas women do not delete at significantly different rates in the dialogue and monologue, men delete significantly more in the monologue than in the dialogue, as displayed in Tables 3.13a and b. Relatedly, whereas there is no significant difference between men's and women's rates of deletion in the dialogue, there is a significant difference between men's and women's rate of deletion in the monologue data, with men deleting significantly more frequently than women, as displayed in Tables 3.14a and b.

To summarize the findings on gender differences so far, men delete both elements significantly more than women, and women delete single elements significantly more than men, resulting in the overall proportion

Table 3.9. *Summary of female and male contraction and deletion of subject pronoun and/or auxiliary/main verb*

	Dialogues					Monologues					Totals				
	Contraction		Deletion		N	Contraction		Deletion		N	Contraction		Deletion		N
	%	N	%	N	N	%	N	%	N	N	%	N	%	N	N
Females															
Subj + Aux	75	(15)	10	(2)	(20)	62	(8)	39	(5)	(13)	70	(23)	21	(7)	(33)
Subj + MV	23	(8)	3	(1)	(35)	50	(15)	3	(1)	(30)	35	(23)	3	(2)	(65)
Subtotal	42	(23)	5	(3)	(55)	53	(23)	14	(6)	(43)	47	(46)	9	(9)	(98)
Males															
Subj + Aux	35	(6)	47	(8)	(17)	50	(7)	14	(2)	(14)	52	(13)	32	(10)	(31)
Sub + MV	52	(29)	16	(9)	(56)	56	(20)	6	(2)	(36)	53	(49)	12	(11)	(92)
Subtotal	48	(35)	23	(17)	(73)	54	(27)	8	(4)	(50)	50	(62)	17	(21)	(123)
Total	45	(58)	16	(20)	(128)	54	(50)	12	(10)	(93)	49	(108)	14	(30)	(221)

Table 3.10. *Deletion of one versus both elements in subject pronoun plus auxiliary/main verb*

	Females		Males		Total	
	N	%	N	%	N	%
One element						
Subj.	1		3		4	
Aux.	4		1		5	
Subtotal	5	55.6	4	19.0	9	30
Both elements	4	44.4	17	81.0	21	70
Total	9	100	21	100	30	100

Table 3.11. *Chi-square test of single versus double deletions by men and women*

	Women		Men		Raw Total
One element	f	5	f	4	9
	F	2.7	F	6.3	
Two elements	f	4	f	17	21
	F	6.3	F	14.7	
Column total		9		21	30 = N

$X^2 = 3.99$.
df = 1.
(p < .05)

Table 3.12. *Proportion of words deleted by gender*

	Females		Males		Raw total
Words deleted	f	13	f	38	51
	F	22.62	F	28.38	
Words not deleted	f	183	f	208	391
	F	173.38	F	217.62	
Column total		196		246	442 = N

$X^2 = 8.31$.
df = 1.
(p < .005)

Table 3.13a. *Women's deletion frequency in monologue versus dialogue*

	Monologue	Dialogue	Raw total
Deletion	f 3 F 5.05	f 6 F 3.95	9
No deletion	f 52 F 49.95	f 37 F 39.05	89
Column total	55	43	98 = N

$X^2 = 4.91$.
df = 1.
(p < .05)

Table 3.13b. *Men's deletion frequency in monologue versus dialogue*

	Monologue	Dialogue	Raw total
Deletion	f 17 F 12.46	f 4 F 8.54	21
No deletion	f 56 F 60.54	f 46 F 41.46	102
Column total	73	50	123 = N

$X^2 = 2.09$.
df = 1.
(p < .25)

of words deleted being significantly greater for men than for women for the corpus as a whole.

When men's and women's language use in the monologues is separated out from the dialogues, we find men delete significantly more than women in the monologues and significantly more in the monologues than the dialogues.

Of the seventeen males who produced juror monologues, twelve deleted at least once, and five of those twelve deleted twice. Of the fifteen females who produced juror monologues, only three females deleted, and all three deleted only once. Thus, neither female nor male deletion was limited to one or two persons, although clearly a much large proportion of the males deleted.

It is also interesting to note that the general pattern is for men to delete once in the first half of the group of monologues in each voir dire and twice in the second half, whereas women delete not at all in the

Table 3.14a. *Deletion by women versus men in monologue*

	Deletion	No deletion	Raw total
Female	f 3 F 8.59	f 52 F 46.41	55
Male	f 17 F 11.41	f 56 F 61.59	73
Column total	20	108	128 ⇒ N

$X^2 = 7.56$.
df = 1.
(p < .025)

Table 3.14b. *Deletion by women versus men in dialogue*

	Deletion	No deletion	Raw total
Female	f 6 F 4.62	f 37 F 38.38	43
Male	f 4 F 5.38	f 46 F 44.62	50
Column Total	10	83	93 = N

$X^2 = .858$.
df = 1.
(p < .5)

first half and once in the second half. Thus, although men generally delete more, both men and women follow the pattern mentioned earlier of more deletion in the second half of the juror monologues.

A closer examination of the monologues also suggests that these differences in frequency and in variable rule form may be accomplished in part through imitation of males by males and females by females.

In both the voir dires with monologues, the form for presentation of material becomes quickly routinized. The jurors tend to follow a format established by the first or second juror in the information they deliver and in the order in which they deliver it (which closely but not exactly follows a written format offered by the court to the jurors). But in addition they also tend to use the same sentence structure to present the same information. This is most evident when the jurors' presentation of information about their jobs is compared in the two voir dires. In one of the voir dires with monologues, the pattern that is established involves breaking the relevant pieces of information up into separate utterances, as in the following examples:

(5) "I'm employed with the city of Tucson. Aah been there over 9 months. I'm a police officer."

(Tape J, side 1, p. 18)

(6) "I'm employed at Davis-Monthan Air Force Base, 'n' I've been there since 1966. Uh I'm a traffic specialist."

(Tape J, side 1, p. 19)

In the other voir dire with monologues, a pattern that gets established early combines much of the same information into a single construction, particularly in providing the number of years worked in a prepositional phrase tacked onto the end of an utterance, rather than in a separate independent construction.

(7) "I'm presently employed with IBS for about 8 months."

(Tape N, side 1, p. 13)

(8) "I'm an advertising copywriter currently employed with Jack Trustman Advertising for about 8 months."

(Tape N, side 1, p. 13)

One consequence of this difference is that even when the same information is being delivered in the two voir dires, the opportunities for contraction and deletion are not the same. Thus, whereas in the first voir dire the environment "I have been working" accounts for five of twelve deletions in that voir dire, that same environment occurs much less often in the second voir dire with monologues, and so such deletion occurs less.

Within each voir dire, there is some evidence of males following males and females following females. In the first voir dire, three males delete *I have* in the environment "I have three children," whereas two females delete only *I* in the same environment. In the second voir dire, three instances of male deletion occur in the environment of "I have had no legal training," and no female deletion occurs in this environment. And, more strikingly, three instances of deletion of subject, auxiliary verb, *and* main verb occur in the second voir dire, produced by two males, whereas no instances of this occur in men's speech in the first voir dire with monologues.

Such data are by no means conclusive, but they suggest that at least some contextual variation in choice among referentially equivalent forms may be due to very local, interactionally constructed patterns of imitation of socially alike cointeractants, in keeping with Giles, Taylor, and Bourhis's (1973) notion that speakers "accommodate" one another.

Relatedly, this data suggests that in some sense the rules that account for variable patterns of use of particular forms should be more abstract than characterizations of statistical frequencies for the occurrence of particular forms. Thus, males with a tendency to delete more and to delete more elements together would manifest that tendency in different ways and in different environments, depending on the environments in which their cointeractants were deleting.

This means that a variable model that attempts to account for the kinds of constraints affecting an individual's naturally occurring speech may need to include a component that accounts for the way in which a speaker is constantly adjusting her or his speech to make it more like that of others present.

Discussion and conclusions

The main difference between women and men in their use of language that emerges from this analysis of prospective jurors' speech is that in the context of a relatively high degree of redundancy in information delivery, men's speech is less redundant than women's. The men, more than the women, allow the redundancy of information to carry their meaning, and they depend more on the hearer's ability to retrieve information that is deleted from the larger context.

If we consider the relation of this finding to the literatures that have addressed subject deletion and auxiliary verb deletion, several points emerge. As our earlier review of this literature indicated, more than one explanation has been offered for deletion in the environments considered here. Discourse analysts see subject deletion as occurring where it is possible to retrieve the subject from the larger social context. This explanation is of fundamental relevance to the explanation of deletion of both subject and auxiliary verb here, where it is evident that as the redundancy in the context increases, so does the amount of deletion. It is also possible to interpret some of the men's deletion as an effort to chain several propositions together in a single sentence, rather than keeping them in paralinguistically separate sentences as the women do, in keeping with Li and Thompson's (1976) and Clancy's (1980) previously discussed suggestions that subject deletion is more common in such constructions.

Akmajian (1979), in contrast, sees the deletion of both subject and auxiliary verb in abbreviated questions as part of an informal style. As was discussed earlier, Akmajian is not the first to associate syntactic deletion with informal speech. The main problem with doing so is that most discussions that associate informality with deletion either indicate or imply that speech is more informal when the social activity or context is more informal, whereas speech is more formal when the social activity or context is itself more formal; and that kind of equation does not apply to the data base at hand. Although there is no evidence that would allow us to argue that anyone perceives the juror monologues as more informal than the dialogic questioning (indeed, if anything, the opposite is the case), there is good evidence for arguing that the monologues are more redundant than the dialogic questionings, particularly with regard to the information being deleted.

The tendency of the women toward greater informational redundancy in their speech in this data is consistent with other findings on American females, as well as females in other societies, including some in this book, which suggest their speech is more often syntactically and morphologically elaborated or complex than male speech (e.g., Gleason this volume; Brown 1980; Goodwin and Goodwin this volume; Sachs this volume; Shibamoto this volume).

But functionally, more frequent surface elaboration by females is explained or interpreted in a variety of different ways when this elaboration is discussed. Elements seen as added to the basic propositional structure by women more than by men are interpreted as feminine (Shibamoto this volume), as polite (Brown 1980; Lakoff 1975), and as relatively powerless (Lakoff 1975). Those elements seen as not having been deleted by women as often as by men cause women's speech to be interpreted or explained as more formal (Labov 1974) or more standard (Fischer 1958; Labov 1974).

Often, however, it is really not clear from whose point of view such meanings are assigned, and they may reflect the analyst's interpretation, the view presented to the analyst by the people being characterized in the study, or some combination of both. Thus, whereas it is possible to characterize differences in form that correlate with gender social identity, as we have in this chapter, it is less clear what role they play at any level in the social construction of gender by parties to the interactions in which they occur. It is clear that differences in women's and men's use of morphological and syntactic surface elaboration contribute to interesting differences in meaning in discourse, but just exactly how is still not yet well understood.

Moreover, it is also clear that men's speech sometimes reveals more grammatical surface explication of meaning than women's, as in Ochs's (this volume) discussion of greater frequencies of ergative case markers in men's speech than in women's.

This finding alone indicates that one cannot readily claim that greater surface complexity in women's speech is universal, and hence possibly related to a biologically based superior linguistic capacity on the part of women of the sort suggested by the papers in Part III of this volume. At this point, then, we still must favor explanations of gender differences that are culturally based.

In the case of the data base at hand, the differences between men and women are still consistent with other characterizations of American gender differences in speech, in that men's speech shows less surface elaboration of meaning. But rather than say this shows women are more standard keepers of the flame of good form, more polite, or more powerless, we see *different strategies for the creation of discourse coherence*, and the imitation by same-sex speakers of one another's speech forms. We reject the view that these differences carry an obvious meaning or function, and we have argued here that such meanings are sometimes too readily assigned to gender differences in the use of particular linguistic forms, when more careful consideration of the nature of the meanings involved is still needed.

The more general point of this chapter is a methodological one. Its purpose has been to show that if gender differences in language form are examined in the context of the interactional and discourse structure of naturally occurring speech, rather than in the context of sentences from only a single interactant, as in research based on sociolinguistic interviews, they look very different and make more sense.

Such a discourse-based approach considers and shows the influence of both cointeractants' speech and naturally occurring contextual variation in the sequential development of meaning on a speaker's language form. Most studies of language variation based on sociolinguistic interviews don't do the former and can't do the latter. There is a need, then, for more research that is based on naturally occurring contextual variation in language use, and that examines such issues, in order to have a clearer basis for claims regarding both how and why meaning and form differ in women's and men's use of language.

Notes

We would like to acknowledge support for this research from the National Science Foundation and the University of Arizona College of Liberal Arts. We have also benefited from the comments on an earlier draft of this paper from Susan Steele, Christine Tanz, and Adrienne Lehrer.

1 Fasold (1972) and Feagin (1980) have not found this clear-cut pattern in their data on gender differences, a fact that may be related to their focus on other than phonological variation.

2 Recently Hendrick (1982) argued that deletion of the auxiliary in yes–no questions does not occur just where there is contraction, and both Hendrick (1982) and Kaisse (1983) dispute Labov's characterization of deletion of AUX as primarily a phonological process, viewing it as syntactically conditioned as well, in keeping with views on AUX developed by Akmajian, Steele, and Wasow (1979).

3 The transcription notations are a modified version of those developed by Jefferson, treated in Sacks, Schegloff, and Jefferson (1974), including:

/something/   Words between slashes overlap with those of another speaker.

[Large brackets connect the speech of speakers who overlap.

(thinking)   Words in parenthesis were not totally clear, so the transcriber was not certain of their meaning.

4. A diversity of voices: men's and women's speech in ethnographic perspective

JOEL SHERZER

The purpose of this chapter is to discuss men's and women's speech from an ethnographic perspective, with a focus on the speaking practices of the Kuna Indians of Panama, among whom I have carried out field research. As I thought about men's and women's speech among the Kuna I found it useful, in fact necessary, to place what I knew about the Kuna in the context of the growing linguistic, sociolinguistic, anthropological, and folkloristic literature on women in relation to language, culture, and society. In order to provide a background for my discussion of the Kuna, then, I first propose a brief overview, based on existing literature, of the types of relationships that exist between men's and women's speech around the world. In the case of the Kuna these relationships are manifested primarily in verbal genres, speaking roles, and ways and patterns of speaking. There are overlaps as well as sharply marked differences in men's and women's speaking practices. Whereas men at one level seem to control and perform most political and ritual activities through public and formalized speaking and chanting, women are also involved in significant ways. In addition women uniquely perform verbal genres that are important in Kuna social and cultural life. Furthermore, from the point of view of the ethnography of communication and of symbolic forms more generally, the *molas* (reverse appliqué cloth blouses) made, worn, and sold by women are probably the primary marker of Kuna ethnicity and culture, as well as being of social and economic significance. The Kuna contrast sharply with the Araucanians of Chile and Argentina, another indigenous South American group I shall discuss briefly, among whom speaking practices are a primary manifestation of the inferior social and cultural status of women. The discussion of the Araucanians and the Kuna leads to a more general ethnographic perspective on language and speech among men and

95

women and in particular to a focus on women's roles in relation to speech, female verbal performers, women's verbal genres, and general patterns of speaking that both relate and distinguish men and women. From this ethnography-of-speaking point of view, the study of language and speech cannot be separated from the social and cultural contexts in which they occur. With regard to men's and women's speech as with regard to other aspects of men's and women's cultural and social lives, there are both universals and differences, remarkable similarities across cultures as well as remarkable diversity. Attention to language and speech in this way reveals cases in which women are in inferior and secondary positions, others in which women are in powerful and dominating positions, and still others in which men and women share or divide significant and powerful speaking roles and practices.

Most of the literature and debate concerning men's and women's speech has dealt with American society, in particular middle-class, Anglo-American society. There does exist, however, enough material about other societies to offer, tentatively, a very general overview of men's and women's speech differences in cross-cultural perspective.[1] This overview is not limited to language structure per se, but involves language use in social and cultural context and is sociolinguistic and ethnographic in orientation. I present the overview in the form of a typology of cases. The types are not mutually exclusive but rather allow for overlaps and intersections. The dimensions involved in the typology include categorical or absolute/variable or frequency differences, differences in grammatical structure/differences in language use, and differences that are perceived by members of the community and are culturally symbolic/differences that are empirically verifiable, whether or not they are symbolically perceived and evaluated.

(1) Obligatory, categorical grammatical (usually phonological and/or morphological) differences between men's and women's speech. These operate not only for literal speech (actual men and women speaking) but also for reported speech (men quoting men, women quoting men, etc.), so that what is involved is not language in relation to sex of speaker but grammatical pattern in relation to gender role, in a very arbitrary, conventional sense. This type of male–female speech differentiation has been reported for Yana, Koasati, and other North American Indian languages and is probably an areal trait that spread by means of contact and diffusion. (See Haas, 1944; Sapir, 1929; and general survey in Bodine, 1975.) It is part of a larger pattern of phonological and morphological marking of social features, common in North American Indian languages, including baby talk, and talking to or about individuals with particular and special physical characteristics.

(2) Whole language differences. Although there is no situation in which men and women speak totally different languages and share none, in multilingual situations men and women sometimes possess distinct repertoires or draw on the same repertoire in distinct ways. In the Vaupés region of the northwest Amazon where residence is patrilocal and individuals speak five, six, or more distinct languages each identified with an exogamous descent group, a village longhouse consists of men, all of whom share a language, defined as the official language of the longhouse, while the women who marry in speak different languages (Jackson, 1974). The women seem to be at a double sociolinguistic disadvantage – their primary language is not the official language of the longhouse and they, as distinct from the men, do not necessarily share a language of easy communication, apart from the lingua franca Tukano. Other bilingual, contact situations are less dramatic. Susan Gal (1978) describes an Austrian community bilingual in German and Hungarian in which women use German more than men, Hungarian being the language of peasant status from which the women want to distinguish themselves. In native American communities of Latin America, bilingualism involving Spanish or Portuguese and the native language is increasingly common. In some communities it is men who are more likely to be bilingual; in others, women.

(3) Differences in style. In some societies, a complex of linguistic features (phonological, morphological, syntactic, and lexical) is associated with women as distinct from men. I use the term "associated" to indicate the point of view and conception of native members of the communities; empirical investigation by outside analysts may show the use of the features in the complex to be variable (type 4) or not even systematically or uniquely related to men and women. The association of certain features with men or women is thus symbolic in the cultural sense of symbolic. Some of the linguistic features, in particular certain lexical items, identified by Robin Lakoff (1975) and others in American English are probably aspects of linguistic style as I have used this concept here.

(4) Variable or frequency differences in a small set of linguistic features. In urban, complex industrial societies, and perhaps in other societies as well, certain phonological, morphological, and syntactic features are found to vary, in statistically significant ways, with a set of social features, including class, ethnicity, education, formality of situation, and gender. A well-known example is the pronunciation of post-vocalic r in New York City and other areas of the eastern United States. More analysis is needed to determine whether the sociological features involved can be grouped under more abstract, basic dimensions, such as power and solidarity or politeness. In any case, it seems to me that

gender should not be separated out of this sociological complex as a totally independent dimension.

(5) Differences in interactional and organizational aspects of discourse, viewed either qualitatively or quantitatively. Thus M. H. Goodwin (1980a) describes differences in discourse structuring between single-sex groups of working-class black American boys and girls. Starting with categories derived from Sacks–Schegloff-style analysis of conversations in American society, Zimmerman and West (1975) found men and women in mixed-sex conversations to vary quantitatively in such features as the distribution of turns at talk, the introduction of new topics, overlaps, and interruptions. Such conversational features can be viewed more generally as part of the complex of sociolinguistic variables of language use, together with such grammatical variables as postvocalic *r*, and similarly related to a complex of sociological features, including but not limited to gender.

(6) Differences in verbal genre and speaking roles. Verbal genres are the culturally recognized, routinized, and sometimes though not necessarily overtly marked and formalized forms and categories of discourse in use in particular communities and societies. While the term genre is often used for more formal and literary forms of discourse, it is also an appropriate concept within a general theory of sociolinguistics and ethnography of speaking for informal, casual, and everyday forms as well as for formal and literary ones. (See discussion in Hymes, 1974b.) Some verbal genres are related to social roles in that they are the defining or primary manifestations of these roles. I shall use the term "speaking roles" as a label for such situations. An illustrative case, to which I shall return in greater detail, comes from the Kuna Indians of Panama, among whom it is mainly men who perform such political and ritual verbal genres as public speeches, tribal myths, and magical and curing chants; whereas women and not men perform two more everyday verbal genres closely linked to the life cycle – lullabies and tuneful weeping or lament. Another example is the Mediterranean areal pattern, in which women perform their own particular verbal genres, such as stories, in their own particular communicative styles, in their own particular settings, especially the home (Harding, 1975; Reiter, 1975a). The Mediterranean pattern has been used as evidence for the claim that women's communicative sphere is always domestic or private and men's is always political and public. A truly cross-cultural and ethnographically contextualized survey does not support this claim, as we shall see.

(7) Differences in patterns of speaking, which cut across and relate particular speech events and verbal genres and are general societal organizing principles for the use of language. These broad patterns and ground rules for speaking must be viewed as part of a larger sociocultural

and sociolinguistic complex and not limited to gender differentiation per se. The most often cited case is probably the Malagasy society, described by Elinor Keenan (Ochs) (1974c), in which there is a basic contrast between two patterns of speaking – direct and indirect. Direct speech is associated with and expected of women; indirect speech is the pattern associated with public, political speechmaking and is the pattern that is positively valued in the society as a whole. Direct speech, though disvalued in general, is useful strategically, for example in bargaining, one of the realms of women.

Types 6 and 7 of my general overview particularly involve a perspective that has come to be known as the ethnography of speaking. The ethnography of speaking is concerned with language use in social and cultural context. The locus of description is discourse: the speech acts, events, and situations in which verbal life is organized and structured. Ethnography of speaking is also concerned with the functions of language use in social and cultural life, including the ways in which forms of discourse and patterns of speaking are related to the various roles in a society, such as those of men and women, my focus here. The ethnography of speaking, like all ethnography, is cross-cultural and relativistic in orientation. It assumes and looks for differences as well as similarities in language use across cultures. And it always situates both these differences and these similarities in the particular social and cultural matrices of actual language use. Finally, of course, like all anthropology, ethnography of speaking does not impose cultural patterns found in our own society on descriptions of others. This final point is particularly relevant to the study of men's and women's language and speech.

In order to illustrate the ethnographic perspective I believe is essential for a truly theoretical understanding of men's and women's speech, I turn now to a comparison of two South American Indian groups, the Kuna, where I have carried out considerable field research, and the Araucanians, where the existing ethnographic literature provides an interesting and instructive contrast. I offer, then, two quite different cases on a single continent of the relationship between men's and women's verbal genres, speaking roles, and patterns of speaking. There are of course others.

First the Araucanians. The Chilean Araucanians are one of the more populous indigenous groups in South America, also living in some of the most horrendous conditions. Most of the over 200,000 Araucanians live on reservations in Chile; others live across the border in Argentina. Araucanian descent is patrilineal and residence is patrilocal. A household consists of a number of brothers with their respective wives and children. Investigators of Araucanian culture and society have noted that everything about Araucanian social structure operates to promote masculine harmony and solidarity while imposing great strains on women. It is instructive to examine the way speech enters into this picture. The ideal Araucanian man is a good orator and general conversationalist and has a good memory. He is expected to speak both well and often; men are encouraged to talk on all occasions, speaking being a sign of masculine intelligence and leadership. To ease relationships and situations that might prove difficult, there exists a ritualized conversation, the *koyaqtun*. Speech, for men, is an instrument of group solidarity and harmony. For women the situation is just the opposite. Upon arrival at her husband's home, a woman finds herself among strangers. The members of her husband's family have their own lives in common; her sisters-in-law are potential rivals. There is no equivalent of the men's *koyaqtun* to draw women together. The ideal woman is quite different from the ideal man. Where the latter is talkative, the former is silent; where the latter is supposed to be a good orator and to lead through language, the former should be submissive and quiet. At gatherings where men do much talking, the women sit together, talking only in whispers or not at all. A woman, on first arriving in her husband's home, is expected to sit silent and face the wall, not looking anyone in the household directly in the face. Only after several months is she permitted to speak, and then only a little.

The literature reports no grammatical differences in the Araucanian language distinguishing men and women, but there are sharp differences in the performance of verbal genres, speaking roles, and patterns of speaking. (These are types 6 and 7 in the general overview I presented.) There are five major Araucanian leadership roles for which speaking ability is the defining characteristic and which are restricted to men, including group leader, public orator, and messenger. On the other hand, there is one significant ritual role which is held by women and which involves a special form of speech. This is the *machi* 'shaman' who in a curing ceremony goes into trance and speaks with the voice of a spirit. The other major women's verbal genre, *ulkantun* 'social singing', is a tuneful lament in which women metaphorically protest their misfortunes and distress and attempt to gain support for their plight. Araucanian child rearing has attracted some attention and it has been noted that boys are specially trained to speak well, including being taken into the woods to practice making speeches to plants and animals. There is no equivalent training for girls.

Thus, with the significant exceptions of the female shaman and tuneful lament, there is a sharp contrast between the ideal Araucanian man and the ideal Araucanian woman with regard to speech. The ideal man is a talker, the ideal woman is taciturn. Patterns of speech use in general seem to favor men over women. In a pattern that in some ways seems to resemble the Malagasy pattern described by Keenan (Ochs), the conception of the ideal Araucanian woman clashes with that of the ideal Araucanian person. Araucanian speaking roles and patterns of speaking, then, are both symbolic reflections and concrete manifestations of the very inferior positions of women within Araucanian social organization and the negative attitudes toward women's behavior that seem to prevail in this society. (See Faron, 1968; Hilger, 1957; Titiev, 1949, 1951.)

I turn now to the Kuna Indians of San Blas, Panama, about whom I know more and who present us with a representative case of the complex nature of men's and women's verbal genres and speaking roles in a traditional, indigenous, mainly nonliterate, lowland, egalitarian South American society. The Kuna have attracted the attention of several generations of anthropologists as a case, perhaps not atypical in lowland South America, of the very central, organizing, and integrative place of language and speech in social and cultural life. There are a variety of related manifestations of this – the large number of Kuna roles, from everyday to ritual, that are defined, conceived, and practiced in terms of language and speech, the very positive attitude taken toward effective speakers and the concomitant negative attitude toward the rare non-speakers, the great amount of time and care devoted to chanting and speaking, and the fact that most aspects of Kuna social and cultural life cannot be adequately understood without approaching them by means of a precise study of the forms of verbal discourse that are central to them. With regard to ritual matters, in my own work I have tended to distinguish three realms, as do the Kuna – public, political gatherings; "curing and magic"; and puberty. The first realm involves humans chanting and speaking to and for humans in a public meeting house. The second and third realms involve humans speaking and chanting to and for spirits, usually in private homes. Three distinct ritual languages, forms of discourse, and sets of roles serve as the distinguishing markers of these three ritual realms. A number of patterns of speaking relate and distinguish the different ritual forms of discourse and relate them to, and distinguish them from, everyday verbal life as well. (See Sherzer, 1983, for a more complete discussion of Kuna ways and patterns of speaking.)

The Kuna ideal of the relationship between language and speech and social organization, often and publicly expressed, is one of egalitarian and harmonious cooperation, integration, and division of labor, involving men and women, old and young. The system of ritual and leadership roles is potentially open to anyone who wants to learn the necessary linguistic skills. In practice things are more complicated. With regard to the general overview and typology I presented, types 6 and 7, verbal genres, speaking roles, and patterns of speaking, most appropriately categorize men's and women's speech differences among the Kuna.

In conventional linguistic terms, differences between Kuna men's and women's speech are relatively slight and involve the tendency for women to delete vowels less than men, to use a small set of words more than men, to use a slightly different range of intonation patterns from men, and to laugh in a very marked conventional and stylized way. The main difference between Kuna men's and women's speech is in the area of discourse, the speech acts and events that are used and engaged in by men and women. The large set of ritual and traditional forms of discourse, verbal genres that are labeled and linguistically and contextually formalized, constitute the essence of the definition and practice of Kuna leadership roles. Ideally available to men and women, these roles are in practical actuality restricted to men.[2] Although the Kuna can point to instances of a woman who once held a political leadership role or a woman who knows and performs a curing chant, these are in fact extremely rare. Let me first examine each of the ritual areas, because each offers different insight into men's and women's speaking roles.

There are three types of public gatherings: those for men only, those for women only, and those for men and women together. It is at men's gatherings that most important political matters are discussed and resolved. Women attend these only when they are accused of wrongdoing, accuse someone else of wrongdoing, or are witnesses. From the point of view of an outside analyst or the Kuna themselves, when women speak at men's gatherings they are as fluent, eloquent, and sure of themselves as male speakers. But at the same time their lack of involvement in (but not knowledge of and personal access to) the ongoing stream of debate in men's gatherings has a certain restricting influence on their rhetorical capabilities. (See Howe, 1986.) In recent years women also have been holding gatherings of their own, with their own leaders, to discuss such matters as their *mola* cooperative and women's tasks in the village. These gatherings are organized and run entirely by women, and they are dynamic, vibrant verbal events. They are strikingly parallel to the men's gatherings, down to the finest detail. Leaders make long speeches, counseling and encouraging the audience to carry out assigned tasks properly. Any woman can and often does stand up and, either agreeing or disagreeing with the leaders, speak as eloquently as they do. At gatherings attended by men and women jointly, women sit together surrounded by the men. They are supposed to make *molas* and listen to the chanting and speaking of chiefs. The chiefs' chants are often specifically addressed directly to the women and insist on explicit moral lessons supposedly needed by them.

In the area of magic and curing, three basic roles are involved: the seer or diagnostician, the medicinal specialist, and the way or chant knower. Medicinal specialists also serve as diagnosticians in the absence of a seer. Seers diagnose disease and discover the sources and causes of wrongdoing by means of communication with the spirit world. They relate their findings and recommendations to the Kuna community in elaborate gathering-house speeches. Men or women can be seers and there are well-known, highly respected female seers today in San Blas. In my experience, official medicinal specialists, who gather medicine and counsel it in a chant, are always men. Unofficially women are extremely knowledgeable in the area of curing and medicine. According to Chapin, who has studied this area extensively, medicinal specialists typically consult with women informally before making a diagnosis and their formal recommendation is often a repetition of the women's informal report to them. (See Chapin, 1983.) Knowers of magical ways perform them to representatives of the spirit world in order to help in the cure of a sick person. Most knowers are men. And only men can learn magical ways by means of apprenticeship to other knowers. But both men and women, especially seers, sometimes learn them in dreams in which deceased individuals or spirits come to them and teach them. Once magical ways are learned in dreams, the knowers, men or women, can be called upon to perform them for curing purposes and to teach them to others. In the cases I am familiar with, women who know curing ways teach them to members of their family, husbands or fathers. Magic and curing may be viewed as a man's world, but it is by no means so to the degree or in the same way in which public politics is. In addition one very important role in the area of magic and medicine is held exclusively by women: the midwife. Midwives are aided in their work by male medicinal specialists and knowers of magical ways.

Puberty rites, which are held for girls, involve a sharp division of labor between women's and men's ritual roles, with women involved essentially in nonverbal activities. In a special enclosure the young girl for whom the rites are held has her hair ceremonially cut. The cutting is done by a ritual haircutter, a woman, and her assistants, all women. Meanwhile, in a large centrally located house, the *inna* (fermented drink) house, the ritual director of the puberty rites, a man, and his assistants, men, perform a long (one-, two-, or three-day) chant to the spirit of a long flute, which ensures the proper unfolding of the ritual.

Each of the Kuna verbal genres, the chanting of chiefs, the speech-making of political leaders, the curing chants of medicinal specialists, and the chants of puberty-rites directors, has specific linguistic properties distinguishing it from everyday speech and from the others. These linguistic properties involve a combination of phonological, morphological, syntactic, and semantic features. The linguistic style of each of these genres is so unique that they are usually unintelligible to nonspecialists and nonpractitioners. The chanting and speechmaking of chiefs are especially characterized by metaphorical language that is in part conventionally predetermined and in part individually created. The long, memorized chants of curing specialists and puberty-rites directors each contain extensive vocabulary unique to these verbal genres. It is important to stress that the linguistic properties of the Kuna ritual verbal genres are not defined or viewed in terms of gender. Rather they are associated with the verbal genres themselves. It is only specialists, those men, and in some cases women, who study and perform these verbal genres, who know the language and style that are used in them. And with regard to nonspecialists, there are women as well as men who have some receptive competence and understanding of the special phonological, morphological, syntactic, semantic, and lexical properties of these verbal genres.

So attention to Kuna ritual genres of speaking provides us with a view of the complex interrelationship of men's and women's speaking roles – some division of labor, some intersection and overlap, and some interplay and contradiction between official conceptions and actual practice.

Examination of broad patterns of speaking provides another insight into men's and women's speech differences. A very basic classification of Kuna discourse opposes flexible, adaptive, and metaphorical and allusive speech on the one hand to fixed, memorized speech on the other. The first occurs in its most elaborate, artistic form, in gathering-house speechmaking and chanting. It is the language of person-to-person communication, the language of rhetoric and the act of convincing. Fixed, memorized speech is the language of magic and curing. It is the language of human-to-spirit communication and comes in the form of named texts that, being unwritten, are preserved through rote memorization and identical performances. The gathering-house flexible speech is indirect in the sense that it encourages creative use of metaphorical, allusive discourse. The magical ways and chants are more direct in that they explicitly state to the spirits what they should do. Neither flexible, allusive speech nor fixed speech is more valued among the Kuna, in contrast to the Malagasy community, in which indirect, allusive speech is more highly valued. Each has its appropriate domain in the Kuna view. And neither is associated more with men than with women. There are women who speak and perform both ways.

Another way to approach women's speech among the Kuna is by focusing on everyday speech, both in and of itself and in relation to the ritual forms of discourse I have described. Kuna women are not at all like the taciturn Araucanian women. In everyday conversation and verbal interaction they are as vociferous as the men, if not more so. And in the large, matrilocal households their verbal presence is strongly felt. Within the home, there are two verbal genres unique to women, lullabies and tuneful weeping. In the performance of lullabies, the singer holds the baby in her lap in a hammock, or sits next to it, moving the hammock back and forth and shaking a rattle. Lullabies have certain basic themes. The baby is told not to cry, that it will soon grow up and perform adult tasks, and that its father is off working in the jungle or fishing. In addition there is improvisation to fit the actual situation of the baby and its family – whether the singer is a mother, sister, or aunt; whether the baby is a boy or girl; whether those off at work are fathers, uncles, or brothers; whether they are farming in the jungle, fishing, or in Panama. The singer describes what she is doing at the moment of the performance, as well as what the relevant others are doing. The language is colloquial Kuna, with certain particular stylistic features.

Tuneful weeping is a lament performed by women to a dying and then deceased individual. Family members surround his or her hammock and cry, either one at a time or several at a time, each in her own words. The weeping continues after the death of the person, on the canoe trip to the mainland cemetery, and until burial. It is in colloquial Kuna, in a sobbing, yet melodic style, involving certain linguistic features particular to this genre. Tuneful weeping deals with the life of the dying and then deceased addressee and the performer's relationship to him or her. The performer improvises on a highly stereotyped basic pattern, incorporating the particular details that are relevant in each case.

Lullabies and tuneful weeping share several features that make it appropriate to group them together. They are both performed by women and are tuneful. They are both addressed directly to an individual who is present and have to do with his or her life and situation and relationship to the performer. And they both involve basic themes that are manipulated and improvised on in order to fit particular situations. It is furthermore interesting to compare and contrast lullabies and tuneful weeping with the chanting of chiefs in the gathering house, because of striking similarities and differences. Lullabies and tuneful weeping share with the gathering-house chanting a structuring in terms of melodic lines, marked musically as well as grammatically and lexically, and a set of relatively fixed basic themes that are elaborated, developed, and improvised from in order to fit in detail particular situations. On the other hand, lullabies and tuneful weeping are different from gathering-house chanting in that gathering-house chanting is performed by men and lullabies and tuneful weeping by women; gathering-house chanting is public and lullabies and tuneful weeping private; gathering-house chanting involves a special esoteric language with a focus on metaphor, and lullabies and tuneful weeping are in colloquial Kuna with no metaphors; gathering-house chanting presents a moral that is then interpreted as part of the total speech event, and in lullabies and tuneful weeping there is no moral and no interpretation.

It is also interesting to consider the significance of lullabies and tuneful weeping in Kuna social and cultural life more generally. The importance of verbal genres having to do with child rearing and death cannot be denied. At the same time, I agree with Howe and Hirschfeld and disagree with Lopez and Joly (in their discussion in the *Journal of American Folklore*, 1981) with regard to the larger place of lullabies and tuneful weeping in Kuna social, cultural, and verbal life. Because it is a public performance, in a ritual language, associated with chiefs and other political leaders, and has linguistic depth and complication in both form and content, the chanting of chiefs in the gathering house, from the Kuna point of view as well as that of outside analysis, is a more significant verbal genre than either lullabies or tuneful weeping. In my own analysis of Kuna language and speech, I have treated lullabies and tuneful weeping as everyday verbal genres, in contrast to the more ritual genres. My criteria are both linguistic and contextual, but I am quite aware that other analytical and classificatory schemes are possible. Tuneful weeping in particular, as a lament for the dead, might very well be viewed as a ritual form of speech. But it is interesting that there exists as well a ritual lament for the dead, "the way of the bamboo cane," which, because it is addressed to a representative of the spirit world (the spirit of the bamboo cane), and is in the spirit language, I classify as a magical way in the classification scheme of verbal genres I outlined above. It is performed by a man, the knower of the "way of the bamboo cane," if the family of the deceased decides to pay for it. So with regard to death there are two laments – tuneful weeping, performed by female relatives, obligatorily and without charge, in a relatively everyday language, and the "way of the bamboo cane," performed by particular male specialists in a ritual language and for a fee.

The question of women's and men's communicative roles becomes even more complicated and, I think, more interesting when we move from the realm of speech per se to communicative and symbolic forms more generally, as we must to fully understand the place of speaking in Kuna life. All women, with few exceptions, make and wear *molas*, which are the symbolic markers, par excellence, of Kuna culture, traditional and modern, and an important source of prestige and income, as well as truly magnificent forms of creative individual artistic expression. It is interesting to compare *mola* making with basket making, an area totally restricted to men, in the light of a most provocative statement from Margaret Mead's *Male and Female*, which I shall quote. For, quite the opposite of Mead's claim, it is the women's *mola* that is the more highly valued material object, in symbolic, economic, and socioesthetic senses. Kuna baskets, though somewhat appreciated in esthetic terms, tend to be conceived of in purely utilitarian terms. A comparison of *molas* with speech is more intriguing. On the one hand we have an element of clothing and a form of artistic expression, a very important nonverbal symbol of Kuna culture, always public and always in production, in addition to being a source of wealth. On the other hand we have the public speeches and chants of men, constantly filling the tropical air with esthetic rhetoric, which at times seems of the highest significance, at times purely esoteric play.

As a final exploration of Kuna men's and women's speech I present some of the actual voices that appear in Kuna discourse, the various ways in which men and women are represented in this discourse and the words they speak. My discussion here is in part an investigation of the Kuna stereotyping of men's and women's speech (which, in American society, has been studied by Kramerae, 1981).

In Kuna gathering-house discourse, especially in the symbolic, metaphorical chanting and speaking of chiefs and other leaders, there is a contrast between the metaphors used to represent women and men. Women, like children, are referred to as flowers, the different types, colors, and sizes of flowers representing the different kinds of women. Women, together with children and like flowers, are delicate and need care and protection, and this is the essence of the chiefly metaphor. In addition, women are directly addressed by chiefs in their chants, counseled without end on proper modes of behavior. Here is a typical example, inserted as a moral into the chanting of a tribal legend and placed in the mouth of the protagonist of the legend, the white seer:

> "Women listen to me well,"
> The white seer chanted.
> "Women clean the house well.
> Don't leave dirt around for me.
> You must throw away the dirt."[3]

Men, on the other hand, are referred to as trees in the jungle or poles and walls in a house, symbolizing their strength but also their personalities as stingy or generous, their moral character, and their location in the Kuna social structure. (See Howe, 1977.)

Insight into the Kuna's own conception and perception of men's and women's speech is further provided by the dramatization of voices in the very common Kuna practice of embedding reported or quoted speech in all forms of discourse, often involving multiple levels of embedding, a pattern I have called telling within telling. Of the many cases of dramatized voices, I have selected a few, which illustrate the diversity of ways in which the Kuna see themselves.

First, two different portrayals of animal people. The Kuna believe that animals were once human and in the spirit world still are. In magical–curing ways, animals have human social organization, perform human activities, and speak to one another in a ritual variety of the Kuna language. Conversations in these texts are stereotyped mirrorings of everyday Kuna verbal interaction, reflecting a strict division of labor between the sexes. Men hunt, women cook, and both mechanically report on these activities to each other. So here are Mr. and Mrs. Rattlesnake talking to each other in "the way of the rattlesnake," a magical chant used to prevent snakebite:

> Rattlesnake says to his wife:
> "For you I will go hunting.
> For you I will kill an animal."
> ....
> Rattlesnake's wife responds:
> "You are going hunting for me.
> You will kill an animal for me.
> I will prepare your beverage for you."[4]

But animal men and women are not always portrayed as this idealized, stereotyped reflection of humans. In the "agouti story," an animal trick-ster tale, which consists of a series of episodes in which Jaguar is miserably tricked by little Agouti, there is an interlude in which Jaguar, his skin badly burned in the latest trick, returns home to his wife to recuperate before taking off again in pursuit of Agouti. Rather than feel sorry for him, Jaguar's wife criticizes and mocks him in several lines of narrative that this particular Kuna audience, consisting almost entirely of men, found quite funny.

Really burned, he got home to his wife; where else could he have gone?
He says to his wife, "Look at me," he says.
"This nephew tricked me," he said.
It's true.
"You're such a stupid oaf always going about this way,"
That wife said to Uncle [Jaguar].
"This same nephew [Agouti] has always been joking with you.
Now he's gone and tricked you again; as far as I'm concerned you're not a man."
[Much laughter]
Aa.
His wife said to him, aa.
"I've got only a husband, no more. [Laughter throughout line]
You don't look like a man to me." [Laughter][5]

This is not the obedient wife who knows her place that was dramatized in the "way of the rattlesnake." Both of these literary models are also found in everyday Kuna verbal reality and are reflections of the complex sociocultural matrix in which speech occurs and from which culturally symbolic interpretations are derived. Both the obedient woman who knows her place and the vociferous woman who boisterously puts forth her point of view are, in different contexts, and sometimes even in the same context, perfectly appropriate.

Significantly, one form of discourse where we do consistently find the stereotyped division of labor and public behavior between the sexes is lullabies, performed endlessly all day long, in house after house, and, presumably, relevant to the socialization process. Here is a typical example, performed by a young girl, and including the uttering of a command by a man and the obeying of it by a woman.

> Father is not here.
> He went to the jungle.
> "I am going to clear out the coconut plantations,"
> Father said as he left.
> ....
> Little girl.
> You will stay in the house.
> You will make a little *mola*.
> You will also sit beside your mother.
> ....
> You will wash clothes.
> You will go to the river.
> With your relatives.
> You will wash small clothes.
> ....
> When your uncles return [from work].
> You will serve beverages to your uncles.
> You will serve them food.
> When your uncles return.
> Your relatives will call to you:
> "Bring me a beverage."[6]

As a final example, I return to a pair of verbal genres I discussed earlier, the Kuna laments for the dead, the tuneful weeping performed by women and the ritual "way of the bamboo cane" performed by a male specialist, in which a woman's tuneful weeping is embedded as reported speech. This particular performance of tuneful weeping, recorded by a young girl out of context, seems to exaggerate stereotypes, as do lullabies.

> It pains me to see grandfather.
> My grandfather died.
> He will be underground.

I say.
......

He would always go with us [to the jungle].
In order to get medicine.
"I am going to get medicine,"
He said to us.[7]

The performance of the "way of the bamboo cane" is interesting in that I recorded it from a man with a very close personal and professional relationship with two women, his wife, like himself knowledgeable in herbal medicine, and his daughter, a seer, who taught him many of the magical-curing ways he knew and which she had learned in dreams. The women's voices in his texts reflect a more biting, complaining, and critical perspective than the voice of the young girl's tuneful weeping. Thus the women's tuneful weeping embedded in the "way of the bamboo cane" talks not so much about the past achievements of the deceased as about the present problems of the living:

"In the big sea there was tarpon.
You always killed tarpon for me.
Now you will never kill tarpon for me again."[8]

This selection of voices provides a literary closure for my discussion of Kuna men's and women's speech, these textual voices mirroring, imitating, idealizing, stereotyping, and mocking the real diversity of voices that constitutes actual Kuna verbal life today. My point in this exploration and description of Kuna speaking practices, and especially my attention to verbal genres, speaking roles, and patterns of speaking, is to illustrate the complex and sometimes seemingly contradictory relationships between men's and women's speech among the Kuna. There is no single, simple dimension distinguishing men's and women's speech, no easy generalization that can be formulated in terms of a neat binary opposition or dichotomy. And it is definitely not possible to make the claim, without considerable qualification, that Kuna speaking practices favor men over women or place women at a disadvantage in Kuna social and cultural life, as seems much more clearly the case among the Araucanians. There is no question that men's ritual, formal, and public speech is more diversified and complex than women's and that men have more access to and control of political authority through such speaking practices. At the same time, women also have ritual, formal, and public speaking roles and these are always positively valued, by men and women alike, and provide women with a certain access to and significant involvement in Kuna political life and power. In addition, women's speech in private and domestic contexts, which involves both their performance of verbal genres unique to them and their active participation in conversations with women as well as men, including political and ritual specialists, is respected and heeded. From the point of view of the ethnography of communication and of symbolic forms, women's constant and public involvement with *molas,* making them, wearing them, talking about them, and selling them, is highly esteemed by Kuna men and women and is of social, cultural, and economic importance.

In sum, investigation of Kuna men's and women's speech and a focus on verbal genres, speaking roles, patterns of speaking, representation of voices, and communicative and symbolic forms shows women sometimes behaving, viewed, and treated as weak, secondary, and inferior, sometimes as equal to, sometimes as different from, and sometimes as similar to men. Kuna speaking practices are reflections of, manifestations of, and play a significant and central role in structuring and organizing the social and cultural contexts in which they occur. In Kuna society there is a fairly sharp division of labor between men's and women's roles. There is also some overlap in certain areas of social and cultural life. At the same time, in all areas of social and cultural life, women's roles and points of view are taken quite seriously. It is in this larger context and perspective of sociological differentiation and cultural framing that gender distinctions in language and speech among the Kuna and indeed any society must be seen, analyzed, and evaluated.

With this illustrative case study of the speaking practices of the Kuna Indians as a background, I now explore the ethnographic perspective on men's and women's speech cross-culturally, drawing on available literature. My focus is on types 6 and 7 of the typology I presented – verbal genres, speaking roles, and patterns of speaking. One way to conceive of verbal genres performed by women is in terms of role in relation to genre, resulting in a category that might be called women performers. A cross-cultural survey reveals a varied class of cases that can be included in this category. These cases, like the types in the general overview I presented earlier, are not mutually exclusive.

(1) Verbal virtuoso performers, individuals who from both the society's point of view and the outside analyst's point of view are truly great verbal artists and, in traditional oral societies, great verbal performers. One of the best examples is Nongenile Mazithathu Zenani, the expert creator of *ntsomi* performances (long oral epic narrations) among the South African Xhosa, discussed at length by Harold Scheub (1972).

(2) Female performers who are part of and who reflect a women's verbal-performance tradition different from that of men. Victoria Howard, Melville Jacobs's Chinookan informant, is such a person, as is stressed by Dell Hymes (1981) in his reanalysis of her narratives. Among the Haya of Tanzania, women are considered the best taletellers (Dauer, 1978).

(3) Women's performances that are not virtuoso, that is, not framed as public, elaborate special events, from the society's point of view, but

significantly different from men's in style and in context, often performed in contexts specifically defined as women's contexts, such as the home. Examples are the British Isles and related areas tradition of women's storytelling (Kodish, 1981; E. K. Miller, 1981), Mediterranean women's storytelling (Harding, 1975), and Siberian storytelling (Azadovskii, 1974). These are instances in which both men and women can be narrators, but men's and women's narrations are framed (in the sense of Goffman, 1974, as developed by Bauman, 1977, for verbal art) in quite different ways in the society.

(4) Women who perform the same verbal genre as men, in the same style and in the same contexts. Examples are all Kuna women who make public speeches in the public gathering house and those who know and perform magical curing chants.

(5) Finally, female performers who have played significant roles as informants, assistants, consultants, or subjects of scholarly study by anthropologists, folklorists, and linguists and thus have enriched these disciplines empirically and theoretically. Examples are Melville Jacobs's Chinookan informant Victoria Howard, Harold Scheub's Xhosa informant Nongenile Mazithathu Zenani, and Natal'ia Osipovna Vinokurova, the Siberian taleteller discussed by Mark Azadovskii. We might also note the interesting case of the wife of Ishi, the last known Yana Indian, the famous informant of Kroeber and Sapir, who was the last and for many years the only person Ishi spoke to and therefore led Ishi to speak women's rather than men's speech and Sapir to write his very important paper on men's and women's speech in Yana.

Another approach to women's verbal genres is to focus on genres that are widely performed by women, thus going beyond particular cases to more general types, categories, and patterns. Two genres that are extremely commonly performed by women, especially in relatively traditional, nonindustrial, and nonliterate or marginally literate societies, and occur at opposite ends of the life cycle, are lullaby and lament. The performance of lullabies by women might be seen as related to women's social and cultural role as mothers, although fathers could just as well and sometimes do perform lullabies. Why it is frequently women who perform laments is not as clear. Laments are often tuneful and wept at the same time and, in fact, have been labeled tuneful weeping, a term I borrow from Tiwary (1975), who describes a North Indian version. Women's tunefully wept laments are extremely common from Eastern Europe through the Middle East to Asia as well as in indigenous South America, from the Panamanian Kuna to the Chilean Araucanians. There is a most interesting and extensive literature about them, which often explicitly makes the point that they are a women's genre, even in societies where both men and women perform them. (See Caraveli-Chaves, 1980, 1982; Danforth, 1982; Feld, 1982; Honko, 1974; Klymasz, 1975; Titiev, 1949; and Tiwary, 1975, among others.) The most common, perhaps basic, type of lament is probably that performed for deceased individuals. Relatives or paid performers recount the life of the deceased and the loss that their death represents, sometimes in explicit and direct, sometimes in allusive and metaphorical, terms. This recounting ranges from such minimal forms as the Kalapalo (an indigenous group in central Brazil) listing of kin terms (Ellen Basso, personal communication) to full narratives such as those of the Kuna, an aspect of the Kuna narrative approach to just about everything from birth to death. This narrative recounting of the entire life cycle of an individual at the moment of his or her death is clearly a most significant form of speech and all alone serves to counter any argument that women are universally restricted to minor verbal genres. Women might also use the occasion of lamenting for the dead to lament their own situation, both before and after the death of the deceased. A not very unusual example is provided by a Ukrainian lament recorded in western Canada by Robert Klymasz (1975), a widow's lament for her dead husband:

> Why don't you say at least one word to me?
> Who will give me advice when you're not around?
> To whom am I to draw near now?
> Why are you abandoning me?
> ....
>
> Little white hands of mine, beloved feet of mine,
> You have toiled much, you have walked much.
> But who will now give me to eat?
> And who will heat up the house for me?
> Now there shall be no one to heat the house.
> ....

This type of lament for the dead provides the link to two other types of women's laments, which focus directly on the problems of women's own situations, their grievances and protests. One, characteristic of patrilocal residence, occurs at the moment of separation from one's parental home and move to the home of one's husband and in-laws. The other complains about and protests one's unfortunate situation, again typically in a new home, surrounded by unfriendly in-laws. This third type of lament is reported for communities as far apart as the state of Bihar in North India and the Chilean Araucanians; there are, no doubt, many other cases.

Several points seem worth making about laments. First, they consist of a class. Some societies have laments for the dead only (for example, the Kuna); others include personal complaining and protesting about one's social situation in the class of laments (Bihar; Araucanian). Second, there is a relationship between social organization and lament, quite clearly reflected in Bihar and among the Araucanians, both of which are reported as cases in which social organization is extremely disadvantageous to women and lament provides for a verbal letting off of steam (psychological) and societal expression of conflict (sociocultural), as well as an individually expressive esthetic form. Third, song, chant, or tune is the appropriate channel for women to express their complaints, grievances, and protests, providing, in the sense of Goffman, both role distance and a clearly, overtly marked frame for messages that would be considered otherwise highly inappropriate for women. Fourth, laments are often sung in groups, but not in unison, so that individual voices emerge, there thus being an interesting interplay between group solidarity and individual expression. Lament is one of only two Kuna verbal genres (the other a highly ritualized greeting among visiting chiefs) in which more than a single individual performs at the same time. Finally, given the wide distribution of lament, questions of areal diffusion of this form of expression and its varieties and features must be raised.

A more general ethnographic approach to women's speech is to search for areal, typological, and perhaps universal patterns of speaking distinguishing men and women. Two in particular attract attention. The first is suggested by the discussion by Elinor Keenan (Ochs) (1974c) of a Malagasy community in which a distinction between direct speech and indirect, allusive speech is associated with the distinction between expected, appropriate behavior for women and expected, appropriate behavior for men; and where furthermore the overall societal cultural value is on indirect, allusive speech, as reflected in such public realms as politics. A similar pattern, particularly with regard to politics, is found to a certain degree among the Kuna and other South American lowland groups, as well as in parts of Africa and New Guinea, but in each case in distinct ethnographic settings, with quite different sociocultural underpinnings and associations. (Dauer, 1978, provides a sensitive and developed discussion of an instance of this pattern found among the Haya of Tanzania.) It is interesting to note that Brenneis (1980) and Rosaldo (1973) have argued that a focus on the use of indirect and allusive speech, typically in public, political contexts, is characteristic of traditional societies professing an egalitarian ideal. The pattern, certainly not universal but apparently widespread, can be stated in terms of an opposition between indirect, allusive, and metaphorical speech, which is highly valued by the society in a socioesthetic sense and is also associated with men, politics, and the public domain, and direct, non-allusive speech, which is not valued by the society in a socioesthetic sense and is associated with women and, perhaps, private and domestic domains.

A second pattern derives from the theory of linguistic politeness as proposed by Penelope Brown and Stephen Levinson (1978). Brown (1979, 1980) has applied this theory to women and argues that women are more polite linguistically in Tenejapan Mayan communities, middle-class America, and perhaps everywhere. The features of politeness Brown discusses vary, but a kind of linguistic indirectness is a central and organizing aspect of them. It is important to point out that the indirectness described by Brown is socially and culturally different from the indirectness that was described by Keenan (Ochs) and that consti-tuted the first general pattern I discussed. Brown's indirectness is a face-to-face interactional indirectness, as in the avoidance or hedging of direct statements. Keenan's indirectness is a metaphorical, allusive, verbally artistic indirectness associated with public and often political discourse.

It seems to me appropriate at this point to raise a question that often looms large in the literature on men's and women's speech differences and that was central to my contrastive discussion of the Araucanian and Kuna Indians, namely, whether differences between the language and speech of men and women are universal and whether such differences are always reflective of an inferior status of women. In thinking about this issue, I have found the recent intensive and extensive anthropo-logical literature about women and usually by women most valuable, not because it provides a focused investigation of language and speech per se, which it does not, but because of significant social and cultural issues it has raised. These issues are an essential background for the study of language and speech as well as for all forms of culturally sym-bolic behavior. One view, most clearly expressed in the papers in the collection edited by Michelle Rosaldo and Louise Lamphere, *Woman, Culture, and Society* (1974), is that a distinction between men's and women's roles and behaviors is universal, involves men in public and women in domestic spheres, can be explained in social and cultural terms, and always finds women in an inferior position. The essence of this view, especially the aspect of it that holds that men and men's activities are always more valued culturally than women and women's activities, was already present in Margaret Mead's *Male and Female* (1949) but not in her earlier and more ethnographically sensitive *Sex and Temperament in Three Primitive Societies* (1935). It is nicely en-capsulated in the provocative quotation from *Male and Female* that together with a quotation from the French philosopher, novelist, and feminist Simone de Beauvoir serves as an epigraph to *Women, Culture and Society*:

In every known society, the male's need for achievement can be recognized. Men may cook, or weave, or dress dolls, or hunt hummingbirds, but if such activities are appropriate occupations of men, then the whole society, men and women alike, votes them as important. When the same occupations are performed by women, they are regarded as less important.

Criticism of this view comes from several directions, mainly from a Marxist approach to modern industrial societies, in particular American society, and from a cross-cultural and ethnographic approach to other, especially more traditional, nonindustrial, and nonliterate, societies. As clearly expressed by Eleanor Burke Leacock (1981), the combined Marxist, feminist, and cross-cultural critique argues that to hold a priori that women are everywhere inferior is to subscribe to a kind of cultural-deficit or culture-of-poverty approach to women, which is just as invalid as the same approach applied to such minority groups as blacks – an approach that has also been eloquently criticized by Leacock, among others. In addition we still have a relative paucity of empirical data concerning the social and cultural roles of women in various societies around the world, language being a particularly poorly studied area; but what we do have suggests that, especially in nonliterate, nonindustrial societies, there is great diversity with regard to the situation and status of women, and that, in particular in societies with egalitarian orientations, women can be on an equal footing with men, as part of a well-worked-out system of divisions, intersections, and overlaps of labor. (See Leacock, 1981; MacCormack and Strathern, 1980; Reiter, 1975b; Rosaldo and Lamphere, 1974; and Sanday, 1981. Atkinson, 1982, and Rosaldo, 1980, are useful survey and review articles.) And, as more Marxist-oriented scholars argue, it is highly class- and caste-structured (traditional as well as modern) societies and imperialist and colonialist situations that have the most developed systems for the subjugation of women, as part of an overall subjugation of the poorer and working classes, ethnic minorities, and dominated third-world countries. To view women's situations as universally inferior, especially in terms of simple dichotomies such as nature/culture, domestic/public, or polite/direct, is to impose our own society's view, in a weird kind of ethnocentrism, on the world at large. A cross-cultural, ethnographically sensitive approach and careful attention to the interweaving of gender with other sociological categories and boundaries reveal other possibilities.

With the anthropological debates with regard to women in culture and society as a backdrop, it is possible to return more directly to the question of language and speech. Two significant and ultimately related aspects of a cross-cultural approach to men's and women's language and speech are the following: First, differences in men's and women's speech are probably universal. Second, these differences are evaluated by members of the society as symbolic reflections of what men and women are like. Let me take up each of these propositions in turn. First, the universality of men's and women's speech differences. Gender, like other major social distinctions in society, such as age, power, and intimacy, is so basic to communication that there will always be some reflection of it in the sociolinguistic system of particular societies, whether in phonology, syntax, semantics, or discourse, including verbal genres and patterns of speaking. It would of course be most interesting if we could say something significant about the relationship between type of society and type of linguistic manifestation of male/female differences, but with available data any such statement must be made with extreme caution. One hypothesis I would like to suggest is the following, offered very tentatively on the basis of available literature. In modern urban, industrial, stratified yet somewhat fluid societies such as our own, in which men's and women's roles are not necessarily viewed as being sharply differentiated, men's and women's speech differences involve statistically significant grammatical variations that are associated with and related to a complex of social factors in addition to gender and are probably best interpreted as surface reflections of such basic social dimensions as power and solidarity. In fact, it has been noted that in contemporary American society, women's language, or a female register, tends to be used by powerless individuals, both men and women, such as courtroom defendants. (See Crosby and Nyquist, 1977; O'Barr, 1982.)

On the other hand, in many traditional societies, and especially in certain relatively small, homogeneous, nonliterate societies in parts of Africa, New Guinea, and South America, in which men's and women's activities are reported to be quite clearly and distinctly defined, it is differences in the verbal genres and the patterns of speaking, which are integral aspects of these activities, that most clearly reflect men's and women's role differences. Each of the terms and assumptions of this general hypothesis requires some discussion, elaboration, clarification, and qualification, in the interest of achieving generality on the one hand without losing sight of cross-cultural and empirical diversity on the other. Oppositions such as modern/traditional, industrial/nonindustrial, complex/homogeneous, and literate/nonliterate are neither simple nor necessarily isomorphic. They involve within them considerable ranges and degrees, subcategories and subdimensions. Furthermore, although the distinction between male and female roles seems to be more sharply defined in traditional societies than in modern societies, this distinction is always cultural, not natural, and symbolic behavior, such as language and speech, including verbal genres and patterns of speaking, is not merely a reflection of this distinction but an important expressive marker, creator, and contributor to it. To claim that statistical variation in surface grammar relates to gender distinctions in modern, complex societies while verbal genres and patterns of speaking are the primary marker of gender distinctions in traditional societies is not to claim also that there is no grammatical variation in traditional societies. Such variation has not been studied systematically in traditional, especially small and nonliterate, societies. It remains to be seen to what degree this variation does exist in such societies and how it relates to such sociological categories as gender. Nor is gender independent of other sociological categories in traditional societies. In groups as far away as the Haya of Tanzania and the Gros Ventre of Montana, gender distinctions expressed in language and speech are related to other sociological dimensions, in particular status. (See Dauer, 1978; A. R. Taylor, 1982.) The Haya case is particularly relevant to my position in this chapter, since, because of the evaluation of women in Haya society as secondary or inferior, female speech styles, which can be used by men or women, mark the speaker as being of lower social status. Finally, there are areal patterns, probably due to diffusion, that might seem to contradict, or at least qualify, my general hypothesis. An example is the common phonological and morphological (categorical rather than variable) marking of gender in North American Indian languages that coincides with differences in men's and women's verbal genres and patterns of speaking. In conclusion and restatement, what I am arguing here is that in certain traditional and especially relatively small-scale, homogeneous, and nonliterate societies, in which gender distinctions are well defined socially and culturally (such as the Araucanians, the Kaluli, and the Kuna, who are discussed in this volume), it is verbal genres, speaking roles, and patterns of speaking that are the primary linguistic manifestations of these gender distinctions.

Why variable grammatical differences rather than verbal genre differences seem to be the primary markers of gender distinctions in modern, complex societies is an interesting question. Perhaps it is related to the fact that there is much more casual, transactional, and impersonal use of language in modern societies, in which there is not always shared knowledge in advance between individuals of their roles and status in society but in which such information is signaled through language and other expressive communicative behavior.

Turning now to societies' symbolic evaluations of men's and women's speech differences, specific, recognized features distinguishing men's and women's speech are interpreted and reacted to by members of a society as valued or disvalued, positive or negative, according to the norms, values, and power relationships of the society, in particular of course those concerning men and women. This simple statement might seem to agree with the quotation from Margaret Mead saying that cultural activities are always evaluated symbolically as a reflection of men's and women's nature. But rather than insist a priori that men's and women's speech differences are always evaluated as reflecting women as inferior, I would instead argue that we should begin with the sociocultural matrix from which the symbolic evaluations and interpretations are derived. If symbolic ranking or typing – inferior/superior, good/bad, similar/different – is involved, the concept of stigma as developed sociologically by Erving Goffman in a classic little book (1963) is useful. To the degree that a society stigmatizes women, women's linguistic behavior, together with other communicative behavior, will be read as indicative of their place in society, an overt mark of their nonnormal and nonnormative status. Or, to borrow another of Goffman's significant concepts, that of frame (Goffman, 1974), the distinguishing features of women's speech place an implicit frame around all of their behavior, a filter that reminds communicative interactants that they are women and, if society views them that way, that they are inferior. What I am arguing for here by drawing on such notions as stigma and frame is a conception of the language–culture–society relationship that begins with the sociocultural and social-interactional matrix of language use and sees language as integrated within this matrix, rather than plugging observed or imagined linguistic differences into preconceived, often ethnocentrically biased, social and cultural categories. This is precisely what I intend to illustrate by means of the comparison of the speaking practices of the Araucanian and Kuna Indians.

In conclusion I want to stress again that according to the ethnographic perspective I have argued for here gender distinctions in language and speech must be seen in the context of sociological differentiation and cultural framing of which they constitute an integral aspect – they are both a reflection of and a contributor to this sociological differentiation and cultural framing. The ethnographic perspective does not rule out the possibility of cross-cultural universals in men's and women's speech and in the symbolic evaluation of this speech. But it insists that any such universals be sought out and analyzed in relation to significant cross-cultural and individual differences as well. Although the Malagasy pattern is like the Haya pattern in some ways, the two differ in important ways. This is the implication of the intended polysemy of my title: "A Diversity of Voices." There is the diversity of Kuna voices, the fact that the Kuna all by themselves demonstrate the complex nature of the relationship between men's and women's speech, including verbal genres, speaking roles, and patterns of speaking. There is the diversity of cross-cultural voices, providing as different pictures of men's and women's speech as the Araucanians, the Malagasy, the Haya, the Kaluli, and the people of Bihar in North India. There is the diversity of disciplinary voices, especially linguistics, anthropology, and folklore, each offering its own special insights. And there is the diversity of scholars and scholarly theories that have been advanced in this area.

The study of men's and women's speech, like other topics of social and political significance in our society, has proceeded by first looking for simple answers, not seeing the complexities offered by cross-cultural and ethnographic investigation, and by projecting our own society's dichotomous ethnocentrism onto the realities of others, always rendering *them* more primitive than *us*. But then the diversity of voices speaks through, reminding us of the complexity of language use in different societies around the world, and that generalizations and universals must come to terms with this complexity and not try to simplify it, and, with regard to my concerns here, that women's language, women's speech, and women's verbal activities are not everywhere socially and culturally inferior, domestic, or polite.

Notes

1   Borker (1980) and Philips (1980) also offer cross-cultural overviews.
2   This distinction between ideal and real or actual is commonly made in social and cultural anthropology. However, much of the literature on language and gender, especially in American society, has mixed or confused these two perspectives, a most unfortunate carelessness from both theoretical and methodological points of view.
3   Chant performed by Chief Olowitinappi.
4   The "way of the rattlesnake" was performed by curing specialist Olowitinappi.
5   Story performed by Chief Muristo Pérez.
6   Lullaby performed by Donilda García.
7   Tuneful weeping performed by Donilda García.
8   The "way of the bamboo cane" was performed by Manual Campos.

5. Women's speech in modern Mexicano

JANE H. HILL

In studies of the role of women in language change conducted among speakers of world languages in urban centers, a paradoxical pattern has been identified (Labov 1978). Women are more conservative than men in cases of stable variation but are more innovative in cases of change in progress, particularly if the change is an assimilation toward an elite norm. Women seem to be more sensitive to such norms than men, and to be more sensitive to the stigmatization of vernacular usage. Women speakers of Mexicano (Nahuatl), an indigenous language of Mexico, who live in rural communities in the region of the Malinche Volcano in the central Mexican states of Puebla and Tlaxcala, display a similarly paradoxical pattern of simultaneous linguistic conservatism and sensitivity to stigmatization. Like most male members of their communities, most of these women are bilingual in Spanish. The most significant variability within the kinds of usage these speakers define as "speaking *mexicano*" results from symbolic work in which they manipulate elements they consider to be *castellano* 'Spanish' in order to produce different speech registers. Women exhibit a different pattern of such manipulations from men. People in the communities hold that women are always "less Spanish" than men, and for some aspects of usage this is so. But for some usages where self-conscious purism in speaking *mexicano* has stimulated male avoidance of *castellano* elements, women are "more Spanish" (or "less Mexicano") than men. This chapter will illustrate some of the intricate patterning of gender differentiation in Mexicano usage. I shall also explore whether we should consider that the women's usages arise from their lack of exposure to Spanish, the active construction of a female gender identity, or their exclusion from patterns of speech appropriate to men and to male-dominated social

121

arenas. I shall present first the background of the research and a brief outline of the social context of the Malinche Volcano communities and the position of women in them. I shall then review evidence from six indices of linguistic variation in speaking *mexicano*, including lexical, syntactic, and phonological variants that derive from contact with Spanish, and attempt to make some suggestions about what these data on Mexicano-speaking women may imply for a general theory about the role of women in language change.[1]

Collection of data

During 1974–5 and the summers of 1976 and 1978, my husband, Kenneth C. Hill, and I tape-recorded a standard interview with ninety-six speakers of Mexicano in eleven communities in the Malinche Volcano region.[2] During this period and continuing to the present, we have recorded additional materials in a variety of contexts from many of these same speakers, as well as from an additional twenty-seven speakers. But all of the materials subjected to the quantitative analysis in this chapter were drawn from the usage of sixty-nine respondents, forty-three men and twenty-six women, for whom we have good information on honorific usage, a pivotal index for speakers of Mexicano that I shall discuss below.

The interview was conducted in the Mexicano language by a native speaker. Thus, all data in this chapter were produced while speakers considered themselves to be speaking *mexicano*.[3] The interview begins with questions about name, age, education, work history, and community responsibilities. Respondents are then asked to tell something about their lives, to tell about an experience in which they believed they were in danger of dying (a technique suggested by Labov 1972b), and to tell a traditional story. They are asked a number of questions about the Mexicano language itself. Finally, they are asked to translate words and sentences from Spanish into Mexicano.

Recruitment of respondents and conduct of the interviews were designed to make people as comfortable as possible. We used existing lines of authority, kinship, and friendship to recruit respondents, rather than conducting a random sample. Interviews were conducted in informal settings in people's homes and fields. Either I or my husband was present at all interviews, which injected a somewhat formal note into the occasion, but other speakers of Mexicano often joined in the interviews, yielding vigorous conversation and argument. As is true of most interviews, however, the level of usage is clearly more formal than that used in casual groups. Nonetheless, it is clear that responses were not as closely monitored as those reported by Bright and Thiel (1965) from a

Mexicano speaker from the Malinche region who participated in a class in Mexicano at UCLA.

Response times to the interviews ranged from twenty minutes to over an hour, with most interviews lasting thirty or forty minutes. The total sample of speech for the sixty-nine subjects includes about 76,900 words. Recent work (Guy 1980) suggests that this sample is too small for the examination of fine-grained variation. The small number of tokens for many variables that proved important, combined with my necessarily preliminary understanding of the structure of this exotic mixed language, makes presentation of the data in terms of variable rules (Labov 1972b) inappropriate. Instead, I have used other statistics to determine whether there is significant variation among different groups of speakers.

Women and society in the Malinche communities

Whereas a detailed account of the histories of the eleven communities would emphasize their diversity, all are evolving in a direction often called proletarianization. Members are shifting from a base of subsistence agriculture and associated rural pursuits such as woodcutting, supplemented seasonally by migratory labor, to integration into a regional and national system of industrial wage labor. The Malinche Volcano is centrally located. No community is more than two hours by bus from the city of Puebla, and Mexico City lies only eighty miles to the west. During the last twenty-five years the enormous labor pool of the region, with one of the highest rural population densities in Mexico, has been tapped by the construction of all-weather roads, a complex network of community bus systems, school construction, rural electrification, the installation of potable water systems, and many other innovations. These render the inhabitants more accessible to the factory complex growing explosively in the Puebla–Tlaxcala corridor, and the needs of the booming industries, particularly construction, of Puebla and Mexico City. The low wages and benefits offered in these wage-labor contexts appear to be predicated on the notion that the rural communities themselves will provide a substantial fraction of the subsistence of workers. This is accomplished in several ways. Road and school construction, electrification, and water systems are often accomplished through *mano de obra*, a contribution of community labor and funds that amounts to a virtual corvée. Bus systems are almost entirely a product of local initiative, although their fares are regulated by public agencies. Families remaining behind migrants continue in subsistence agriculture, with women and children accomplishing all but the heaviest agricultural tasks. Finally, the communities exhibit complex systems of support through reciprocity that members enter into in two major ways: participation in the hierarchy of community offices and *mayordomías* (the sponsorship of the adoration of holy images) and association through *compadrazgo*, in which ties of ritual kinship are formed between members. This system, documented by Nutini and Bell (1980), may be the most complex system of ritual kinship in the world. Successful participants in it have hundreds of *compadres* (coparents) and *ahijados* (godchildren), who serve as an important source of assistance and support. The community members believe that their subsistence comes from wage labor and farming. They believe that access to wage labor is gained entirely through education and the use of Spanish. Access to farm land is increasingly difficult, but cultivation is critical to an identity as a *campesino* (peasant) and a speaker of *mexicano*. Members consider the system of *compadrazgo* and the hierarchy of community service as outside the sphere of the economy, having an exclusively sacred character, but it can be shown that up to three-fifths of the financial outlay of families in these communities takes the form of investment in these systems (Olivera 1967). Access to them is greatly facilitated by the use of Mexicano, and most community members say that bilingualism – *titlahtoah de ōme* 'we speak two' – is a good thing.

The variable situation of women in the communities displays some general patterns. It seems clear that the uncompensated work of women stay-at-homes is crucial to the "superexploitation" of the communities by the industrial system. Women appear to be far less likely to engage in regular wage labor than men.[4] Those who do so work mainly in a stigmatized occupation – domestic service – although a very small number of women work as teachers, secretaries, or sales clerks. But women engage in a bewildering variety of nonwage economic activity, which is important to both domestic and community economies. This activity is characterized by independence and entrepreneurship, as opposed to the regular wage labor of men. Women may hire themselves out as casual agricultural labor. Many women practice traditional embroidery. One woman in our sample ran a small putting-out system in which she distributed raw materials for embroidered blouses and collected the finished products for sale. Women engage in a variety of small trade, commuting to the weekly market round and trading in flowers, fruit, small animals, pottery, and other products that can be transported by women and children on buses. One woman of our acquaintance is a distributor of such products. She attends the markets and purchases on contract for *clientas* in her home community, who have lines of credit with her (she is illiterate and keeps all her accounts in her head). Women raise such small animals as turkeys, chickens, and pigs. They raise money by the collection and sale of eggs, firewood, wild-plant products, parched squash seeds, and so forth. Most of the women in our sample from Tlaltepango, a ward of the large town of San Pablo del Monte, Tlaxcala, earn money by preparing tortillas daily and selling them in the central market in the nearby city of Puebla. In addition to these innumerable independent enterprises, women support the work of male relatives in many spheres. Women perform many of the tasks in the agricultural cycle, such as *destapando* (uncovering the young maize plants when these are covered by earth in the second plowing), weeding, and planting seed. Women in the families of weavers clean, skein, and dye yarn. They assist men in the production and sale of *pulque*, a local beverage (the consumption of which is an important marker of self-conscious indigenous identity for some people), and in the production and sale of charcoal. They may be in charge of the pasturage of sheep, goats, or milk cows (draft animals seem to be in the charge of men). Women and children collect the manure that supplements expensive chemical fertilizer. They assist as clerks in small shops owned by male relatives, and a few women have tiny shops of their own. Within the domestic sphere, women are versatile and participate in many tasks beyond their main role in food production and the care of small children. In spite of the intensive schedules and the multiple responsibilities of these women, they see their lives as having been greatly eased in recent years, primarily by the introduction of electric or gasoline-driven corn mills. Until the coming of the *molino* (mill), women rose before dawn to spend up to four hours grinding corn. Today, twenty sociable minutes in line, and perhaps a half-hour's regrinding by fastidious cooks, will supply a household with the day's tortillas. Women say that in the old days girls were brought up "under the *metate*" (grinding stone); the life of a woman without daughters old enough to help her in this task was drudgery indeed. Little girls begin to make tortillas when they are about ten years old, and a woman who can do this job is an essential component of a household, as none of the communities have tortillas for sale. The primacy of women in domestic food production is virtually absolute. Men assist in *desgranando* (shelling corn) and prepare certain kinds of cooked meats such as *barbacoa* (roast meat) and *chicharrón* (fried pork skin). (These communities follow the Lévi-Straussian rule: Women produce boiled meats, such as chicken and turkey for feast-day *mole* [meat eaten with sauce], and men produce meats that are not boiled in water.)

In contrast to the diversified entrepreneurship of women's economic participation, their formal position in households can be one of great subservience. The preferred pattern of residence is for a man to bring his bride (who is usually in her teens) to live in his father's household. After a couple of years, if money is available, a new house will be constructed for the couple. As the inheritance pattern is ultimogeniture, a woman who marries a *xōcoyōtl* (youngest son) will live with her mother-in-law until one of them dies. (Women are largely excluded from inheritance, according to Nutini and Bell 1980.) Some couples do live neolocally. A stigmatized pattern of living *al yerno*, with the wife's natal family, is universally believed to reveal a falling out between father and son or economic catastrophe in the husband's natal family. It should be said that although women say they resent the domination of their in-laws, extended households do provide support in the form of child care for the entrepreneurial thrusts that supplement family income. Several women, however, report that their husbands and mothers-in-law objected to their leaving the household to earn extra money.

In recent years abandonment and widowhood have perhaps replaced the mother-in-law as the most feared threat for women. Abandonment can take place outright – a man goes to the city and never comes back – but it is far more common for men to be absent from the household for long periods of time, leaving women lonely and without financial support. Work in factories and construction seems to produce a high level of accidental death or serious injury, and death by violence is also relatively frequent. Abandoned and quasi-abandoned women seem to fall back on the support of blood relatives. Widows and orphans may also be supported by in-laws. Such single women, however, are in general excluded from the formation of important *compadrazgo* relationships, which ideally are contracted between married couples in the hope of lifelong mutual support. (Some minor *compadrazgos* involve women's making ties with other women.) People believe that women alone will not have the resources to enter and sustain a major *compadrazgo*. Single mothers may even be forced to go to the city and throw themselves on the charity of strangers in order to find someone to stand up with their child for baptism or confirmation. We found that a high percentage of our own *comadres* were widows; we are a last-ditch source of ritual kinsmen for these low-status women. Participation in the reciprocal feasting of the *mayordomías* is also considered to be a male affair. The *mayordoma* basks in glory reflected from the *mayordomo*, although she may undertake the largest share of the work in organizing the great feasts that are a part of his responsibilities. Women have their own religious societies, but participation in these involves only small ceremonies such as the lighting of votive candles or the award of medals and scapulars, rather than the public manifestations made by the *mayordomo*, in which he calls on the assistance of a wide range of friends and blood and ritual kinsmen. It is important, however, to emphasize that women have wide-ranging social networks. Much as female economic entrepreneurship may be contrasted with the structured wage work of men, female social activity tends to involve a strategy of flexibility and informality compared to the formal affiliations of men. Nutini and Bell remark that, whereas men control the system of institutionalized ritual kinship, women may have more and stronger friendships than men, and "it is usually through women that men are led to think about particular friends as potential *compadres*" (1980:208).

The evolution of female personality during the life cycle reflects the realities of female independence rather than the ideal of subservience. Although all young people are quieter and less assertive than adults, young women exaggerate this pattern. It is very difficult to collect linguistic data from young women, who perform as stereotypical "muted" females: They blush, giggle, give one-word answers, "play dumb" on the translation tasks, and speak in tiny voices. The ideal of "muting" in this age group seems to be expressed also by a quirk of manipulation of the *rebozo*, the six-foot length of dark cloth that is the universal uniform of rural and working-class Mexicano women. The *rebozo* is held over the mouth in public, clenched between the teeth if a woman's hands are occupied.

As people grow older, they become more outgoing, and again women may exaggerate the pattern. By the time women are in their forties, some seem to be cultivating a reputation for outspokenness and rowdy wit, even joking blasphemously in circumstances where men are very serious. Women in their middle years and beyond often criticize and nag their husbands in public. Older women often talk very fast and are mistresses of the interruption and the quick comeback. Older men, however, become slow and pompous in their speech. It is often difficult to interview such men when their wives are present; the women grow impatient and interrupt their husbands. Women, however, do accept the authority of their husbands in principle, and we have collected many recollections from women of the "suffering" that stems from adherence to the principle of obedience.

Perhaps the most visible difference between these women and their men is dress. Very few elderly men still wear traditional rural costume; most men are indistinguishable from working-class urban men of their age group. Many women, however, wear traditional clothing of several types. But this lag in costume will probably change within the next generation, and I am acquainted with several mothers who dress their daughters in polyester slacks and polo shirts while they themselves wear embroidered petticoats, wraparound skirts, red sashes (the *faja*), and satin blouses cut in the style of the turn of the century.

Language in the Mexicano communities: the syncretic continuum

The language system of the communities of the Malinche Volcano can be analyzed as a syncretic continuum with two major zones, for which the local labels are *mexicano* and *castellano* or *castilla*.[5] Almost everyone in the communities is to some degree bilingual. Some speakers are self-identified, or identified by others, as unable to speak *castellano*, but these must be considered to be at least "incipient bilinguals" (Diebold 1961). Speakers consider their usage in both the languages, however, to lie in a zone of imperfection somewhere between the ideal versions of them. One ideal pole is called *legítimo mexicano* (genuine Mexicano). This is considered to be a pure form of the language, without Spanish loan words, which existed at some time in the past and is documented in old books. It is not believed that any modern speaker in the communities can produce such a usage. All modern speech is considered *revuelto* (mixed up) with Spanish loan material. In spite of the availability of education, which speakers believe leads to competence in *castellano*, speakers consider their usage inadequate because, they say, they make *cuatros* (absurd errors). Thus, all speech is considered to be dominated by mixing and error. Within this zone of imperfection, speakers do distinguish speaking *mexicano* from speaking *castellano*, monitoring particularly inflectional material. But the differentiation between the two languages is the object of active ongoing negotiation, and people can speak *mexicano* in a manner that involves using an enormous amount of loan vocabulary and syntax, as well as frequent switching.

Within the sector of the zone of imperfection that people consider to be speaking *mexicano*, I describe most of the socially meaningful variation in terms of two principles of "coding": the power code and the solidarity code. Coding is used as a term for a principle of selection from the enormous range of symbolic materials available to speakers, to produce a particular "way of speaking" (Hymes 1962). The power code "opens" *mexicano* to *castellano*, raising the frequency of this material in a symbolic invocation of the power and prestige of the Spanish-speaking world. Speech encoded in this manner becomes more elevated and authoritative. The solidarity code is a principle of selection that "closes" *mexicano*, restricting (more or less unsuccessfully) the frequency of *castellano* material as an expression of ethnic self-consciousness and solidarity. The power code is not acknowledged by speakers, but the solidarity code is salient and is expressed in vigorous purism, particularly among men.

Evidence for the power code is indirect. It is discussed in detail in Hill and Hill (1980) and in Hill and Hill (1986), but I shall review it briefly here. First, Spanish loan words reach high frequencies in the speech of senior men, the *tiāchcātzitzīn* or *principales*, who have reached the highest levels in the hierarchy of community service. Only young men who are semispeakers (often they have learned Mexicano as a second language as their ethnic self-consciousness develops in adolescence) use as high frequencies of Spanish loan material. One apparent contradiction is that speakers will criticize such usage by young people while singling out as relatively good speakers of Mexicano elderly men who, by objective criteria, use the same frequency of Spanish loans. In terms of the power code, this may suggest that to use too high a frequency of loans in speaking *mexicano* is presumptuous if one's social station is not appropriate. Thus, there is some evidence that many speakers, both male and female, monitor down Spanish loans to avoid such presumption. Evidence for such monitoring comes indirectly, from drunken speech, which exhibits inflated frequencies of Spanish loans and is considered to be "out of control," or unmonitored, in these communities (although it is important to recognize that drunken speech, like all speech, has aspects of deliberate performance).

The contextual distribution of Spanish loan words, as well as their stratification among types of speakers, is also evidence that the power code exists. Loans are most frequent in speech about matters of public importance, such as government and religion and money. In narrative discourse, Spanish loan words tend to be clustered in sections that are "evaluative," that is, that indicate why the narrative should be taken as important (Labov 1972b). It is common for speakers to clinch an argument by a switch into Spanish for an aphoristic coda.

The use of the symbolic resources of an elite language in a local vernacular, as in the Mexicano power code, has of course been attested from many other speech communities. The classical languages have served this function for English (as have French and German); Sankoff (1980) documents a similar usage of English and Tok Pisin by speakers of Buang, a New Guinea language. Spanish-speakers in urban Mexico use English and French. Such usage often collides with indigenous purism when this emerges as a strategy of firming up ethnic boundaries, and this is occurring today in the Mexicano communities. The overt attitude of all members is that the use of *castellano* words in *mexicano* is bad. Thus, the principle of usage that speakers are willing to acknowledge is not the power code but the solidarity code. I have given this coding principle this name because I believe that it is an attempt by speakers to protect access to community resources by defining this access as a privilege of indigenous ethnicity, which becomes highly self-conscious, solidary, and egalitarian, and has as an important marker the ability to speak *mexicano*. In a previous study (Hill and Hill 1980) I showed that the density of solidarity-code manifestations in a community can be correlated with its relative dependency within regional and national economic systems. Thus, as the frequency of participation in wage labor increases, speakers in a community will tend more and more to be dominated in their usage by the solidarity code. Not only does wage labor, along with the ever-increasing pressure against successful culti-vation, make the economic situation of people increasingly precarious,[6] but it makes the boundaries of the communities more permeable. Thus, the purism of the solidarity code is considered by speakers to be part of *respeto* 'respect', particularly in the establishment and conduct of *compadrazgo* relationships. The emphasis on accomplishing these in *mexicano* is so strong that, if no one in a family is able to perform the appropriate ritual language, a *huēhuētlahtōqui* 'old speaker' (always an elderly man who is considered competent in *mexicano*) will be brought in to speak for them. Networks of *compadrazgo* are, of course, a crucial support system for families struggling to make ends meet.

The most widespread manifestation of the solidarity codes is lexical purism. The stigmatization of aspects of usage that speakers identify as *castellano* mixing in speaking *mexicano* makes etymology a subject of much local attention. It is important to note, however, that in this vernacular etymology many features of Mexicano usage that the linguist would trace to Spanish are not considered to be *castellano* by speakers. Additionally, purists will often identify grammatical patterns that are obviously modeled on Spanish and have no attestation in the classical language (the records of the sixteenth century) as *legítimo mexicano*. Lexical purism is largely a losing battle, as precisely those speakers who are most concerned with it are also the most exposed to Spanish influence through participation in wage labor.

Lexical purism in Mexicano probably dates to the sixteenth century (Karttunen and Lockhart 1976). But it is becoming particularly em-phatic, and particularly problematic, in the modern communities. This occurs because the usage of many people is apparently shifting from a continuum of registers in Mexicano that included the power code and the solidarity code (with Spanish reserved as a language used only with outsiders) to a diglossic division in which Spanish functions as a public language, even within the communities themselves, and Mexicano func-tions as a private language. In this context, the symbolic weight of the Spanish loan material incorporated into Mexicano through hundreds of years, which functions in the power code to manifest the elevation and seriousness of public usage of important people, contradicts the new function of Mexicano as exclusively a private language used among intimates who emphasize egalitarianism and ethnic solidarity. Thus solidarity-coding purists evaluate hispanized Mexicano speech not as elevated but as spoiled and polluted. This stigmatization of the usage of all speakers of Mexicano is combined with the very real limitations of community support systems, which speakers compare unfavorably with the perceived opportunities of wage labor in a Spanish-speaking environment. Even parents who value Mexicano may reluctantly abandon its use in the family in order to prepare children for school. Thus, Mexicano can disappear very rapidly from most of the linguistic repertoire of a community, and be driven underground into the *reductio ad absurdam* of the solidarity code, in which the Mexicano competence of speakers extends only to a few toasts used in the drinking of *pulque*, or the obscene challenges used to "test" strangers (Hill and Hill 1980).

Honorific usage as an index of language functions

Modern Mexicano usage in the Malinche area offers a convenient index by which we can distinguish those speakers who have probably completed the functional shift of Mexicano to that of a private language of ethnic solidarity from speakers who may use the language over a wider range of functions, including "elevated" and public speech. This is the index of narrow versus broad honorific usage.[7] All speakers use a system of honorifics to express degrees of social distance and deference. The levels within the system are distinguished by pronoun choice and by derivational affixes on nouns and verbs. Level I forms are used to intimates and subordinates. Level II is used to strangers, parents, and by some women to their husbands. It is marked by the addition of the honorific suffix *-tzīn* to pronouns, and the use of the deferential prefix *on-* (away) on verbs. Level III has two sublevels, which are used together, with Level IIIb appearing about 20 percent of the time, or more frequently if extra deference is required. It is used to very old people, to very high-status people such as priests, bishops, state governors, and the like, and to sacred beings. Many women use Level III with their in-laws. Level III is marked by reflexive morphology in addition to the affixes of Level II. Thus, the reflexive prefix *mo-* is added to verbs; this requires in turn that the verb be marked with an "applicative" suffix *-lia* and *-lih*. In Level IIIb, the pronoun can shift to the term *māhuizotzīn* (reverence), and the verb can be suffixed with the honorific *-tzīn*. Level IV shifts to the third person for direct address and is used in speaking to compadres. Otherwise it is like Level III. The examples given below all mean "You give it to me." (Note that only one object can be marked on the verb, so the third-person object "it" is not present. The reflexive object is, of course, an exception to this rule. Third-person subject is not marked in Mexicano; cf. the example for Level IV.)

Level I: *teh ti-nēch-maca* 'you you-me-give'
Level II: *tehhuā-tzīn ti-nēch-on-maca* 'you-honorific you-me-away-give'
Level IIIa: *tehhuā-tzīn ti-nēch-on-mo-maqui-lia* 'you-honorific you-me-away-reflexive-give applicative'

Level IIIb: *mo-māhuizo-tzīn ti-nēch-on-mo-maqui-lih-tzīn-oa* 'your-reverence-honorific   you-me-away-reflexive-give-applicative-honorific-theme'

Level IV: *ī-māhuizo-tzīn nēch-on-mo-maqui-lih-tzīn-oa* 'his/her-reverence-honorific me-away-reflexive-give-applicative- honorific-theme'

All speakers use the entire system in direct address; not to use the appropriate construction is at best a youthful error and at worst a serious breach of politeness or an insult. However, the system contracts somewhat when speakers are referring, rather than addressing (that is, talking about someone rather than speaking directly to him or her). The morphology of the system in reference is identical with that shown above; of course the subject prefix *ti-* (you) does not appear, and instead of the second-person pronouns *teh*, *tehhuātzīn*, and *momāhuizotzīn* the third-person pronouns *yeh*, *yehhuātzīn*, and *īmāhuizotzīn* are used. (To save space I give only singulars; of course the system can be used in the plural as well.) The possible contractions of the system in reference can be expressed in terms of an implicational series:

Sacred beings < The verb "to die"<Speaking of the dead<Speaking of priests, etc.<Speaking of other living persons

Thus, if a speaker uses Level II to speak of living persons – say, her in-laws or grandparents – that speaker will use at least Level II in all other environments as well. All speakers use Level III in speaking of God and the Virgin. But a speaker who uses Level III forms for the verb "to die" (*ōmomiquilih* [he/she died]; the Level I form is *ōmic*) will not necessarily use anything except Level I in any environment rightward on the series. Within the series, we have identified the environment "speaking of the dead" as the critical index of differentiation between narrow-honorific-speakers, who use Level I forms in that environment, from broad-honorific-speakers, who use at least Level II. Narrow-honorific-speakers, like all speakers, use Level III to refer to sacred beings, and they use the full system in direct address. However, some such speakers will say *ōmic* (he/she died) (Level I) even of a mother or father.

It is important to understand that narrow-honorific usage does not mean that a speaker does not control Mexicano. These speakers can and do use complex Level III morphology in appropriate environments. Whereas it is certainly the case that narrow-honorific-speakers are more likely to be poor speakers of the language than broad-honorific-speakers, this is not the cause of the contraction of the functional range of honorific usage. Indeed, some superb speakers exhibit narrow-honorific usage, and the sample discussed here includes a self-defined monolingual Mexicano speaker (S11) who exhibits narrow-honorific usage. The appearance of the narrow-honorific pattern is, I believe, one aspect of the shift of Mexicano into a function as a language of solidarity exclusively, where the intricate distinctions of status rendered in the honorific system are no longer appropriate. The system is retained in direct address, but in the less dangerous environment of reference it can be abandoned. Thus, we are presented with the contradictory situation of speakers who hold that *respeto* (respect) is an important advantage of Mexicano over Spanish, yet who are suppressing the usages that manifest *respeto* most dramatically. This functional shift of Mexicano is being led by male factory workers who are on the cutting edge of the increasingly precarious economic situation of the communities and of the increasing influence of Spanish through education and wage labor. Narrow-honorific usage is one way in which they encode the ethnic self-consciousness and ethnic solidarity by which, as they often say, one "defends oneself."

The usage of narrow-honorific-speakers is not, at all points, sharply differentiated from that of broad-honorific-speakers. For instance, drunken narrow-honorific-speakers can exhibit extreme versions, which may be intended as parodies, of the power code. Broad-honorific-speakers are sometimes very purist. No doubt additional data would make it clear that some speakers in our sample are misclassified. (For instance, four women who otherwise appear to be very conservative speakers of Mexicano are classified as narrow-honorific-speakers because they mention their deceased husbands using Level I. There may be personal reasons for this usage in each case.) Honorific usage, however, offers a relatively objective index for grouping speakers, which enables us on reasonable grounds to differentiate more and less ethnically self-conscious speakers. In the present study, it is important to control for honorific usage so that gender differentiation can be separated from manifestations of ethnic self-consciousness, which one might expect would be differentialy developed in men and women because of their different economic situations.

The Mexicano speech of women

Speakers in the Malinche Volcano communities believe that women "lag" linguistically. The term "linguistic lag," introduced by Dorian (1980), describes a situation in which women would be more likely to be monolingual in Mexicano than men, that their Mexicano would exhibit less Spanish influence, and that their Spanish would be more influenced by Mexicano. Many speakers believe this to be the case, and express astonishment that "even women" are turning to Spanish. Thus, in answer to a question about whether people are ever ashamed to speak Mexicano, a young man remarked:

(1) *hasta in zoāmeh yōpīnāhuih* 'Even the women were ashamed.' (24.92)

Reflecting on the usage of young people, a middle-aged woman said:

(2) *hasta māz ichpocatzitzīn ācmo ctenderoah, huān ōcatca quēmah.* 'Even the young girls no longer understand it [Mexicano], and before they certainly did.' (28.4.4)

My informal observations of women's usage in Spanish suggest that some women exhibit stereotyped patterns of modifying Spanish sounds that are not found in men's speech. Thus, women may shift Spanish /f/ to /p/, as in /josepa/'Josefa'. This shift is a shibboleth *cuatro* (error), so hypercorrections appear where Spanish /p/ becomes /f/. For instance, one woman described to me a cure which used /fumada/'salve' (from Spanish *pomada*; the shift /o/ to /u/ occurs in men's Spanish as well). Women have other interlingual forms in Spanish that, as far as I know, do not appear in men's usage. Most prominent among these is the overgeneralization of the first-person plural form of verbs, yielding sentences like

(3) *Ya venimos in Concho* 'Concho is coming now.'

Women are also more likely than men to use the Mexicano element *in* in speaking Spanish, as in (3). This usage is also stereotyped, and hypercorrections yield forms in both speaking *mexicano* and speaking *castellano* in which initial /n/ disappears from its position, as in *ce úmero* ('a number', from Spanish *número*).

As I shall show, not only is women's Spanish more likely to be conspicuously interlingual than the Spanish of men, but they exhibit on many variables (although not all) less hispanization of their Mexicano usage than do men. Women use significantly fewer Spanish loan words than men. The use of noun-incorporating verbs, a conservative Mexicano way of speaking that is disappearing from modern varieties of the language, persists in women's usage at a significantly higher rate than in the speech of men. Women appear to be less influenced than men by Spanish syntax in the construction of relative clauses. Examining these indices, one might conclude that women are simply conforming to the purist male ideal of the solidarity code, closing their speech to *castellano* mixture. On other indices, however, women are more Spanish, or, in solidarity-code terms, less Mexicano, than men. For instance, an important and salient phonological pattern assimilates stress-final Spanish words to Mexicano by shifting their stress to the penultimate syllable. Women retain the Spanish final stress at a higher rate than do men who are otherwise at a comparable level of hispanization, as measured by the loan-word index. In the case of Spanish influence on the syntax of Mexicano possessive constructions, all women and some men appear to be relatively unselfconscious about this mixture, using hispanized constructions with relative freedom. However, some men are apparently self-consciously nativistic on this index. Based on evidence from these two indices, we might conclude that women are simply ignorant of male norms for nativization. We find, however, that in the important area of number purism, women are just as self-conscious as men, given comparability of other usages. Finally, we find that whereas women are apparently aware of male nativism, they do not share this value. Nor do men value the speech of women; their speech, although conservative in many ways from the linguist's point of view, apparently is not considered by men to exemplify the purist norm.

In the present section I shall review three indices of variation where women's usage can be shown to be less Spanish than men's usage in speaking *mexicano*. These indices are the frequency of Spanish loan words, the use of noun-incorporating verbs, and the use of Spanish-style relative clauses.

The measure of frequency of Spanish loan words in speech is calculated as follows: Each Spanish loan word used by a speaker is counted the first time, and only the first time, it appears in that speaker's interview. The total of first appearances is divided by an estimate of the total number of words in the speaker's interview. This total is derived by multiplying the number of lines in typed transcript by the average number of words per line. Frequency of Spanish loan words is thus expressed as a percentage of total words. Spanish loan words that local vernacular etymological practice holds to be *legítimo mexicano*, such as *axno* (donkey), *tomīn* (money), and *xolāl* (downtown, from Spanish *solar*, an area enclosed by walls and open to the sky), are not included in counting Spanish loans. Nor are Spanish words that appear in "switches" (that is, sequences in Spanish of clause or sentence length that include Spanish inflection and definite articles, except where these are fixed expressions that have been borrowed by Mexicano). Since each item is counted only the first time it appears, no speaker gets credit for creating a densely hispanized texture by the frequent repetition of forms such as *entonces* (then), *pues* (well), or *este* as a hesitation form. Thus, the measure may bear some relationship to a speaker's actual knowledge of the Spanish lexicon as this is expressed in the ability to use a variety of borrowed words. However, as I noted above, Spanish loan-word frequency is apparently monitored down by speakers, either through solidarity-code purism or observation of the power-code constraint on presumptuous elevation, so the index should not be taken as a reliable indicator of bilingual skills.

Table 5.1 shows the distribution of the total number of first appear-

Table 5.1. *Spanish loan-word frequencies*

	NH male (N = 27)	NH female (N = 16)	BH male (N = 16)	BH female (N = 9)
Spanish loan	2,393	1,222	1,424	900
Other words	25,263	16,404	18,310	13,158

	X^2	p
A. Total distribution	87.78	≤ .001
B. Male vs. female	46.64	≤ .001
C. NH vs. BH	34.07	≤ .001
D. NH male vs. NH female	43.34	≤ .001
E. BH male vs. BH female	8.49	≤ .01
F. BH male vs. NH male	32.10	≤ .001

ances of Spanish loan words (hereafter simply "Spanish loans") compared with all other words. Data are sorted into the four categories of speakers. The results of significant pair comparisons are given. If a pair is not given, the difference proved not to meet the .05 level of significance. In this, as in all succeeding tables, NH means "narrow-honorific-speaker" and BH means "broad-honorific-speaker."

Table 5.1 shows a significant gender differentiation for Spanish loans. However, there is also a significant differentiation according to honorific usage. Note that among narrow-honorific-speakers, the genders are more different from one another than among broad-honorific-speakers (a result consonant with the findings of Rothstein 1982), and that narrow-honorific men use significantly more loans than broad-honorific men. This suggests that the principal source of the gender differentiation is that narrow-honorific men are pulling away from other speakers, reflecting their increasing involvement in the Spanish-speaking world. Of course, these speakers are also the most active stigmatizers of Spanish loan materials. However, broad-honorific men are also moving away from women in the same category. Thus, this index seems to reflect a gender lag (Dorian 1980) and to confirm community opinion. It is important to determine whether the lag of women on this index is the result of relative lack of exposure to Spanish or the result of monitoring down Spanish loan frequency. The best evidence that women are monitoring down comes from the speech of S48, a narrow-honorific woman who was very drunk during the interview; she has the highest frequency of Spanish loans of any speaker, including all men. (Her frequency is 18 percent; recall that this counts only first usage. Her absolute frequency would be about 70 percent.) Narrow-honorific women are usually good speakers of Spanish; the extreme "mexicanoisms" I cited at the beginning of this section were all heard in the usage of broad-honorific women, with one exception.[8] If women are monitoring down, we need to know whether this is in response to the power code, which reserves Spanish for prestigious senior men, or in response to the solidarity code, which urges a "pure" usage. I shall return to this question after other indices of variation have been discussed.

A second index of variation where women appear to be "less Spanish" than men is the frequency of noun-incorporating verbs. Records of Mexicano from the sixteenth century (representing the so-called classical language) are famous for this feature of morphology. Many students of the modern language have noted that noun incorporation is now rare, giving way to the influx of borrowed Spanish verbs and to an increasing tendency toward Spanish-influenced "analytic" syntax, as opposed to morphological polysynthesis. The examples below will illustrate the difference between a "synthetic" construction with a noun-incorporating verb, and an "analytic" construction. The two sentences occurred consecutively from a single speaker, who glossed (4) with (5); such glossing of noun-incorporating expressions is common.

(4) *ni-c-tlahzol-tequi-tih* 'I-it cornstalk-cut-go in order to' (I am going in order to cut cornstalks)
(5) *ni-yah ni-c-tequi-tih in tlahzol* 'I-go I-it-cut-go in order to *in* cornstalk' (I am going in order to cut cornstalks)

Such forms are very rare. Only 114 noun-incorporating verbs appear in the sixty-nine interviews. Thus, many speakers exhibit no such forms. A definitive study of the verbs would require far more text than is possible here, and should incorporate an account of the lexical, syntactic, and discourse constraints on noun incorporation versus "analytic" constructions. The assumption implied here, which is that each time a verbal element appears there is an equal chance that it will incorporate a noun, is clearly not the case. It is, however, important to note that both transitive and intransitive verbs can incorporate nouns (for a discussion of noun incorporation in another variety of Mexicano, see Merlan 1976).

Table 5.2 shows the distribution of noun-incorporating verbs compared with all other verbs for each category of speaker. Only significant results of pair comparisons are indicated. There is a significant gender effect for frequency of noun-incorporating verbs. Unlike the case of Spanish loan frequency, there is no significant effect for narrow- versus broad-honorific-speakers. In addition, in this case the difference between broad-honorific men and women is greater than that for narrow-honorific men and women, the reverse of the Spanish loan index. While the pair chi-square comparison of broad-honorific women and narrow-honorific women does not yield a significant difference, a comparison of these two groups when each woman is ranked according to frequency

Table 5.2. *Frequency of noun-incorporating verbs*

	NH male (N = 27)	NH female (N = 16)	BH male (N = 16)	BH female (N = 10)
N-I Verbs	26	35	15	38
Other verbs	5,073	4,045	3,771	3,136
		X^2		p
A. Total distribution		20.25		≤ .001
B. Male vs. female		16.67		≤ .001
C. NH male vs. NH female		4.16		≤ .05
D. BH male vs. BH female		14.66		≤ .001

of usage does yield a significant difference. Using the Mann-Whitney U Test for comparison of ranks, broad-honorific women have higher frequencies of noun-incorporating verbs (U = 46, z = 1.83, p≤.0336). Thus, noun incorporation seems to be a good index of "conservative" female speech. The fact that broad-honorific men depart significantly from broad-honorific women in this usage may mean that this way of speaking is to some degree a female register.

Although from the point of view of the linguist the use of noun-incorporating verbs seem to be a very "Mexicano" way of speaking, no Malinche speaker has ever mentioned such constructions to me as *legítimo mexicano* usage, or indeed mentioned them at all. On several occasions, however, speakers who uttered such constructions immediately glossed them as in (4) and (5) above, which may have reflected their belief that the interviewer, a bilingual male teenager, was not likely to understand the usage.

The third index where women appear to be "less Spanish" in the performance of speaking *mexicano* than men is another case of a very rare construction, in this case a calque on the Spanish construction of relative clauses.[9] (A calque is a borrowed syntactic form, where a construction in the donor language is translated word for word into the target language. An example in English is "attorney general," which exhibits noun–adjective word order, a calque on French that occurred in the medieval period of language contact.)

Classical Mexicano – and the usage of many modern speakers – does not exhibit true relative pronouns, such as English "who" in (7):

(6)   I just met the man who will be our next president.

In Mexicano such relative clauses are formed by conjoining the verb in the relative clause directly to the head noun (sometimes the verb is set off by the particles *de* or *in*).

(7) ōyec cē tēnāntzīn ōyah Puebla
     was one old woman went Puebla
     'There was an old woman who went to Puebla.'

Mexicano has forms that function as indefinite nominals and question words, which include *āquin* (someone, whoever, who?), *tlen* (something, whatever, what?), *can(-)* (somewhere, wherever, where?), *cuac* (whenever, when?). Modern Mexicano has borrowed several Spanish nominals which also function as indefinite nominals and question words in Spanish, but which in Spanish have the additional role of relative pronouns, appearing with nominal heads in sentences like (8) below. These include *que* (what, whatever, which), *donde* (where, wherever), and *cuando* (when, whenever).

(8) *En el mes del febrero, cuando hay mucho aire, sufrimos del frio.*
     'In the month of February, when there is a lot of wind, we suffer from the cold.'

Presumably under the influence of bilingual usage, some Mexicano-speakers use both the borrowed Spanish forms and the indefinite nominals of Mexicano origin as true relative pronouns. This syntactic change can be definitely identified only when the speaker uses such an item with a nominal head. In (9) the word *personahtin* (people) heads the relative clause that follows it and begins with the element *āquin*, which is functioning as a true relative pronoun. Note that this sentence also exhibits a syntactically conservative relative clause: *personas [cpiah; . . .]* 'people [(who) they have it . . .]

(9) Pues, cateh personahtin, āquin cmatih tlatōzqueh, personas cpiah ocachi edad.
     'Well, there are people, who know how to speak, people who are older.'

Table 5.3 displays the data on relative clauses with nominal heads and true relative pronouns (the innovative Spanish type) compared with the number of all other relative clauses. Data are sorted into the four categories of speakers, and significant pair comparisons are given. The distribution is rather like that for Spanish loan words. On the one hand, gender differences are clearly significant. But so is the difference between broad- and narrow-honorific-speakers. Again we see that the difference between the genders is greater for narrow-honorific-speakers (although a Mann-Whitney U Test comparing ranks for broad-honorific men versus broad-honorific women narrowly misses significance ($U = 52.5$, $z = 1.64$, $p \le .0505$); the chi-square statistic is not significant at the .05 level). Again we see the significant difference between broad-honorific and narrow-honorific men. This grammatical innovation is apparently moving first into the "exposed" narrow-honorific male popu-

Table 5.3. *Frequency of relative clauses with true relative pronoun*

	NH male (N = 27)	NH female (N = 16)	BH male (N = 16)	BH female (N = 10)
RC with true RP	49	15	14	6
Other RC	490	435	330	255
			X^2	p
A. Total distribution			24.75	$\leq .001$
B. Male vs. female			13.79	$\leq .001$
C. Narrow honorific vs. broad honorific			7.54	$\leq .01$
D. NH male vs. NH female			13.44	$\leq .001$
E. BH male vs. NH male			7.99	$\leq .01$

lation. Although no speaker ever mentioned this type of clause as an example of mixture, it is interesting to note that the speaker with the highest rate of use of the innovative type of relative causes (S44, a narrow-honorific man with six of eight relative clauses of the innovative type) was very drunk at the time of the interview. S44 may have been parodying the power code. I have the impression that such clauses are more likely to appear in relatively elevated contexts, so they may be a manifestation of power coding among narrow-honorific-speakers. However, they are not part of the broad-honorific power code, which emphasizes the use of Spanish adverbs and adjectives.

In summary, we can see that women's usage can be said to be significantly less Spanish on the three variables discussed above. But the structure of each index is distinctive. Only noun incorporation is stratified exclusively by gender. Spanish loan frequency and relative clause syntax are also stratified according to honorific usage, which I am taking here to be an index of a self-conscious reaction of ethnic solidarity, in response to the exposure in a dependent relationship to the Spanish-speaking world of wage laborers. Thus it may be that gender differentiation on these indices is simply an epiphenomenon of the fact that women are less exposed than are men, simply because they do not participate in wage labor. The degree to which their Mexicano is less Spanish than that of men because of their lack of exposure, or because of other factors, cannot be ascertained until we have examined other indices of variation.

There are two indices where women can be shown to be less *mexicano* than men in their Mexicano usage. These two indices are stress shift, a phonological pattern that nativizes borrowed Spanish nouns, and the construction of the possessive. The index of stress shift is a complex variable, and the distinction between women's and men's usage can be seen only when stress shift is examined in combination with the index of Spanish loan frequency. When we control for Spanish loan frequency, women not only emerge as less *mexicano* than men, but exhibit a hypercorrect crossover from their casual usage to the usage of the interview, of a type that Labov (1972b) has suggested indicates sensitivity to stigmatization.

Stress in Mexicano is always on the penultimate syllable of words (except in the vocative, which is rare). Many borrowed Spanish nouns, however, have final stress in Spanish, including forms such as *mamá* (mother), *doctor* (doctor), *revolución* (revolution), *ciudad* (city), *lugar* (place), and so forth. Many speakers shift this stress variably to the penultimate syllable in speaking Mexicano, yielding *mámā, dóctōr, revolúciōn, cíudād* or *ciúdād, lúgār*, and the like. The main constraints on stress shift seem to be lexical; a few nouns never shift, such as *edad* (age) and *verdad* (truth). Stress shift is salient for speakers. In speaking *mexicano* it is considered purist and authentic to shift stress. But in speaking *castellano* stress shift is a shibboleth *cuatro* (error). A narrow-honorific-speaker used stress shift to exemplify the extreme *mexicano* nature of a community near his own (his conversational partner is a narrow-honorific woman):

(10) S55: Aquí en Aztatla, ōmpa quēmah, allí te van a decir, pos, "Tlā quēmah tlā nopápān."
        'There in Aztatla, there yes, there they're going to say to you, well, "Sure, yes, sure it's my father (*nopápān*)." '
      S53: Hahaha.
      S55: Es su papá, esto es, nopápā es su papá.
        'It's his father, that's what it is, *nopápā* means his father.'
      S53: Su papá.
        'His father.'
      S55: Mjm, nomámā, es su mamá.
        'Mhm, *nomámā*, it's his mother.'

To fail to shift stress is "mixing." Thus, a young narrow-honorific man from Canoa, criticizing the Mexicano usage of the rival town of La Resurrección, described the faults of speakers there as follows:

(11) Pero nihqui ōtomomacac cuenta quēnin, in acento ctlāliliah al último, eh?
      But also you've noticed how they put the stress on the last syllable, eh?

Table 5.4 shows the frequency of stress shift, followed by the frequency of Spanish loans for all speakers who have at least four environments where stress shift could have occurred. Stress-shift frequency is expressed as the percentage of environments in which stress is shifted to the penultimate syllable. Speakers are grouped according to these two indices into four categories:

Table 5.4. *Stress-shift frequency and frequency of Spanish loan words*

	Low Spanish loan			High Spanish loan		
	NH male:	S11 (20)	(4) M	NH male:	S31 (20)	(10) D
		S19 (21)	(7)		S42 (0)	(12)
		S57 (17)	(5)		S44 (12)	(14) D
		S77 (21)	(8)		S51 (0)	(12) D
	BH male:	S12 (0)	(7)		S52 (0)	(15)
		S16 (20)	(5)		S63 (14)	(15)
		S18 (20)	(7)		S80 (0)	(15)
Low		S38 (21)	(5) M		S90 (10)	(12)
stress		S98 (20)	(8)	BH male:	S5 (0)	(11) D
shift	NH female:	S36 (17)	(6)		S15 (8)	(10)
		S43 (0)	(7) M		S33 (0)	(13)
		S50 (8)	(8)		S37 (4)	(9)
		S53 (6)	(8)	NH female:	S48 (20)	(18) D
		S59 (0)	(6)	BH female:	S29 (0)	(10)
		S75 (6)	(7)			
		S91 (10)	(5)			
	BH female:	S14 (0)	(5) M			
		S20 (15)	(7)			
A		S78 (20)	(5)	B		
		S84 (17)	(7)			
	NH male:	S2 (83)	(3)	NH male:	S10 (29)	(12)
		S46 (57)	(6)		S24 (22)	(13)
		S47 (67)	(5)		S25 (57)	(14)
		S56 (22)	(8)		S55 (50)	(14)
		S60 (22)	(8)	BH male:	S26 (54)	(9)
		S61 (100)	(8)		S39 (25)	(9)
		S65 (24)	(8)		S102 (23)	(16)
High		S73 (25)	(7)	NH female:	S54 (40)	(14)
stress		S83 (50)	(7)		S58 (100)	(9)
shift	BH male:	S13 (29)	(5) M			
		S76 (31)	(6) M			
	NH female:	S62 (100)	(8)			
		S74 (22)	(5)			
	BH female:	S17 (22)	(7)			
		S23 (83)	(8)			
C		S41 (54)	(6) M	D		

Key: D = Drunken speaker; M = monolingual.
Read information for each speaker as follows: S11 (20) (4) = Subject 11 shifts stress to the penult in 20 percent of possible environments and has a Spanish loan frequency of 4 (4 percent of all words are first-time occurrences of Spanish loans).
Average stress shift: 22%.
Average Spanish loan: 8.32%.

A. Speakers with stress shift below the average for all speakers (22 percent) and Spanish loan frequency below the average (8.32 percent)
B. Speakers with stress shift below the average but Spanish loan frequency above the average
C. Speakers with stress shift above the average and Spanish loan frequency below the average
D. Speakers with stress shift above the average and Spanish loan frequency above the average

This yields a distribution along two axes: the AD axis, with Low stress shift/Low loan and High stress shift/High loan speakers, and the BC axis, with Low stress shift/High loan and High stress shift/Low loan speakers. The utility of the two axes can be proposed as a priori grounds. I have suggested that the main coding principles in the communities are the power code, which opens Mexicano to Spanish, and the solidarity code, which closes Mexicano to Spanish. We would expect that power-coding speakers would be in box B. That is, they would keep stress shift low, failing to nativize Spanish loans in order to make their source salient. At the same time, they would use a relatively high rate of Spanish loans. Conversely, we would expect to find solidarity-coding speakers in box C, nativizing Spanish loan material to conceal its provenance and using a relatively low rate of Spanish loans. Thus the speakers on the BC axis should represent the mainstream of Mexicano speech variation. If we examine the speakers on the main axis, taking into account what we know of their biographies, we find nothing to seriously challenge this proposal. For instance, box B contains all the speakers (S51, S44, S31, S5, and S48) whom we know to have been drunk at the time of the interview. As I have noted above, drunken speakers use greatly inflated Spanish loans and may parody the power code. Box B also includes several genuine *tiāchcātzitzīn*, senior community leaders: S52, S63, S80, S37, and S15. It contains the wealthiest broad-honorific man in our sample, S33. Box C, which should be dominated by solidarity-coding speech, in fact does contain mostly narrow-honorific men whom we know to be avid purists. It also contains two monolingual speakers of Mexicano (S76 and S41).

On the AD axis we find most of the speakers whom we know to be very poor speakers of Mexicano. S24, S25, and S57 are all second-language speakers of Mexicano.[10] (S57 simply switches to Spanish when he cannot remember a word; S24 and S25 use a strategy of Spanish roots and Mexicano inflections.) S55 is a rambling and incoherent speaker (note his switching in Ex. II above). S26 and S18 are literate in Mexicano (S18 has taught the language in school), are extreme purists,

Table 5.5. *Distribution of speakers on axes defined by stress shift and Spanish loan frequency*

	NH male	NH female	BH male	BH female
AD axis	8	9	8	4
BC axis	17	3	6	4
A.	NH male vs. NH female		$X^2 = 4.43$	$p \leq .05$

Chi-square on the total distribution cannot be computed, as expected frequencies fall below 5.

and exhibit very peculiar usage on many indices. S10, S39, and S102 are all very young and have education through the ninth grade. In box A are two monolingual men, S11 and S38, who are the opposite of the *tiāch-cātzitzīn* (community elders): Both are elderly and claim never to have held a community office. S38 laughingly rejected the idea, noting that all the *tiāchcātzitzīn* from his time were burning in hell, while he was still vigorous. Of the remaining speakers, all in box A, S77, S19, S98, S16, and S12 all have perfectly normal biographies. Note that all of them are quite close to the average on stress shift. S12 was a new compadre of our interviewer's and was using very "elegant" language with him, which may account for his nonexistent stress shift but not for his low rate of Spanish loans. Needless to say, this review has merely anecdotal significance. There is, however, much that supports my contention that the BC axis is the power–solidarity code mainstream, and little that poses a serious problem for this contention in the distribution of speakers.

Let me now turn to a discussion of the female speakers. It is important to understand that there is no significant difference for gender or honorific category for stress shift taken alone. We can see the differences only when we treat stress shift together with Spanish loan frequency along the AD–BC axis. Table 5.5 shows the distribution of speakers by axis. Recall that BC is the mainstream axis. Here, the sample is so reduced that no significant values emerge for any groups except narrow-honorific men and women, who show a significant gender differentiation. Note, however, that the distribution of the broad-honorific-speakers is in the direction we would expect. In any case, it is clear that narrow-honorific women are not behaving like narrow-honorific men. Instead, they are combining a failure to nativize Spanish loan words (a spectacular failure, with stress being shifted at extremely low frequencies) with a low rate of Spanish loan usage, whereas men who fail to nativize by stress shift use a high rate of Spanish loan words. Thus, narrow-honorific women appear to be very much out of the mainstream of variation. This additional evidence helps us to address the question I raised in connection with Spanish loans: Are women monitoring down in response to solidarity-code purism or the power-code sanction against presumptive elevation? Since solidarity coding seems to be associated with a high rate of stress shift, apparently female monitoring down of loan words must be in response to the power code. It seems unlikely that they use a low rate of Spanish loans because of lack of knowledge of Spanish, since they seem to be quite sensitive to the more subtle issue of Spanish stress patterns.

The fact that narrow-honorific women failed to use stress shift in the interview may be an instance of hypercorrect crossover. Labov (1966) described this process for lower-middle-class women in New York City. In informal speech these women used stigmatized vernacular variants at a high rate. In more careful styles, they actually exhibited a lower rate of stigmatized variants than did middle-class speakers. My attention was originally drawn to the stress-shift variable by listening to informal chatting in casual groups of Mexicano-speaking woman. Here, it was easy to overhear personal names such as Miguel and Pilar and place names such as San Martín and La Resurrección. In these casual conversations women shift stress at a rate close to 100 percent, and I examined the stress-shift variable in the interview data in the expectation that it would provide a good example of female lag, with women using the Mexicano penultimate stress at a higher rate than men. Thus, the actual distribution of usage in the interviews was a surprise. As I have noted, stress shift is a stereotyped error in speaking *castellano*. Thus, it seems likely that female retention of the Spanish stress pattern in the interviews is the result of a sensitivity to stigmatization. Women apparently are more self-conscious about the Spanish pattern, whereas men are more self-conscious about Mexicano purism and the differentiation of the two grammars, at least on this index.

A second index of variability where women appear to be more Spanish and less Mexicano than men is the possessive construction. In Mexicano, possession is expressed as below in (12). The possessed noun is prefixed with an element that agrees in person and number with the possessor noun, and the possessor is juxtaposed directly to the possessed noun.

(12)   nin ī-coneh nin tlācatl 'This is this man's child.'
       This his-child this man

Speakers often use Spanish *de* in such constructions:

(13)   nin ī-coneh de nin tlācatl 'This is this man's child.'
       This his-child of this man

Such a construction is a partial assimilation to the Spanish possessive:

(14)   *este es el hijo de este hombre*   'This is the child of this man.'

Table 5.6. *Frequency of possessive constructions with* de *in extemporaneous speech*

	NH male (N = 13)	NH female (N = 7)	BH male (N = 9)	BH female (N = 4)
With *de*	3	4	6	4
Without *de*	21	7	11	11

A. NH male vs. BH male   Fisher Exact Probability: p = .00004
B. NH male vs. all other speakers X^2 = 4.07   p ≤ .05

Chi-square on the total distribution cannot be computed, as expected frequencies fall below 5.

Possessive contructions with overt possessor nouns are relatively scarce in the interview texts, but there are enough so that some of the constraints of variation between the two types can be identified. Spanish *de* is more likely to appear if the possession is alienable. Inalienable possessions, such as kin terms and body parts, are distinguished from alienable possessions, such as *tlalli* (land), *comitl* (pot), and so forth. Spanish *de* is most frequent with inanimate possessors, in which case many speakers abandon the possessive prefix and assimilate the construction completely to the Spanish model, as in (15):

(15)   In   tepāmitl den   teōpantzīntli 'The wall of the church'
       THE WALL OF THE CHURCH

Certain types of expressions never appear with *de*, such as constructions involving *-tōcā* 'name.'

Table 5.6 shows the distribution of possessive constructions with overt, animate possessor noun and inalienable possession that appeared in extemporaneous speech during the interview. Results of significant pair comparisons are given in the table. For this index in extemporaneous speech, there is no gender effect as such. Instead, we find narrow-honorific men apparently avoiding the use of the *de* possessive in this environment. Since women apparently are not avoiding it, at least for this small sample, we can tentatively say that on this index they are less *mexicano* than men. But when we compare the data from extemporaneous speech with the data from possessives gathered in a translation task, the relationship between male and female speakers shifts. Each speaker was asked to translate from Spanish two sentences with an animate possessor of an inalienable possession. The first sentence was (14) above. The second is (16):

(16)   *Ella es la hija de un rico* 'She is the daughter of a rich man.'

Table 5.7. *Frequency of possessive constructions with* de *in translations*

	NH male (N = 21)	NH female (N = 15)	BH male (N = 10)	BH female (N = 8)
A. Distribution by number of constructions				
With *de*	25	23	14	3
Without *de*	17	7	6	15
A. BH male vs. BH female	$X^2 = 8.85$		$p \le .01$	
B. Distribution by number of speakers				
De only	9	10	7	1
Without *de* only	5	2	3	7
Variable	7	3	0	1

A. Narrow-honorific vs. broad-honorific, comparing variable with invariable usages: Fisher Exact Probability = .04

The distribution of responses to the two sentences is given in Table 5.7 in two ways. In section A, the distribution is given according to the number of sentences translated with *de* possessives versus the number translated without *de*. This can then be compared to the distribution from extemporaneous speech in Table 5.6. In section B, the distribution is given by the number of speakers who (a) translated both sentences with a *de* construction, (b) translated both sentences without *de*, and (c) translated one sentence with *de* and one without ("variable"). The distribution shown in (A) in Table 5.7, when compared with the distribution from extemporaneous speech shown in Table 5.6, makes very clear the danger of using translation from a dominant language as a way of eliciting data from bilingual speakers of a subordinate language. In translation, the distributions simply reverse, showing *de* constructions in the majority for every category of speakers except broad-honorific women, who apparently were not much swayed by the presence of the Spanish model. The distribution shown in Table 5.7, section B, shows that narrow-honorific self-consciousness extends to women. We can take variable behavior in response to the translation task to suggest that the speaker is caught in a sort of double bind. On the one hand, the speaker is confronted with the prestigious Spanish model, and we know that purist speakers often claim that calques on Spanish syntax are more *legítimo mexicano* than the historically attested Mexicano construction types. On the other hand, speakers know that they are supposed to speak *mexicano*, and no speaker is ignorant of the characteristic Mexicano possessive construction. Narrow-honorific-speakers should be more susceptible to the double bind, as they tend to be more self-conscious about the differentiation between the two grammars. Indeed, we find that there are significantly more narrow-honorific- speakers who are variable. There is no significant difference between males and females in each category of honorific usage; in this salient, monitored environment, women are as susceptible (or as unsusceptible) as men to self-conscious doubt. This suggests, then, that we probably should not attribute the failure of narrow-honorific women to use mainstream solidarity coding, discussed with the stress-shift index, to ignorance of the solidarity code.

As a final example of an index of variation that can suggest some of the intricacies of the development of grammatical self-consciousness among these speakers, I shall review the example of number purism and the grammar of noun-number constructions. Mexicano speakers use many Spanish numbers. These are old borrowings and apparently were among the earliest targets of purist stigmatization (Karttunen and Lockhart 1976). The second question on the interview asks for the speaker's age. This apparently innocent question caused great distress for speakers (this was not expected), who protested that they could not give their ages in *legítimo mexicano*. Men and women equally expressed this concern. But all of the speakers who gave their ages in compound numerals in the Mexicano vigesimal system – forms such as *yēyi pōal huān nāhui* (three twenties and four) for 64 – were men: eight narrow-honorific and two broad-honorific. The two broad-honorific-speakers were S18 and S26, the two literate, educated speakers of Mexicano who are off the mainstream axis in Table 5.4. But in spite of number purism, all speakers, including narrow-honorific men, were equally unlikely to use Mexicano numbers greater than given in extemporaneous speech, and all varied quite freely on numbers below five, using numbers of both types.

Number purism suggests that the differential grammar of noun-number constructions between Spanish and Mexicano is a likely target on which purist self-consciousness might focus, and this turns out to be the case. In Mexicano, noun-number agreement is not required. In the classical language, inanimate nouns were never pluralized, although Karttunen (1978) has shown that this option developed during the colonial period (it is rare in my data). Animate nouns are optionally pluralized. In Spanish, nouns must of course be pluralized with plural numbers, regardless of animacy. Many Malinche-area Mexicano-speakers exhibit exuberant mixing of the grammar of noun-numeral constructions in extemporaneous conversation when speaking *mexicano*. Such mixing can exhibit almost all the possibilities allowed by either grammatical system. Table 5.8 shows the possibilities, illustrated with examples that appear in my data. Note that all speakers avoid constructions of type (3). A great many examples appear in the interviews of

Table 5.8. *Possible noun-number constructions in mixed usage*

	Mexicano noun		Spanish noun	
Mexicano number				
Singular N	(1)	*ōme tlahtōl* 'two word'	(5)	*nāhui peso* 'four peso'
	(2a)	*nāhui ilhuimeh* 'four feast days'	(6)	*ōme cajetitos* 'two little bowls'
Plural N	(2b)	*nāhui tlātlācah* 'four men'		
Spanish number				
Singular N	(3)	—	(7a)	*noseis hijo* 'my six child'
			(7b)	*tres tonelada* 'three ton'
Plural N	(4)	*siete cōconeh* 'seven children'	(8)	*tres pesos* 'three pesos'

Table 5.9. *Distribution of mixed and unmixed noun-number constructions*

	NH male ($N = 21$)	NH female ($N = 12$)	BH male ($N = 14$)	BH female ($N = 9$)
Mixed	9	6	29	26
Unmixed	101	59	63	37

	X^2	p
A. Total distribution	37.78	$\leq .001$
B. Broad-honorific vs. narrow-honorific	30.46	$\leq .001$

numerals with Mexicano singulars such as *xihuitl* (year), *mētztli* (month), and *tōnal* (day). These invariably appeared with a Mexicano numeral.

The constructions in Table 5.9 can be divided into mixed versus unmixed constructions. Constructions of types (2a), (6), (7a), and (7b) are mixed; that is, they do not follow the grammar of the language of the numeral. Other constructions are unmixed, following the agreement pattern that one would expect, given the language of the numeral.

In a previous study (Hill and Hill 1980) I attempted to distinguish "mixing" from "sorting" speakers, assigning a speaker to a "mixer" category even if that speaker produced, as did S73, twenty-one unmixed constructions and only one mixed one. S73 produced such triumphs of grammatical sorting as *ōme ciento de varas* (two hundred varas, a unit

Table 5.10. *Distribution of two types of mixed constructions*

A. *Spanish numbers with singular nouns*				
	NH male	NH female	BH male	BH female
Mixed	4	4	26	34
Unmixed	44	19	31	7
A. Total distribution			$X^2 = 57.04$	$p \leq .001$
B. Broad-honorific vs. narrow-honorific			$X^2 = 40.68$	$p \leq .001$
C. BH female vs. BH male			$X^2 = 12.46$	$p \leq .001$
B. *Mexicano numbers with inanimate plural nouns*				
	NH male	NH female	BH male	BH female
Mixed	5	2	3	3
Unmixed	51	12	28	15

Figures for mixed constructions are too small to allow assessment of significance.

of measurement), where *ciento* is singular, as prescribed by the preceding *ōme*, but *varas* is plural, since it is preceded by *ciento*. (The Spanish usage is *dos cientos varas*; here S73 has also calqued Spanish *de* on Mexicano *in*.) We achieve a more reliable count, however, if we group the data from all speakers. Table 5.9 shows the distribution of mixed and unmixed constructions, by speaker category. It is obvious from the distribution that mixed constructions are a property of broad-honorific speech, regardless of gender. It is instructive to examine precisely what types of mixed constructions occur. There are two major types: Spanish numbers with singular nouns and Mexicano numbers with pluralized inanimates (which are very unlikely). Table 5.10 shows the distribution of these two major types of mixed constructions.

We can see from these distributions that mixed constructions with Spanish numbers and singular nouns are the most frequent type, with all categories of speakers about equally unlikely to produce the second type, Mexicano numbers with inanimate plurals. The common types of mixed constructions are conspicuously concentrated, however, in broad-honorific usage, and broad-honorific women use the most of all speaker types. We might explain these distributions as a reflection of influence from Spanish, since this is lowest among broad-honorific women. However, I believe that what they actually indicate is the degree to which speakers are self-consciously sorting the grammars of the two languages. Recall that what speakers are doing is speaking *mexicano*. Thus, it is entirely appropriate to observe Mexicano grammatical patterns with borrowed numerals, and this is what broad-honorific-speakers do. However, narrow-honorific-speakers appear to sort in their Mexicano usage.

If they use a Mexicano number, they will use a singular noun (I have not included constructions that must have plural nouns, such as nouns suffixed with *-tzīn*). If they use a Spanish number, they will use a plural noun, almost without exception. Thus, we have a situation where the same grammatical self-consciousness that stimulates Mexicano purism actually pushes usage toward Spanish on this index. Narrow-honorific women are sorting on this index just as much as men.

Although there is no significant differentiation among the four groups of speakers for the use of Mexicano numbers and pluralized inanimates (Table 5.11, section B), in one conversation evidence turned up that narrow-honorific men are focusing on the problems raised by such constructions. Two men, S46 and S46, were talking about the digging of wells. In the first exchange, S47 used the construction *mācuilli pozo* (five well). S46, the poorer of the two speakers, gave him an immediate back-channel: *macuilli pozohtin* (five wells). A few minutes later, they returned to the topic again. This time, however, their usages reversed. S46 first said *yeyi pozo* (three well). This time the back-channel was from S47: *yēyi pozohtin* (three wells). There seems to be little question that this was a conscious negotiation on this grammatical point. (Note the position of S46 and S47 in Table 5.4; they are both very self-conscious purists who do some of the most dramatic "vocabulary tests" on outsiders of any purist speakers I have met.)

Thus, to summarize, on indices where purist self-consciousness emanating from the solidarity code is in play, differentiation between genders is sharply complicated by stratification according to honorific usage. On stress shift, narrow-honorific women are less *mexicano* (or more Spanish) than narrow-honorific men, and apparently are not self-consciously differentiating the two languages. On translations of possessives, and in noun-number usage, however, narrow-honorific women display a level of self-consciousness quite like that of narrow-honorific men. Thus, these women are apparently sensitive both to stigmatization from Spanish itself and to stigmatization from the Mexicano solidarity code, making their usage a tangle of contradictory tendencies. Broad-honorific women apparently are not very self-conscious about differentiation between the two languages. On the index of possessive construction, broad-honorific women are less *mexicano* or more Spanish, along with other speakers, than the self-conscious narrow-honorific men. On the noun-number constructions, they appear to be more Mexicano – but in an environment where purism shifts speakers toward the Spanish pattern through sorting. Thus, they are not *mexicano* in a way being emulated by solidarity-code speakers; by this standard, they are less *mexicano*.

In addition to the data presented above on patterns of usage in Mexicano, I gathered some information on language attitudes. Of this information, the most important appears to be the answers to five questions for which the answers can be sorted into "positive," "negative," and "evasive" types:

1. Do you want your children to speak Mexicano?
2. Are you ashamed to speak Mexicano?
3. Do you think other people are ashamed to speak Mexicano?
4. Do you think Mexicano should be taught in school?
5. Are you sad that Mexicano is disappearing?

"Yes" answers to questions (1), (4), and (5) and "No" answers to (2) and (3) are taken to reflect a positive attitude about Mexicano. Some answers are evasive, such as "I don't know" or "Who knows?" Table 5.11 shows the distribution of positive, negative, and evasive answers by category of speaker.

In calculating the differences among groups of speakers, we consider evasive responses to reflect negative attitudes, since such attitudes are less publicly acceptable in the communities. When we make this adjustment, we find that different groups of speakers are significantly different in the following ways:

A. Narrow-honorific-speakers are much more likely than broad-honorific-speakers to say they want their children to learn Mexicano ($X^2 = 5.76$, $p \leq .02$).
B. Men are more likely than women to say they want their children to learn Mexicano ($X^2 = 5.76$, $p \leq .02$).
C. Men are more likely than women to say they want Mexicano to be taught in the school ($X^2 = 11.28$, $p \leq .01$).
D. Men are more likely than women to say they are sad that Mexicano is disappearing ($X^2 = 4.04$, $p \leq .05$).

All groups of speakers appear to be in general agreement on questions (2) and (3), about whether or not they are ashamed to speak Mexicano. There is, however, a significant difference between broad- and narrow-honorific-speakers when we compare those who answered positively to both questions (2) and (3) with those speakers who gave a positive reply to (2) and a negative reply to (3), that is, who claimed that whereas they themselves were not ashamed to speak Mexicano, other people were. Narrow-honorific-speakers were significantly more likely than broad-honorific-speakers to be in the second group ($X^2 = 4.68$, $p \leq .05$).

It is clear from these results that women express more negative attitudes about the Mexicano language than do men. Significantly more women than men do not want Mexicano taught in the schools, do not want their children to learn the language, and are not sad that it is

Table 5.11. *Responses to language-attitude questions*

Question	Speaker type	Positive response	Negative response	Evasive response	No response	Total
(1)	NH man	14	2	1	8	25
	BH man	2	1	0	12	15
	NH woman	6	4	1	8	19
	BH woman	1	7	1	2	11
(2)	NH man	20	5	0	0	25
	BH man	11	4	0	0	15
	NH woman	16	2	0	1	19
	BH woman	5	6	0	0	11
(3)	NH man	3	15	3	4	25
	BH man	3	12	0	0	15
	NH woman	3	10	4	2	19
	BH woman	2	5	3	1	11
(4)	NH man	20	3	2	0	25
	BH man	11	3	1	0	15
	NH woman	7	7	4	1	19
	BH woman	3	6	1	1	11
(5)	NH man	18	4	3	0	25
	BH man	7	6	1	1	15
	NH woman	8	9	1	1	19
	Bh woman	4	6	1	0	11

disappearing. Broad-honorific women, who are by linguistic standards the most "Mexicano" of all speakers, have the highest proportion of negative attitudes. Women have a higher (although not a significantly higher: $X^2 = 3.75$, $p \leq .10$) rate of evasive responses to the language-attitude questions than do men. This suggests that women are aware of male support for the Mexicano language but are dubious about whether or not they agree with it and are reluctant to contradict men in public.

The negative language attitudes of women compared with men in regard to Mexicano appear to have a practical foundation. Broad-honorific women, and some narrow-honorific women, feel hampered by their inadequacies in Spanish. As wearers of traditional dress, as illiterates, and as poor Spanish-speakers, they are easily identified as low-status "Indians" and feel that they are unable to "defend themselves" when commercial activity brings them in contact with Spanish-speakers. As the lowest-status adults in their home communities, they have little of the economic or political capital that is essential collateral for participation in the intracommunity systems of reciprocity and are able to see the serious limitation of these support mechanisms, to which solidarity-code Mexicano gives access.

Women feel that their usage is highly "controlled." The older women believe that their illiteracy and lack of Spanish are results of education's having been denied them by parents or unenlightened community elders. Even today education for girls is not taken as seriously as that for boys, and in most communities the sixth-grade graduation will have few young women stepping forward for the graduation waltz.

Women now feel controlled and pushed toward Spanish. Several women report that their husbands insisted they learn Spanish so that they could do their own shopping. This suggests that men who at one time found it convenient to control the disposition of family funds now find that the demands of wage labor and cultivation make this impossible. Many women report that their husbands or in-laws insist that they speak Spanish to their children. Children are said to nag their mothers and grandmothers not to speak Mexicano. The same children are said, on reaching adolescence, to reproach their mothers for not teaching them enough Mexicano to understand and respond to the obscene challenges that are part of the enforcement of ethnic solidarity. A typical remark about these problems is (17):

(17) S78: Āxān conēntzitzīn chocotzitzīn yōcmo tlahtoah īca mexicano. Āxān puro castilla, hasta contrario cualānih in conēhtzitziñ, ye tēchahhuah in tehhuān nicān, hasta in totlahuīcalhuān ye tēchahhuah. In tlā itlah tquil-īzqueh ye tēchhūalregañaroah, "Āmo tpīnāhua ōhuāllah cē compadrito huān ttlahtoa īca mexicano. Xtlahto īca castilla, āmo xtonta!"

'Now as for the little children they no longer speak Mexicano. Now it's nothing but Spanish; to the contrary, the children even get mad, now they scold us here, even our husbands scold us now. If we say something, they scold at us "Aren't you ashamed that when a compadre comes you speak Mexicano. Speak Spanish, don't be stupid." '

Women who are under this kind of pressure report that they go to great trouble to speak Spanish, even in their own homes:

(18)   S20: Nēchiliah "Ay mamá porque hablas ansina? Yo quiero que hables ansina!" A ver, pues ya voy diciendo aunque sea cuatro.

'They say, "Ay mama, why do you speak that way. I want you to speak this way!" Let's see, well I go speaking even if it's a mistake.'

This pressure on women to speak Spanish appears to contradict the purist prescriptions of the solidarity code. Speakers who endorse the solidarity code and the values of *legítimo mexicano* believe that women lag linguistically. This belief in women's linguistic conservatism does not mean, however, that their speech is valued. One of the interview questions asks the respondents who they think are the best speakers of Mexicano. Of ninety-six replies to this question, all but four mentioned only "the old men": *in ancianohtin*, or *in tētahtzitzīn*. (Some speakers mentioned other towns.) Of the four respondents who suggested that the best speakers were "the old women" – *in ancianitas, in tēnāntzitzīn* – three were middle-aged women. One teenaged boy mentioned his grandmother, S41, who is in fact a superb monolingual speaker of Mexicano (with very negative attitudes about the language).

Let me return to the problem raised at the beginning of the paper: From what factors do the different patterns of women's speech arise? Table 5.12 summarizes the patterns revealed in analysis of the six indices of variation. Each index is indicated as "conscious" if there is evidence that speakers are aware of it, whether from direct comment or from apparent self-conscious avoidance of a construction, as in the case of *de* possessives. In addition, the social stratification of the index along gender and honorific lines is indicated, and whether female speech can be said to be more Spanish or less Spanish on that index.

Table 5.12 shows a complex patterning of differentials that stratify according to gender and honorific usage. Each index appears to have its own pattern, making a unified explanation for the diversity quite difficult. Gender differentiation is complicated by honorific differentiation. Recall that honorific usage is being used here as a linguistic index to exposure to the Spanish-speaking world that precipitates a nativistic reaction, of which one manifestation is narrow-honorific usage, which emphasizes solidarity and equality among community members. In exposed communities women are as likely to be narrow-honorific-speakers as are men, in spite of the fact that women do not participate in the wage-labor system. Gender differentiation along honorific lines is by no

Table 5.12. *Summary of stratification of usages*

Usage	Consciousness	Stratification	Women
(1) Spanish loan	Yes	Gender split and honorific split Gender split greatest for NH-speakers	Less Spanish
(2) Noun-incorporating verbs	No	Gender split only; greatest for BH-speakers	Less Spanish
(3) Relative pronouns	No	Gender split for NH-speakers only	Less Spanish
(4) Stress shift	Yes	Gender split for NH-speakers only	Less Mexicano
(5) Possessives	Yes	Gender split for NH-speakers in extemporaneous speech	Less Mexicano
(6) Noun-number agreement	Yes	Honorific split only in translation task Honorific split. Gender split for BH-speakers only	Same as men More Spanish (in purist perspective, less Mexicano)
(7) Language attitudes	—	Honorific and gender split	More negative about Mexicano

means neat. Leacock (1983) has suggested that role differences between men and women, and the intensity of relationships of domination and subordination between them, will increase as indigenous communities move into increasingly dependent relationship with national and world capitalist economies. The Mexicano language data do not give unequivocal support for that position. On indices (1), (3), (4), and (5) we do see greater gender differentiation among narrow-honorific-speakers, as her suggestion would predict. On indices (2) and (6), however, we see a greater split for broad-honorific-speakers. In addition, the direction of the differentiation along the more Mexicano/less Spanish to less Mexicano/more Spanish continuum differs. Broad-honorific women are always less Spanish (except in the case of the possessives, where they are not differentiated from other speakers except for narrow-honorific men). Narrow-honorific women, however, are less Mexicano than narrow-honorific men on indices (4) and (5); less Spanish on indices (1), (2), and (3). Narrow-honorific women clearly are aware of purist solidarity-code norms and behave according to them in translation tasks and in their sorting of noun-number-agreement patterns. They do not, however, conform to them in stress shift, and they often reject them in direct questioning.

It seems clear that we cannot accept the indigenous theory of women's speech, that they lag because they know less Spanish. On some indices, such as stress shift, women show a high sensitivity to the Spanish norm. In the case of noun-number agreement, the sorting behavior of narrow-honorific women again suggests a keen awareness of Spanish grammar. It is probably the case that many broad-honorific women know less Spanish than most other speakers, but they are clearly very much influenced by it. There is a difference of self-consciousness about language differentiation, rather than a difference in knowledge of the language.

It seems likely that women may experience active exclusion from male patterns and that this is the reason they are at once both less Mexicano and less Spanish than men. Such an explanation would run counter to several recent studies of gender differentiation in language, which have suggested that women are merely "marginal" or "diffused" in relation to male norms. Cheshire (1978) and Milroy (1980) have suggested that in communities where women are more "domestic" than men, and are not involved in close-knit peer groups that form at places of employment or on street corners, women will be less tightly constrained by vernacular norms, which are maintained by peer monitoring and may have "covert prestige" (Trudgill 1972). Thus, women will be more open to elite norms. I might propose that women in Mexicano communities are, in fact, marginal to major social arenas dominated by men: the system of community offices, with which power coding is associated, and the system of *compadrazgo* and male friendships with which the solidarity code is associated. Clearly, male peer groups have elaborated a system of sanctions that enforce solidarity coding: vocabulary tests on purist shibboleths, negotiation on grammatical points, and obscene challenges in Mexicano to outsiders. One young man noted that his peers behaved as if it were shameful to speak Spanish, and the amount of second-language learning of Mexicano in the communities suggests that these sanctions are effective. Women are fully aware of these practices of linguistic terrorism but do not participate in them. Women in these communities do, however, feel that their usage is very much controlled, by men and by young people. They are clearly sensitive both to stigmatizations that emanate from the norm of speaking *castellano* and to stigmatizations that emanate from solidarity-code purism about speaking *mexicano*. Thus, they probably should not be considered "diffuse" speakers. Instead, they are often sanctioned linguistically: told "Don't be stupid, speak Spanish" or "It's your fault that I can't reply when they curse me, because you didn't teach me Mexicano" or introduced as "not speaking Spanish" when in fact they are bilingual. Rather than think of the speech norms of women as marginal to a core of male norms, we might instead think of women's speech as highly constrained within a narrow range of possibilities, at the same time less Mexicano and less Spanish than men's speech, whereas men are able to use the full range of code variation. This would conform to the women's own view of their language problems rather than to the male belief in female linguistic lag. Such a constraint on women would make sense in terms of the local political economy. To use the power code and the solidarity code in Mexicano brings access to the resources of the communities. To speak Spanish gives access to wage labor and the marketplace. When women do not have access to these codes, their uncompensated labor in the community – what Ivan Ilich has called "shadow work" – provides support for male wage laborers and makes it possible for local industry to employ these men at very low wages and with few benefits.

The linguistic behavior of Mexicano women suggests also that we might wish to question the widely held belief that women lead in change toward an elite norm because they have some kind of natural sensitivity to such norms. This belief led Nordberg (1975:596) to suggest that women's tendency to embrace prestige forms "could almost serve as criterion for determining which speech forms are stigmatized and which carry prestige in a given community." In the matter of Mexicano, however, nothing of what women do is valued by men. If they become more Spanish they violate the solidarity code; if they remain more Mexicano they are said to lag. In many of the cases that led to Nordberg's statement, vernacular male usage in fact had enormous covert prestige. In

Mexicano the situation is particularly clear because the solidarity code that is the male norm has not covert prestige but overt prestige supported by the romanticization of the Mexicano language among urban Mexicans. We might revise Nordberg's generalization, suggesting that, in whatever direction women are moving, it is probably *not* toward the usage valued by men in the same community. Thus, the failure of women to conform to male norms may be a result of exclusion from them rather than of some special affinity of women to elite norms.

In exploring the possibility of analysis of gender differentiation in terms of exclusion of women from male patterns of usage, it is important to recall that feminist scholars have cautioned us against automatically assuming that men are the only sources of relevant norms. Women may have their own norms, quite independent of men. Women may find that the symbolic resources emanating from an urban elite are a good alternative to male usage patterns, offering benefits that may be more attractive to women, who are excluded from scarce resources in their own communities, than to men. Gal (1978) has pointed out that in the bilingual community of Oberwart in Austria the Hungarian language is associated with a peasant way of life that women find unattractive. Women in Oberwart are leading the shift to German, which is associated with urban opportunity. It may be that women in the Malinche Volcano communities have the potential for this kind of independence. Although they believe that they are dominated and controlled by men, their spirit of independence and entrepreneurship is highly developed, and the language-attitude data make it clear that they are prepared to reject male values. Since they appear to have less to lose than men by abandoning the norm of conformity to community values, they may represent a potent force for change. However, if the uncompensated labor of these women is a pivotal component of the regional system of industrial wage labor, it seems unlikely that the educational opportunities and other support that would enable the women of the Malinche Volcano to fulfill their potential for change will be made available to them.

Notes

1 Work on Mexicano has been funded by the National Endowment for the Humanities (NEH-RO–20495–74–572), by the American Council of Learned Societies, and by the Penrose Fund of the American Philosophical Society. I would also like to thank Carole Browner, Susan Philips, and the participants in the Conference on Sex Differences in Language for many useful suggestions.
2 Communities in which interviews have been conducted, and their approximate populations at the time of the work, are:

San Miguel Canoa, Puebla (15,000)
La Resurrección, Puebla (5,000)
San Lorenzo Almecatla, Puebla (800)
San Pablo del Monte, Tlaxcala (20,000)
San Antonio Acuamanala, Tlaxcala (1,000)
Santiago Ayometitla, Tlaxcala (500)
Santa Maria Acxotla del Monte, Tlaxcala (800)
San Luis Teolocholco, Tlaxcala (1,000)
San Rafael Tepatlaxco, Tlaxcala (1,000)
San Felipe Cuahutenco, Tlaxcala (1,000)
Santa Ana Chiauhtempan, Tlaxcala (15,000)

3   Needless to say, speakers often switch briefly to Spanish while "speaking *mexicano.*" I have rather arbitrarily defined a switch as a sequence of clause or sentence length that is not a fixed expression such as *presidente de la República* 'President of the Republic'. No material that occurs in a switch is included in the analyses in this paper; switching is treated in detail in Hill and Hill (1986).

4   Farrell (1977) found that the majority of migrants from the town Santa Maria Aquiahuac, near San Felipe Cuahutenco in our sample, were women. However, his sample of migrants from this community of two hundred included only eighteen subjects. Rothstein (1982), working in San Cosme Mazatecochco near Acuamanala, has confirmed our observation that women do not enter the factory labor market. Indeed, she finds that women in proletarian families are more limited to the domestic sphere than are women in the families of cultivators.

5   I have used the term syncretic in preference to "mixed" because it does not have the pejorative connotations of the latter term, and because it suggests the complex remodelings of symbolic material from both languages that are distinctive of modern Mexicano. In addition, students of language contact have used the term "mixed language" (*Mischsprache*) as a technical term for intensive exchange of morphological elements; this has hardly happened at all in Mexicano.

6   Rothstein (1982) has pointed out that wage laborers can make more money than cultivators. She also points out that wage laborers experience frequent unemployment, and it is to this aspect of their lives that I refer with the term precarious.

7   Honorific usage is discussed in detail in Hill and Hill 1978 and 1980.

8   Pellicer (1982) has found that speakers of indigenous languages who work as sidewalk vendors in Mexico City, the so-called Marías, who have been thought to be very inadequate in Spanish, in fact are quite fluent in a variety of Spanish that she calls *español indígena* 'indigenous Spanish'. The EI of the Marías has some features shared by Mexicano-speaking women in our area in speaking *castellano.*

9   Relative clauses are discussed in detail in Hill and Hill 1981.

10 We have documented a number of cases of second-language acquisition of Mexicano, and this is probably even more common than our data reveal. Chick (1980) has found it in San Rafael Tepatlaxco on the Malinche. Waterhouse (1949) has discussed it for Oaxacan Chontal.

Part II

Gender differences in the language of children

Introduction

CHRISTINE TANZ

The question of whether gender differences exist in the language of children has been a subject of investigation for many years. A review by Harris (1977) cites empirical research dating back to 1913. McCarthy published her much cited summary of then-existing research in 1954. An enormous variety of language phenomena have been investigated with respect to this question: clarity of articulation, age at first word, voice pitch, grasp of various syntactic constructions, rate of vocabulary growth, incidence of stuttering, skill in making verbal analogies, simple loquacity, and so forth. (See Maccoby and Jacklin, 1974.) But there has been little conceptual unity in this work, partly because until the 1960s no attempt was made to develop an overall theoretical perspective about what children learn when they learn language. In fact, it is difficult to draw conclusions from the research done to date. Recent reviews of the field have come to opposite conclusions. Maccoby and Jacklin (1974) in their extensive survey state that "female superiority on verbal tasks has been one of the more solidly established generalizations in the field of sex differences and recent research continues to support the generalization to a degree." Harris (1977) agrees with this assessment. On the other hand, Fairweather (1976) and Maccauley (1978) disagree, the title of the latter's review stating his position: "The Myth of Female Superiority in Language."

Few patterns of gender differences in language acquisition have been reported that have been replicated and remain noncontroversial. The following brief summary is drawn from a review by Klann-Delius (1981). Some researchers have found that preverbal girls vocalize more frequently than boys, but others have failed to replicate this difference. Her review, however, does not report any findings that boys vocalize more frequently than girls. Perhaps this constellation of results is suf-

163

ficient to justify a claim that there is a difference, detectable under some circumstances. Studies of onset of speech as measured by age at use of the first words also show a slight tendency for girls to be earlier, but this is not statistically significant. Mean length of utterance (MLU) has been shown to correlate at early ages with the complexity of a child's grammar. Measures of MLU, however, have sometimes favored girls, sometimes boys. The one area in which there seems to be widespread agreement about robust gender differences does not involve normal language acquisition at all but is the domain of pathologies of language and speech. Here boys emerge as significantly more vulnerable than girls. (For more details and references about this, see Maccoby and Jacklin, 1974); Fairweather (1976; Harris, 1977; Maccauley, 1978; and Klann-Delius, 1981.)

Despite their opposing conclusions, the first four reviews just cited share a perspective: They examine the data for evidence that one sex is *superior* to the other. In this "psychometric" approach, differences are seen as indicating different degrees of proficiency. There is some relatively recent research that maintains this perspective. For example, Nelson (1973) found that girls were more rapid than boys in reaching a fifty-word vocabulary. Schachter, Shore, Hodapp, Chalfin, and Bundy (1978) found that two-year-old girls were ahead of two-year-old boys in MLU, which has been shown to correlate with level of syntactic development. And Ramer (1976) found that girls were faster than boys in progressing from their first two-word utterance to the use of syntactically more advanced subject–verb–complement constructions.

Against this background, certain similarities among the chapters in this section on the development of sex differences in language are striking. First, they deemphasize or ignore the question of relative proficiency; differences are construed as differences in style. In this respect, the chapters are more closely aligned with those in Part I, on cross-cultural comparisons of men's and women's speech, than with those in Part III, on differences in the biological substratum of language. None of the cross-cultural chapters entertains the possibility that one gender is "better" at language than the other, although several discuss the fact that within their respective cultures the language attributed to one gender may be evaluated as being better – and persons of that gender, therefore, may be regarded as more proficient. (By contrast, the chapters in the section on biological aspects of language continue the tradition of emphasis on relative proficiency. At the least, they imply that behavioral differences reflect differences in language *capacity*.)

Whether sex differences in children's language are construed as a matter of differences in style or differences in capacity has implications for our notions of how the differences arise and for answering the classic developmental question about the roles of nature and nurture in establishing them. Whereas alleged differences in proficiency have been attributed to both biological factors and socialization, differences in style tend to be attributed to social factors. It is possible, however, to interpret stylistic differences in terms of biology as well. Sachs pointed out in Chapter 6 of this section that if a higher general activity level is a contributing element in the verbal style of boys, that activity level itself might be traceable either to environmental factors or to innate characteristics. Therefore, biological causation is not excluded in explaining stylistic differences. But it is interesting to note that the biological causative factors entertained in these chapters do not include any aspects of language-specific biology. None of the chapters even mentions such topics as sex differences in brain lateralization.

A second property that the chapters in this section share is an emphasis on language development at the same broad conceptual level, the level of communicative competence, rather than, for example, at the level of syntax, morphology, phonology, or semantics. (In this respect, again, they align with some of the chapters in Part I, which include discussions of language use in social interactions, rather than with those in Part III, which employ language variables at an entirely different level.)

This second property that the chapters in this section have in common is, by far, the most pervasive and is the aspect I shall concentrate on in this introduction. After beginning with a review of the major issues in research on communicative competence, I shall discuss the chapters in terms of their treatment of sex differences in communicative competence and conclude with a consideration of the most important points of convergence among the chapters.

Bates (1976), Bruner (1975), and Hymes (1972) were among the early researchers to point out that children must learn how to use language in interaction as well as how to construct sentences. Topics in the acquisition of communicative competence range from the very narrow (e.g., when to say "trick or treat") to the extremely broad (e.g., adopting the general communicative stance of the Kaluli, which avoids making verbal attributions of someone else's internal state) (Ochs and Schieffelin, 1984).

In her review of communicative development, Shatz (1983) divides the topic into three major lines of research: acquisition of discourse knowledge, illocutionary knowledge, and sociolinguistic knowledge. Each of these domains is relevant to the issues raised in the chapters that follow. They will be discussed briefly here to indicate the range of component skills and patterns in their acquisition.

The maintenance of discourse requires some skills that are purely formal and content-free, such as taking turns at speaking, and others that incorporate substantive information, such as tying one's turns to those of a conversational partner. Very young children are limited in their discourse skills. They are more likely to respond to adult utterances than to initiate conversation. And their responses frequently do not relate in form or substance to the prior utterance. Children apparently sense the obligation to respond before knowing how to do so in a meaningful, appropriate way. They devise a variety of means to satisfy this obligation, such as simply imitating the prior turn (Boskey and Nelson, 1980) or choosing at random between the canonical yes or no to answer a question, even though the answer may be incorrect. Relevant responses are more likely to be made (Bloom, Roussano, and Hood, 1976) in some contexts than in others, for example, in response to questions rather than to nonquestions.

Extending dialogue beyond two-turn sequences is apparently quite difficult (Kaye and Charney, 1980), but ingenious ways to do this have been documented even for some very young children. Keenan (Ochs) (1974b) analyzed extended dialogues of her two-year-old twins, focusing on their use of repetitions and repetitions with modifications for different pragmatic purposes such as agreeing and disagreeing.

In addition to giving substantive responses, mature listeners participate in discourse by providing feedback to the speaker. They signal that they can follow the speaker by nods of the head, saying "Yeah," "Mm-hmm," and the like. These listener responses promote the flow and integration of conversation. If they cannot follow, listeners can signal this by looking puzzled or by asking, "What?" or by making any of a set of more specific requests for clarification, which Garvey (1977a) has called "contingent queries." Mastering such devices is one of the tasks of discourse development. The age at which children start to make listener response of the "Mm-hmm" variety during ongoing speech is apparently not known. Six-year-olds make them, but only at about one-quarter of the adult rate (Dittmann, 1972). Three-year-olds are able to request clarification in some contexts, as in an experiment where they receive ambiguous requests from adults (Revelle, Karabenick, and Wellman, 1981), but do not do so often in playroom conversation (Garvey, 1977a). At age three their contingent queries or requests for clarification tend to be nonspecific, whereas four-year-olds can tailor their requests to specific types of ambiguity (Revelle et al., 1981).

In turn, speakers must respond to listeners' requests for clarification. Peterson, Danner, and Flavell (1972) looked at children's responses to implicit and explicit indications of communication failure. All four-year-olds reformulated their messages when explicitly requested to do so, but only a small minority did when their addressee merely looked puzzled or said, "I don't understand" without asking an additional question. Two-year-olds are likely to respond to what-questions simply by repeating what they have already said, although some do make revisions (Gallagher, 1981).

Most of the studies reported here do not analyze for sex differences despite reporting on the sex of subjects. But several do. Esposito (1979), in line with her expectations from the literature on adults, found that in conversations in boy–girl pairs, boys interrupt twice as much as girls. Dittman (1977), contrary to his expectations, found that in a setting where they were listening to an adult speak, boys gave more listener responses than girls. Karabenick and Miller (1977) report that in a communication task, boys spontaneously gave more confirmations of information than girls.

The second line of research is illocutionary knowledge. One of the most intensively studied aspects of the development of communicative competence falls within the framework of speech-act theory (Austin, 1962; Searle, 1969). Speech-act theory attempts to provide a taxonomy of possible functions of messages (e.g., to inform, to promise, to convince), a description of the social contexts and sets of expectations that must exist in order for those functions to be successfully carried out, and an analysis of how particular language structures are systematically linked to the expression of these functions.

In an early paper, Holzman (1972) showed that very young children (age two) are able properly to infer a wide variety of communicative intentions behind utterances that take the syntactic form of questions. They can go beyond the syntax to interpret questions as requests for information, requests for action, and even prohibitions (e.g., "May I have my coffee?" as a request for the child to stop running about).

A number of subsequent studies have taken as their focus not one surface form and its many pragmatic interpretations but, rather, one speech act and its many surface realizations. The most intensively studied category of speech acts is directives. Ervin-Tripp (1977) provides a taxonomy of types of directives used by adults and a review of children's acquisition of them. The taxonomy includes imperatives ("Gimme a match"), personal-need statements ("I need a match"), imbedded imperatives ("Could you give me a match?"), permission directives ("May I have a match?"), question directives ("Have you got a match?"), and hints ("The matches are all gone"). As she points out, two developmental questions can be asked about this taxonomy: How do children come to infer directive function in utterances that are not explicitly directive? Is there an order in which the various forms are mastered? Garvey (1975) reports a constant level of direct requests to peers between the ages of 3;6 (3 years 6 months) and 5;7 and a doubling of the number of successful indirect requests over this age range. Bates (1976) also found in a study of Italian children that the youngest in a sample between 2;10 and 6;2 tend to use simple imperatives and need-statements ("Give me a candy"; "I want a candy") and gradually to add more complex conditional and modal constructions. Thus there is a developmental progression of indirectness in making requests. Ervin-Tripp (1977) concludes that the most difficult forms and the last to be acquired are those that do not explicitly refer to what the speaker wants.

Comprehension clearly precedes production in the mastery of indirect requests. In naturalistic situations, the context often provides additional information about the intended directive force of an indirect request. Holzman (1972) and Shatz (1978) both show two-year-olds capable of understanding directives couched as questions. And yet Carrell (1981) shows that precise decoding of complex indirect requests is a skill still being mastered at age seven. Knowledge of how to interpret and carry out speech acts begins early and continues to develop for a long time.

Finally, consider sociolinguistic knowledge. The material discussed so far relates to the problem of discovering the connection between a particular communicative intention (wanting someone to do something) and the various means available for expressing it. A final problem relates to the selection of one set of means from the multiplicity available. This selection is made on the basis of social knowledge with regard to considerations of status, solidarity, familiarity, and so forth. Mitchell-Kernan and Kernan (1977) report that children of ages seven to twelve who control all six forms in Ervin-Tripp's taxonomy of directives are much more likely to use simple imperatives to people of equal or lower rank than to people of higher rank. Shatz and Gelman (1973) show that four-year-olds are sensitive to this distinction, using unmodified imperatives to two-year-olds, softened directives to adults. There is evidence that even two-year-olds use different request types according to age and rank of their addressee. (See Lawson reported in Ervin-Tripp, 1977.) Very young children apparently have notions of speech appropriateness and politeness.

Bates (1976) claims that children organize request forms on a gradient of politeness at about the age of two and a half. It was at this age that the two Italian-speaking subjects of her longitudinal research began to repair failed imperatives by reducing rather than augmenting their force. Bates then tested children's emerging knowledge of what language devices serve to make a request polite (again in Italian). In her experiment, children heard two frogs ask for candy. They were required to decide which frog asked most nicely. For instance, one frog might say, "Give me candy," and the other might add "please" or ask, "Could I have a candy?" In Bates's middle-class sample, two-year-olds were able to choose requests with "please" as more polite. Gradually other devices such as soft intonation and interrogative directives were discriminated.

Thus children can scale directives in terms of degree of politeness, and they can select among directive forms on the basis of some listener characteristics. They also have models of how speaker characteristics influence the choice of directive forms. Andersen (1978) asked children to role-play fathers, mothers, children, doctors and nurses, and teachers and students. Gender was a factor in their choice of directive forms. "Fathers" used more direct imperatives; "mothers," more hints. "Doctors" and "nurses" repeated this pattern. Children playing female teachers, however, used many direct imperatives to their "students." Children also have some knowledge of the politeness dimension in the semantic structures of discourse verbs such as "ask" and "tell." When given instructions to ask someone to do something, they use more polite request forms than when they are given instructions to tell (Bock and Hornsby, 1981).

Do boys and girls differ with respect to these communicative skills? The studies reported above do not tell us. Most of them are primarily concerned with age as a subject variable. Although sex is often reported or controlled, its effects are usually not analyzed. One exception is Bates (1976), who reports that there were no sex differences in her polite-frog study. Boys and girls were equally adept in making judgments about which of two request forms is more polite. She concludes that even though girls were shown to deploy politeness devices more often, boys match them in their passive knowledge of politeness rules. Bock and Hornsby (1981) found girls to be more polite, but not significantly so.

The chapters in this section of the book touch on aspects of all three of our broad categories of comunicative competence. Sachs's chapter investigates the form of "obliges" used by five-year-old upper-middle-class children as they play "pretend" games with each other. "Obliges" are defined as utterances that require a response on the part of the addressee. They include directives, prohibitions, questions. Sachs analyzed the form of these obliges in terms of their directness or the degree to which they were mitigated. Mitigating devices included tag questions, question imperatives, imperatives with joint focus ("Let's sit down"), pretend directives, and "state" questions ("Are you sick?"). Sex differences were found in all categories except question imperatives, which at this age were used by few children of either sex. Girls used more of each remaining type of mitigating device except "state" questions. Since "state" questions do not fall as clearly as the others into the category of mitigating devices, the overall profile is one of girls very broadly using mitigating devices more than boys.

Sachs also reports the provocative finding that while, overall, girls use as many obliges as boys, boys produce five times as many prohibitions. The form of the prohibitions, however, is not analyzed. Perhaps these "negative directives" are also susceptible of degrees of mitigation. A future analysis might examine the form of prohibitions as well as their number for results as fruitful as Sachs's work on the form of positive directives.

Gleason reports a series of studies on sex differences in the language of two- to five-year-old American middle-class children and in that of their caretakers. An explicit effort is made to draw connections between the language produced by the children and the inputs made to them. Gleason argues that language input to children is linked to gender in two ways: according to both the target and the source of the message. Girls and boys are spoken to differently in certain respects, and they are shown that adult men and women speak differently in certain respects. The language variables she analyzed were lexical selection (precision and level of sophistication of vocabulary) and politeness as indicated by the use of politeness routines such as "Thank you," by approaches to the control of discourse through interruptions, and by directness or mitigation of directives.

On some variables, she found differences in input language tied to the gender of the parent as speaker but not to the gender of the child as addressee. For example, Gleason reports that fathers used more sophisticated vocabulary items than mothers to their children of both sexes (in talking about cars). This finding is provocative but must await additional evidence before it can be interpreted. Are fathers more specific and mothers vaguer across semantic domains? Or, as seems more likely, is each sex more specific in its "domains of practical knowledge"? (See Schieffelin, Chapter 9 in this section.) Should sophisticated vocabulary be viewed as a progressive aspect of the input, showing greater cognitive demandingness on the part of the parent and leading to faster vocabulary development in the child, or as a regressive aspect reflecting an inability to adapt to the child's level (as Gleason argues in the case of MLU)?

With respect to other variables, Gleason found differences in language use tied to the gender of both source and target. Fathers interrupt children more than do mothers. Parents of both sexes interrupt girls more than they interrupt boys. Fathers use more direct imperatives than do mothers, especially to boys. (Whether mothers also differentiate between boys and girls in this way is not indicated.)

What follows from these variations in input language? On the empirical level, Gleason reports that by the age of four, boys use more direct imperatives than girls. Interruptions and lexical specificity have not yet been studied in the children.

On the theoretical level, the mechanisms of transmission remain too complicated to disentangle. Do boys produce more direct imperatives because their fathers model more of them or because they receive more? And if the latter is at all the case what predictions should be made about interruptions? Girls receive more interruptions; therefore they should interrupt more? Obviously this is not the outcome we expect, which suggests that the operative factor in our tacit theory of the influence of input language is not simply frequency of exposure but a much more complicated cognitive structuring of that input by the child. Although the Gleason chapter does not deal with this cognitive structuring directly, it makes an important contribution in demonstrating a framework for research that will supply us with the empirical data necessary for developing theories of transmission.

The Goodwins' chapter applies discourse analysis to the language of children in American black urban culture. They focus on arguments, examining broad questions of what boys and girls argue about and what general strategies they use to advance their arguments. With respect to the question of sex differences, their conclusions are two-sided. They wish to demonstrate that, contrary to previous claims, black girls are as adept as black boys at carrying arguments forward. They advance this claim both in a loosely quantitative way (comparing the number of turns in argument sequences of boys and girls and the time frame encompassed in arguments) and qualitatively (comparing the complexity of patterns of accusation, denial, and counteraccusation). They also identify differences between boys' and girls' arguments. In terms of topics, boys' arguments often deal with establishing relative rankings of power and skill, girls' arguments with inclusion in shifting social alignments. In terms of technique, boys' arguments are characterized as more direct. Girls arguing among themselves frequently use an indirect device for making accusations, what the Goodwins call "he-said-she-said" statements, which deliver an accusation by reporting what someone else said about the accused party.

One important contribution of the Goodwins' chapter is to expand the scope of language examined beyond sentences and their component parts and even beyond speech acts. In this respect, their chapter connects with discussions of sex differences in adult language that invoke the concept of genre (see Sherzer, as well as Schieffelin, in this volume). But they differ from this approach in that they identify similarities and differences in boys' and girls' performance within the same type of global speech genre (arguing), rather than focus on different speech activities in which they take part.

An important variable the Goodwins introduce in their analysis is the distinction between same-sex and opposite-sex conversations. They find that sex differences are exaggerated when one examines only same-sex disputes. They report that when boys and girls argue together there are fewer distinctions in style, with girls matching the gambits of the boys. This finding is used to strengthen the point that girls are as adept at arguing as boys. The observation prompts some additional questions: Are boys, then, less adept at arguing because they control one style whereas girls control two? Or, from a different perspective, why does the boys' style set the framework for cross-sex disputes?

The Goodwins' observation that in their data sex differences decrease in cross-sex interactions raises a number of questions. First, how widespread is the applicability of this variable? How much does the sex mix of groups affect the manifestation of sex differences in speech? Sachs's study does not bear on this question, since she used only same-sex dyads in her experiment; and Gleason's studies did not control for this variable. In the chapters on adults in Part I, a number of contextual factors are examined, but same-sex versus cross-sex interaction is not one of them. When sex differences in speech arise in the context of genres in which only one sex participates, this variable becomes moot; but in analyses such as Hill's it is applicable and might yield interesting information.

According to the Goodwins, in the cross-sex context, sex differences are reduced because girls move toward the norms of same-sex boys' groups. Other patterns are possible. For example, each sex might move toward the norm of the other. Does this also occur?

Finally, where there are differences between cross-sex groups and same-sex groups, is it always the same-sex groups that exaggerate sex differences? The answer appears to be negative. Esposito's (1979) study of conversational interaction shows boys and girls interrupting their conversational partners at identical rates in same-sex pairs. It was only in boy–girl pairs that boys interrupted twice as often. In this case, it is a mixed-sex group composition that exaggerates sex differences. Similarly Haas (1979) found that girls laugh more than boys in conversation, but only in mixed-sex dyads, not in a comparison of two-girl with two-boy pairs. Therefore, it appears that cross-sex interaction leads sometimes to convergence of styles and sometimes to polarization.

The fourth chapter in this section, by Schieffelin, is concerned with gender differences in children's speech among the Kaluli of the New Guinea Highlands. Schieffelin claims that although there are highly elaborated gender-role differences in this society, these differences are not reflected in the ordinary conversational language of either adults or children. Men and women do perform different "genres" of speech, which in turn are distinctive in language form; but these genres occur in the context of specific activities, and Schieffelin believes they should be associated with the activities rather than directly with gender.

Two of the identifiable genres are "sung-texted weeping," performed by women, and narratives, performed by men. They employ distinct word orders, both of which occur frequently in conversation, but with differing functions. In daily speech AOV (agent, object, verb) word order is used for reporting and announcing. This is the order used almost exclusively in narratives spoken by men. The OAV order is used for requests or to focus the agent. Women's sung-texted weeping employs this order almost exclusively. Children of both sexes learn both word orders very early, but they will not learn the more gender-specific speech genres until well after they have joined same-sex peer groups, around the age of three years. This pattern of later discourse–genre specialization is the same one discussed in Part I by Joel Sherzer for the Kuna.

Although boys and girls are socialized in explicitly different ways – for example, girls are encouraged to be submissive to their brothers, and boys to be aggressive to their sisters – Schieffelin finds no reflections of these differences in the children's language. This claim is all the more striking in light of her observation that "Kaluli everyday life is overtly focused on face-to-face verbal interaction . . . . Talk is a primary way to be social and a primary indicator of social competence."

An element of Kaluli socialization is the notion that children must be explicitly taught language. This is done primarily by mothers, who are responsible for caretaking in general, and who in the course of inter-action tell their child, in effect, "Say this: . . . ." Although one might expect to see differences in these instruction sequences according to whether the student speaker is a boy or a girl, Schieffelin reports that there are none to be found, whether at the phonological, syntactic, or even pragmatic level.

One intriguing sex difference does emerge in connection with the instruction sequences. The term for "Say this" is *ɛlɛma*. Both boys and girls are exposed to this routine frequently in the course of early language acquisition. Young girls, however, adopt it and use it in caretaking games with other children and in role-reversal games with their mothers, but little boys do not. Boys, like girls, learn the dialect of their mothers, having little exposure to the dialect of their fathers. But in the case of *ɛlɛma* they somehow filter the common input to reject a fragment that presumably is "inappropriate" for their use. These data about parental input and child output, like Gleason's, demonstrate that in the acqui-sition of gender differences (and communicative competence in general), just as in the development of grammatical competence, children organize and structure the language they hear and do not merely reflect it directly.

There are a number of points of convergence and contrast in the findings of these authors. The most obvious convergence is the general agreement in Chapters 6–8, all of which examine language use in American sub-cultures, that boys are more likely to use direct imperatives than girls. Gleason, Sachs, and the Goodwins all make this claim. They also agree that girls are more likely to use a variety of mitigated forms. But here their results diverge slightly within categories of mitigated forms. For example, Gleason reports that four-year-old girls, like their mothers, use more question imperatives than boys. Sachs did not find sex differences in this particular category among her five-year-olds.

The categories of directives used by different researchers overlap but do not correspond exactly. For example, Sachs has a class of "declarative directives" (e.g., "You have to push it") that has no counterpart in Gleason. Gleason has a category of "implied indirect directives" (e.g., "The wheel is going to fall off") that has no counterpart in Sachs. Gleason's example happens also to be declarative, but the directive trust of the utterance is implied rather than explicit as in Sachs's example.

In these categories there are some deviations from the general pattern of sex differences. Sachs classifies the declarative directives as unmitigated but finds them to be used equally by both sexes rather than more frequently by boys. Gleason's "The wheel is going to fall off" is mitigated in that it does not make explicit its directive intent, but in her data boys and men use this mitigated form more frequently than girls and women.

Another convergence occurs in this domain of what might be called state directives. "The wheel is going to fall off" (see Gleason's chapter) asserts a state of affairs and leaves the inference of directive intent to the listener. "Are you sick?" as a way of telling one's playmate to "be" sick questions a state of affairs and likewise leaves the inference of directive intent to the listener. In Sachs's study it is the only mitigating category in which boys' productions exceed girls'. Thus boys seem to use both more assertions and more queries about state.

The agreement on the finding that boys use more direct imperatives is particularly striking considering the contrasts between the sources of data, especially those of Sachs and the Goodwins. Sachs examined an upper-middle-class population; the Goodwins, a lower-class one. Sachs's subjects were primarily white; the Goodwins' black. The age ranges they studied overlapped only slightly, with Sachs looking at two- to five-year-olds and the Goodwins at four- to thirteen-year-olds. Sachs elicited speech in semiartificial "pretend play" situations. The Goodwins recorded speech that occurred in completely natural settings. Sachs characterizes the broad framework of her research as the "ability of preschool children to coordinate their play behavior." The focus is on the language of cooperation. By contrast, the Goodwins focus on disputes and the language of conflict.

Although girls used more polite varieties of directives, the studies reported here do not support the notion that they are more polite in all possible ways. According to Gleason, they did not use conventional expressions of politeness such as "Thank you" and "Good-bye" more than boys – this despite the fact that their presumed models, mothers and fathers, did differ in this respect. It is somewhat puzzling that children would pick up gender differentiation in a rather subtle domain such as the form of directives and not do so in the more conspicuous matter of saying "thank you." Perhaps the solution of the puzzle lies in the fact that Gleason reports sex differences not in parents' use of "thank you" as a sincere expression of gratitude on their own behalf but, rather, in the special case of thanking on behalf of their children. This use of "thank you" has as part of its purpose teaching the child to say "thank you." Perhaps in actual contexts in which parents express gratitude, mothers and fathers would not differ but all approach a ceiling level as they did for saying hello to the experimenter.

All of the comparisons made so far apply to comparable data at the level of speech-act analysis. There may also be some convergence across levels of communicative competence, for example, comparing data about speech acts with data about organization of discourse. The Goodwins point out that in the scripts for arguments used among girls, offenses are presented as being known by hearsay. Accusations are made relatively indirectly rather than as bald statements of truth. It is tempting to draw a connection between girls' preferences for less direct accusations and less direct directives. Both give greater latitude for responding to the addressee.

Differences in boys' and girls' choices of directives to peers may also bear some relation to the differences in the goals of their arguments discerned by the Goodwins, who state that the purpose of boys' arguments is usually to establish superior rank in terms of power and skill. Research previously discussed in my comments on "sociolinguistic knowledge" indicates that young children vary their directive forms according to the rank of their addressees. Direct imperatives are more likely to be used to individuals of lower rank than to those of higher rank. Perhaps, then, the boys' preference for more direct forms of directives toward children who are their peers reflects a more pervasive orientation to establish their position in a hierarchy. Perhaps they use direct imperatives as a way of establishing their superior rank and not just as a response to the preestablished lower rank of others.

Given the convergence among the first three chapters in this section, the fourth, introducing as it does material from another culture and language, offers particularly valuable points of contrast. In Schieffelin's chapter we find that it does not follow from a heavy cultural emphasis on gender-role differences that boys' and girls' speech will be differentiated earlier and more than in a society with a less heavy emphasis on gender-role differences. In fact, the chapters in this section display the opposite pattern, because it is the white middle-class American children from a purportedly less gender-role-differentiated society who show early significant differences in the frequencies of use of particular (pragmatic) language devices.

In attempting to explain the absence of gender differences from Kaluli conversational language, Schieffelin offers some provocative speculations about the type of society that is likely to produce such a pattern. She reasons that because Kaluli society clearly defines male and female spheres of activity, and because it lacks general stratification, there may be no "need" for linguistic marking of gender. But Brown's (1979,1980) work on Tzeltal, a society similar in these parameters where style differences between men's and women's language do exist, undermines the generality of this claim and challenges explanations of gender differences based on need. Conclusions about such questions are, of course, premature; but the questions are valuable and fascinating.

Overall, these chapters, like those in Part I, make it evident that very different aspects of language use may be involved in the behavioral differences associated with gender. Thus, whereas the Sachs and Gleason chapters focus on everyday use of directives by preschoolers as they are contained within a single utterance, the Goodwins' chapter is concerned with disputes among grade schoolers that take place over a number of turns at talk and have distinctive features of sequential structure that differ between boys and girls. The Schieffelin chapter focuses on discourse, as does the Goodwins', but on a form of discourse that is set apart from everyday speech, unlike the form covered by the Goodwins, and that does not become clearly gender-differentiated until adulthood.

Although these chapters give evidence of a diversity of ways in which gender differences appear in the speech of children, all make a case for the social basis of these differences. Gleason argues that differences must arise from exposure to different adult models or from being spoken to differently by adults. The Goodwins share Labov's opinion that children come to speak not like their parents but like their peers. Presumably both sets of influences, parent and peer, are operative, with the balance varying according to the ages of the children (the Goodwins' subjects were older) and patterns of socialization in different cultures. Both Sachs and Gleason do acknowledge the possible contribution of biological factors – arguing, for example, that boys might elicit more direct imperatives because they are physically more aggressive – but neither of them refers to language-specific biological factors in her explanations of the gender differences she found.

Finally, while essays from both of the disciplines represented in this section, psychology and anthropology, are concerned with issues of generalizability of findings, they ascribe different priorities to different types of generalizations. The psychologists are especially interested in establishing the reliability and significance of their results (the statistically defined presumption that their findings will apply equally to other sets of similar children in similar circumstances and that their findings, whether of gender differences or absence of differences, are not spurious or accidental). The anthropologists, to varying degrees, are concerned more with providing information that will allow us to make or test generalizations across human groups. Therefore, the two psychologists studied white middle-class American children, and they establish (or allude to) the reliability and statistical significance of their findings. The Goodwins, though also on American territory, report on a group of black adolescents. Schieffelin moves farther afield in her study of Kaluli, potentially increasing our opportunities for generalizing at one level, but perhaps at the expense of generalizability at the other (and logically prior) level. Her conclusions about gender differences (and the lack thereof) in Kaluli child language are based on detailed data from one girl and two boys. With such a small sample, there is a danger that spurious factors can either create differences where there are no systematic ones or obscure differences that do exist. As Schieffelin herself admits, individual differences among children and mothers in the sample made some points of her analysis problematic. One hopes that the process of addressing similar questions jointly will alert members of each discipline to the other's concerns about generalizability and stimulate each to apply the other's criteria more widely.

6. Preschool boys' and girls' language use in pretend play

JACQUELINE SACHS

Despite the rapid growth of research on communicative competence in children, we have little information as yet about the similarities and differences between the speech styles of boys and girls. This lack of information is somewhat surprising, since authors of most studies carefully include half boys and half girls. However, the use of gender as a variable for data analysis is less common than one might imagine. In this chapter, I shall present data from a study of language use in children's pretend play, discuss these data in relation to other studies of communicative competence, and offer suggestions about possible bases for the sex differences observed.

The data come from a larger study that is being carried out by me and two colleagues, Jane Goldman at the University of Connecticut and Christine Chaillé at the University of Oregon. The main purpose of that study is to look at the development of the ability of preschool children to coordinate their play behavior (see Sachs, Goldman, Chaillé, and Seewald, 1980; Sachs, Goldman, and Chaillé, 1984, 1985; Chaillé, Goldman, and Sachs, 1983). I concentrate here on whether the boys and girls spoke differently in the situation in which we observed them.

Method

The children observed were twenty boys between 26 and 61 months (mean age, 47 months) and twenty-six girls between 24 and 64 months (mean age, 48 months). The children were enrolled in a preschool program at the University of Connecticut and were primarily from educated, upper-middle-class families. All but two of the children were Caucasian. Dyads were formed of same-sex children within four months of age,

178

Table 6.1. *Coding categories*

Nonplay	Literal reference to objects, events, feelings
Nonpretend play	Using play objects but not in pretend mode
Pretend play	Utterances within sequence of utterances or behaviors showing role-appropriate or nonliteral use of objects

from the same preschool class. The pairings were screened for incompatibility by a teacher.

Three boy dyads started play sessions but were not used in the study. In two cases, the sessions were stopped because of aggressive behavior and in one case the data were not used because the boys discovered that they could look through the one-way mirror into the filming room. One dyad of 2-year-old girls was not used because the children were afraid to stay in the room without an adult.

Each dyad was taken to a playroom by a familiar adult. The children were told that they had a long time to play and that the teacher would come back to take them to their classroom.

The playroom was a small room furnished with two couches, low tables, and a lamp, with a one-way mirror on one wall. Play objects were arranged on the couches and tables. There were many objects suggesting a doctor theme, such as a toy stethoscope, Band-Aid box, syringe, medicine bottles, and cotton. Some other objects not specific to the doctor theme were also available, such as pieces of fabric, hats, blocks, some pieces of styrofoam, and two dolls (a baby doll and a dog).

The doctor theme was chosen because: (1) It reflects the child's own experiences as well as material from TV, movies, and books, (2) both boys and girls play the game spontaneously, (3) the theme calls for the reciprocal roles of doctor and patient, and (4) the theme is complex enough to allow a wide range of behavior during make-believe.

The sessions were videotaped from the next room. Each session was sixteen to thirty minutes in length. The data used in the analyses discussed here derive from the first sixteen minutes after the adult left.

The utterances were transcribed with notes about context by an experimenter who had been present at the taping. Immediate self-repetition was not counted or coded as a separate utterance. The utterances were coded using the transcripts while viewing the tape. The coding system represented a continuum from utterances that were least like pretend play to those that were enactments of pretending. The coding categories are shown in Table 6.1. Each dyad was analyzed by two coders. One coded all utterances from sixteen minutes and the other coded a four-minute sample to provide a reliability assessment. The reliability of coding was .87. All statistical analyses were performed on dyad data rather than on individual children's data.

Pretending

In 2-year-olds, 26 percent of the utterances were in the pretend category. There was a significantly higher percentage of pretend utterances in the older dyads (56 percent in 3-year-olds and 63 percent in 5-year-olds). Most older dyads began pretend play within the first few utterances, drawing upon a preestablished schema for doctor play. Here is an example from two 5-year-old girls, MO (age 64 months) and MI (age 61 months), who went straight to the doctor's kit upon entering the room and explicitly mentioned the theme of the play:

MI: What's this? (indicating blood-pressure gauge)
MO: Wanna play doctor?
MI: Well, yeah. Pretend we were both . . .
MO: Doctors.
MI: Yeah. Will you be the patient for a few minutes?

There was no difference between boys and girls in the amount of pretend play. Other studies of pretend play in young children have sometimes found that boys pretend more (e.g., Rubin, Maioni, and Hornung, 1976; Singer, 1973) and sometimes that girls pretend more (e.g., Fein and Robertson, 1975). It may be that the equipment or locale influences the amount of pretend play that one finds in boys and girls.

There were some sex differences in what was said during pretending. One important topic during pretend play is the assignment of roles. The youngest subjects (2-year-olds) did not talk about roles at all, but all of the older children did. Boys and girls used similar numbers of utterances about roles but differed somewhat in the content of their speech. For boys, doctor was the role chosen by the child for himself 79 percent of the time, and there were many long arguments over which child would be doctor. In a study of role playing with puppets, Andersen (1977) also found that boys preferred the high-status roles of doctor or father and refused to play the role of patient or baby. (Similar results have been reported by Garvey, 1977b, and Miller and Garvey, 1984.) In this study, the girls wanted the doctor role only 33 percent of the time, often wishing to be a baby, a patient, or a mother in the game.

In suggesting roles for the other child, the boys usually (in 72 percent of cases) told the other child what to be, as in:

CH: Come on, be a doctor.

The girls, on the other hand, asked what the other child would like to be (in 80 percent of cases), as in:

MI: Will you be the patient for a few minutes?

The girls also sometimes talked about joint roles (roles of both children), as in:

LA: I'll be the nurse and you be the doctor.
MO: Now we can both be doctors.
SH: We both can be sick.

It appears from these findings about role utterances that the girls may have become more aware of the needs of the other child in the dyad. To examine this possibility further, we turn to a broader category of utterances, looking now at all utterances that call for a response from the other child.

Obliges

We call the utterances that demand a response from the listener "Obliges," taking the label from a coding system for conversational behavior developed by Blank and Franklin (1980). An Oblige in Blank and Franklin's scheme is an utterance that sets up an obligatory environment for a reply or a behavior. Thus "What is your name?" is an Oblige, and so is "Tie your shoe."

The reason for looking at Obliges rather than at the narrower category of Directives is that some types of speech that influence the other child's behavior are not ordinarily coded as Directives and yet may be of interest. For example, if a child asks the other, "Do you want to be the patient?" the question may have directive intent but, on the other hand, may simply be a question about the other child's wishes. We wished to include such questions without presupposing whether they functioned as directives or not.

Studies have shown that utterances used to control the behavior of the listener are sensitive to variables such as situation and status (Ervin-Tripp, 1977; Ervin-Tripp and Gordon, 1984). Such utterances can be in the most direct form, such as imperatives, or can be "mitigated" (Labov and Fanshel, 1977) in various ways to be more polite. In adults, it has been suggested that women are more likely to use mitigated forms (e.g., Brown and Levinson, 1978; Lakoff, 1975). In children's speech, it has been found that imperatives are used by young children and that indirect forms appear as the children get older (Garvey, 1975). In this analysis of the use of Obliges in pretend play we wish to ask whether there is a difference in the use of Obliges by boys and girls.

The transcripts of four 5-year-old boy dyads and four 5-year-old girl dyads were coded for types of Obliges. This coding was done as follows:

Table 6.2. *Coding categories for Obliges*

Coding	Example
Imperative	Bring her to the hospital.
Prohibition	Don't touch it.
Declarative Directive	You have to push it.
Pretend Directive	Pretend you had a bad cut.
Question Directive	Will you be the patient?
Tag Question	That's your bed, right?
Joint Directive	Now we'll cover him up.
State Question	Are you sick?
Information Question	What does she need now?
Attentional Device	Lookit.

Table 6.3. *Percentage of Obliges in various categories, for boys and for girls*

Category	Boys	Girls
Imperative	25	10
Prohibition	11	2
Declarative Directive	6	5
Pretend Directive	4	11
Question Directive	0	2
Tag Question	16	35
Joint Directive	3	15
State Question	11	2
Information Question	22	16
Attentional Device	2	2

1. Only utterances in pretend episodes were coded.
2. Utterances with parts that could not be understood were omitted.
3. Clarification requests were omitted.
4. Utterances were coded in subcategories (see Table 6.2).

The results of the coding of Obliges are shown in Table 6.3. The reliability of this coding was .91. Owing to the small number of dyads, we shall not make inferences about the generalizability of the results to other children but shall merely present the data descriptively for these children.

Whereas boys and girls used about the same total number of Obliges (186 for the boys and 174 for the girls), the results shown in Tables 6.3 and 6.4 support the hypothesis that the girls in this study were talking in a manner that was more mitigated than were the boys. The conclusion is suggested by many differences found:

Table 6.4. *Percentage of Obliges unmitigated, mitigated, or other*

Category	Boys	Girls
Unmitigated	42	17
Mitigated	34	65
Other	24	18

1. Boys used the simple Imperative form much more frequently than did the girls, as in:

CH: Lie down.
JA: Get the heart thing.
SE: Gimme your arm.
TY: Try to give me medicine.

One boy was especially eager to give directions, and said:

SU: Then take your medicine and put some of these – then do everything.

In fact, only one girl used more than one Imperative during the sixteen-minute interaction. In contrast, 25 percent of the boys' Obliges were Imperatives, the least polite form of attempting to change the partner's behavior.

Since the boys preferred the role of doctor, one might wonder whether the Imperative utterances were being used to represent the role of doctor. Even when we eliminate utterances spoken in the role of doctor, the boys still used Imperatives much more frequently than did the girls (18 percent).

2. The boys used Prohibitions five times as frequently as did girls. These Prohibitions were often uttered in arguments over activities or possessions, as in:

CH: Don't touch nothing.
SU: Don't take my things.

3. Declarative Directives were found about equally in the boys' and girls' speech.

4. Taken together, the Imperative, Prohibition, and Declarative Directive are directive forms showing no mitigation. As is shown in Table 6.4, many more of the boys' Obliges were unmitigated (42 percent as compared with 17 percent for the girls).

5. Pretend Directives show some mitigation in that they posit a transformation from reality. The girls used the Pretend category more frequently than did the boys. Eleven percent of the girls' Obliges were Pretend utterances such as:

SH: Pretend he cried.
KA: Pretend you had a chill.
MI: Pretend this was the next patient.

Another 9 percent of the utterances coded as Tag Questions and Joint Directives also included an explicit "pretend."

   6. Question Directives represent the type of mitigation found often in adult speech (e.g., "Could you give me the stethoscope?"). In the children's speech, there were few Question Directives by either sex.

   7. Tag Questions mitigate in that they provide an opportunity for the listener to concur or disagree with the content of the utterance. The girls made heavy use of Tag Questions, as in:

KA: That's for the shot, OK?
MI: Oh yes, she needs the little pill, right?

   8. Joint utterances are mitigating because they imply cooperation between the listener and hearer. Fifteen percent of the girls' Obliges were Joint, five times as many as were spoken by the boys, and they talked about joint activities and roles, as in:

SA: Let's sit down and use it.
LA: OK, and I'll be the doctor for my baby and you be the doctor for your baby.

   9. Some girls' utterances used a combination of devices for mitigating the Oblige, as in the following utterances that have an explicit "pretend," are Joint, and have a Tag:

JE: Pretend we each took a different kind of drugs in our eyes, right?
SH: Pretend I was waking up and you were tired and you wanted to take a little nap in here, right?

   10. The only mitigating category in which we find more utterances by boys than by girls is State Questions. Boys more often asked what the other wanted or how he felt, as in:

JO: Do you need a shot?
JA: Are you sick?

   11. Looking overall at categories with mitigation, we find that many more of the girls' utterances were mitigated (65 percent as compared with 34 percent for the boys), as is shown in Table 6.4.

Discussion

The results of the analyses of utterances that call for a listener response suggest that the 5-year-old girls in this study differed from the boys in a number of ways. The girls seemed to soften their Obliges, perhaps being more concerned to include the other child in the play-planning process. The boys, on the other hand, were more assertive, often simply telling the other child what to do.

One question that arises is whether the differences observed here represent a developmental difference or a stylistic difference. As mentioned earlier, the indirect forms of requests are developmentally later than the imperative forms (Garvey, 1975). Perhaps the boys are mastering the same linguistic style as girls but are less mature linguistically. On the other hand, perhaps boys control the same devices for mitigation as do girls but simply use them less frequently, resulting in a style difference. Several types of evidence bear on this issue.

First, when the boys got into arguments, they often used mitigating utterances in order to make peace. In the following example, SU, the boy who was being the patient, has gone off with the toy stethoscope. The italicized utterances are ones that were coded as mitigated Obliges.

CH: No. You're not the doctor. Now take that off.
SU: No. Stop that. You pinched me on the eye.
CH: I didn't mean to.
SU: Then be my friend.
CH: Then don't talk like that.
SU: And you too.
CH: And you too, cause I didn't mean to do that.
SU: Not me either.
CH: *Can you take that off?* Just one person can be the doctor. One person. *So can you take that off?*

Note that the mitigation here is using the form that is often found among adult speakers, The Question Directive. Furthermore, it is supported with a justification: "Just one person can be the doctor."

Here is another argument that resulted in mitigating utterances. JA had become angry with CH, and CH tried to make amends by offering the desirable role of doctor:

CH: *You wanna be the doctor?*
JA: No.
CH: Why?
JA: Cause I hate you.
CH: Please, I won't do that anymore. *Never, never again, all right? Let's be friends. Now let's get up, right? You wanna do something? You wanna be the doctor forever and never change? Wanna do that?*

A second reason for thinking that the differences observed here between boys and girls represent style differences rather than developmental differences is that the same pattern of results has been described for adults. Lakoff (1975) argued that men use a more forceful style, whereas women hedge their statements. Gleason (1975) has compared the speech of mothers and fathers talking to children and found that fathers use the simple imperative form of directive more than mothers do.

Third, our finding of a less mitigated style for boys is consistent with M. H. Goodwin's (1980a) findings in a population that differs from this one in both age and ethnic background. Goodwin, observing working-class black children between 8 and 13 years of age in same-sex groups, found that boys used mostly imperative forms, whereas girls used various devices to mitigate their language when attempting to control the other children. Goodwin found that the girls she observed could use a more assertive style when arguing or in mixed-sex groups. Our data do not include mixed-sex pairs, but our finding that the boys could use mitigated utterances when the situation called for them seems quite similar to Goodwin's finding for girls.

Finally, there is evidence from other studies suggesting that boys as well as girls can use mitigated styles when called upon to do so. James (1978) tested twenty-one children between ages 4;6 and 5;2 in a situation where the child gave requests and commands to dolls representing three groups: adults, peers, and younger children. The children were polite to all three categories of "listeners," and there were no significant differences between boys and girls in politeness. Andersen (1977) also found that both boys and girls used politeness markers in their role-playing speech. Looking at older children, D. Gordon et al. (1980) found that boys and girls from kindergarten through grade five avoided simple imperatives when making a request of an adult in an experimental task.

What was the source of the style difference between boys and girls that we observed? I wish to raise three types of explanations, although they are not mutually exclusive and may well interact, each to play some role. First, children may learn patterns appropriate for their gender from observing the way adults talk, either to one another or to children. As noted above, fathers use imperative directives to their children more than mothers do (Gleason, 1975). Other kinds of assertiveness are also present in male speech. Greif (1980) found that when parents talked to children, the fathers interrupted more often than the mothers did. More generally, in mixed-sex conversations between adults, men interrupt women much more than women interrupt men (Zimmerman and West, 1975). There is independent evidence, too, that children notice these differences in adults' speech. In a puppet play task, both boys and girls role-playing fathers used many imperatives, but when role-playing mothers used few (Andersen, 1977). The difference in interruption patterns is also picked up by children. Esposito (1979) found that boys interrupt girls more than girls interrupt boys in mixed-sex conversations. Sachs (1982) and Sachs, Donnelly et al. (1984) found that young preschool boys were less polite than girls when they attempted to enter into on-going conversations. Children can also make judgments about the sex of a speaker from stylistic cues. Edelsky (1977) asked children to judge whether utterances were said by men or women, and found that by the third grade, children judged an indirect request form ("Won't you please...") to be said by a woman. By the sixth grade, children identified Tag Questions as being from women. All of these studies show that children are being influenced by the conversational patterns of the adults around them.

A second possible reason that children differ in assertiveness in language is that they have been treated differentially by adults when they behave assertively. Assertiveness may be more tolerated and even rewarded in boys but not in girls. To explore this possibility, it would be necessary to have research on the consequences for the child of various types of speech. For example, Ervin-Tripp, O'Connor, and Rosenberg (1982) have looked at compliance with requests in children (both sexes) and found that, surprisingly, when the "cost" of the request was held constant, polite requests were less successful than requests using a more direct form. They argue that children do not go on to learn to be polite in order to be successful in getting their way but because politeness is part of the linguistic system they are exposed to.

Thirdly, the possibility exists that boys' and girls' linguistic behavior reflects other differences in their behavior. It has been consistently noted that boys are more physically active and engage in more "rough and tumble" play (DiPietro, 1981; Halverson and Waldrop, 1973; Pederson and Bell, 1970; Pulaski, 1973; Tauber, 1979). The activity differences show up quite early (Goldberg and Lewis, 1969; Smith and Daglish, 1977). It has been noted that girls engage in more construction and sedentary play, whereas boys are more active (Rubin et al., 1976). The differences in play activity level may reflect inborn differences or may reflect treatment or may reflect both. For example, Power and Parke (1980) found that adults' play with boys was more physical, and it has frequently been noted that parents supply boys and girls with different sorts of toys (e.g., Rheingold and Cook, 1975). Whether the differences in activity level are influenced by environmental differences or not, it may well be that more physically active children are more accustomed to struggles for dominance and that these struggles come out in their language as well as their nonverbal behavior.

A concluding word about the implications of finding differences in assertiveness even in 5-year-olds: A number of years ago, I was involved in research on differences between boys' and girls' voices. In one study (Sachs, Lieberman, and Erickson, 1973), we found that although girls' voices were no higher in pitch than boys', judges could identify the gender of a child from a short sample of speech. We suggested that one way of achieving the speech-quality difference that judges seemed to be responding to was lip spreading on the part of the girls. That is, the girls "said it with a smile." In the study described here, where boys and girls both try to influence the other child in a pretend-play interaction, the girls appear to "say it with a smile" in content, too.

On the surface it might seem that the girls were linguistically more advanced than the boys because politeness in language is seen as a goal. But although we appear to value politeness in our culture, in some situations we respect assertive language. It has been suggested many times before that one problem for many women may be that, unlike the girls observed by Goodwin, they do not know how to be effectively assertive when the situation calls for it. Furthermore, when women are assertive, it is seen as not suitable for them. One important goal for future research is a more complete understanding of the effects of the speech styles that are used by men and women.

In a review of the motion picture *Tootsie*, Ellen Goodman noted that the society traditionally values sensitivity as a female strength and fighting for oneself as a male strength. Dustin Hoffman as Dorothy seemed to succeed by turning himself into a woman, but actually he succeeded by being a woman who acted like a man. "If 'Tootsie' pushes the idea that men are nicer in their personal lives when they are acting like women, it also sells another subliminal notion: Women are more successful in public life when they are really men" (1983). The difference between the film and real life is that the actress who behaves like Tootsie – not tolerating sexual harassment, speaking her mind, confronting her director – runs the risk of being fired. Like the little girls in this study, if she wants to say it, she had better "say it with a smile."

Note

I wish to acknowledge Jane Goldman and Christine Chaillé, who collaborated in collecting the data used in this analysis. Debbie Pierson, James Donnelly, Richard Seewald, Julia Dwyer, Bianca Lauro, and Elaine Dickinson helped with various aspects of the data collection, transcription, and coding. The University of Connecticut Preschool Laboratory generously made the children and facilities available to us.

7. Sex differences in parent–child interaction

JEAN BERKO GLEASON

Since by now it is well documented that there are differences in the ways grown men and women speak, it seems reasonable at this point to ask where those differences originate. There are, of course, a number of plausible explanations of the origins of sex differences in language: They can arise either from inborn differences or as a result of environmental forces, or perhaps as a result of an interaction between the two. In this chapter, the emphasis will be on environmental forces, especially the role mothers and fathers play in shaping the language of their daughters and sons. This is not an attempt, however, to say that there are no inborn differences. The work of McKeever (Chapter 10 of this volume), Witelson and Pallie (1973), and many others has shown that it is entirely likely that the language areas of the brains of males and females are not identical: Specialization for language appears to develop earlier in the brains of females, and males appear to be more vulnerable to every kind of insult that affects language development and retention at every age from early childhood through advanced old age.

Even if there were no differences in the neuroanatomical bases of language in males and females, there would be other obvious differences that, though not themselves linguistic, could have a differential effect on language development. Young males, for instance, are more physically aggressive than females in all cultures that have been studied (Maccoby and Jacklin, 1974). It should not surprise us, therefore, to find adults uttering more negative statements and more prohibitions to boys than to girls, and that is exactly what Cherry and Lewis (1976) found. Adults spent more time trying to control young boys, and adult language, of course, reflected those efforts. If children's language development is affected by the kinds of language they hear when interacting with adults, girls and boys may develop different kinds of language

189

because they are spoken to differently. Thus, males and females may produce and elicit different kinds of language because of their different neurological and behavioral dispositions; and these possibly inborn differences may be amplified by society.

There are also powerful environmental forces that shape the way individuals speak and that lead to stylistic variation: Males and females speak differently as a reflection of their gender roles. The use of certain lexical items, syntactic forms, and intonation patterns cannot be reasonably tied to either neurological or inborn behavioral differences, since they are culturally constrained. The use of the adjective "darling" in English, for instance, or a special set of pronouns in Japanese, may be limited to women, but not for any intrinsic reason.

There is general agreement that, for whatever reason, men and women speak differently as adults. Presumably, these differences began to emerge at some point in childhood, and the most likely context of their development lies in the arena of parent–child interaction.

Input Language

We may well ask the questions, When do little boys and girls first begin to sound like males and females? and What role do parents have in the development of whatever differences there are? But questions of this sort are very recent indeed. The ontogenesis of sex differences in language has hardly been explored, and only very recently have we had any information at all about the possible differences in the speech directed to girls and boys by their mothers and fathers.

One major reason for the dearth of information on what is obviously an interesting and important topic lies in the nature of the theories that have dominated the study of children's language development in the years since Chomsky first published *Syntactic Structures* (1957). The models of child language acquisition that dominated the field in the 1950s and 1960s were child-centered and did not consider the role of adults, except insofar as they were thought to provide a rather degenerate sample of language that the young language-learning child could feed into her or his Language Acquisition Device. It was generally assumed that differences in the language the child heard (and this language was called Input Language) did not matter, since the child's Language Acquisition Device was equipped with suitable filters for processing out those elements that were not of use at a given time. The search was for universals, with an emphasis on the acquisition of syntax. The burden of acquisition lay on the child, and the role of adults in the child's environment was minimized; it was assumed that all the child needed to set the Language Acquisition Device in motion was to overhear a sufficiently large sample of the target language.

In the late 1960s this picture began to change for a variety of reasons. Among other things, a number of researchers (for instance, Gleason, 1973; Remick, 1971; Snow, 1972) began to wonder if it was really true that young children had to learn the rules of language from listening to a complex and degenerate corpus of adult speech. This led investigators to study the language of mothers of young language-learning children. The results of those studies are well known: Mothers' speech to young children is much less complex than their speech to other adults and appears to contain design features that may make the learning of language easier. The language of mothers to their 2-year-olds is slow, redundant, simple, and, above all, grammatical. This special speech may or may not make the acquisition of syntax simpler: There is still a raging controversy in the field on this subject, with some (e.g., Moerk, 1975) claiming that mothers' speech contains all of the elements necessary to teach children grammatical language, and others (e.g. Gleitman, Newport, and Gleitman, 1984) claiming that what appears to be simple in mothers' speech is not and that mothers' speech at best can have only a superficial influence on children's acquisition of language.

No one contests, however, that mothers' speech has the particular form that has been described by so many researchers, and it is that very special kind of speech that is now referred to as *input language*. (Those who think it is unimportant and uninteresting tend to call it "Motherese," but for a number of reasons that will soon become apparent, this is a misnomer.) Another name for input language is Child Directed Speech (CDS), which is a bit more accurate, since the special features of this speech are necessitated by the child who is being addressed rather than by the person, who may or may not be a mother, who produces it.

Once it became clear that mothers have a special way of speaking to young children, a number of questions arose in addition to those that center on the acquisition of syntax. These questions have to do with stylistic (or registral) variation: Input language, or CDS, is clearly a separate style, or register. It appears in the speech of women who are not mothers, in the speech of fathers, and, indeed, in the speech of all speakers, child and adult, who are addressing young children. Shatz and Gelman (1973) showed that even 4-year-olds make some modifications in their usual speech when they speak to 2-year-olds. Other researchers (Giattino and Hogan, 1975; Golinkoff and Ames, 1979) showed that fathers' speech also contained the simplifying and clarifying modifications that had been noted in mothers' speech. Thus, input language (CDS) containing some special features is produced by all speakers addressing young children. Bohannon and Marquis (1977) suggest that it is children themselves who cause these modifications, because it can be demonstrated that speakers adjust the complexity of their utterances in accordance with the signals of comprehension or noncomprehension produced by their addressees. While this can be shown experimentally, it is also true that speakers have preconceived notions of how to talk to young children: Adults simplify and clarify their speech when they only think they are talking on the phone to 2-year-olds (Snow, 1972), and young children in preschool produce typical "baby talk" when playing with dolls (Sachs and Devin, 1976; Andersen, 1977). Some of the features of CDS are undoubtedly tied to communication pressure (for instance, clear enunciation), but others are part of a conventionalized speech register (for instance, calling a rabbit a "bunny"). Young children acquire this register as part of their developing communicative competence, and adults use this register in speaking to young children.

Input language is not a unitary phenomenon, however. It changes over time and becomes more complex as children's ability to comprehend it changes. By the time children are 4 or 5, adults speak to them in a "language of socialization" that emphasizes not so much syntactic clarity, or the rules of language, as the rules of society. Speech to a 2-year-old contains many phrases like "See the bunny. It's a nice bunny. Pat the bunny," while speech to a 5-year-old contains many phrases like "Look both ways before you cross the street," "Say thank you to Mrs. Williams," and "Sit up at the table."

CDS thus occurs in different forms, depending on the *age* of the child being addressed. There may be some argument about the relation between the syntax used by adults in their CDS and the acquisition of syntax by children, but there is general agreement that adults explicitly teach children social conventions and that the adult language is the medium of that education.

What remains to be determined is whether the *sex* of the child as well as the age of the child has an effect on the CDS, and, additionally, whether CDS varies according to the *sex of the speaker*. Unless girls and boys are exposed to different adult models or are spoken to differently, we are hard pressed to provide an environmental explanation for how sex differences in their own language might possibly originate. In the rest of this chapter, a number of studies originating in our own laboratory will be discussed. The questions to be considered involve: (1) differences between mothers' and fathers' speech to children, regardless of the child's sex, (2) differences in parents' speech to boys and to girls, and (3) emerging sex-associated differences in the speech of children.

Research settings

The research was carried out in both naturalistic and laboratory settings. Initially, we obtained a small sample of families whom we visited in their homes, making audiorecordings of family interaction. At the same time, for comparison, we made recordings of male and female teachers in a day-care setting (Gleason, 1975). We then obtained funding to conduct a laboratory and home study of a much larger sample of families. Twenty-four families participated in this study. Each family had a child between the ages of 2 and 5; the mothers were the primary caretakers, and the fathers worked outside the home in professional occupations. Twelve of the child subjects were girls and twelve were boys, about evenly matched for age.

Methods

In the laboratory portion of the study, each child was seen and videotaped twice, once with the father and once with the mother, in a counterbalanced design. Recording sessions lasted a half hour, which was divided among three activities: "reading" a picture book that had no words (Mercer-Mayer's *The Great Cat Chase*); taking apart (and attempting to put back together) a toy Playskool car; and playing store with a number of grocery items, paper bags, and a toy cash register. Toward the end of the session a research assistant entered the laboratory playroom with a gift for the child. This assistant followed a script, designed to maximize the likelihood that the parent and child would say, "Hi," "Thanks," and "Goodbye" (see our article of that name: Greif and Gleason, 1980). This was accomplished by, for instance, holding out the gift; saying, "Here's a little gift just for you"; and then waiting expectantly. Obviously, the pressure on a parent under the circumstances is to tell the child to say "Thanks" or personally to say "Thanks." In this way we were able to look at sex differences in politeness behavior in fathers, mothers, girls, and boys.

The laboratory videotapes were transcribed and analyzed in all of the standard ways (e.g., for mean length of utterance and sentence type), as well as for features thought to be differentially represented in the speech of females and males. We looked for tag questions, for instance, as in "It's hot in here, *isn't it?*," a construction often claimed to be used more by women than by men.

The home and day-care studies relied only on audiotapes, since we felt that taking a videocamera into subjects' dining rooms was too intrusive; the same held true in the day-care center. Since these studies have been reported in detail elsewhere, the major findings, along with their implications for the study of sex differences in language, will be reported here rather than the means and standard deviations associated with their statistical analyses. The interested reader is referred to Bellinger and Gleason, 1982; Gleason, 1973, 1975, 1980; Gleason and Greif, 1983; Gleason and Weintraub, 1976; and Masur and Gleason, 1980. These report on both the laboratory and home studies. It should be added here that the twenty-four families who participated in the laboratory study were also seen at home: A recording of a family dinner where both parents and the child were present was made in each family. Our current work centers on these dinner transcripts (Gleason, Perlmann, and Greif, 1984).

Differences in the speech of mothers and fathers to girls and boys

Home studies

Our first study was of several families at home. Like other researchers, we found that there were very few substantive differences in the speech of the mothers and fathers; but there were some notable exceptions. It should be noted here that in this first home study a male research assistant participated and remained with the family while the recording was made. This may have led to some exaggerated "macho" behavior on the part of the fathers. In our later home study, where we recorded the dinner interactions of our twenty-four families, we learned to leave a small cassette player with them, with the instruction to turn it on when they were about to have dinner. This much less intrusive method resulted in what seemed to be a more natural interaction.

In the first study (with the male assistant in attendance) we found that the syntactic measures of males and females were roughly equivalent. The only real syntactic difference was that the mean length of utterance of the fathers was less closely related to the child they were addressing than the mothers' MLU was to the child they were addressing. This seemed to reflect two things. The first is that the mothers appeared to be more "in tune" with their child than the fathers. Other evidence for this lies in the fact that in our study and others (see Stein, 1976) mothers were better able to understand what their child was saying than fathers were, and misunderstood less often than fathers did. The second thing that the disparity between father and mother MLU reflects is the fact that in the home sample fathers, especially when they talked to their sons, used many more imperatives than mothers did. Since an imperative lacks a subject (e.g., "Stop that"), the MLU is quite short. The fathers used many more direct imperatives than the mothers did, especially when talking to their sons, and so had disproportionately short MLUs when talking to boys. In one family, which had two children, the father had a longer MLU when talking with his 3-year-old daughter than with his 5-year-old son. Needless to say, he used many imperatives with his son.

In these home samples, the fathers produced approximately twice as many direct imperatives as the mothers – in fact, 38 percent of the fathers' utterances were in this form. Mothers were more likely to couch their imperative intentions in conventionalized polite forms (e.g., "Would you take your plate off the table, sweetie?"). It should be noted that this tendency to give orders is somewhat mitigated in the laboratory, where the differences in imperatives were slight, since, apparently, public behavior is a good deal more polite than private behavior at home.

The other major differences we found, which appear to be robust, were in choice of lexical items: Fathers used rarer vocabulary than mothers. Again, this finding has been replicated elsewhere, including in our own laboratory, where a father talking to his very young son referred, for instance, to a "construction site." The fathers at home also used a number of rather disparaging terms of address with their sons: One father called his son "dingaling"; another referred to his preschooler as "nutcake" and "Magoo." Again, we observed similar nomenclature in the laboratory, where one father called his son "wise guy." The fathers at home also had a tendency to threaten their sons, e.g., "Don't go in there again or I'll break your head." We did not see threats in the laboratory. Thus, rare lexemes, direct imperatives, threats, and rather pejorative names marked the fathers' speech at home. All of these features except the rare vocabulary were more likely to be found in speech to boys than to girls.

Unfortunately, these results have been neither replicated nor disconfirmed by others, since home studies are rare. Each of the features mentioned is a good candidate for emerging differences in the speech of boys and girls; but, with the exception of imperatives, which will be discussed shortly, these features have not been found (or sought) in the language of young children. If fathers serve as models for their sons, we would expect young boys, when compared with girls, to use more threats, more imperatives, more "funny" names. The research remains to be done, however, and if early sex differences of this type are found, they cannot all be attributed to the influence of parents, since children also find models among their peers and in society's stereotypical representation of the sexes.

Laboratory studies

A number of our own studies in the laboratory revealed sex differences in parents' speech, some of them also confirming earlier home findings. In addition to those already discussed, several might be mentioned here.

Lexical differences. In this study (Masur and Gleason, 1980) we looked at the speech of mothers and fathers to their children in the laboratory situation where they played with an automobile that could be disassembled. The auto, of course, is not a neutral toy; most observers would agree that it is male-oriented. In their conversations with their children in this situation there were several differences between mothers and fathers but few in the way boys and girls were addressed. Basically, the fathers were more likely than the mothers to provide the actual names of the car parts and to ask their children to produce them. The fathers were more cognitively demanding, expecting their children to display their knowledge by naming the car parts and tools and explaining their function. Thus, in this laboratory situation, fathers modeled different behavior from mothers while treating boys and girls in roughly equivalent fashion.

The mothers, rather than name the car parts or associated tools, said things like "That's the turn thing" rather than "wrench," and they frequently referred to nuts as bolts and vice versa. If children follow the models of their same-sex parent, we might expect to find among the emerging differences in children's language a greater specificity and demandingness among boys, at least when dealing with topics perceived as in their domain, such as sports and tools, and more lexical vagueness among girls, perhaps reflected in the use of more general vocabulary – more use of words like "thing" and "whatsis."

Politeness. In this study, we looked at politeness behavior in the laboratory situation described above, where the child was given a gift (Greif and Gleason, 1980). We did not find differences in the ways boys and girls were treated: Both sexes were encouraged (actually urged) to say thank you when given a gift and, to a lesser degree, to say "Hi" and "Good-bye" as well. There were large differences in the mothers' and fathers' own politeness behavior, however: The mothers were much more likely to say thank you to the assistant when their child was given a gift than the fathers were. There were also some differences in the children's own spontaneous behavior: Boys were more likely to say "Hi" than girls were. If parents provide models for their same-sex children, we would, therefore, expect to see in the emerging language of the little girls more conventional expressions of politeness than in the speech of boys. The greater percentage of greetings in the speech of boys is quite interesting, since it may reflect either less shyness on the part of boys, which itself may be related to sex-role expectations, or it may be more directly related to the fact that there is more emphasis on greeting behavior among males than among females in our society – adult males are obliged, for instance, to rise and offer their hands, whereas females have a great deal more latitude in what is permissible. It is impossible to discuss differential modeling of greeting behavior by parents, since virtually all of the parents said hello when the assistant said hello to them.

Interruptions. This study (Greif, 1980) examined the frequency of interruptions in the speech of parents and children across the three laboratory situations (playing store, reading a book, taking apart the toy auto). Greif looked at both simultaneous speech, where the speakers overlap, and outright interruptions, where one speaker wrests the floor from another. Here she found differences in the amount of interruption experienced by girls and boys, as well as differences in the number of interruptions produced by mothers and fathers. Fathers interrupted their children more than mothers did, and both fathers and mothers interrupted little girls more than they interrupted little boys. Children interrupted their parents less frequently than parents interrupted their children, despite a cultural belief that it is children who often interrupt. Given the large number of interruptions produced by parents, it seems likely that the cultural strictures against interruptions are more related to status considerations involving who may interrupt whom than to a belief that interrupting per se is unacceptable behavior. Interruptions are therefore another area where we might look for emerging sex differences in the language of girls and boys, but they might be expected to be found only in certain permissible contexts, as, for instance, among peers.

Directives. A competent speaker can produce many different surface structures in order to express a directive intent. We looked at the production of directives in the situation where parent and child were playing with the toy car (Bellinger and Gleason, 1982). Three forms of directives in particular were examined: direct imperatives, conventionalized polite imperatives that occur in question form, and implied indirect imperatives. Examples are:

Direct imperative: "Turn the bolt with the wrench."
Conventionalized polite imperative: "Could you turn the bolt with the wrench?"
Implied indirect imperative: "The wheel is going to fall off."

In this study we found that mothers were more likely to use the question forms and that fathers' speech had a higher proportion than mothers' speech of both the direct imperatives and the implied indirect forms. If children follow the model of their same-sex parent, we would expect little girls to use the polite question forms more and little boys to begin to use the direct imperatives and the implied forms more than the girls. As they get older, we would expect, for instance, that females would say, "Would you move your car, please?" to a person who has double-parked next to them, whereas males would be more likely to say, "Your car is blocking mine." Looking at the speech of the young children in our laboratory situation (for purposes of this study ten families were used, five with boys and five with girls), we found that by the age of 4 these young children were indeed producing the same forms of directives as their same-sex parent: Boys produced more direct imperatives and more implied forms than girls, and girls produced more polite question forms than boys.

Sex differences in the language of children

As this paper has tried to indicate, very little work has been done on the emergence of sex differences in the language of children. Yet we know that since men and women speak differently, those differences must begin to emerge at some point in time. The research cited here has described differences in parents' speech to children in the use of jocular names, threats, directives, complex vocabulary, politeness, and interruptions. For directives, we were able to show that preschoolers were already stylistically similar to their same-sex parent. Some researchers (e.g., Lakoff, 1973a) have suggested that all children speak "women's language" until the age of 5 or 6, but this is probably a reflection less of the facts than of our lack of sophisticated methods of analysis and good hypotheses about what to look for when seeking differences: Differences can be found in the speech of even very young children when we have precise features to investigate. This observation is provocative: Developmental psychologists representing various theoretical schools (Freudian, cognitive, social learning) have suggested that children do not have a firm sex-role identity until about the age of 5. Others (e.g., Money and Erhardt, 1972) have pointed out, however, that after the age of 18 months it is very difficult to reannounce the sex of a child if there has been an initial misidentification; that is, a child who was thought to be of one sex cannot after this point easily make the transition to the other sex, even when the chromosomes say it must be so. Perhaps one of the reasons for this is that the child has already begun to absorb sex-role related behaviors at some level. These may include specific linguistic features.

This chapter has attempted to suggest some areas for further research. More careful research on the language of parents and other adults is certainly in order, but it is also time to turn our attention to the emerging language of children in order to find the earliest evidences of linguistic sexual dimorphism.

In doing this research it will be important to examine children's language in a variety of contexts that allow us to separate out age, sex-role, and status considerations. Since, for instance, status factors militate against children's using imperatives with their parents and with older people, one area to look for these differences is in peer language. The speech children use when talking with one another is, of course, a separate register itself, and one that has hardly been studied. Some of the features of peer language must surely be learned from other children or other models: Male parents rarely make noises like dive-bombers or machine guns; yet these sound effects are common in the speech of young boys and not in that of young girls. By the same token, male and female teenagers undoubtedly use different features in their speech. Since communicative competence requires appropriate linguistic use even before adulthood, all of these populations are worth studying in order to understand the nature of sex differences in language. Transitory phenomena should be noted, along with those enduring features that ultimately mark as distinct the language of grown women and men.

8. Children's arguing

MARJORIE HARNESS GOODWIN
AND CHARLES GOODWIN

Whereas a great deal of research in sociolinguistics has been directed toward the investigation of politeness as an organizing feature of conversation (and, in particular, of women's conversations),[1] far less attention has been given to how people manage opposition, a type of talk that is generally evaluated negatively and viewed as disruptive.[2] The present study will present an ethnographically based description of how girls and boys carry out the activity of arguing.[3] When this activity is examined in detail, it is found that, rather than being disorderly, arguing provides children with a rich arena for the development of proficiency in language, syntax, and social organization. Moreover, in contrast to the prevalent stereotype that female interaction is organized with reference to politeness and a dispreference for dispute (Gilligan 1982:9–10; Lever 1976:482; Piaget 1965:77), we find that girls are not only just as skilled in argumentation as boys but have types of arguments that are both more extended and more complex in their participation structure than those among boys.

In this chapter we first provide some background information on the Maple Street group and fieldwork methods. Then we examine how everyday instances of conflict are conducted in cross-sex situations, paying close attention to the formulation of opposition moves. Finally we turn to a consideration of how more serious confrontations, in which one's reputation is at stake, are managed in girls' and boys' same-sex groups.[4] By looking at how children handle conflict in cross-sex as well as same-sex groups, we hope to avoid the problems of studies that exaggerate differences between females and males and that, in Thorne's (1986:168) words, "tend to abstract gender from social context, to assume males and females are qualitatively and permanently different."

200

The children and the methods used to study them

The children whose conversations are examined in this chapter are working-class black preadolescent girls and boys from Philadelphia, ages 4–14, whom I (Marjorie Harness Goodwin)[5] audiotaped for a year and a half as they went about their everday activities while playing on the street. The "Maple Street group," as the children will be referred to, includes forty-four friends living within a block's radius of one another who talk and play together after school, on weekends, and daily when school is not in session.

Fieldwork

As an anthropologist I was interested in documenting the ordinary activities of the people I was observing in their natural environment. Focusing on activities, rather than communities or groups, for the study of culture is congruent with Goodenough's analysis of the relationship between culture and activity. Goodenough (1981:102–103), noting that members of any society have not one culture but many, which become appropriate on different occasions, observes with concern that

... in practice, anthropologists have rarely considered simple clusters associated with one or only a few activities as the units with which to associate the phenomenon of culture. ... Culture has been so strongly associated with social groups and communities – as distinct from activities – in anthropological practice that one often reads about people as being "members of a culture," a truly nonsensical idea.

Analysis in this chapter will focus on the activity of arguing and seek, through qualitative analysis of its structure, to explicate the procedures used to construct it.

In order to disturb as little as possible the activities I was studying I attempted to minimize my interaction with the children while I was observing them. In this respect my role was quite different from that of other ethnographers of children (see for example Corsaro 1981) and, indeed, most anthropologists, in that I was more an observer of their activities than a participant in them. The phenomena that were being examined in my fieldwork, the ways in which the children used language, would have been especially sensitive to more intrusion on my part. As research in conversation analysis has demonstrated, talk, rather than being performed by an abstract, isolated speaker, emerges within particular speaker–hearer relationships and indeed can be modified by interaction between speaker and recipient even as the talk is emerging (C. Goodwin 1981; Schegloff 1972). If I had acted as a principal recipient of the children's talk I would necessarily have influenced that talk. In brief, I was interested more in how the children interacted with one another than in how they interacted with an adult ethnographer. For similar reasons I chose to ask as few questions as possible.

My actual methods of working consisted of traveling with the children as they went about their activities, a Sony TC110 cassette recorder with an internal microphone over my shoulder. The children knew they were being recorded. I did not use a movie or video camera because of its intrusiveness. I recognize, however, that visual phenomena are an important part of the organization of face-to-face interaction, and in other work (for example, C. Goodwin 1981 and M. Goodwin 1980c) we have studied them intensively.

Data and transcription

This study draws on a collection of more than five hundred argumentative exchanges; however, only a few representative argument fragments are included in this chapter. Texts of actual instances of the phenomenon we are discussing are provided so that others may inspect the records that form the basis for my analysis.

Data are transcribed according to the system developed by Jefferson and described in Sacks, Schegloff, and Jefferson (1974:731–733). The following are the features most relevant to the present analysis:[6]

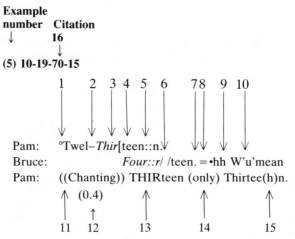

1. Low volume: The degrees sign indicates that the talk following is low in volume.

2. Cutoff: A dash marks a sudden cutoff of the current sound. Here, instead of bringing the word "twelve" to completion, Pam interrupts it in midcourse.

3. Italics: Italics indicate some form of emphasis, which may be signaled by changes in pitch and/or amplitude.

4. Overlap bracket: A left bracket marks the point at which the current talk is overlapped by other talk. Thus Bruce's "*Four*teen" begins during the last syllable of Pam's "*Thir*teen." Two speakers beginning to speak simultaneously are shown by two left brackets at the beginning of a line.

5. Lengthening: Colons indicate that the sound just before the colon has been noticeably lengthened.

6. Overlap slashes: Double slashes provide an alternative method of marking overlap. When they are used, the overlapping talk is not indented to the point of overlap. Here Pam's last line begins just after the "*Four*" in Bruce's "*Four*teen."

7. Intonation: Punctuation symbols are used to mark intonation changes rather than as grammatical symbols:
   –A period indicates a falling contour.
   –A question mark indicates a rising contour.
   –A comma indicates a falling–rising contour.

8. Latching: The equal sign indicates "latching"; there is no interval between the end of a prior and the start of a next segment of talk.

9. Inbreath: A series of *h*'s preceded by a dot marks an inbreath. Without the dot the *h*'s mark an outbreath.

10. Rapid speech: Apostrophes between words indicate slurred, rapid speech.

11. Comments: Double parentheses enclose material that is not part of the talk being transcribed, for example a comment by the transcriber if the talk was spoken in some special way.

12. Silence: Numbers in parentheses mark silences in seconds and tenths of seconds.

13. Increased volume: Capitals indicate increased volume.

14. Problematic hearing: Material in parentheses indicates a hearing that the transcriber was uncertain about.

15. Breathiness; laughter: An *h* in parentheses indicates plosive aspiration, which could result from events such as breathiness, laughter, or crying.

16. Citation: Each example is preceded by a citation that locates the tape and transcript where the original data can be found.

Subgroups and their play preferences

The children divided themselves into four separate clusters with members of each cluster interacting more with each other than with outsiders.

The clusters were differentiated from each other by the age and sex of the participants in each:[7]

Younger girls	Ages 4–9	5 children
Younger boys	Ages 5–6	3 children
Older girls	Ages 10–13	15 children
Older boys	Ages 9–14	21 children

Children 14 and older generally interacted in couples, and not necessarily with friends from the neighborhood; companions were chosen because they had similar interests rather than because they lived nearby. In this chapter we shall primarily be investigating conversation of children aged 9–14.

There were marked differences in the play preferences of older girls and older boys. The activities of the older boys included flying kites, yo-yoing, walking on hands, playing coolie and dead blocks, playing football and basketball, pitching pennies, playing halfball, making and riding homemade go-carts, flying model airplanes, shooting marbles, practicing dance steps, and playing musical instruments in a small group. The older girls seldom engaged in organized sports activities or indeed played games of any kind. Instead they liked to jump rope, play house and school, practice original dance steps, organize club meetings, and make things such as crocheted and knitted scarfs and hats, glass rings from bottle rims, and food, such as cake, pizza, and water ice, to sell. Older boys and girls on occasion would participate in similar activities, playing cards, house, or school, skating, riding bikes, yo-yoing, or jumping rope.

Most of children's activities took place outside their homes. Except for special activities such as practicing dance steps to music, playing instruments, or having a club meeting, the inside of the house was generally designated off limits by parents. With the exception of jump rope, many of the girls' activities took place on the shaded steps of their row houses, where boys often played as well. From this location they were in range of most of the boys' activities, which were characteristically conducted on the sidewalk and street. Only on occasion did boys make use of backyards (as an area for making such things as go-carts or slingshots) or parks (for flying kites, sledding, and conducting acorn or slingshot fights). Given the preferences for playing near one's house as well as girls' and younger children's obligations not to wander too far from home, girls and boys were frequently in one another's presence and had ample occasion to talk with one another. The relationships of girls and boys in the Maple Street group were characterized by a type of "arrangement between the sexes" (Goffman 1977) that involved an alternation between joining with and separating from each other for various activities.[8]

Argument structures used by both girls and boys

We begin by investigating some of the basic structures and procedures used by the children to construct argument. Two phenomena will be focused on: (1) the construction of opposition and (2) format tying, ways in which return moves tie to the detailed structure of the talk that they are opposing. Though there are some differences in the ways in which girls and boys organize their arguing (to be discussed in a later section), the features they use in common are far more pervasive. Were one to focus just on points where girls and boys differ, the activity itself would be obscured. Although we shall not focus on gender per se in analyzing this activity, the reader will observe in many of the data to follow that girls not only use the same structures as boys but frequently emerge as the victors in their disputes with boys.

Opposition moves

Displaying deference to others present is implicated in the organization of a range of behavior that occurs in human interaction (Goffman 1967:47–95, 1971). This is accomplished in part through watchful concern that potential discord not emerge as an explicit event in encounters. Looking at talk from such a perspective has provided a focus for much research on the pragmatic organization of language, with extensive investigation being made of such phenomena as how disagreements between participants might be stated while preserving the face of each. For example, Brown and Levinson have studied how a speaker in conversation avoids the extreme of acting "baldly without redress" (1978:74) and assumes an orientation toward both positive and negative politeness. Such an orientation characterizes a range of speech actions, including the "hedged request" reported for American English-speakers by Lakoff (1973a:56 – "Won't you please close the door?") and Labov and Fanshel (1977:85 – "This room is going to be dusted, isn't it?"), and for Tzeltal by Brown (1980:120 – "You don't, perhaps, have any chickens, it is said").

The opposition moves of Maple Street children are built in ways that contrast with actions designed to display deference to the other. The children frequently seek opportunities to test or realign the current arrangement of social identities among their peers (M. H. Goodwin 1980b, 1982a, 1982b); opposition provides an effective way to accomplish this.[9] When the actions of another can be construed as a violation, the offended party can take action to remedy such an affront, an event that provides the opportunity to display character. Thus, instead of attesting to "the actor's current willingness to accept the status quo" (Goffman 1967:254), the children create miniature versions of what Goffman (pp. 237–258) has termed "character contests" – "moments of action [during which] the individual has the risk and opportunity of displaying to himself and sometimes to others his style of conduct" (p. 237). In brief, rather than organizing their talk so as to display deference to others, the children frequently seek opportunities to display character and realign the social organization of the moment through opposition.

In order to highlight as clearly as possible the structures used to build opposition it is useful to compare the organization of opposition turns with that of talk that displays a preference for agreement. In her work on agreement and disagreement in assessment sequences Pomerantz (1984:64) distinguishes a *preferred-action turn shape*, which maximizes the salience of actions performed with it, from a *dispreferred-action turn shape*, which minimizes the action performed with it. In the data she examined, disagreement was a dispreferred activity and its occurrence was minimized through use of phenomena such as delays before the production of a disagreement and prefaces that mitigated the disagreement. Indeed, these prefaces sometimes took the form of agreements that were followed by the disagreement.[10] The following provide examples:

(1) SBL:L:03

A: She doesn't uh usually come in on Friday, does she.
B: Well, yes she does, sometimes,

(2) G.26(T)7:30

```
1   John:  You could live in thih– in this area.
2          I belie:ve you c'd really live in this
3          area inna tent.
4              (0.7)
5   John:  Y'know?
6   Don:   I think you'd if– if– if (you did it
7          you'd be) ro(h)bbed,
```

The disagreement in (1) is mitigated by both the hesitant "Well" that precedes it and the qualifier "sometimes" that follows it. In (2) the statement being disagreed with is followed by a long pause (line 4), and the explicit disagreement occurs only when initial speaker in line 5 explicitly requests a response. The disagreement that is at last produced is further modulated by being prefaced by a hedge ("I think"). In these examples, though disagreement occurs, it is organized as a dispreferred activity through use of phenomena such as delays in its occurrence and prefaces that mitigate the disagreement when it at last emerges.

By way of contrast, when the Maple Street children oppose one another they organize their talk so as to highlight that opposition. For example, rather than being preceded by delays, turns containing opposition are produced immediately. Moreover, such turns frequently contain a preface that announces right at the beginning of the turn, characteristically in the first word said, that opposition is being done.

(3) 9–25–70–13
Chopper: Get outa here you wench! You better get outa here.
Pam: No! You don't tell *me* to get out!

(4) 10–24–8–20
   ((talking about Sharon's hair))
Eddie: Wet it!
Sharon: No. I don't *w*anna wet it.

(5) 8–28–70–3
Earl: ((asking for rubber bands)) Just *two*.
Darlene: No! Y'all losin all my rubber bands up.

(6) 10–21–70–3
Eddie: ((singing)) You didn't have to go to school today did you.
Terri: Yes we *did* have to go to school today!

In these data opposition is signaled immediately through the expression of polarity (Halliday and Hasan 1976:178) that is used to initiate the turn.[11] The shape of these disagreements is such that they do not delay or disguise the alignment a participant is taking up with respect to a prior move but instead emphasize opposition.

A second type of preface used to begin opposition turns consists of repetition of part of the talk that is being opposed:

(7) 8–2–71–4
   ((on reaching a city creek))
Pam: Y'all gonna walk in it?
Nettie: *W*alk in it, You know where that water come from? The toilet.

(8) 8–2–71–28
   ((The girls are trying to trick the boys into believing that they have found some frogs.))
Pam: We found a frog.
Chopper: A *frog*, y'all did not.

Partial repetition of prior talk occurs in a variety of conversational activities including disagreements with prior speakers' self-deprecations (Pomerantz 1984:83–84) and other-initiated repair (Schegloff, Jefferson, and Sacks 1977). In these activities, as well as in opposition, the partial repetition is used to locate a trouble source in another's talk. But the partial repetitions that occur at the beginning of opposition moves differ from the repetitions in some other activities in several important respects. In other-initiated repair the discovery of error is characteristically modulated through use of markers of uncertainty, for example pronouncing the partial repetition with rising intonation. Moveover, locating the trouble source is frequently the only activity performed in the turn. For example:

(9) GTS1:II:2:54

A: 'E likes that waider over there,	A: Trouble source
→ B: Wait-*er*?	B: Find trouble
A: Waitress, sorry.	A: Provide remedy

In these data the activities of locating the trouble and providing a remedy are separated into distinct turns performed by different individuals. Although B points to something problematic in A's talk, A is allowed to do the correction himself. By restricting the activity in his or her turn to locating the error, B proposes that the party who made the error has the competence to remedy it, and provides him or her with an opportunity to do so (see Schegloff, Jefferson, and Sacks 1977 for further analysis of this process).

By way of contrast in aggravated opposition, such as that performed by the Maple Street children, the partial repeat does not characteristically stand alone, but instead is immediately followed by further talk that explicitly opposes what prior speaker said.[12] If subsequent speaker's opposition proposes that prior speaker has made an error of some type (e.g. Ex. 7) that party is not portrayed as having the competence to remedy the error himself or herself; and, since speaker moves on to oppose prior speaker immediately after the initial challenging, he or she is not given an opportunity to modify or correct the statement being opposed.[13] As these examples make clear, actions of this type are used by both boys and girls.

A second way in which opposition prefaces differ from other-initiated repair is in terms of the intonation pattern used. Rather than modulating the discovery of a trouble source with a tentative, rising intonation, opposers use distinctive contours that not only focus attention on the trouble as trouble, but also call into question the competence of the party who produced such an object. The partial repeats in Exx. 7 and 8 are spoken with falling–rising contours (Gunter 1974:61), a pattern that Ladd (1978:150) notes may be used to "do something like a holistic 'contradiction' or questioning of speaker A's assumptions." Challenge can also be conveyed by affiliating "who" or "what" with a partial repeat produced with falling intonation (as in Exx. 10 and 11) or the words "what" or "huh" produced with emphatic rising intonation (as in Exx. 12 and 13).

(10) 10–12–70–12

Juju: Terri go and get your pick.
Terri: *Wha*t pick. I'm not goin in the house now.

(11) 9–2–70–7

Sharon: When it snows outside where y'all have gym at.
Eddie: In the basement.
Vince: *Wha*t basement. *No* we ain't.

(12) 9–28–70–40

           ((discussing bottles for making rings))
Poochie: Can't use this kind.
Terri: *What?* We already– sh– Candy show him them things.

(13) 11–11–70–7

           ((discussing a foster child))
Eddie: Her mother didn't want her.
Pam: Huh? She said cuz her sister ran away and she ain't have nobody
           to take care of her while she go to work so,

Rather than simply disagreeing with something in prior talk, the aggravated character of the intonation used in opposition prefaces actively challenges what has just been said.

In brief, both the intonation structure of opposition prefaces and the sequential organization of the turns begun by such prefaces (e.g. the way in which opposer does not provide a space for prior speaker to deal with the trouble source located by the preface) treat prior speaker as someone who is not only wrong but unable or unwilling to modify the talk being objected to on his or her own. Looking at such phenomena from a slightly different perspective, we can see that in such opposition what is being called into question is not simply the trouble source in the prior talk but the competence or status of the party who produced that talk. In essence what is being opposed is not simply a position but also an actor responsible for stating such a position. In view of this it is not surprising that another phenomenon found quite frequently in opposition turns is an explicit characterization of the person who produced the talk being opposed. For example:

(14) 10–19–70–110

           ((Boys are discussing slings they are making for a slingshot fight.))
Tokay: All right we *got* enough *al*ready.

→ Michael: No– man! *You* must be *crazy*. (0.8) *M*ust be. (0.6) Talkin about I got e*nough*. = Boy. You must– I *know* you have never played *now*. Thinkin I got e*nough*. (0.8) Ma:n you need three *thous*and to have e*nough*. (1.8) I *al*ways like to have– I *al*ways like to have more than my enemy has. Cuz if *I* don't have more than my enemy ma:n *I* is *doom*ed.

(15) 10–19–70–119

                ((Discussing slings))
Chopper: I don't want these big thick ones.
→ Michael: You is crazy boy. I swear to god. You need that– thick like that. Cuz that hurts people.

In both of these examples the party who produced the talk being opposed is characterized as "crazy" for having said what he said. In Ex. 14 this is elaborated to include the judgment that a party who would produce such talk must be unfamiliar with the activity being talked about ("I *know* you have never played *now*"). Opposition can thus call into question not only what has been said, but also the general competence of someone who would produce such talk. Moreover such an action provides the opportunity for a reciprocal display of opposer's expertise. Thus the talk does not simply portray its recipient as defective but rather invokes a particular relationship between speaker and addressee that categorizes each of these participants in an alternative way. Data such as these emphasize the fact that in analyzing opposition it is not sufficient to focus exclusively on the talk through which opposition is done; one must also take into account how actors are portrayed and constituted through that talk.

Looking at opposition from such a perspective sheds light on another frequent component of opposition turns: pejorative person descriptions and insult terms. Such objects provide resources that are used quite frequently to build a turn that not only opposes prior talk but also explicitly characterizes the person who produced that talk. For example:

(16) 9–23–70–9

Michael: Me and Huey saw– we saw um: the Witch and the Hangman.
Huey: The *H*angman and the *W*itch knucklehead.

(17) 9–15–70–11

Sharon: It's something like Johnny bike. It's
                hot hot– // (   )
Terri: Johnny's bike is *or*ange you egg.

(18) 10–19–70–58

Huey: *Gi*mme the *things*.
Chopper: You sh:ut up you big lips.

Data such as these demonstrate how a single opposition turn can contain a variety of components that attend to and operate on differential phenomena (e.g. one component of the turn might deal with something said in prior talk and another address the character of the person who produced that talk). The multiplicity of action within individual turns raises questions about the common practice of analyzing argument by glossing a turn as an instance of a particular kind of speech act.

As the data just examined demonstrate, opposition can be signaled at many places within a turn. One of the most common ways of displaying opposition in the midst of a turn is through use of what Halliday and Hasan (1976:146) call "substitution," or "the replacement of one item in a sentence with another having a similar structural function." For example:

(19) 10–10–70–144

Chopper: Get your four guys.
Michael: You get *three* guys.

(20) 11–2–71–7

Deniecey: An that happend *last* year.
Terri: That happened *this* year.

(21) 9–25–70–5

Michael: How'd you lost those two games.
Chopper: *One* game.

(22) 10–26–70–2

Robby: You got on a blouse too. I can see the
sleeves.
Terri: I got a *sweat*er on dear heart.

As is the case with the talk following an aggravated preface, opposition done through substitution does not provide the party being opposed a place to remedy the trouble source on his or her own. For example if Terri in Ex. 22 had wanted to do her correction as other-initiated repair rather than as opposition, a turn consisting only of "Blouse?" could have been produced. Such a turn would have provided Robby an opportunity to attempt a remedy on his own.

When the substitution format is used to do opposition, a number of phenomena are used to heighten the salience of the term being offered as a correction. First, the utterance containing the correction characteristically repeats some of the prior talk, with the exception of the item being replaced. Such repetition of another's talk frames the item being corrected and helps to emphasize that what is being done is a correction of something he or she said. Second, the replacement term is typically spoken with heightened emphasis, giving it "contrastive stress" (Ladd 1978:78).[14] Such a way of signaling a correction differs from that found by Yaeger-Dror (1974, in press) for talk among adults in which a preference for agreement was operative. In her data nonsalient intonation was used in expressions of disagreement.[15]

We shall now briefly investigate how the components of opposition turns can engender more extended disputes. To examine this process it is useful to distinguish two types of opposition moves.

1. Disagreement (Ex. 23) or refusal to perform some requested action (Ex. 24):

(23) 10–13–70–13

Raymond: Boy you broke my skate board.
Earl: No I *di*dn't.
Raymond: Did *too*.
Earl: Did *not*.
Raymond: Did *too*.

(24) 10–24–70–20

           ((discussing Sharon's hair))
Eddie: Wet it.
Sharon: No I don't *w*anna wet it.

2. Return and exchange moves (Pomerantz 1975:26), in which a move equivalent to the one being opposed is returned:

(25) 9–23–70–6

Sheridan: You cheat.
Chopper: *You* cheat.

Although both types of action can occur in a single opposition sequence, these procedures are alternative to each other in that they provide for quite distinctive types of sequencing. Disagreement and correction sequences involve the assertion (and reassertion) of positions. Such assertions can be buttressed by accounts that have sequential consequences of their own. Exchange and return sequences, by contrast, are constructed not out of moves that assert the validity or invalidity of a position but, rather, from actions that return a reciprocal action. Note that even though the words may be the same (as in Ex. 25), the action is a reciprocal one, not an identical one, since features of it, such as who is referred to by the pronouns in it, change as the participation framework changes. What is preserved is the relationship of action, current speaker, and current recipient.[16]

The most common way of sustaining contradiction is through "recycling." Each of two opposing parties repeats a prior position with the effect that an extended series of disagreements is produced (see M. H. Goodwin 1983:672–675).[17] For example in the following Sharon and Pam playfully object to Johnny's version of his age, 14, and recycle their version of his age, 13, through several turns.

(26) 9–28–70–18

((Johnny, age 12, going on 13, is discussing his upcoming birthday.))

1 Johnny: Till I be fourteen,
2 Sharon: How old are you? Thirteen?
3 Johnny: *Fourteen.*
4 Sharon: *Thir//teen.*
5 Johnny: *Four//teen.*
6 Pam: *Thir*teen.
7 Johnny: *Four*teen.
8 Pam: *Thir//teen.*
9 Sharon: *Thir*teen.
10 Johnny: *Four//teen.*
11 Sharon: *Thir*teen.
12 Pam: Thirte(hh)n. heh.
13 Johnny: I'll be thirteen next week.

Only after Pam embeds laughter in her talk, shifting its framing, does the argument reach closure. In line 13 Johnny concedes.

Participants may, alternatively, attempt to effect closure in a dispute by justifying their point of view through an account or explanation of the position taken up.[18] Some research has postulated that a justification "is significantly more likely to lead to a termination of the episode" (Eisenberg and Garvey 1981:166). However, in the following the accounts themselves engender extended dispute. With the introduction of a justification for a position, the focus of the argument shifts to the new account. In this example accounts are indicated in the left-hand column by #.[19]

(27) 10–7–70–5

((While children skate Raymond bumps into Terri.))

1	Terri:	Get off Raymond. Get off!
2	Sharon:	Now Terri just aim at Raymond butt and
3		let's see if we could knock him down.
4	Terri:	Oh yeah you– you be // you better
5	Raymond:	Y'all better *not* knock me *down*!=
6	Terri:	Yeah?
# 7	Sharon:	If we do that's what we // playin.
# 8	Terri:	Play and you gonna get knock down.
9	Raymond:	Nuh *uh*:!
10	Terri:	Mm *hm*!
# 11	Raymond:	Nuh *uh* y'all. I ain't playin.
12	Terri:	Yes you *are* playin.
13	Raymond:	I can't af//ford
# 14	Terri:	If you– if you put a skate on you
15		playin.
16	Raymond:	*No* it ain't.
17	Terri:	*Yes* it is.
18	Raymond:	I ain't playin // nuttin!
19	Terri:	Is you playin Sharon,

```
    20  Raymond:  Nope!
    21  Terri:    Huh // aren't we playin Sharon,
#   22  Sharon:   If you–
    23            if you put that skate on // you are.
#   24  Terri:    Yeap. If you put the skate on you
    25            playin.
    26                  (2.2)
    27  Terri:    Pam! If they
    28            p//ut a skate on // aren't they playin,
    29  Raymond:  This her skate.
    30  Sharon:   You want this?
    31  Terri:    If they put a skate on?
    32                  (1.4)
    33  Terri:    All except Earl.
```

This argument is composed of two sequences in which recycling of positions (similar to Ex. 26 above) and arguments about accounts occur. In this interaction Sharon and Terri treat Raymond's bumping into them while skating as an offense, as demonstrated by their command for him to "get off" (line 1). In response they propose a reciprocal action, knocking him down (lines 2–3), which Raymond first objects to in line 5: "Y'all better *not* knock me *down!*" In lines 7 and 8 Sharon and Terri legitimate their proposed course of action – knocking Raymond down – by stating that such actions are appropriate within the context of the activity: "If we do that's what we playin." "Play and you gonna get knock down."

The first recycling of positions follows this first justification:

(27) 10–7–70–5

```
#    7  Sharon:   If we do that's what we // playin.
#    8  Terri:    Play and you gonna get knock down.
     9  Raymond:  Nuh uh:!
    10  Terri:    Mm hm!
#   11  Raymond:  Nuh uh y'all. I ain't playin.
```

Raymond's justification for his position of disagreement, "I ain't playin," becomes the lead-in to a new series of recyclings of positions.

(27) 10–7–70–5

```
#   11  Raymond:  Nuh uh y'all. I ain't playin.
    12  Terri:    Yes you are playin.
    13  Raymond:  I can't af//ford
#   14  Terri:    If you– if you put a skate on you
    15            playin.
    16  Raymond:  No it ain't.
    17  Terri:    Yes it is.
    18  Raymond:  I ain't playin // nuttin!
    19  Terri:    Is you playin Sharon,
    20  Raymond:  Nope!
```

```
21   Terri:      Huh // aren't we playin Sharon,
# 22  Sharon:    If you–
23              if you put that skate on // you are.
```

The dispute is eventually dissipated following a display of Terri and Sharon's alignment with a single position. Sharon in lines 22–3 explicitly agrees with Terri's question in line 21. The account that a position is shared by two people is a move children offer in their attempts to assert their positions. In line 29 Raymond begins a nonargumentative move.

In this section we have investigated a number of different procedures for carrying out disputes and examined both how opposition is accomplished and how more extensive argument sequences are constructed. As these examples have shown, boys and girls have access to similar types of ways of disputing. These data are thus important with regard to the relationship of language and gender. Researchers investigating black language and culture have repeatedly argued (e.g. Abrahams 1970, 1975, 1976; Abrahams and Bauman 1971; Hannerz 1969:129–130; Kochman 1970, 1981; Reisman 1970, 1974) that such character contests are peculiar to Afro-American males. But as studies of everyday arguments among black and white families (Vuchinich 1984) and in white middle-class Anglo-American children's groups (Brenneis and Lein 1977; Cook-Gumperz 1981; Corsaro and Rizzo 1985; Eisenberg and Garvey 1981; Genishi and Di Paolo 1982; Hughes 1983; Maynard 1985a, 1985b), as well as among Italian (Corsaro and Rizzo 1985) and part-Hawaiian (Boggs 1978), children and children in a multinational suburban American school setting (Adger 1984), have shown, contest frameworks for interaction occur among other groups as well. Moreover, as both previous research (M. H. Goodwin 1980b, 1985b; Hughes 1983) and this chapter demonstrate, the opportunity to create and display character within oppositional interaction is not confined to males, but is quite important for females as well. Indeed, some of the interactive frameworks available to females for doing this, the "he-said-she-said," for example (to be examined below), are both more extended and more elaborate than anything yet reported for males.

Format tying

Much of the work on discourse and pragmatics has made a distinction between the surface structure of the utterance (that is, the actual words spoken) and the actions embodied by the utterance (that is, the actual words spoken) and the actions embodied by the utterance (that is, its illocutionary force), and has argued that sequencing between utterances occurs on the level of action. For example, Labov and Fanshel

(1977:25)[20] state; "Sequencing rules do not appear to be related to words, sentences, and other linguistic forms, but rather form the connections between abstract actions such as requests, compliments, challenges, and defenses." One effect of such a position is that sequential and discourse phenomena, such as speech acts, are treated as distinct and separable from the phonological, syntactic, and semantic phenomena traditionally analyzed by linguists. There is, however, evidence that approaching sequencing entirely from the perspective of larger speech acts misses much of the work participants in conversation are doing. Thus the work of Sacks (1967) on tying techniques has demonstrated that much of the connectedness between separate turns is achieved through systematic syntactic operations. Such a perspective sheds important light on a range of phenomena central to the use of language in argument sequences.

In producing a subsequent argumentative move, participants frequently tie not only to the type of action produced by last speaker but also to the particulars of its wording.[21] Consider the following:

(28) 10–24–70–20

((Eddie, who has been teasing Sharon about her hair, has just laughed.))

Sharon: I don't know what you *l*aughin at.
Eddie: I know what I'm laughin at.
        Your *h*ead.

If all that were at issue in this sequence were an exchange of information, the second line of Eddie's turn by itself could constitute a complete reply to Sharon: "Your head" tells Sharon what is being laughed at. Eddie, however, precedes this component of his turn with another longer sentence that semantically seems to state the obvious – that he knows what he is laughing at. If this sentence is not providing relevant information, what is it doing? When we look at it in relationship to Sharon's talk we find that it is not only closely tied to the particulars of what she just said, repeating many of the exact words that she used,[22] but that it in fact constitutes a systematic transformation of her sentence. The skeleton of her structure is retained, but Sharon's "you laughin" is changed to "I'm laughin" and the negation in her sentence is deleted.[23] These are precisely the minimum and adequate changes necessary to transform her talk into a reply to that very talk. In an almost literal sense Sharon's own words are used against her. To focus analysis of this sentence on its information content, the presuppositions it embodies, or the speech act it makes visible would be quite misleading. This sentence constitutes an adequate reply to what has just been said by virtue of the way in which it reuses the materials provided by that talk to shape a counter to it.[24]

Some demonstration of how important such format tying is to the organization of the talk that is occurring here is provided by what happens next:

(29) 10–24–70–20

		((Eddie has been teasing Sharon about her hair.))
1	Eddie:	heh heh!
2	Sharon:	I don't know what you *l*aughin at.
3	Eddie:	I know what I'm laughin at.
4		Your *h*ead.
5	Sharon:	I know I'm laughin at your head too.
6	Eddie:	I know you ain't laughin cuz you ain't
7		laughin.
8	Sharon:	((mirthless laughter)) Ha ha.
9	Eddie	Ha ha. I got more hair than *you*.
10	Sharon:	You do not. Why you gotta laugh. You
11		*know* you ain't got more hair than me.
12	Eddie:	((taking out shoestrings)) Fifty-four
13		inches.

The talk examined earlier is found in lines 2–4. In line 5 ("I know I'm laughin at *your* head too") the "I know I'm laughin at" framework provides a point of departure for yet another return, this time from Sharon to Eddie. In line 6 it is used again, and indeed, the same types of transformations that were applied to line 2 to produce line 3 – changing pronoun structure to keep action constant over shift of participants and adding or deleting negation – are used on line 5 to build line 6. Although speakership changes, the underlying pattern used to construct the utterance of the moment is preserved.

Conceptualizing what happens here as a sequence of abstract actions obscures the way in which the participants, in an almost musical way, are exploring one after another the possible variations provided by the detailed structure of the utterances they are producing. The surface structure of the talk in these data is anything but superficial in terms of its power to provide organization for the sequencing of the exchange.

In line 8 the particular pattern that we have been examining is abandoned when Sharon shifts from talking about laughter to laughter itself. However, in line 9 the practice of building a return action from the materials just provided by the other party continues as Eddie uses laughter to begin his reply to her laughter. In line 10 Sharon challenges what Eddie has just said, and in line 12, rather than dispute with her, Eddie shifts to a different topic.

Format tying can occur in many different ways. The following provides an example of one of the simplest, that is, exact repetition of what the other has said:

(30) 10–21–70–1

((Cameron is sitting on Terri's top step as Joey approaches him from the street.

The initial talk refers to an incident in which Cameron was reported to have cried because he lost a key.))

```
1   Joey:      He– he was gettin ready to cry.
2   Cameron:   But that wasn't mine.
3                  (1.0)
4   Cameron:   Mole!
5                  (1.0)
6   Joey:      Mole.
7                  (0.3)
8   Cameron:   Ah shud up.
9                  (0.4)
10  Joey:      Ah shud up.
11  Cameron:   Make me.
12                 (0.3)
13  Joey:      Make me!
14                 (0.4)
15  Cameron:   Why donchu make me.
```

In lines 6, 10, and 13 Joey constructs a counter to Cameron by using the exact words Cameron himself has just used.[25] But although the surface structure of the original and that of the repeat are identical, the meanings are not; the change in discourse structure produced by the change in speakers requires a new interpretation of each utterance. Thus "me" in line 11 refers to Cameron but in line 13 to Joey, and in all cases agent and recipient of action are changed. By holding the linguistic form constant Cameron is able to highlight changes in interactive organization by reversing the participation framework created by Joey's prior utterance.

In line 15 a more complex type of format tying occurs. Rather than simply repeat what Joey has said, Cameron, by prefacing Joey's "*Make me*" with "Why donchu" (and stressing "*me*"), creates a new sentence that includes Joey's prior talk as an embedded component within it[26] and reverses the agent of the proposed action.

Embedding such as this is, in fact, one of the prototypical ways of taking the words of the other and using them against him or her in a reciprocal action. Consider the following in which Chopper transforms Huey's command into a challenge. This is achieved by reusing the structure of the prior utterance and adding the words "make me" (while dropping the possessive reference to the yard that the children are in). Huey's sentence is now embedded within a new sentence of Chopper's:

(31) 10–20–70–59

Huey: Why don't you get out my yard.
Chopper: Why don't you *m*ake me get out the yard.

Huey's request that Chopper leave is thus transformed into a challenge to Huey to enforce such an action.

As Ex. 29 demonstrated, transformations of prior speaker's talk can occur by the deletion of elements of a prior utterance as well as by the embedding of such talk within a new action. Consider the following:

(32) 10–19–70–58

Chopper: Don't gimme that. I'm not *t*alkin ta y:ou.
Huey: I'm talkin ta *y*:ou!

Here, rather than embed prior talk in a new sentence, Huey constructs a return to Chopper by deleting the negation in Chopper's sentence.

The format tying and embedding that occur in Ex. 31 and 32, rather than operating on a "linguistic" level that is distinct from the "discourse" level of speech acts, are intrinsic components of the way in which the actions produced in these examples are constructed to be the things that they are. Whereas it is possible to escalate an argument with a subsequent action whose structure is unrelated to that of the action being dealt with, the utterances of Ex. 30 and 31 display their status as escalations[27] of prior actions, and challenges to the producers of those actions, by making use of the talk of prior speaker and transforming it to their advantage; in essence they turn the prior action on its head. Indeed, there is a nice fit between the social activity of escalating a sequence and challenging a prior move and the syntactic structure of these utterances, in which the prior move becomes an embedded sub-component of the sentence used to answer it. Looking at these data from a slightly different perspective it can be noted that by performing such embedding the children are openly making use of, and creatively playing with, the syntactic resources provided by their language as they transform prior sentences into new sentences appropriate to their current projects.

Huey's talk in Ex. 32 consists of almost the same words as Chopper's (with the exception of the negation). It is not, however, a repetition of what Chopper has just said. First, as was noted in Ex. 30, both pronoun reference and participation framework change when the party producing the talk changes. Second, in reusing the words provided by prior speaker subsequent speaker can substantially modify what is being done with those words by the way in which he or she speaks them.[28] For example, in these data the emphasis in Chopper's sentence falls on the action that is the topic of the sentence, "*t*alkin," whereas in Huey's version the emphasis is shifted to the recipient of that action, "*y*:ou!" The focus and import of the sentence are thus modified by the way in which it is spoken.

The following provides a more vivid example of how the way in which something is spoken can substantially change what is being done with those words:

(6) 10–21–70–3

Eddie: ((singing)) You didn't have to go to school today did you.
Terri: Yes we *did* have to go to school today!

Terri's utterance maintains a structure parallel to that of Eddie's with two major exceptions: (1) the word "Yes" at the beginning of her talk, which, through its display of polarity, constitutes an opposition preface, and (2) the replacement of Eddie's "didn't" with "did," which is spoken with contrastive stress (Ladd 1978:77).[29] Both the contrast replacement and the opposition preface enable Terri to modify substantially the import and focus of the talk she is reusing, that is, to turn it into a challenge of what that talk originally proposed. But the changes she is able to accomplish through her pronunciation of the talk go beyond this. Eddie's statement, with its singsong intonation, could have been interpreted as a bid for an alliance with its recipient against the school establishment. Instead of participating in the proposed alliance, Terri focuses on Eddie's error in having said what he did. Through the way in which she speaks, Terri is able to display indignation, something that contrasts quite strongly with the playfulness that was found when Eddie spoke these words. In essence, Terri not only changes the semantic meaning of the prior utterance but also the affect it had conveyed.

Looking at the change from "didn't" to "*did*" from a slightly different perspective, we can see that such replacement in fact constitutes an instance of contrast-class replacement or substitution. Since the use of substitution in the construction of counters has already been examined, it will not be looked at in detail here, except to note that it is common in format tying. Indeed, the repetition of structure provided by format tying frames the substitution so that it becomes highlighted as a noticeable event. Format tying and substitution thus work hand in hand, the similarity of structure between two utterances provided by format tying making the relevant difference in the second utterance, the substituted term, stand out with particular salience.[30]

In addition to operating on the semantic, syntactic, and propositional structure of a prior utterance, the children may also play with its phonological structure. Consider lines 14–15 of the following:

(33) 6–3–71–2

((Nettie is sitting on top of Pam.))
1   Pam: Get off!

2	Nettie:	No. Ain't there's another way?
3	Pam:	Come on, Nett*ie*.
4	Nettie:	Come on, Where we *goin*. Don't say that
5		*ei*ther.
6	Pam:	Come on. // Get off. All y'gotta do–
7	Nettie:	Cuz I gotta answer.
8	Pam:	Get off.
9	Nettie:	All ya gotta say *is* (0.2) I mean get –
10		I mean um – um – *Move* please and I can't
11		get no rhymes on that one.
12	Pam:	°Move please.
13	Nettie:	Where the *move* at.
14	Pam:	I'm tryin to get off rather,
15	Nettie:	*Wa*ther, wh– oh: the weather you want?
16		The day is sunny and tomorrow's gonna
17		be ra–

In line 15, by systematically varying its phonological structure Nettie transforms "rather" into "weather." This is accomplished by first changing the *r* in "rather" to *w* and then changing the *æ* in "rather" to *ε*.

rather

wather

weather

Through this stepwise transformation Nettie is able humorously to change Pam's request for her to move into a request for information about the weather.

This sequence also contains a number of other playful mishearings that demonstrate yet other ways in which children might transform a prior utterance in a subsequent move. For example, within the sequence occurring here, the words "Come on" in line 3 are clearly a recycle of the request made in line 1, that Nettie get off Pam. But when abstracted from a particular context, the words could have a range of different meanings, and in line 4 Nettie plays with this fact, first repeating what Pam has said and then treating it as a request to go somewhere, rather than as a request to get off. In line 12 Pam makes a request ("Move please") that has the following format:

[Verb (action requested)] + [Please]

A similar format, however, is used with nouns when asking for objects (for example "Salt, please" to request salt at the dinner table):

[Noun (object requested)] + [Please]

In line 13 Nettie treats the verb in line 12 as a noun by asking, "Where the *move* at." A similar creative reorganization of the syntactic categories provided by a prior utterance is found in the following, in which Huey transforms an adjective in Chopper's utterance into a verb:

(34) 10–19–70–58

Chopper: Ah you better sh:ut *up* with your *dingy* sneaks.
Huey: I'm a *dingy* your hea:d. How would you like *that*.

While sitting on top of Pam, Nettie is in fact playing in rather abstract ways with a range of basic structures used by her group not only to construct their talk but also to interpret is meaningfulness. In lines 10–11 she refers to the process through which she is able to avoid providing next moves to Pam's requests as "having rhymes" on Pam's utterances. Such an expression describes as aptly as any outside analyst could the process of playful but systematic transformation she is engaged in.

We are now in a better position to investigate how a range of different strategies for format tying might be combined in a single dispute. In the following a group of girls are practicing steps for a future dance contest against the boys:

(35) 9–28–70–25

		((Girls sing as they practice original dance steps.))
1	Huey:	You sound terrible.
2	Sharon:	We sound just like you *look*.
3	Michael:	What's the matter.
4	Terri:	What's the matter with *you*.
5	Michael:	Same thing that's the matter with *you*.
6	Terri:	Well *nothing's* the matter with me.
7	Michael:	Well nothing the matter // with *me* then.
8	Terri:	Well then *go* somewhere.
9	Michael:	Well I wanna stay *here*.
10	Terri:	Ah: I hate you.
11	Sharon:	Go ahead, go ahead. Go ahead y'all.
12		Act like he just ain't even here.

In these data a variety of argumentative actions are organized through format tying into a series of rounds. Moreover, while attending to the details of the structure of prior talk, the participants also play with the operations used by that talk to reference phenomena.

In line 1 Huey delivers an insult to the girls: "You sound terrible." In her return action Sharon reuses the "[girls'] sound" structure but replaces "terrible" with talk that equates how the girls sound with an attribute of the boys': "We sound just like you look." Instead of producing an explicit insult term of her own, Sharon uses the power of talk to refer to other talk to create a boomerang so that the boys now become the target of their own insult.

For clarity, format tying has so far been discussed in terms of the operations on explicit phonological, syntactic, and semantic elements of prior talk. It can, however, be more abstract than this, as is demonstrated by lines 3–5 of this exchange. Michael's talk in line 3 is disjunctive with the talk that just preceded it, but it quickly becomes the template for a new sequence of format-tying operations in lines 4 and 5. Since the way in which actions such as these reuse the materials provided by prior talk has already been examined, this process will not again be looked at in detail here. We wish rather to focus attention on the way in which Michael in line 5 makes the pejorative attribute of himself being asked about by Terri (i.e. the answer to the question "What's the matter with *you*") an attribute of Terri as well ("Same thing that's the matter with *you*"). In effect he constructs another boomerang. Thus, although the surface structure of the talk in lines 3–5 is completely different from that found in lines 1–2, Michael nonetheless makes use of material from that earlier sequence. What is being reused, however, is not specific words or phrases but, rather, a particular structural solution found by Sharon to the problem of building an appropriate return.

The talk in lines 3–5 refers to a phenomenon, the answer to the "What's the matter" question, that has not yet been specified. In lines 6 and 7 this issue is resolved in a way that takes into account the fact that it has now become an attribute of both contesting parties, i.e. it is defined as "nothing." Parenthetically it can be noted that if one were to approach argument from the perspective of resolving conflict, this would appear to constitute a prototypical example of conflict resolution; that is, the contesting parties come to agreement, and moreover agree in a way that is not pejorative to either of them. Clearly such an approach to what is happening here would be seriously in error.

In lines 8 and 9 the pattern of providing reciprocal actions through format tying is broken. In line 9 Michael provides an account rather than a reciprocal move to Terri. Despite the fact that similarity in action is not achieved, similarity in structure is maintained. Michael's utterance ("Well I wanna stay *here*") repeats the "well" of the talk just before it and produces contrast-class substitutions for both verbs ("stay" is substituted for "go") and adverbs ("here" replaces "somewhere"). In addition both tied utterances share the same stress and rhythmic pattern.

The way in which format tying poses the task of using the immediately prior talk to build an appropriate return casts light on how this process might be related to a range of other phenomena. For example it would appear to have close structural ties to "sounding" or "ritual insult" (Abrahams 1970; Kochman 1970; Labov 1972a, 1974). The recipient of an initial ritual insult (an insult about the target recipient known not to be literally true) must use the scene described in prior speaker's talk to produce a second description that turns the initial insult on its head and is even more outrageous. As noted by Goffman (1971:179), "the structure of these devices establishes a move that is designed to serve as a comparison base for another's effort, his object being to exceed the prior effort in elegance or wit."[31] A successful return insult leaves the other party with nothing more to say and is responded to with laughter (Labov 1972a:325). The following are excerpts from a lengthy playful ritual-insult battle:[32]

(36) 6–3–71–4

		((Simplified transcript))
39	Nettie:	One day– (0.2) *my br*other was spendin'
40		the night with *you*, •h And // the next
41		mornin' he got up,
42	Michael:	I don't wanna hear about it. Your
43		brother // ain't *never* been in *my*
44		house.
45	Nettie:	THE NEXT TIME HE GOT UP, •heh He was
46		gonna brush his teeth so the roach
47		tri(h)ed ta(h) bru(h)sh hi(h)s!
48	Michael:	Don't // swag.
49	Nettie:	•h *Ha ha ha ha ha* •hh!
50		[[•h Eh heh heh // *heh* he he he he he
51	Michael:	An if he was up there If the roach was
52		tryin' ta *brush* it // he musta brought
53		it up it up there *with* him.
54	Nettie:	•heh!
55		•h *Eh* // he heh heh heh he he he he
56	Michael:	•h eh heh!
57	Robby:	((falsetto)) Ha // he! he
58	Nettie:	He he he he ha // ha ha // ha
59	Johnny:	•heh!

In this fragment Nettie (lines 45–7) describes her brother's finding roaches brushing their teeth in Michael's house. Michael's response builds upon this description in lines 51–3, stating that if that is so, her brother must have brought the roaches with him. The point is not to negate or contradict prior talk but to show that second speaker can take a feature of first speaker's talk (here, the statement about roaches) and transform it.

In the following a three-part insult sequence occurs. Nettie's initial description of talking roaches at Michael's door is answered by a return insult from Michael in lines 99–100, which is subsequently overturned by a response in lines 101–2.

(36) 6–3–71–4

74	Nettie:	Ah ha:. (0.2) And one *more* thing! One
75		day (0.2) *I* went in your hou– *I* was
76		gonna walk in the door for *two* sets

```
77                    ⌈ a roaches.
78    Michael:  ⎩⎩ For what.
79                     For what.
80    Nettie:    One roach here (0.2) and one roach here.
81               THE ONE RIGHT HERE,
82    Michael:   Oh you tryin' ta *sell* // em for him.
83    Nettie:    THE ONE RIGHT HERE W–
84    Michael:   You tryin' to se(hh)ll e(hh)m.
85    Nettie:    THE ONE RIGHT HERE // WAS UP HERE SAYIN'–
86    Michael:   *Some*body gonna buy your // damn roach.
87    Nettie:    THE ONE RIGHT here was up here sayin–
88               (0.2) "People movin' *ou:t*?" (0.2) And
89               the one right here was sayin' (0.2)
90               "*Peo*ple movin' in–"
91                    ⌈ Why? Because of the odor of their // ski(hh)n.
92    Michael:   ⎩⎩ You understand their language. You
93               must be one of 'em.
94    Johnny:    ((falsetto)) Eh *heh!* Heh he heh!
95    Nettie:    What'd he s(hhhh)ay? Wha(h)d he(h)
96               say(h)y? •H What he(h) sa(hh)y? What
97               he sa(heh heh)y? What you say? Whad's
98               he // say Candy?
99    Michael:   You understand their language cuz you
100              *one* of 'em.
101   Nettie:    I(h) *know(h)* you(h) ar(hh)re! You was
102              *born* from the roach fam//ily.
```

In each of these insult sequences speaker does not refute prior statement but instead accepts the description and builds upon it, arguing that if the statement is so, then the consequence is that an even more pejorative description can be made of prior speaker. In lines 87–91 Nettie sketches a scene of roaches on either side of Michael's doorway speaking the words of the Jackson Five song "Ball of Confusion" with her quotes "People movin ou:t" and "People movin in." Michael then in lines 92–3 states that Nettie is able to understand talking roaches because she herself is "one of 'em." In response Nettie (101), using the preface "I know," transforms Michael's insult about her into a statement authored by him about himself and tops his insult; she argues that Michael "was born from the roach family." In brief, ritual insults do not constitute an activity or genre that is totally distinct from other, less stylized talk. Rather, through the way in which participants use the material provided by prior talk to construct return actions, ritual insults build from resources that are already present in opposition sequences.[33]

In this section of the chapter we have attempted to demonstrate that within argumentation children do not simply tie to the action contained in a prior utterance but also to a range of features implicated in its construction and that such format tying provides an arena for the productive creation of new structure through systematic operations on existing structure. Such findings have a number of larger implications.

First, in sociolinguistics context is frequently treated as something external to the talk being examined; for example, it may be described in terms of attributes such as the setting in which talk occurs or the characteristics of the participants. Such an approach to discourse is compatible with categorizing talk as instances of different types of "actions" and then focusing analysis on the sequencing of those actions rather than on the details of the talk through which those actions become visible. But a most important context for any talk is the talk that has just preceded it, in all of its multifaceted complexity. If preadolescent children are able to attend in detail to the rich variety of structures found there and to use those structures for the organization of subsequent talk, discourse analysts must attend to them as well. Trying to describe how participants in conversation move from one utterance to another without close attention to the details of their talk is like trying to describe the work that a musician does while ignoring the music being played.

From a slightly different perspective it can be noted that arguing has generally been evaluated negatively by adults, for example treated as behavior to be both stopped and sanctioned by parents and teachers. Thus children who engage in arguments at school, even on the playground, are treated as troublemakers. Work on children's arguments (Eisenberg and Garvey 1981) has been concerned with the study of how conflicts can be "resolved"[34] rather than with how they might be sustained. Instead of viewing argumentation as an activity to be pursued for its own sake (as, indeed, psychologists [Hartup 1978:138] have argued it should be viewed), researchers consider it something to be remedied and moved past as quickly as possible so that harmony can be restored. But as the data presented here and previous work among urban black children (M. H. Goodwin 1982b, 1983), as well as naturalistic studies conducted among middle-class preschool white children (Corsaro and Rizzo in press; Genishi and Di Paolo 1982; Maynard 1985a, 1985b), part-Hawaiian children (Boggs 1978), and Italian children (Corsaro and Rizzo in press) have shown, children do not share this bias against argumentative behavior.[35] The present data would suggest that, despite the tendency to cast argumentation in a negative light, there might be rather good reasons for children to treat argument as they do. When arguments are looked at as natural phenomena, it is found that, rather than being disorderly, argumentation gives children an opportunity to explore through productive use the structural resources of their language. When format tying, a child must immediately produce an appropriate subsequent utterance by transforming the prior utterance in a way that shows integrated attention to both the action embodied by it and the details of its linguistic structure.

Moreover, since this process occurs within argumentation, an activity where the stakes are high for the participants and one's character and reputation are not only on the line but in fact being created and evaluated, there is a strong motivation for the child to display as much quickness, skill, and inventiveness in her or his transformations as possible.[36] It would be difficult to imagine adults constructing for children, in the classroom or any other learning setting, drills for practicing and experimenting with the underlying resources of their language that are as effective or creative as the ones the children spontaneously perform with each other when engaged in argumentation, an activity that adults systematically try to ban from the learning situations that they administer.[37]

Finally, as Labov (1970:33, 34) has noted, although children initially learn to speak from their parents, surprisingly they *"do not speak like their parents* [italics in original]. . . . Instead it is the local group of . . . children's peers which determines this generation's speech pattern." The present data, by locating a domain of action specific to the peer group within which creative use of language structure is not only made salient but also evaluated by other peers in contests of some moment, locate one place where children can and do affect one another's talk in complex ways, away from adult supervision, models, or intrusion.[38]

Disputes with members of the same sex

Although they had much in common, when the boys and girls on Maple Street interacted in same-sex groups they displayed different interests, engaged in different activities, and constructed different types of social organization. This had consequences for the types of disputes that occurred within each group. To illustrate some of the differences between the groups, it is useful to describe briefly how girls and boys performed two types of action: making comparisons and organizing tasks.

One of the major activities of the children involved comparing oneself with others. In a group where individuals share similar types of living conditions, have parents with roughly the same income, and within which there is no fixed status hierarchy or division into specialized roles,[39] making comparisons is one of the ways group members can differentiate themselves from one another. Older girls and older boys differ with respect to the criteria they use for making comparisons. Girls focus on the types of relationships they can be seen as maintaining with others, both peers and adults, and their appearance. For example:

(37) 3–23–71–2

Terri: And Johnny gave me his phone number when I first moved around here?
He done *gave* em to me.

(38) 10–20–70–2

Maria: These are my *m*other earrings.

Within the girls' group, statements such as these may be heard as attempts by speaker to show herself superior to others. Recipients frequently counter such claims by showing that prior speaker is, in fact, not special (Ex. 37), or by turning the attempted boast on its head (Ex. 38):

(37) 3–23–71–2

Terri: And Johnny gave me his phone number
when I first moved around here? He
done *gave* em to me. And they– and
they was talkin bout– wanna call him?
Maria:→   ⌈⌈Talk that sweet talk.
‌   ⌊⌊He gave me his phone number *too*.

(38) 10–20–70–2

Maria: These are my *m*other earrings.
Pam: → She let you wear your– her stuff now.
She don't hit you no more. First–
first she didn't hit Jeanie no more and
now she don't hit you no more. And now
she just hittin Antony and them. = Right?

In Ex. 38, after Maria's claim to special status Pam indicates that she is, in fact, in a relationship that is certainly not to be envied.

The importance of such claims about relationships in the girls' dealings with one another is further demonstrated by the fact that hearers of such statements do not simply counter a speaker who makes them but also talk about the making of such claims when the speaker is no longer present:

(39) 9–12–71–4

Terri: Maria going around tellin everybody that– that Pam– that Pam mother like her more than anybody else. She said she think she so big just because um, Miss Smith let her work in the kitchen for her one time.

By contrast, when boys talk to other boys, they rarely discuss relationships with the opposite sex or make claims about privileged status vis-à-vis their relatives. Instead, they openly compare themselves with each other on the basis of individual skills and abilities. A rotating cycle of games among boys provides for changing realms in which ranking can take place; different activities may rank the same participants in different ways, and each boy knows his relative position in a variety of pastimes:

(40) 11–10–70–5

((during a yo-yo contest))
Earl: Who *w*innin? Who *w*innin? Earl Masters.

(41) 9–24–70–1

Raymond: I could walk on my hands better than anybody here. Except him.
And Chuckie. *R*obert can't walk.

Actions of this type are interpreted as attempts to view oneself as superior to another, and quite frequently they are followed by counters.

(42) 10–19–70–105

((concerning pliers))
Poochie: Hey these– hey these cut better than yours.
Michael: So good. Good.

(43) 11–12–70–6

((discussing whose bus arrived first at school))
Chuckie: We was first this afternoon!
Vincent: We was first this *morn*in baby!

In brief, the comparisons made by girls characteristically deal with ties they have to others or their appearance, whereas the boys employ a variety of criteria to explicitly rank themselves against each other.

Differences between the girls' group and the boys' are also found in the way in which they organize task activities. Since these have already been analyzed in detail elsewhere (M. H. Goodwin 1980a), at present we simply note that the boys organize their talk so as to display hierarchy (for instance, with imperatives from "leaders," e.g. "Gimme the pliers," and mitigated requests from their subordinates, e.g. "Can I be on your side Michael?"). Girls, on the other hand, choose directive forms that minimize differences between the party being requested to do something and the party making the request (e.g. "Let's do x"). It should be noted, however, that in situations other than task activities the girls make use of the entire range of directive forms, (M. H. Goodwin 1980a:170–171, 1985a, 1985b:324–325).

The ways in which disputes are organized within each group are consistent with the differences found in other activities. The themes of boys' disputes frequently involve issues of relative power, as can be seen in some of the disputes between boys that have already been examined (e.g. Ex. 30), as well as in the following:

(44) 10–19–70–58

((Nate is using Huey's pliers.))
Huey: *G*imme the *things*.
Chopper: You shut up you big lips.
Huey: *Sh*ut up.

Chopper: Don't gimme that. I'm not *t*alkin ta you.
        (1.4)
Huey: I'm talkin ta *y*:ou!
Chopper: Ah you better sh:ut *up* with your *din*gy sneaks.
        (1.2)
Huey: I'm a *d*ingy your hea:d. How would you like *that*.
Chopper: No you won't you little– •h *Gue*ss what.

Since most of the opposition structures used here – and indeed many of the couplets found in this exchange – have already been examined, this dispute will not be looked at in detail here.[40]

In boys' disputes, opposition is generally restricted to two opposing positions, though a number of parties may side with a particular position. The shape of argument will vary, depending on both the type of actions used to promote conflict and the parts of utterances selected out to be countered. When commands, insults, and threats are used, argument may be constructed in rounds of exchange and return moves, with each round daring the other party to take steps to make good his actions and visibly prove he can carry out the action he proposes. This was particularly evident in Ex. 30, which was discussed above in terms of format tying.

Though issues of power are not the dominant themes of girls' disputes, the forms of action we have been examining, as well as the strategies for sequencing cycles of these actions, are used by both girls and boys. Boys use rounds of insults, commands, or accusations when disputing among themselves as well as in cross-sex interaction. Girls, however, tend to use them more often in their interactions with boys than when by themselves, reserving actions that are "face-threatening" for acting out hypothetical confrontations (M. H. Goodwin 1982a:810) or to be performed as deliberate affronts to girls whose offenses are deemed especially serious.

The structure of girls' accusations reflects their concerns with what others say about them and their use of indirect speech forms (Mitchell-Kernan 1972). Rather than confronting someone directly with an accusation such as "Boy you broke my *skate* board!" girls talk about offensive actions of others in their absence. Through an elaborated storytelling procedure called "instigating" (M. H. Goodwin 1982a) girls learn about offenses of absent parties that have been committed against them – principally having talked about them behind their backs – and commit themselves to future confrontations with such individuals. The stories of girls used in he-said-she-said disputes contrast with those used by boys in several ways. (See M. H. Goodwin 1982b for more detailed analysis of stories used by boys in disputes.) First, they deal with pejorative actions of absent parties rather than present ones; second, they function not to counter others' argumentative moves in the present but, rather, to elicit commitments to courses of action against which moral judgment can be diverted in the future; third, they transform the impending dispute into a large public event that others can anticipate and participate in.

Such instigating can lead to a formal accusation. In pursuing such character contests the girls use actions that are distinctive to their way of handling grievances; these differ from baldly stated accusations both in terms of their syntactic structure and with regard to the participation framework they make available for those present. For example the types of embedded structures girls use to open a type of argument they call he-said-she-said[41] are of the form "A said you said I said x":

(45) 10–20–70–76

Flo: They say y'all say I wrote *every*thing over there.

(46) 10–19–71–19

Darlene: And *Ste*phen said that *you* said that *I* was showin off just because I had that *bl:ou*se on.

(47) 6–7–71–1

Pam: Terri said *you* said that (0.6) I wasn't gonna go around *Pop*lar no more.

Each of these accusations provides an ordering of participants and events in a past culminating in the present. This pattern can be diagramed as follows:

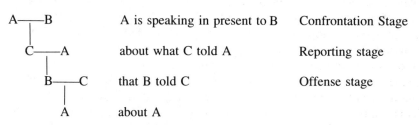

A——B	A is speaking in present to B	Confrontation Stage
C——A	about what C told A	Reporting stage
B——C	that B told C	Offense stage
A	about A	

The pattern contains three basic stages. At each stage two parties in the immediate presence of each other are situated as speaker and hearer. A third party, neither speaker nor hearer, is talked about. Participants change positions within this basic triad[42] at each stage in a regular fashion:

Time 1	Speaker	Hearer	Spoken about
Time 2	Spoken about	Speaker	Hearer

The ordering of events at each stage and the rules for sequencing stages through a regular rotation of participants provide a past with a particular structure that makes relevant specific types of next moves in the present. In essence the current hearer is charged with the offense of having talked about the current speaker behind her back, with the report of the third party establishing the grounds for that charge.

It is traditional in the social sciences to treat language, culture, and social organization as essentially different types of phenomena, and indeed frequently to relegate them to entirely different disciplines (linguistics, cultural anthropology, and sociology for example). Thus Radcliffe-Brown (1973:310) was of the opinion that whereas there may be "certain indirect interactions between social structure and language . . . these would seem to be of minor importance." Here, however, we find these apparently separate phenomena being dealt with by the girls as integrated parts of a single whole. Thus the structure of the utterance, and in particular the pattern embedding it makes visible, creates not simply a linguistic form but also what Goodenough (1981:110) has termed an operating culture, a small activity system providing relevant social identities for participants (e.g. accuser and offender/defendant), a set of relevant actions for them to perform, and a formulation of the types of events they are engaged in. In addition to being this cultural organization, the utterance functions socially to shape the behavior of the participants into a particular type of coordinated action, and makes relevant specific types of future action.

Examining the organization of a he-said-she-said confrontation in more detail, one may note that the framing of offenses in an indirect way as the girls do allows for next actions that protect the face of both accuser and the accused. By including in the accusation a statement that another party supports the charge being delivered, a girl establishes a warrant for her action and argues that an alignment of "two against one" is maintained against the offender. In that a third, generally nonpresent, party, rather than current speaker, is stated to have originated the report of the offense, the offender cannot counteraccuse her accuser. This contrasts with the situation found in Exx. 24 and 25 for baldly stated actions that can receive similar actions as returns. Denials to he-said-she-said accusations address the actions in the third stage from the present, the offense stage – either denying the charge or attributing blame to another party:

(48) 10–12–71–71

Naynay: *Uh* uh. I ain't *say* anything.

(49) 10–20–70–76

Pam: *UH* UH. = *THAT* WAS *VINCENT* SAID.

Alternatively, the accused may charge that the reporter (the nonpresent party) lied during the second stage from the present:

(50) 11–2–71–18

Deniecey: Well I know that *they* tellin a *lie* cuz I know I ain't *say* nothin about you.

(51) 10–12–71–78

Naynay: I don't know who said it but– now– I– now if I ain't say it, whoever told you musta said it.

In that the offense is known about only through a report, the accuser cannot definitively establish whether or not the act at issue was in fact authored by the defendant. Therefore answers to the offending party's denials tend to be recycles of the initial accusation or refutations of accounts that the defendant provides. Consider the following short he-said-she-said dispute:

(52) 6–7–71–1

```
 1  Pam:      Terri said you said that (0.6) I wasn't
 2            gonna go around Poplar no more.
 3  Darlene:  You said you weren't.
 4  Nettie:   She– Terri say–
 5  Pam:      And Terri said that um that you said
 6            that Pam wasn't gonna go around Poplar
 7            no more.
 8  Darlene:  That's what Terri said.
 9  Pam:      Well, I know what Terri said that you
10            said. She said– She sat there and
11            looked at you. And Terri– And she
12            said– And if you have anything to say
13            about me you come and say it in front
14            of my face. And here and right here
15            you say whatever you got to say cuz
16            everytime you go around Poplar you
17            always got something to say.
18  Nettie:   Terri said it too.
19  Pam:      And I'm tellin Terri too that she said
20            it.
21  Darlene:  I gotta go somewhere.
```

After Darlene's defense (line 3), Pam, the plaintiff, recycles the initial accusation (lines 5–7).[43] When Darlene provides a second defense (line 8) addressing actions at the reporting stage, Pam refutes Darlene's account – "Well I know what Terri said that you said" – and provides a descriptive detail of her previous encounter with Terri to justify her position. Pam closes up the he-said-she-said sequence with an admonition to Darlene, as well as with a framing of this particular offense as representative of Darlene's more general way of behaving: "Everytime you go around Poplar you always got something to say."

An even more complex type of floor may be created, however, when the intermediary (the reporter) is present, as well as a number of spectators who can affiliate themselves with the changing arrays of identity relationships made operative as the dispute unfolds. Consider the type of field created through the utterance "They say y'all say I wrote everything over there" (line 7) in the following example:

(53) 10–20–70–76

```
 1   Maria:     WE AIN'T SAY THAT PA:M.
 2   Flo:       You said that // I said–
 3   Pam:       °Where. Where.
 4   Maria:  [[ °Sh'said–
 5   Pam:       (°Lemme see.)
 6   Maria:     Um–
 7   Flo:       They // say y'all say I wrote everything
 8              o//ver there. I ain't // wrote
 9              everythi:ng.
10   Maria:     They say– (0.2) Y'all said that she
11              (0.2) Wrote that um, They wrote // that
12              bi:g
13   Terri:     You // said –
14   Flo:       Only thing // is the car.
15   Terri:     H Pam tol: // me–
16   Pam:       UHUH. = THAT WAS VINCENT SAID.
17   Terri:     But y//ou told me that
18   Flo:       I know it was Vincent cuz Vincent was
19              the one that wrote that // on that car.
20   Sharon:    ((falsetto)) Uhuh. = We started to tear
21              that– •h uh that out. We tol– we said
22              that we– all said– •h I said // all–
23   Maria:     ((falsetto)) I said, "Who wrote it on
24              the car." Sharon say "Either Vincent,
25              (0.2) or, Vincent or um– // Florence.
26   Pam:    [[ Florence.
27   Sharon:    Florence. I put th//is
28   Flo:       Vincent di:d it. Vincent had that
29              crayon more than anybody.
30                         (0.7)
31   Sharon:    •h An plus– an =
32   Flo:       Oo this's cold out here // t'day.
33   Terri:     WELL WHY YOU TELL HER I said it.
34   Pam:       YEAH BUT RIA– YEAH BUT RIA WAS SAYING WE
35              WRO:TE ALL OVER THE STREET AND WE
36              DIDN'T. =
37   Flo:    [[ We ain't write over no street nothin.
38   Terri:     I'm'not'talkin'bout' B'//t why did–
39   Maria:     Vincent say he wrote in the street. ((sigh)) =
40   Sharon:    = Well I ain't write // in the street.
```

41	Flo:	Oh *you* fin' s'n in the st//r:eet then.
42	Pam:	I ain't *wrote nutt*in in no str:ee://t,
43	Terri:	Well how come *you told Flor*ence that I
44		said that *she* wrote it.
45		(0.6)
46	Sharon:	I said that *who* wrote it. =
47	Terri:	= *No*t you. = *P*am.
48	Pris:	°Well // who did.
49	Pam:	That *she* wrote it,
50	Pam:	°That– that you was–
51	Pris:	All they hadda do is // look in the street.
52	Sharon:	Well come on out here. Let's see it.
53		(1.2)

(Lines 50–51 joined at left by a large bracket `[[`)

((Girls move to the site where pejorative things were written about Terri on a car and garage door.))

54	Flo:	I only said– // so that when I– when we
55		were goin to the car.
56	Pam:	That *she* that *she* wrote it, I TOLD YOU
57		THAT // FLORENCE WROTE,
58	Sharon:	( )
59	Maria:	I'm gonna stay *out* from *now* on.
60	Terri:	Well cuz you– you said that she wrote it.
61	Flo:	U*H*UH. U*H*UH CUZ I ONLY WROTE *ONE* THING
62		IN *RED*.
63		(0.4)
64	Pam:	S:o did I. *I* only– •h // Besides– I
65		only di:d that where *A*isha did cuz
66		Aisha wrote on that *thing*.
67	Flo:	Vincent did *that*. Aisha wrote where.
68	Pam:	Aisha wrote on that thing. = And // I
69		only traced what– Aisha wrote on it,
70		•h cuz Aisha wro//te it *sm*:all.
71	Sharon:	On the side?
72	Terri:	I know. = I'm not *tal*kin bout *that*. But
73		how come you told her that I that I was
74		*talk*in about her.
75	Pam:	= YOU WA:S.
76	Terri:	When.

((The division of the conversation at this point into two groups is indicated by separate columns. Simultaneous talk occurs on the same horizontal line.))

77	Pam:	Remember when um– um– that's when um:		
78		(0.8) Uh: uh: remember when you sai:d,		
79			Flo:	(°Well he started it) cuz
80				he got
81		that um,		some of it off.
82			Sharon:	Yeap.
83		nuh–		
84		remember when you	Flo:	( )

85		jus– When you		Vincent did that.
86		sai:d, When you		
87		sai:d,	Sharon:	'N who
88		"Fla-uh	Pris:	Fla:,
89		Florence don't	Flo:	All this the same hand-
90		got nuttin to do		writin an it ain't *mi:*ne.
91		with it."		
92	Terri:	*Uhuh. Ma*ria said	( ):	How bout right up there.
93		that.		
94	Pam:	Oh Ma*ria* said that.	Flo:	Mm *hm.*
95	Maria	((from distance)) SAID WHAT. =		
96	Flo:	= Maria // said what.		
97	Pam:	said– // that you ain't		
98	Terri:	That Florence don't have nothing to *do* with		
99		it. = Member? // We was arguin?		
100	Maria:	Y:OU DON'T– She's not– (1.0) Cuz– She		
101		ain't mean nuttin° t'do nuttin to you.		
102		(1.4)		
103	Flo:	I was just writin for *fun* cuz I ain't		
104		do it till nuttin was happenin.		

Generally the intermediary party is absent from the confrontation. Here Terri's presence provides for the multiple parts of an accusation to be addressed in rapid succession. In line 7 the dispute begins with Flo's accusation to Pam:

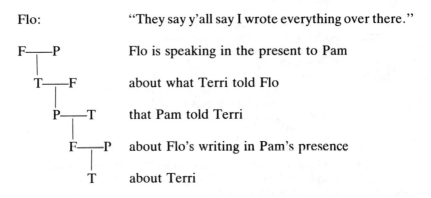

Flo: "They say y'all say I wrote everything over there."

F——P   Flo is speaking in the present to Pam

T——F   about what Terri told Flo

P——T   that Pam told Terri

F——P   about Flo's writing in Pam's presence

T   about Terri

As Flo begins her rebuttal to the accusation implied against her, Maria in line 10, taking up a position with Flo, provides a repeat of Flo's initial accusation. In line 15, Terri, the party implicated in the plural pronoun "they," begins a defense to the charge located in the second stage from the present. Pam (line 16) addresses her defense to the charge that is located in the third stage from the present and states that Vincent, an absent party, is responsible for having reported the offense. By introducing an absent party into the dispute, Pam forecloses certain next moves in the sequence. Vincent's absence prevents him from countering the charge against him and makes it impossible for Florence to question him.

Terri then reenters the dispute with a recycling of her prior talk (line 17) and a countermove to Pam's talk. She is, however, interrupted by Florence (line 18), who now finds a way to agree with Pam: "I know it was Vincent cuz Vincent was the one that wrote that on that car." She both discontinues her opening accusation to Pam through this action and charges that Vincent, rather than herself, is to blame for the offense of having written about Terri (located as the fourth stage from the present). Sharon (line 20), answering to Terri's incomplete counter to Pam (and thereby aligning herself with Pam), argues that Terri is incorrect in her thinking: Sharon states that she and Pam deleted what Terri was about to charge them with having said. Sharon's utterance, accounting for "all she had said" before, is continued in line 23 by another party, Maria, who now takes up an alignment with rather than against Pam, as she had in lines 10–12. At the tail end of Maria's utterance, three people – Maria, Pam, and Sharon – collaborate in producing an utterance that claims that Florence was in part guilty of the offense (lines 25–7).

In that the action on the floor has now shifted to a charge against Florence, Terri does not again attempt to answer Sharon's counter. The statement that Florence was in part to blame is answered by Florence in line 28 with a restatement of her counterclaim that Vincent was the perpetrator of the offense in question. Argument now shifts from Florence's complaint to Pam to Terri's action vis-à-vis Pam: "WELL WHY YOU TELL HER *I* said it" (line 33). This accusation appears two other times, in line 43 – "Well how come *you told Flor*ence that I said that *she* wrote it" – and in lines 72–4 – "But how come you told her that I that I was *talk*in bout her." Pam attempts to sidetrack this issue each time Terri poses the question. Her first response to the accusation is an account (line 34), that provides a counteraccusation: In that Maria was saying something about her first, she was justified in saying something about Maria (a friend of Terri's).

Pam's defense becomes the new action on the floor to which participants respond, first with a series of denials and a challenge to the reported accusation (lines 37, 40–2) and then with a repair sequence (lines 46–57). When in 60 Terri reintroduces the offense, writing about Terri, Florence in 61 provides a justification/denial, which is followed by a similar type of justification/denial by Pam (64–6). Terri's third recycling of her accusation to Pam (lines 72–4) is answered by "YOU WA:S" (line 75), which is immediately challenged by Terri: "*WH*en."

An elaborate recounting of the incident at issue takes place during simultaneous talk by Florence and Sharon (lines 77–91). This is then answered by Terri's denial (lines 92–3) that she was the principal party involved in the incident recounted by Pam. Instead Maria is found to have been the author of the deed that is the offense being dealt with in the confrontation. When Pam acknowledges that it is actually Maria rather than Terri who is the guilty party, Maria becomes the new defendant (to Florence), and talk now shifts to Maria's defense.

When conducting a dispute, children make selections from a range of cultural alternatives. In dealing with serious affronts learned about through the elaborated storytelling of an instigating sequence, girls select utterances with a particular embedded structure to carry out their argumentation. The utterance opening up the he-said-she-said dispute provides for an ordering of past events and participants that remains the topical focus throughout (indeed, there is only one utterance – Florence's "Oh this's cold out here" in line 32 – that is outside the frame of dispute). Moreover, it creates a highly ordered and legalistic conversational domain – one in which rights and obligations with respect to the taking of turns and defending of points of view are of primary importance. Nonetheless throughout this dispute the alignments of principals to the argument shift as different stages of the initial accusation statement are dealt with. This provides for a speaking floor of much greater complexity than exists when only two positions to an argument are debated, the general situation in most boys' and cross-sex disputes. Moreover, because of the topical focus they provide, he-said-she-said disputes can become significantly more extended than the disputes found in the boys' groups. Indeed, because of the way in which it creates both a relevant past and an anticipated future, he-said-she-said can provide an arena for action and drama that lasts for days. From a slightly different perspective, the entire he-said-she-said sequence can be seen as an elaborate way to play out games of shifting coalitions, a theme common in the girls' social structure.

Conclusion

Most efforts at defining argument (Brenneis and Lein 1977:61–62; Corsaro and Rizzo in press; Eisenberg and Garvey 1981:150) have sought to specify its distinctive attributes, the features that set it apart from other activities and provide for its characteristic organization. The concept of opposition has emerged as a key feature of many of these definitions, and considerable attention has been paid to a range of actions that are used to display opposition within arguments. Such a perspective toward argument has led to fruitful research that has revealed much about its characteristic structure. Focusing entirely on how argument differs from other modes of interaction, however, can obscure some important aspects of its organization. Argument has much in common with many other types of discourse. Indeed, one of its crucial features is its ability to incorporate other forms of speech. Thus within argument one can find a wide range of speech events including stories (M. H. Goodwin 1982a, 1982b), requests, commands, insults, explanations, excuses, threats, and warnings (M. H. Goodwin 1982b). Many of these actions provide occasion-specific social identities for participants (e.g. accuser–defendant).

The ability of argument to encompass disparate phenomena extends as well to intonational and other paralinguistic operations on the talk in progress (including a rich set of "voices" for doing such activities as ridicule, teasing, insult, etc.) and to displays of affect such as anger and righteous indignation. With these resources, participants are able not simply to occupy particular social identities but also to construct fully articulated social personae in the midst of argument (e.g. an offended party bristling with hurt and righteous indignation performing the accusations and challenges appropriate to one in her position). Insofar as such characters exist only as elements in a larger field of action that also encompasses their opponents (and frequently others, such as an audience, as well), dynamic social drama becomes possible. Thus, although argument is usually analyzed as conflict, it can in fact be done in many different ways, some of them, as we have seen here, quite playful; indeed, this playfulness can be elaborated into distinctive artistic genres such as ritual insults. The ability of argument to incorporate such a diversity of modes of discourse within its scope provides a rich arena for research.

In this chapter, rather than attempt to delineate broad categories of differences between female and male speech, we have restricted study to a single activity, arguing, and focused analysis on detailed explication of the procedures used by both girls and boys to accomplish this activity. When data are examined in this way, it is found that the mode of talk that characterizes girls' disputes shows an orientation that differs from that described elsewhere as characteristic of adult black female speech and of female speech more generally. For example, the talk of the argumentative sequences examined here displays anything but a "tone of relaxed sweetness, sometimes bordering on the saccharine," which Hannerz (1969:96) states typifies black female adult speech and is contrastive with black males' argumentative style. Girls' use of dispute structures quite similar to those of the boys was evident both in their interaction with each other (Exx. 7, 17, 20, 33, 52, 53) and in their interaction with boys (Exx. 3, 4, 5, 6, 10, 12, 13, 22, 24). Indeed, they frequently outmaneuvered the boys in more extended dispute sequences (Exx. 26, 27, 28, 35, 36). Abrahams (1976:77) has suggested that the "contest element" in speech lasts for a shorter duration among black females than among males; however, as we have seen, girls' confrontations can be far more expanded than boys' arguments, and in fact talk about the confrontation and repercussions from it may extend over several weeks (see M. H. Goodwin 1980b:688). In addition, in Abraham's work, female values of respectability and the home are contrasted with male values of reputation and the public world (1976:64); however, displaying one's character in a public arena is precisely what is at issue in he-said-she-said.

The form in which opening accusation statements in he-said-she-said are shaped works to protect the face of the parties to the dispute in ways that explicit accusations do not; nonetheless, the extensive debate that ensues in this type of dispute (as well as in cross-sex arguments) is anything but an expression of powerless speech, and neither is it organized in terms of careful attention to forms of politeness. Indeed, the argumentation occurring in he-said-she-said creates a situation of far greater complexity than has generally been discussed for either male or female speech. Moreover, these data show females' skill in domains of talk, such as legalistic debate, traditionally associated with male concerns. McConnell-Ginet (1983:378), for example, has proposed that women's "informal theories of conversation" do not deal with "individual rights and obligations." Within he-said-she-said, however, preadolescent girls formulate charges that their individual rights about the way they are to be treated in the talk of others have been violated. They do so by constructing opening accusation utterances of considerable sophistication that not only state the charge formally but also provide the grounds for it – invoking what is in fact a vernacular legal process.[44] Although within this process participants work together to sustain a coherent activity with a well-defined structure, the specific type of collaboration exhibited does not resemble "supportive" forms of collaboration described elsewhere as characteristic of female speech (see Maltz and Borker 1982:211). For example, there is no "underlying esthetic or organizing principle" of "harmony," as Kalčik (1975) found in the adult female storytelling group she studied.

This does not, however, mean that the talk of the girls studied was the same as that of the boys. Indeed, although legalistic argumentation is usually associated with males, he-said-she-said occurred only among females, and the males studied had no structure for extended debate of comparable complexity. Thus, although the speech of the Maple Street girls does not conform to many of our current stereotypes about female speech, it does show clear differences from that of their male agemates. What these results suggest is that if we are to describe accurately the organization of male and female language, we shall have to go beyond global generalizations that contrast all men with all women in all situations and instead describe in detail the organization of talk within specific activity systems. Such an approach permits study of the similarities as well as differences in female and male language usage and relates specific utterance forms to both ongoing practical activities and the cultures that underlie them.

Appendix A: Ages of the children who appear in transcripts

Boys		*Girls*	
Cameron	6	Damey	7
Joey	7	Priscilla	7
Stephen	7	Dishunta	8
Robby	9	Aisha	10
Raymond	10	Darlene	10
Vincent	10	Naynay	10
Earl	11	Deniece	10
Chuckie	11	Deniecey	10
Lee	11	Nettie	11
Chopper	12	Maria	12
Eddie	12	Pam	12
Sheridan	12	Sharon	12
Johnny	13	Terri	12
Juju	13	Florence	13
Michael	13		
Poochie	13		
Tokay	13		
Huey	14		

Appendix B: Ritual-insult sequence

Example 36: 6–3–71–4

```
1  Michael:    Shoes all messed up.
2                  (1.0)
3  Nettie:     You say somp'm? I– come on let me have
4              it.
5  Michael:    You been che(hh)win' o(hh)n e(hh)//m.
```

6	Nettie:	Eh heh heh heh heh!
7		•h I *know* you been. *You* all me://ssed
8		up.
9	Michael:	•h You bee(h)n chewin' o(h)n e//(h)m.
10	Nettie:	Eh heh!
11		No I *ha*ven't.
12	Michael:	*Yes* you ha://ve.
13	Nettie:	You took a(h)n got your dog your dog 'd
14		chew 'em up cuz he ain't have nothin'
15		ta // eat.
16	Michael:	If he pick up a piece of wood and I say
17		no ( ) then it's in the– in the // ( )
18	Nettie:	Ah you shu:t up.
19		You can't even kees // a
20	Michael:	You slap
21		You just slappin' on wood!
22	Nettie:	You can't even *keep* a (0.2) a decent
23		(0.2) pair a shoe://s.
24	Michael:	Don't swag.
25		(0.3)
26	Nettie:	I'm not *swa*:ggin.
27	Michael:	You // are too cuz you go to the (0.2)
28		you go to the John
29	Nettie:	Mole mole cheek cheek. Psychedelic
30		(0.2) that'//s all.
31	Michael:	You go to the John Baldwin's store and
32		get them five dollar shoes.
33		(0.8)
34	Michael:	Eh // heh!
35	Nettie:	What?
36	Michael:	Cuz the closest thing is the Thrifty
37		Sto(heh-heh // heh)re!
38	Nettie:	You go and get them *one* dollar. Okay?
39		One day– (0.2) *my* brother was spendin'
40		the night with *you*, •h And // the next
41		mornin' he got up,
42	Michael:	I don't wanna hear about it. Your
43		brother // ain't *ne*ver been in *my*
44		house.
45	Nettie:	THE NEXT TIME IIE GOT UP, •heh He was
46		gonna brush his teeth so the roach
47		tri(h)ed ta(h) bru(h)sh hi(h)s!
48	Michael:	Don't // swag.
49	Nettie:	•h *Ha ha ha ha ha* •hh!
50		•h Eh heh heh // *heh* he he he he
51	Michael:	An if he was up there If the roach was
52		tryin' ta *brush* it // he musta brought
53		it up it up there *wi*th him.
54	Nettie:	•heh!
55		•h *Eh* // he heh heh heh he he he he
56	Michael:	•h eh heh!

57	Robby:	((falsetto)) Ha // he! he
58	Nettie:	He he he he ha // ha ha // ha
59	Johnny:	•heh!
60	Johnny:	•H!
61	Nettie:	•h and I // saw– I sawed you on (0.2)
62		Ni:nth Street tryin' ta catch a *knit* on
63		*sale* for a dollar!
64	Johnny:	•H heh.
65	Michael:	Don't swag.
66	Nettie:	Ah: shut up. ((singsong)) Poor liddle
67		Michael
68	Michael:	What? Do you have a knit?
69	Nettie:	[[Sittin' onna fence.
70	Michael:	Do you have a knit?
71	Nettie:	Troyina make a dollar outa ninety noine
72		cents. He heh!
73		(0.3)
74		Ah ha:. (0.2) And one *more* thing! One
75		day (0.2) *I* went in your hou– *I* was
76		gonna walk in the door for *two* sets
77		[[a roaches.
78	Michael:	For what.
79		For what.
80	Nettie:	One roach here (0.2) and one roach here.
81		THE ONE RIGHT HERE,
82	Michael:	Oh you tryin' ta *sell* // em for him.
83	Nettie:	THE ONE RIGHT HERE W–
84	Michael:	You tryın' to se(hh)ll e(hh)m.
85	Nettie:	THE ONE RIGHT HERE // WAS UP HERE SAYIN'–
86	Michael:	*Some*body gonna buy your // damn roach.
87	Nettie:	THE ONE RIGHT here was up here sayin'–
88		(0.2) "People movin' ou:t? (0.2) And
89		the one right here was sayin' (0.2)
90		"*Peo*ple movin' in–"
91		[[Why? Because of the odor of their // ski(hh)n.
92	Michael:	You understand their language. You
93		must be one of 'em.
94	Johnny:	((falsetto)) Eh *heh!* Heh he heh!
95	Nettie:	What'd he s(hhhh)ay? Wha(h)d he(h)
96		say(h)y? •H What he(h) sa(hh)y? What
97		he sa(heh heh)y? What you say? Whad's
98		he // say Candy?
99	Michael:	You understand their language cuz you
100		*one* of 'em.
101	Nettie:	I(h) *know(h)* you(h) ar(hh)re! You was
102		*born* from the roach fam//ily.
103	Michael:	Don't swag.
104		(1.2)
105	Nettie:	Don't *you* swa::g.
106		(1.2)
107		You know one thing ((tch!)) uh when

108		you was *li*ttle, All you did every roach
109		you see crawl on the floor you get it
110		and save it for a souvenir. =
111	Michael:	Don't swag. You used to go out there
112		and put the roaches in the– in the– in
113		the jar at night. (0.2) And put 'em and
114		let 'em out in the mornin.'

Notes

The fieldwork constituting the basis for this study was carried out by Marjorie Harness Goodwin and was made possible by a National Institutes of Mental Health research grant (17216–01) administered through the Center for Urban Ethnography, University of Pennsylvania. We are deeply grateful to Erving Goffman, William Labov, John Pfeiffer, Susan Philips, Barrie Thorne, Sharon Veach, and especially Samuel Vuchinich for comments on earlier versions of this analysis. The deficiencies that remain are our own responsibility.

1   For reviews of the literature on these issues, see Brown (1980); Kramarae (1981); McConnell-Ginet (1980, 1983); Philips (1980); Thorne and Henley (1975), Thorne, Kramarae, and Henley (1983); West and Zimmerman (1985).

2   See for example McLaughlin's (1984:180) description of argument as a "troublesome" conversational event.

3   Various definitions have been proposed for arguing. Eisenberg and Garvey (1981:150) describe the "adversative episode" as "the interaction which grows out of an opposition to a request for action, an assertion, or an action. . . . An adversative episode is a sequence which begins with an opposition and ends with a resolution or dissipation of conflict." For a critique of this definition, see Maynard (1985a:4–5). Brenneis and Lein (1977:61–62) define an argument sequence as an arrangement of content and/or stylistic categories according to one of three different patterns: (1) repetition, (2) inversion, or (3) escalation. Boggs (1978) uses the term "contradicting routine" in describing the patterning of arguing among part-Hawaiian children. Genishi and Di Paolo's definitions (1982) are built on those of Boggs (1978) and Eisenberg and Garvey (1981).

4   Analysts of conversation (see, for example, Schegloff, in press) have noted that there are serious problems with using categories such as gender to classify participants for purposes of analysis without demonstrating that the participants themselves are attending to such categories as a constitutive feature of the activities they are engaged in. We are in complete agreement, and have used such a perspective to organize much of our other research. For purposes of exposition in this chapter, however, we frequently talk about participants as "girls" and "boys." Despite such terminology, most of the findings presented here buttress rather than refute the position taken by such conversation analysts as Schegloff. For example, despite many previous claims about strong gender differences in the ways that men and women disagree and argue, we find that girls and boys make extensive use of the same resources for building argumentative exchanges. Beginning analysis from a perspective that assumes the relevance of gender differences and focusing study on how the sexes might differ from each other grossly

distort the data being examined and hide many crucial phenomena (for example organizing structures used by both sexes) from detailed investigation. Such an approach also leads to the reification of stereotypes that may be quite inaccurate. Finally, an exclusive focus on gender differences shifts investigation away from analysis of the procedures utilized by participants to construct the activities they are engaged in. In our opinion the explication of such structures should be the primary object of study. Thus we consider the analysis of how the gossip activity that the children called he-said-she-said was constructed and organized to be more basic and more important than the finding that on Maple Street only the girls engaged in this activity, and indeed we should not be surprised if future research revealed that use of these structures was not restricted to women (which would not of course invalidate the underlying analysis of the activity). Detailed investigation of the procedures used to build appropriate events makes it possible to study in detail how alternative choices from these resources can be used to build different types of social organization, some of which may be more appropriate to the interests of one group (the girls' group on Maple Street, for example) than another (such as the boys' group), while leaving open the possibility that in other circumstances the same participants might make quite different choices.

5   Since both authors contributed to the analysis, the pronoun "we" is used throughout the analytic sections of the chapter. But, since only Marjorie Harness Goodwin actually worked with the Maple Street group, the pronoun "I" is used when describing fieldwork.

6   This example has been constructed to contain a variety of relevant transcription devices for a brief example. It is not an accurate record of an actual exchange.

7   A listing of the names and ages of children who are cited in this chapter appears in Appendix A for researchers interested in competencies displayed by differing age groups.

8   A similar type of social organization has also been observed by Thorne (1986) in a study of primary-school children in California and Michigan.

9   Mitchell-Kernan and Kernan in their analysis of role-playing activity of black American preadolescent children (1977:201) have made similar analyses regarding the use of directives and their responses, which "were constantly used to define, reaffirm, challenge, manipulate, and redefine status and rank." See also Ervin-Tripp (1982:31).

10   See also Sacks (in press) regarding preferences for agreement.

11   Such procedures share the principle of opposition observable in the "contradicting routines" of part-Hawaiian children described by Boggs (1978:328). For review of child-language literature dealing with the development of children's "discourse negation" see Maynard (in press).

12   This same pattern was found in Pomerantz's (1984:83–84) examples of disagreements with prior speakers' self-deprecations. Indeed, in such circumstances the disagreements are opposing what prior speaker said in an environment in which prior speaker would not be expected to modify his or her initial position on his or her own.

13   Corsaro and Rizzo (in press) note that initial opposition prefaces of this sort occurred rarely in their data of middle-class children's talk; only the black children in their data sample made use of such structures.

14 Lein and Brenneis note similar patterns of stress in the arguments of black American migrant children they studied. The Fijian Indian children in their sample also used contrastive stress, though far less frequently than did blacks, and "white children did not use stress for contrast in the way which the other two groups did" (Lein and Brenneis 1978:305).

15 For detailed analysis of how correction can be formulated either as a salient or as a nonexplicit event see Jefferson (in press).

16 See Pomerantz (1975:26) for an analysis of how return assessments maintain the relationship between referent and speaker.

17 It has been noted that such types of disputes are less complex in structure than disputes with justifications by such researchers as Eisenberg and Garvey (1981:167), Genishi and Di Paolo (1982:55), Keller-Cohen, Chalmer, and Remler (1979), and Piaget (1926:68). Genishi and Di Paolo (1982:55) argue that more complex arguments include "an acceptance, appeal to authority, compromise or supporting argument."

18 Boggs (1978:341) found that "arguments (statements that attempt to prove other statements, explanations, and explications) are more frequent in the older boys' disputes than in those of younger boys and girls." Similarly in my data younger children more frequently constructed their arguments out of exchange and return moves than out of positions buttressed with accounts. Nevertheless, the linguistic skill of embedding displayed in format tying in return and exchange moves is highly developed, and we do not consider providing accounts "a move beyond inversion or the assertion/counterassertion format of opposition," as does Maynard (in press).

19 Here line numbers are used to mark talk, though clearly the argument originates before the talk, with Raymond's bumping into Terri while skating.

20 For a more recent statement of this position see Maynard's (1985b:213) distinction between "surface level" characterizations of an utterance and deeper analysis of what that talk presumes and presupposes.

21 Although the present data were drawn from the arguments of children, format tying is not restricted to either children or argumentative exchanges. Consider, for example, the following, which is taken from an adult male joke-telling session (simplified transcript):

Mike: She said– You better hurry on up. For I get outta the mood. She says. He says. I gotta get outta the mood before I can get outta the car.

Here second speaker not only repeats the exact words of prior speaker ("get outta the mood") but also uses the structure provided by that talk as a framework for his subsequent talk ("before I can get outta the car"). The following (reported in the New York Times, August 8, 1985, p. 10) occurred at the White House between presidential spokesman Larry Speakes and reporter Helen Thomas:

Speakes: Do you want to say that I did not tell the truth?
→ Thomas: Aw, come on, get off of that.
→ Speakes: No, you come on. You've accused me of something.

22 Keenan (Ochs) (1974b) and Keenan and Kelin (1975) describe conversations of 2- and 3-year-olds, in which replication of form in terms of phonological shape occurred between paired utterances. Keenan (1974b:179) states, "It is often acceptable to reply to a comment, command, question

or song with an utterance which attends only to the form of that talk." In the data being examined in this chapter, although the children attend closely to the form of the prior talk, that in itself is not adequate for the construction of a proper return move; it must also provide an appropriate next action to the action being countered. The work of Ochs (see, in particular, the collection of articles in Ochs and Schieffelin 1983) on substitution, sound-play, focus operations, and repetition, though dealing with children younger than those being studied here, is relevant to a range of phenomena that we are discussing as format tying.

23   Such a procedure is also used in part-Hawaiian children's arguments. Boggs (1978:332–333) states, "One way of contradicting is by grammatically incorporating and negating another speaker's clause."

24   Semantic shifts with minimal changes in form are observable in verbal duelling of the Chamula (Gossen 1974) and of Turkish boys (Glazer 1976) and provide a key structural feature of ritual-insult events (Labov 1972a:349).

25   Such a type of counter is also characteristic in arguments of part-Hawaiian children (Boggs 1978:329) and among white middle-class children (Lein and Brenneis 1978:305). Note also the strict attention to turn taking observable in these data. Such a patterning is similar to that observed by Lein and Brenneis for the black migrant and white middle-class children they studied (p. 306) while contrasting with that for Fijian Indian children (pp. 306–308).

26   We use the term "embedding" here in a way slightly different from the way it is usually used in linguistic analysis. However, we know of no other term that captures as aptly the way in which specific material from prior talk is implanted within the current talk. We are indebted to Don Brenneis for bringing this issue to our attention.

27   On the principle of escalation see Lein and Brenneis (1978:301).

28   For more extensive analysis of what happens to the talk of another when it is repeated by someone else see Vološinov (1973).

29   Ladd is careful to state that, on the other hand, "contrastive stress" may not be signaling explicit contrast but rather "narrow focus"; that is, it may be doing nothing more than "focusing on the points of difference in otherwise identical phrases" (1978:79).

30   Cook-Gumperz (1981:45) notes the importance of stylistic contrast in children's "persuasive talk" and argues that "prosody carries a very significant part of the signalling load as does rhythm." See also Schriffin (1984:318) for a discussion of such features in adult arguments.

31   Lein and Brenneis (1978:302) note that "among the black migrant children and the Indian children insults are repeated or improved on by each succeeding speaker."

32   The entire sequence from which this is taken appears in Appendix B.

33   Ritual insult of this type was not observed in the younger children's group. The younger child, however, generally constructs his or her extended arguments in rounds of moves attempting to outmaneuver the other (as contrasted to moves that attempt to validate a particular point, which will be discussed later). The content of these moves generally refers to comparisons of ascribed rather than achieved attributes – for example, ages of children and their relatives – reflecting the idea "more is better" (Genishi and Di Paolo 1982:57–58).

34 For a critique of such a position, see Adger (1984:50, 104), M. H. Goodwin (1982b:87), and Maynard (1985a).

35 Vuchinich (1984, in press) has made similar findings for American families of various classes and ethnic types.

36 Goffman (1981:27) argues that it is children rather than adults who are "the mature practitioners" of comebacks or "inversionary interchanges."

37 For other analysis of how apparently disruptive events in spontaneous conversation might contribute to a child's ability to master the underlying structure of his or her language see C. Goodwin (1981:170–172).

38 Also relevant to this issue is the observation by Ervin-Tripp and Mitchell-Kernan (1977:7) that "Many of the speech events in which children engage typically occur among children apart from adults, and they are explicitly taught, in many cases by children."

39 Such a situation contrasts with male peer groups studied by Keiser (1969), Savin-Williams (1976), Sherif and Sherif (1953), Suttles (1968), and Whyte (1943).

40 For more extensive analysis of this dispute, including the way in which movement to talk with a different type of social organization, a story, is consequential for participation in the dispute, see M. H. Goodwin (1982b).

41 For more extended analysis of he-said-she-said, see M. H. Goodwin (1980b, 1982a).

42 Generally the arguments of children analyzed by previous researchers (e.g. Eisenberg and Garvey 1981) have been dyadic in structure. This may be in large part due to the fact that characteristically such researchers have themselves set up or created the situation to be observed. Looking at argumentative phenomena from another perspective, the structure of argumentation itself seems to bias the interaction so that it becomes focused upon two opposing positions (see M. H. Goodwin 1982b). Even in such cases, however, participants other than the principals may align themselves with one of the positions on the floor, so that although the arguments are bipolar in terms of position, they are not intrinsically dyadic with respect to numbers of participants. Moreover, as the present data demonstrate, within he-said-she-said children may operate on several positions concurrently. In brief, a dyadic model does not adequately conceptualize the richness of organization that children bring to their spontaneous arguments.

43 Note that Nettie aligns herself with Pam against Darlene; she delivers actions similar to those of Pam, yet as actions that are fragmented rather than complete and as actions that echo other actions rather than direct the confrontation.

44 Hughes (1985) and von Glascoe (1980:229–230) describe similar forms of legalistic debate by girls in the context of games.

9. Do different worlds mean different words?: an example from Papua New Guinea

BAMBI B. SCHIEFFELIN

Many anthropologists working in Papua New Guinea have focused on the social relationships between the sexes (Brown and Buchbinder 1976; Langness 1967; Malinowski 1929; Mead 1935; Meggitt 1964; O'Brien and Tiffany 1984). For example, there have been extensive accounts of sexual antagonism and the separateness of men and women in a variety of social spheres in the Highlands. Indeed, the range of male–female relationships and ideologies found in Papua New Guinea has fascinated researchers for many years and has been the basis for developing theories in several different areas.

On the one hand, interest in male–female relations has been directed to issues of initiation, pollution, and self-concepts (see, for example, Faithorn 1975; Hays and Hays 1982; Herdt 1982; Poole 1981; Read 1954). Another direction has been away from the focus on individuals and toward seeing individuals as the vehicles for the creation and validation of social alliances. Out of this framework have come theories of social organization, marriage and exchange, and conception (e.g., Clay 1977; Glasse and Meggitt 1969; R. Kelly 1977; A. Strathern 1973; M. Strathern 1972; Wagner 1967; Weiner 1976). More recently, anthropologists have investigated the relationships among gender, nature, and culture in order to understand better the organization and ideology of social life (Gewertz 1983; Gillison 1980; Goodale 1980; Meigs 1976; A. Strathern 1979; M. Strathern 1980). These anthropologists, among others, have worked with both the men and the women in a society and have been fluent speakers of the local language. Several have focused on language more directly (Feld 1982; Goldman 1981; McKellin 1980; Sankoff 1980; B. B. Schieffelin 1986, in press).

When one looks at the relevant cultural and linguistic literature for Papua New Guinea, however, it is striking that for all of the descriptions

249

of the differences in the worlds of men and women, there has been virtually nothing written about the differences in their words. That is, there is a notable absence of reports that examine patterns of language use with regard to possible gender-based differences. This is particularly surprising given the attention paid to other types of linguistic variation in Papua New Guinea, variation based on dialect and language choice, genre differences, special ritual and magical languages, and language change. One's first worry is that there has been some great oversight. Could it be that everyone has just overlooked the gender differences in language? Asked another way, *are* there relevant differences in language used by men and women in these societies? If so, where are these differences located and what do they mean? This chapter explores these questions in order to understand some of the relationships between culture and language among the Kaluli. Data on adult as well as child language use will be examined.

In order to understand developmental issues concerning Kaluli children's language acquisition and use with regard to the possibility of gender differences, it is important to set up a larger frame. First, relevant aspects of Kaluli culture and language are presented. If one starts with an anthropological approach to language, one must consider how social organization and gender ideology relate to linguistic resources and language use. Although I shall focus on the Kaluli, I suspect that what I have observed holds for other Papua New Guinea societies that are organized along similar lines and hold similar beliefs. Data on the Kaluli are drawn from three sources of ethnographic research, which has been collaborative at many different stages: E. L. Schieffelin's work on cultural and social aspects of Kaluli life (1976, 1979, 1981); Steve Feld's work on Kaluli ethnography of communication (1982); and my own work on family interaction, language acquisition and socialization (B. B. Schieffelin 1979, 1981a, 1986).

Kaluli culture and language

The Kaluli (population 1,200) can be characterized as a nonstratified, small-scale, traditionally nonliterate society. They live in a rain forest on the Great Papuan Plateau in the Southern Highlands Province of Papua New Guinea. They are one of four small groups who collectively refer to themselves as Bosavi people (*Bosavi kalu*) and to their language as Bosavi language (*Bosavi to*). The Kaluli, Ologo, Walulu, and Wisesi people are culturally identical, and the dialects they use are marked by predominantly phonological and lexical differences. These dialects are, nonetheless, mutually intelligible.

The Bosavi people are subsistence horticulturalists who live in about twenty longhouse communities, separated by a walk of an hour or so through the rain forest. Each longhouse community is a residential grouping, averaging about sixty to eighty individuals. The longhouse, which has no internal walls, has a men's and women's section, separated by a low partition over which food and other items can be passed. Two or three named patrilineal descent groups, approximately fifteen families, live in a village community. Marriage is exogamous; residence is patrilocal. This system promotes large networks of relations between affines and matrilateral relatives across longhouse communities and dialect groups.

In the traditional anthropological sense, Kaluli society can be characterized as egalitarian. That is, adults may dominate children, and men may dominate women. In terms of the division of labor, men and women have their own spheres of domestic activities that are different, that is, a group of activities they customarily perform. For example, women generally take responsibility for the children, pigs, and sago beating. Men generally take care of fighting and warfare, hunting with bows and arrows, and arranging marriages. But men and women sometimes do perform domestic and subsistence tasks normally associated with the sphere of activities of the opposite sex. For example, men can take care of young children, and when the opportunity presents itself women do trap and catch small animals but never use bow and arrows to do so. That is, some domestic activities are not in and of themselves gender-marked. If a man must beat his own sago it is because he is either poverty-stricken or has no wife or sisters. He is consequently pitied by members of his village or clan. He is not considered effeminate or unmasculine, but unfortunate.

While these spheres of activity are not as strongly marked as they are in Highlands societies, it is the usual participation in those appropriate spheres that demarcates sex roles. Among the Kaluli, the daily routines of men and women are quite separate. However, the antagonism between the sexes reported in the New Guinea Highlands is not present in Bosavi. Unlike many Highlands societies, Kaluli do not have separate men's and women's houses, nor do they have the extensive male and female initiations reported in the Eastern Highlands and elsewhere in Papua New Guinea (Herdt 1982). Among the Kaluli, complementarity and cooperation best describe the majority of daily interactions between men and women.

Kaluli is a non-Austronesian language that is part of the Central and South New Guinea stock of the Trans–New Guinea phylum. It is a verb-final split-ergative language tracking reference predominantly through a system known as switch reference (B. B. Schieffelin 1986). For Kaluli

this means that when the agents of a dependent clause and its following
independent clause are not the same, verbal morphology on the nonfinite
dependent verb signals this switch. Foley and Van Valin (1984) and
Heath (1975) have noted the inverse relation between gender systems
and switch reference in languages throughout the world. Kaluli, like
other languages with elaborate switch-reference systems, lacks gender
distinctions throughout the nominal system.

Most Kaluli are monolingual speakers, but more contact in the last
twenty years has brought about an increase in multilingualism for the
men. Some younger men know Huli and Tok Pisin mainly through their
experiences with contract labor and the Christian mission in the area,
but their use is limited in village affairs. Kaluli everyday life is overtly
focused on face-to-face verbal interaction. Talk is thought of and used
as a means of control, manipulation, expression, assertion, and appeal.
It gets you what you want, need, or feel owed. Extensive demarcation
of the kinds of speaking and speech acts further substantiate the observation that Kaluli are energetically verbal. Talk is a primary way to
be social and a primary indicator of social competence. The same linguistic resources, however, are not part of every individual's productive
repertoire. Furthermore, there are differences in the distribution of
linguistic resources that one draws on according to which activities one
engages in, what aspects of expressive culture one participates in, and
what genres or modes one uses.

Modes and codes

Here we shall briefly examine three modes: conversation (*to*), stories
(*malolo to*), and sung-texted weeping (*sa-yelɔ*). These three modes share
a feature in that the language used is considered by Kaluli to be "hard"
(*halaido*) (Feld and Schieffelin 1982). Unlike the language of song, which
is cast in a special poetic grammar, the language of conversation, stories,
and sung-texted weeping is well formed according to the rules of colloquial Kaluli. Even though sung-texted weeping is similar in vocal
production to song, because of its "hardness" Kaluli classify it with
other forms of speaking. While these three modes share many features,
there are a number of important phonological, morphological, syntactic,
semantic, and pragmatic differences, as well as differences in context
and content that set them apart. As we shall see, where there are different expressive and linguistic modes for men and women, different
social and linguistic codes will be drawn on.

Within modes shared and participated in by all members of society,
such as conversation, ways of speaking follow preferred forms of other

appropriate behavior. Consistent with the egalitarian nature of Kaluli society, there are no specially designated speaker roles. No one speaks for you – what an individual gets for himself or herself is determined by ability to use language effectively. There are no marked male or female forms or registers; men and women use the same linguistic strategies, sequences, and routines when discussing the same topics. For example, since the organization of domestic affairs and caregiving is predominantly the domain of women and girls, one frequently hears them talking to babies, making household arrangements, and discussing and arguing about issues relevant to their social spheres. Since men are involved more publicly in political and economic affairs (such as arranging bridewealth and negotiating breaches in relationships), the content and organization of their talk are appropriate to those activities. When men do involve themselves in domestic affairs and caregiving, however, they use many of the same forms of talk as do the women in similar situations. Likewise, when women are negotiating in the political arena or are involved in arguments, they make use of the same linguistic resources as do the men. This holds for both the phonological and syntactic organization of utterances, as well as for the multitude of expressive, emphatic, and affective forms that appear throughout Kaluli speech.

In everyday talk much is taken for granted, allowing casual, often very rapid speech to appear the conversational norm. In this rapid speech, vowels are noticeably centralized. There is a wide range of speech speeds and volume. Intonation is used both for emphasis and disambiguation. For daily conversation, speakers use two word orders, AOV and OAV. Each serves a set of pragmatic purposes and has a corresponding set of nonfocused or focused pronouns and nominal case markings for agents. AOV is used in announcements and reports or when the agent is not in focus. OAV is used in requests or when the agent is in focus. Tense is more frequently used than aspect on serialized and concatenated verbs. There is frequent use of quotatives, emphatic and pragmatic particles, and expressives.

The Kaluli do not have such expressions as "That sounds like men's talk." Nor would anyone ever say that a man "talks like a woman" or vice versa. Kaluli metalinguistic notions support sociolinguistic analyses. In any type of speech-related identification, individuals are most often characterized by their dialect. Dialect in turn usually carried information about one's natal village or clan of origin. Identification in this way is primary. One sees the clearest differences in the distribution of linguistic and expressive resources when one compares conversation with two other major expressive modes, stories and sung-texted weeping. We examine stories first.

There are two major genres of stories. One concerns a trickster and his good-guy cross cousin, and the other concerns birds and animals. These stories are told primarily by men at night for entertainment and are not esoteric or embedded in any ritual context. Plots are commonly known and easily understood by all. Length and elaboration in actual narration are determined by the storyteller, but as a rule bird and animal stories tend to be short and unelaborated, whereas trickster stories, when told by an animated teller, may be very elaborated, particularly around sexual themes. Speakers use normal vocal register with frequent prosodic shifts marking the changes between narrator and character roles being portrayed. A skillful teller uses sound effects to advantage over description. Speed range is as variable as in other modes, but there are more pauses. Emphatic speech is marked by repetition and emphatic particles.

Stories use AOV word order, usually referring to third-person agents. OAV order is usually reserved for direct quotation within the story. Introductory and concluding formulae function as both boundary and mode markers, as do the various narrative particles on verbs. Agents are often dislocated, and listing devices and repetition are used for dramatic effect. The full range of tense and aspect is utilized in complex syntactic constructions of switch reference.

In contrast to these two modes, we examine *sa-yelc*, one of five varieties of Kaluli expressive weeping. *Sa-yelc* are the most elaborate from the textual and melodic points of view. They are performed by women at funerals and other occasions of profound loss. These personal improvised laments are spontaneously sung while weeping. The degree of intricacy depends on age, skill, and experience; hence, older women do the longest and most complex *sa-yelc*. Owing to the continual shedding of tears and choked-up breathing, the *sa-yelc* differs from phonological production in talk. There is marked nasalization, and when the singing is rapid, vowels centralize and the tones dearticulate to a *sprechgesang*. All *sa-yelc* are framed by the melodic contour ♭ D–C–A–G in descent. Phrases are expanded by duplications, embeddings, and conjoinings of these pitches; the phrases ranges from four to twenty-two seconds, and the texts can be unelaborated, using single kinship terms, or be fully elaborated sentences.

In the area of syntax, (O)AV with focused first-person pronouns emphasizes the personal nature of the message, and the theme of remembrances is accentuated by the use of place names, often in verbless formulaic phrases. Extensive use of two aspectual forms, past habitual and future imperative continuous, emphasizes the repeated shared past experiences and the predictability of continuous future loss. In addition, subjunctive hypotheticals are used to frame lines (Feld 1982:104–6).

In addition to these examples of differences in the distribution of code features across modes, several other domains of speaking should be mentioned. For example, there are hunting as well as other ritual and magical formulae involving particular lexical items and idiomatic expression. These are used by men during appropriate ritual and hunting situations; women are not supposed to hear or know them.

Men perform as spirit mediums in seance performances for the entire community, bringing both male and female spirits up to speak through them. Men compose and perform three major types of song and dance in major exchange and ceremonial contexts, *gisalo*, *heyalo*, and *koluba* (Feld 1982). Women compose a more limited number of ceremonial song types. In these seance and ceremonial contexts, while the men do the majority of the composing and performing, the language used (both poetic grammar of song and the language used by mediums) is understood by women as well as men. What it is important to emphasize, however, is that the different code features and their relationships have more to do with the nature of the mode in which they occur than with the gender of speaker or participant. Stratification is most extensive in complex expressive forms, such as song and sung-texted weeping. These forms are most marked linguistically, as well as metalinguistically. Finally, it is important to remember that in Kaluli society what is specialized is also complementary.

Socialization and language acquisition

The social and linguistic aspects of Kaluli life presented above set the framework for making sense out of the socialization and developmental data that follow. The data on which the following discussion is based were collected in the course of two years' ethnographic and linguistic fieldwork (1975–7). This study of the development of communicative competence focused on four children who were approximately 24 months old at the start of the study. But an additional twelve children aged from birth to 10 years were included in the study (siblings and cousins). The spontaneous conversations of these children and their families were audiotape-recorded for one year at monthly intervals, with each monthly sample lasting an average of three hours. Detailed contextual notes accompanied the audiorecording. These annotated transcripts along with interviews and observations form the data base. A total of eighty-three hours of audiotaped conversations were collected and transcribed in the village. (Analyses of Kaluli language acquisition are reported in B. B. Schieffelin 1981b, 1986, in press.)

Kaluli see all newborns as helpless: "One feels sorry for babies" (*tualun lɛsu nofolan*). Infants are said to be "soft" (*taiyo*) in the early months, and one of the goals of the primary caregiver, the mother, is to facilitate "hardening" (*halaido domɛki*) – referring to the physical as well as mental firming up that takes place as the child matures. One of the critical aspects of social development concerns the acquisition of language. Unlike other types of behaviors and activities that the Kaluli say the child picks up by himself or herself, language must be "shown" or taught (*widan*) to the child. The child's mother has primary responsibility for this instruction. As with other domestic and caregiving activities, fathers' participation is quite minimal. Once a child has uttered the two words Kaluli take to indicate that language has begun (*nɔ* 'mother' and *bo* 'breast'), direct and explicit instruction begins. In ongoing interactions with siblings and others, mothers tell their language-learning child what to say. This takes the form of Proposition + *ɛlɛma* 'say like that', an imperative. This direct instruction frequently occurs in interactions involving three individuals, the mother, the young child, and another child or adult. The young child may not be particularly interested in repeating the mother's instructed utterances, but mothers structure these sequences so that the child gets involved in arguments, teasing, making claims on food and objects, and other exciting verbal routines that often have some type of payoff for the child. In the majority of cases, young children cooperate in these routines. These sequences may last for only two turns or continue up to forty consecutive turns, and may involve a number of different individuals to whom the young child is to speak (B. B. Schieffelin 1979). This type of language-teaching situation continues until the child is almost 3 years old, or until the mother has her next child. At that point she redirects her focus to the younger child, and the older one, equipped with strong language skills, enters a mixed-age peer group, no longer under the watchful eye of the mother.

Kaluli patterns of socialization differ quite dramatically for boys and girls in many respects. Girls are encouraged to be independent at an early age so that they can take care of themselves as well as assist with the care of infant siblings. They are taught to give up things they like, especially foods, to please a begging brother or younger sibling. Mothers are attentive to their young daughters' needs but treat them in a somewhat matter-of-fact way. Boys, on the other hand, are given food preferentially and are rarely asked to help with domestic chores. Mothers are physically quite affectionate with their sons and engage in playful teasing games with them. The boys are encouraged to be more aggressive than their sisters, especially in games. Little girls are encouraged to be submissive when their brothers make demands on them. In games they are instructed and encouraged to let their younger brothers chase and hit them. However, for all the differences in the ways in which boys and girls are treated, there do not seem to be any significant linguistic reflections of these differences.

The direct instruction sequences are one area in which gender-based language differences would show up in terms of input, since mothers are actively involved in shaping their children's communicative development and want them to speak appropriately. Since utterances are shaped to be socially appropriate between child speaker and intended addressee, they carry a great deal of cultural material. Here is where one might expect to find linguistic differences in the mother's speech to the child related to the child's gender or based on the gender of the child's intended addressee. There are, however, no significant linguistic differences at the phonological, syntactic, or pragmatic levels that are gender-based, either in the language spoken by the mother to the child or in the language the child is expected to address to the mother. There is variation between the mothers in the amount of language spoken to their male and female children, but this variation seems to depend more on the mother's own style of speaking than on the gender of the child.

The linguistic environment of the young child consists primarily of participation in and overhearing of conversations among a wide range of individuals in the village. Seances and other ritual and ceremonial contexts occur late at night when young children are asleep, and are infrequent enough to have little direct effect on their early language. The only adult expressive form that young children acquire is the melodic contours of *sa-yelc*, sung-texted weeping. Two of the young children in this study, one boy and one girl, used these melodic contours when wistfully talking about objects they wanted but did not have.

Given that systematic gender-based differences were found neither in the mothers' direct instruction language nor in their spontaneous language directed to the children, we next examine the child's linguistic production for possible gender-based differences. The most important and salient aspect of children's language is that children of both sexes learn the dialect of their mother and not that of their father, which is almost always different. Dialect, therefore, is the most marked characteristic of their language. In conversation, which is the major mode of communication for children, boys and girls tend to speak in much the same ways. A developmental analysis of the acquisition of the nominal case-marking and pronominal systems, word order, verb morphology including the tense system, and several aspects of pragmatic development showed individual variation to be the rule in all aspects of acquisition. Any differences found in the linguistic structure of children's utterances are due to individual variation rather than to any systematic variation according to gender.

We do not as yet fully understand the ways in which subtle differences in language use might interact with individual variation in the learning process. The data base for these analyses was substantial and documented adults' and children's language use in a range of contexts. But the in-depth developmental data focused on three children, and a small sample does raise the question of individual differences. It is possible that the reason for not finding gender-based differences in these data lies in the fact that strong individual variation might interact with subtle differences in language use. Systematic differences should have been apparent, however, given the contextually grounded data base of this study.

As I mentioned earlier, though, the roles and activity spheres of men and women are clearly demarcated, and children learn the ways of speaking appropriate to those roles and activities. It is in this area that there are some interesting differences between boys and girls in the ways in which they use language. The most salient of these has to do with using language as part of taking on the role of mothering and caregiving. For example, just as Kaluli mothers tell their young children what to say to others, Kaluli girls, as young as 28 months old, use the same routine involving *elema* 'say like that' in telling even younger children what to say. The frequency of this type of verbal interaction increases with age, and older girls, from 6 years on up, take an active role in instructing younger children in teasing, making claims, and using language to get things for themselves. Boys, on the other hand, almost never engage in this type of caregiving behavior. If they did so in more than a limited way, their behavior would be considered somewhat inappropriate. Girls spend a lot of time with young children and thus are in a position to tell them what to say when protecting, nurturing, and supporting them. Telling a younger child what to say is consistent with how females are supposed to act.

Another aspect of language use that follows appropriate role behavior concerns verbal play. In this study only girls were observed to play with the direct instruction routine, *elema*, and they did so with their mothers. It is one of the few contexts in which mothers and daughters engaged in playful interactions. These sequences are interesting in a number of respects. First, they are evidence of sophisticated socio- and metalinguistic skills on the part of girls as young as 30 months of age. Second, these sequences of verbal play involve role reversal (daughter telling mother what to say) and reciprocity (mother following daughters' turn-taking and instructions to repeat). In addition, these sequences represent one of the few instances of what might be a kind of role play in a society where it has not otherwise been observed. In these sequences, the young daughter is enacting the role of mother, doing what mothers repeatedly do: tell their children what to say. Furthermore, in general, girls seem to be involved with verbal play and sound play to a greater degree than boys (B. B. Schieffelin 1981a). From an early age (30 months) their verbal play follows the continuously overlapping style of Kaluli singing, as described by Feld (1984). Learning appropriate social behavior necessarily involves learning appropriate verbal routines and skills. Young children spend a great deal of time with their mothers, who teach them appropriate gender-based roles and activities. Therefore, it is not surprising that girls engage in verbal routines that are considered within the women's domain and boys do not.

When children are very small they appear fairly similar. As they reach their second year, the differences become more marked in terms of dress. In the third year their activities become more differentiated. As girls reach the age of 4 or 5, they associate with same-sex peers and older women, thus acquiring more specialized knowledge and skills. They learn about gardening, food preparation, and the expressive forms and genres in which they will participate as they get older. The same is true of boys. In the company of peers and older boys, they learn hunting lore, botanical information, and the expressive forms they will use in ceremonial and ritual contexts. Men and women do acquire different bodies of lexical knowledge, especially in the area of botany and animal lore. However, this does not affect the ways in which they use language in the sense of traditional studies of language and gender. It reflects different domains of practical knowledge. The social and linguistic differences among genres, as outlined above, concern the different distribution of linguistic resources across modes of language use.

We should start any inquiry into language use with the notion that speech communities have available a set of linguistic and expressive resources. These resources may be distributed in a variety of ways. For example, some are stylistic, others are grammatical, and additional ones are genre-based. One cannot assume that everything that is socially salient and marked will be linguistically marked. What is strongly marked in the social sphere may not necessarily be marked linguistically. The absence of gender-based grammatical distinctions in Kaluli and other Papua New Guinea societies that have strong gender dichotomies should caution us against assuming that gender distinctions will always be reflected in grammatical encoding. For the Kaluli, there may be both linguistic and sociological reasons for the absence. The tremendous amount of dialect variation may inhibit the development of stable stylistic or grammatical indicators related to gender. Alternatively, there may be ideological or social-structural reasons for their absence. Given the clear definition of male and female activity spheres, and the lack of stratification and specialized role differentiation throughout Kaluli society, perhaps no linguistic markers are needed. In all contexts it is very clear who and what you are. As yet we do not fully understand the very complex relationships between the worlds of women and men and the words of women and men.

Notes

The research carried out in Papua New Guinea was funded by grants from the National Science Foundation and the Wenner-Gren Foundation for Anthropological Research. Their continued support is gratefully acknowledged. Many helpful suggestions from Steven Feld, Gillian Sankoff, and Edward L. Schieffelin have improved this chapter, parts of which draw from a paper co-authored with Steven Feld presented at the 1979 Meetings of the American Anthropological Association.

1   The issue as to the balance of expressive resources in song in Kaluli society is taken up by Feld (1984).

Part III

Sex differences in language and the brain

Introduction

Susan Steele

The chapters in Part III address the question of whether there are any differences between males and females in cerebral organization and neurological maturation that have linguistic effects. The question has two subparts: First, are there any biologically based differences in brain organization or maturation that can be correlated absolutely or partially with sex? And, second, if such differences exist, what consequences, if any, are there for cognition in general and language in particular?

The volatility of the topic must be admitted at the outset. Scientific research is presumably objective, but it is difficult to ensure that research into this particular topic is value-free. The study of the implications of biologically based sex differences raises the specter of genetic determinism, of using the results of scientific inquiry to substantiate cultural prejudices and biases. I admit the presence of the specter; I believe that anyone working in this area must face squarely the possible political ramifications of his or her work. Having laid my political cards on the table, I do not intend to play out the hand. I focus only on the scientific aspects of this investigation.

Investigation of the correlation between sex and brain organization or maturation has a long history, spanning two millennia. Men and women have been perceived, through the ages, as different on physical, emotional, and intellectual grounds – essentially with respect to every parameter. The issue, then, has been how to account for such differences. From the time of Aristotle until the beginning of this century, the explanation of the assumed differences has been a neurophysiological one. So it has been proposed that the reason men and women are "mentally" different devolves to their relative brain size, the relative complexity of their brains, or differences in the organization of their brains.

One major difference between current work and what preceded it has to do with the empirical nature of modern research. As the foregoing suggests, earlier investigators into the topic began with the assumption that women were inferior to men – that they were, for example, less intellectual, more emotional. The issue, then, was simply to show that some biological precondition accounted for male superiority. Modern researchers, at least optimally, begin with experiments designed to test for the existence of neurophysiological differences. The experiments have focused largely on testing for differences in lateralization; that is, while brain-size and brain-complexity proposals are not found in the current literature, differences in localization play a major role in modern theories as to the differences between males and females.[1] The experiments testing for male–female differences in lateralization probe the asymmetricality of responses localized in the right and left cerebral hemispheres. There are dichotic hearing tests (Lake and Bryden, 1976, for example), that is, experiments testing the dominance for certain tasks of the right or left ear; visual-field tests (Andrews, 1977, for example), that is, experiments testing the dominance for certain tasks of the right or left eye; and comparison of the EEGs (electroencephalograms – records of brain-wave activity) of the right and left hemispheres (Galin and Ellis, 1975, for example).

No consensus exists that such tests unequivocally reveal basic neurophysiological differences between males and females. Some researchers have concluded on the basis of such experiments that the brains of males and females are differently organized. For example, McGlone (1980), in a general overview of the literature, concludes that the evidence points to the brain of a male being more asymmetrically organized than that of a female. And Kimura (1980, 1983) argues that, for speech in particular, the critical areas for the female are concentrated in the left anterior part of the brain, while the critical areas for males are both anterior and posterior. In contrast, some researchers have concluded that males and females exhibit no critical difference in laterality. For example, Fairweather's (1982) review of visual-laterality studies reports the vast majority finding no sex differences whatsoever. Finally, some researchers argue that sex is a factor in differential patterns of lateralization but intersects with (and is perhaps ultimately less important than) such other variables as handedness. McKeever's chapter in this section is an example of this contention.

In their attempts to investigate the correlation between sex and brain organization or maturation, the two chapters in this section should be viewed against this background of controversy and conflicting results. In fact, the two chapters reflect the conflict in that one comes down much more strongly on the side of sex differences than does the other.

The chapter by Shucard, Shucard, and Thomas is concerned with the development of hemispheric specialization of brain functions. The authors note the existence of innate hemispheric differences in anatomical structure and the possibility that there may also be a functional correlate; for instance, infants as young as a month old have been claimed to be able to discriminate among linguistically relevant sounds. But hemispheric specialization is also a function of maturation. (See Bryden and Allard, 1978, for discussion of this issue.) On the basis of electrophysiological evidence, the authors argue for a pattern of hemispheric development that is different for male infants than for female infants.

For 3-month-old infants, speech and musical stimuli produced a pattern of evoked potential asymmetry that was more dependent on the sex of the infant than on the stimuli themselves: For females [the left hemisphere appears to be the] area of the brain that was more involved in the processing of both types of stimuli, whereas the opposite pattern shown by the 3-month-old males indicates that the right hemisphere played a more active role in the processing of both speech and musical stimuli.

At 6 months, males showed essentially the same pattern of asymmetry as at 3 months. However, 6-month-old females tended to show the pattern found in adults.

Shucard, Shucard, and Thomas are not alone in their proposal that hemispheric specialization for some tasks comes earlier in females than in males. D. Taylor (1969), for example, considering the relationship among sex, the age of onset of seizure activity, and hemisphere affected, found that in females, but not males, the inception rate of left-hemisphere seizure activity drops off sharply after one year. He reasons that the hemisphere undergoing the greatest development is less vulnerable to damage and argues that therefore lateralization occurs earlier in females than in males. A most striking element of the Shucard, Shucard, and Thomas study is the tender age at which there are measurable differences between males and females: At three months, males and females differ in hemispheric specialization. Such a pattern could be the result of even earlier developmental differences or of an innate difference; Shucard, Shucard, and Thomas do not address this question.

The chapter by McKeever is concerned not with developmental differences in cerebral organization but, rather, with the question of whether adult males and females differ in hemispheric specialization. He reviews recent dichotic and tachistoscopic studies of right-handed, English-speaking adults, assumedly testing relative hemispheric specialization, and concludes that with minimal exceptions they do not support the hypothesis that adult males and females differ in hemispheric specialization. He presents evidence, however, that sex is a factor, if it is considered relative to familial sinistrality (i.e., relative to the presence in the subject's family of left-handedness). In brief, in a tachistoscopic task, females lacking familial sinistrality and males with familial sinistrality have smaller right-visual-field superiority than females with familial sinistrality and males without.

As noted, McKeever's findings in regard to hemispheric specialization and sex suggest a weaker correlation than those of Shucard, Shucard, and Thomas. This difference – and other such disagreements mentioned – may be a result of the different tests involved. Electrophysiological studies involve more direct tests of brain activity than do dichotic hearing and tachistoscopic studies, but, on the other hand, electrophysiological activity need not translate directly into performance. The commensurability of the results remains, then, an open question.

While the two chapters in this section differ in the relative importance they ascribe to sex as a variable, they both find some correlation between sex and hemispheric specialization, and so they represent what seems to be the majority opinion in the literature. That is, the first subquestion raised at the outset – Are there any biologically based differences in brain organization or maturation that can be correlated absolutely or partially with sex? – is most commonly answered in the affirmative (although, as indicated, there is no absolute unanimity on this score). Given this conclusion, one direction of research is toward refining the experimental base. (Both chapters touch on this problem.) Another is providing an explanation of why such a difference should exist. (Compare recent work on the interaction between hormones and the brain, e.g., Nottebohm, 1977.)

I turn, then, to the second subquestion raised at the outset, to the implications drawn from this research for cognition in general and language in particular. One issue follows immediately from the preceding discussion. There is no reason to doubt that tests such as those just described measure some type of brain activity. The question is whether the observable brain activity has any direct relationship to cognition or language. Most studies are reasonably tentative about the conclusions to be drawn in this regard, depending rather on indirect chains of inference. So, for example, specifically in regard to language and sex differences, one might (as Shucard, Shucard, and Thomas do) note the existence of studies that suggest that "girls begin to speak earlier than boys . . . express themselves more frequently . . . show earlier use of two-word sentences . . . and develop a larger vocabulary at an earlier age," and comment that the evidence of differences in hemispheric specialization is at least consistent with these findings. The issue is obvious: If it is difficult to argue that the experiments discussed in the two immediately preceding sections of this introduction test cognitive behavior, it is at least equally questionable to propose – or implicitly assume – that observed differences in such experiments are indicative of differential cognition.

Let us consider the issue of language specifically, since that is the focus of this book. What a linguist would consider the cognitive aspect of language – what it suggests about the organization of the mind (as distinguished from the brain) – is not revealed by differential rates of vocabulary acquisition any more than it is revealed in responses to tachistoscopic tests. But, viewed from this perspective, there is a very interesting result in these studies for the issue of whether, given the existence of biologically based differences in brain organization according to sex, these differences have any consequences for language. The chapters in this section are representative of the field in that they offer no evidence that males and females differ in their ability to construct a grammar, that is, to acquire a language from primary data. Thus, if there are differences between males and females in terms of hemispheric specialization and the like, the conclusion can only be that the differences do not matter for this basic cognitive capacity.

This is an important result in two different respects. First, if males and females are indistinguishable on basic cognitive grounds, investigation of the differences they exhibit becomes less loaded. Second, if there are neurophysiological differences between males and females and if males and females are cognitively indistinguishable, it suggests that the same cognitive task can be accomplished by different organizational systems. The question then shifts to delimiting the range of organizational systems.

The chapters in Parts I and II of this book report systematic differences between males and females. The neurophysiological literature suggests the same conclusion. There is no reason, however, to think that the types of differences discussed here are the bases of the differences discussed there. The link between the two kinds of work is more abstract. The literature on language and sex differences allows a focused investigation of the range of possibilities (socially based, developmentally based, and neurophysiologically based) available to humans, given an essentially invariant innate linguistic capacity.

Note

1 Witelson (1985) is one obvious exception to this generalization about the modern literature. She reports that "there may be no sex difference [in regard to the weight of the corpus callosum] in right-handers, but there may be in mixed-handers, with males tending to have a relatively larger posterior half" (p. 666).

10. Cerebral organization and sex: interesting but complex

WALTER F. MCKEEVER

With the increased interest in hemispheric specialization of function that has evolved since the end of the 1960s, a number of hypotheses have been put forward regarding the "strictness" or "degree" of hemispheric specialization as a function of subject, or person, characteristics. Among the characteristics that have been suggested as influencing the degree of hemispheric specialization are handedness, familial left-handedness, handwriting posture, and, most relevantly, sex. With respect to sex differences, Levy (1969), McGlone (1978, 1980), and Waber (1976) have all suggested that females may be less hemispherically specialized for language and spatial processing than males.

According to Levy (1969), the hemispheric organization favorable for conjointly optimizing verbal and spatial abilities is one of very strict lateralization of language functions to the left cerebral hemisphere and of spatial functions to the right hemisphere. Levy hypothesizes that when language is relatively bilateralized, that is, when some aspects or types of language function are partially or wholly mediated by the right hemisphere, language skills may be augmented, but spatial ability will be correspondingly diminished. The assumption is that while the right hemisphere is sometimes capable of some language functions, the left hemisphere is unable to compensate for reduced right-hemisphere spatial competence. Since there are data showing females to be superior to males in at least some aspects of language ability and showing males to be superior to females in visual-spatial abilities (Maccoby and Jacklin, 1974), the hypothesis that females are more bilateralized for language accords well with the pattern of consequences for ability that Levy (1969) predicts. One must realize, however, that the hypothesis of greater female bilaterality of language processing is perhaps deduced from the already established pattern of ability differences between the sexes.

268

Table 10.1. *Auditory verbal laterality studies of adults*

Author(s)	Task	Sex more lateralized
1977		
Schulman-Galambos	Word report	—
McKeever & VanDeventer	Digit recall	—
Lishman & McMeekan	Word report	—
1979		
Scott et al.	Syllable report	—
Kelly & Orton	Word report	—
1980		
Young & Ellis	Word report	—
Piazza	Syllable report	Males
Searleman	Syllable report	—

Source: Adapted from McKeever (1981), courtesy of the Orton Dyslexia Society.

What is needed therefore is direct evidence that females do possess greater bilaterality of language processing and execution than do males.

With the availability of many techniques for assessing language function lateralities one would assume that unequivocal direct evidence regarding a possible sex difference in language functioning would be readily obtainable. We have dichotic listening tasks, lateralized tachistoscopic tasks, electroencephalograph (EEG) techniques of various sorts, procedures for chemically deactivating one or the other hemisphere, clinical studies regarding the incidence of aphasia following unihemispheric lesions, and so forth. But both positive and negative results with respect to the question of sex differences have been found.

In my own research I have employed mainly tachistoscopic procedures and, to a lesser extent, dichotic listening procedures. Although some positive results regarding Levy's hypothesis have been obtained with such procedures by others, I believe any objective assessment of the entire literature casts the most serious doubt upon the proposition that females are less lateralized than males. To demonstrate this I want to present the results of a review of studies published from 1977 through 1980 in the three journals that seem to publish the most laterality research – *Neuropsychologia*, *Cortex*, and *Brain and Language*. I chose the period arbitrarily to keep it manageable and restricted the review to dichotic and tachistoscopic studies with normal, adult, right-handed, English-speaking subjects.

Table 10.1 summarizes the various dichotic studies, and Table 10.2 summarizes the tachistoscopic studies, by year. Of the eight dichotic studies, only one, that of Piazza (1980), found a significant sex difference. Piazza found males more lateralized than females, but an exam-

Table 10.2. *Visual laterality studies of adults*

Author(s)	Task	Sex more lateralized
1977		
McKeever & VanDeventer	Letter report	Females
Bradshaw et al.	Lexical decision	Males
Ellis & Young	Word report	—
Andrews	Letter, word report	—
1978		
Bradshaw & Gates	Lexical decision	Males
Bradshaw & Gates	Homophone decision	—
Bradshaw & Gates	Word naming latency	—
Bradshaw & Gates	Word nonword naming	—
Kail & Siegel	Digit report	Males
1979		
Leehey & Cahn	Word report	—
Bradshaw & Taylor	Word naming latency	—
Segalowitz & Stewart	Letter name matches	—
Schmuller & Goodman	Word report	—
McKeever & Jackson	Object naming latency	Males
McKeever & Jackson	Color naming latency	—
1980		
Miller & Butler	Letter report	—
Piazza	Word report	—
Madden & Nebes	Target digit RT	—

Source: Adapted from McKeever (1981), courtesy of the Orton Dyslexia Society.

ination of Piazza's data will show that among right-handed subjects the lesser lateralization of females was in fact restricted to those females who had left-handed relatives. Of the eighteen visual laterality task studies, only five found a significant sex difference, and one of these (McKeever and VanDeventer, 1977) found females more lateralized than males. In three of the four studies that found males more lateralized (Bradshaw and Gates, 1978; Bradshaw, Gates, and Nettleton, 1977; McKeever and Jackson, 1979) there is the possibility that the apparent sex differences could actually have been due to sex–familial sinistrality interactional influences. The Bradshaw et al. (1977) and the Bradshaw and Gates (1978) studies did not include FS+ subjects (i.e., persons positive for familial sinistrality) and the McKeever and Jackson study included virtually no FS+ males. The latter investigators noted that among their female subjects it was only those who were FS− (i.e., lacking familial sinistrality) who appeared responsible for the apparent sex difference. These results, in general, are not supportive of the hypothesis of greater verbal function bilaterality among females, since only

12.5 percent of the dichotic and 27.2 percent of the tachistoscopic study results found females less lateralized.

That this selective review is not biased against sex differences is suggested by the results of a recent review of visual laterality studies not restricted to particular sources (Fairweather, 1982). Fairweather found only five of forty-nine (10.2 percent) studies that showed males more lateralized, with two studies finding females more lateralized and forty-two studies finding no sex difference whatever. More recent evidence derived from dichotic listening experiments also fails to support the sex-differences hypothesis. Using a dichotic consonant–vowel recognition task, McKeever et al. (1984) found no sex effect in a sample of 104 right-handed subjects. Hiscock and MacKay (1985) found no sex difference in a sample of 477 right-handed subjects pooled across dichotic digit recall and consonant–vowel recognition experiments.

Despite these negative findings regarding sex differences, I would suggest there is reason to believe that sex may be a somewhat influential factor in language laterality differences between individuals. I suggest that the influence of sex, however, is not a simple one but, rather, an influence moderated by familial sinistrality and possibly other variables yet to be identified.

Evidence of sex–FS interactional influences on language lateralization

The original data I want to present are largely from a lateralized tachistoscopic task we call the Object Naming Latency Task (ONLT). We have administered this task to three separate samples of normal right-handed college students. The original study was by McKeever and Jackson (1979). We chose the task of naming pictures of common objects as one that would not allow the possibility of learned directional memory scanning artifact. The possibility of directional scanning bias (Heron, 1957) had raised the question of artifactual right-visual-field (RVF) superiority in nearly all lateralized verbal tachistoscopic tasks, since these had almost universally employed letters or words as stimuli to be recognized. Additionally, we were aware that one of the most common "tests" for aphasia is naming pictures of familiar objects, and there is irrefutable evidence that it is a clearly left-hemispheric function in nearly all right-handers (Fedio and VanBuren, 1974; Ojemann, 1978). Finally, the decision to employ a latency measure rather than a simple recognition accuracy measure was made because we felt reaction time could provide a more valid measure of hemispheric differences. In the recognition accuracy paradigm the subject can take as many as five seconds or more to respond. This lengthy poststimulus preresponse interval allows ample opportunities for interhemispheric information interchange. In the latency paradigm, however, where recognition is made easy via appropriate experimenter choices of stimulus size, contrast, and exposure time, the subject responds as quickly as possible. Thus, if one hemisphere can name the stimulus without recourse to "consultation" with the other hemisphere, it will do so. If, on the other hand, a hemisphere cannot perform the task without such assistance from the other hemisphere, that assistance will be manifested in slower reaction time for stimuli channeled initially to it.

In the ONLT five different object drawings are randomly and unilaterally presented in 100-msec exposures. The object pictures (an apple, a clock, a lamp, a moose, and a shoe) are taken from the Peabody Picture Vocabulary Test (Dunn, 1959). The nearpoint of each object picture to fixation is 1° of visual angle. A total of 210 trials (seven blocks of thirty stimuli) are run, with the first block serving strictly as practice in the procedure of naming the flashed pictures as quickly as possible and then, when asked by the experimenter, reporting a fixation-point digit (2 to 9) that appeared at fixation during each lateralized stimulus exposure. Trials on which the subject is unable to report the fixation control digit correctly are discarded as trials on which improper fixation may have occurred. In this task, after the practice block of trials, subjects make very few errors of any kind. A total of 180 trials, 90 LVF and 90 RVF, provide the raw reaction-time data. A median is computed for LVF and RVF trials and a difference score is then obtained. Positive difference scores indicate RVF superiority and, inferentially, left-hemispheric dominance for the process of object naming.

In the original McKeever and Jackson (1979) experiment only ten men and ten women served as subjects. The results of that study showed clearly that the task yielded a strong RVF superiority. Ninety percent of the subjects named RVF-presented objects more quickly than LVF objects. The familial sinistrality of the subjects was also assessed. Subjects who had at least one first-degree or two second-degree left-handed (for writing) relatives were designated as positive for familial sinistrality (FS+). All others were designed FS−. McKeever and Jackson (1979) found, as indicated earlier, that males were more lateralized than females. Although FS was not included in the analysis because only one male and four females were FS+, McKeever and Jackson noted that FS− females appeared to be mainly responsible for the smaller RVF superiority of females as compared to the (overwhelmingly FS−) male sample.

To examine the possibility that sex–FS–visual-half-field interaction might exist, McKeever and Hoff (1982) administered the ONLT to sixty-four subjects of balanced sex–FS composition. The results replicated the strong RVF superiority elicited by the task. Eighty-six percent of the subjects were RVF-superior. No *sex*-by-*field* nor *FS*-by-*field* interaction was found. A significant *sex*-by-*FS*-by-*field* interaction was, however, obtained. The FS− females and FS+ males had smaller RVF superiorities (18.1 msec and 19.2 msec, respectively) than did the FS+ females and FS− males (30.0 msec and 29.6 msec, respectively). Thus, McKeever and Jackson's suspicion of a possible sex-by-FS-by-field interaction was confirmed.

More recently McKeever et al. (1983) undertook to attempt a replication of the McKeever and Hoff findings. Fifty subjects, not balanced for sex and FS status, were administered the ONLT. The results again confirmed the strong RVF-superiority of the task, with 90 percent of the subjects naming RVF stimuli more quickly than LVF stimuli. No differential sex or FS-by-visual-field effects were obtained, but as in the earlier study, a significant sex-by-FS-by-field interaction was obtained. The FS− females and FS+ males had smaller RVF superiorities (22.2 msec and 16.3 msec, respectively) than the FS+ females and FS− males (41.5 msec and 33.3 msec, respectively).

These tachistoscopic task indications of a less strict left-hemisphere dominance for object naming in FS− females and FS+ males, though basically empirical and originally unhypothesized, are consistent with an as yet little appreciated but important finding of Hécaen, De Agostini, and Monzon-Montes (1981). These investigators reported the frequencies of aphasia (all types combined) in right-handed patients who had suffered unilateral cortical brain lesions. Hécaen et al. reported their findings for each sex and FS status group. Their data indicated that among those suffering left-hemisphere lesions, 70 percent of the FS+ females were aphasic but only 35 percent of the FS− females were aphasic; 62 percent of the FS− males were aphasic but only 36 percent of the FS+ males were aphasic. Hécaen et al. noted this reversed influence of FS within the two sexes but said only that it was nonsignificant. The conclusion of nonsignificance, however, was based solely on the comparisons of FS+ and FS− patients within sexes, since these were the only comparisons made. The pattern of sex-by-FS interaction suggested by the ONLT results can be tested by contrasting the frequencies of aphasia in the presumably strongly left-hemispheric-dominant groups (FS+ females and FS− males) with the frequencies for the more "bilateral" groups (FS− females and FS+ males). When a chi-square test is applied to these contrasted groups there is a statistically significant difference in the susceptibility to aphasia ($X^2 = 5.54$, df = 1, p < .02). The FS+ female and FS− male group shows aphasia in 64.2% of the sample (twenty-five of thirty-nine patients) while the FS− female and FS+ male group shows aphasia in only 35.5 percent of the sample (eleven of thirty-one patients). In addition, although the numbers are too small to allow meaningful statistical tests, the Hécaen et al. data also indicate that FS – females and FS + males seem more prone to aphasia than the FS + females and FS – males following *right*-hemisphere lesions.

Figure 10.1 shows, first, the RVF-superiority magnitudes obtained in the McKeever and Hoff (1982) and McKeever et al. (1983) experiments. Figure 10.2 shows the frequencies of aphasia following left-hemisphere lesions in the four sex–FS groupings. It is apparent that the groups having lesser RVF superiorities on the ONLT are the same as those having greater resistance to aphasia following left-hemispheric lesions. This data is consistent in suggesting that sex and FS factors interact to influence the degree of language lateralization.

Evidence of sex–FS interactional influences in spatial ability

In addition to the evidence of sex–FS interactional influences on language lateralization, we have also found evidence of sex–FS interactional influence on spatial visualization ability (McKeever et al., 1983). Factor analytic studies have consistently indicated that at least two types of spatial ability exist. These are referred to by McGee (1979) as spatial visualization ability and spatial relations ability. Spatial visualization involves the ability to recognize a shape despite the rotation of the shape in space, and it is this type of spatial ability we have tested. The spatial visualization test we have used is the Stafford Identical Blocks Test (SIBT) (Stafford, 1961). This is a thirty-item test in which an oddly shaped "block" test item is presented and the examinee must choose from five response blocks the one he thinks is the same shape, though rotated to a different perspective, as the test block.

Four samples of right-handed college students were individually administered the SIBT. In the first sample, eighty-two subjects were administered the first, middle, and final fifths of the test, with a time limit of twelve minutes. In the remaining three samples, all thirty items were administered with a total time limit of fifteen minutes. In all four samples FS – females were found to score significantly higher than FS + females; and in three of the four samples FS + males scored significantly higher than FS – males. Figure 10.3 shows the results across all four samples and plots percentage-correct scores. The same groups who appear to be more "bilateral" for language lateralization (FS – females and FS + males) can be seen to be superior to the other two groups in spatial visualization ability. Males were found to be superior to females generally (p < .0001), a well-replicated finding on the SIBT (Stafford, 1961;

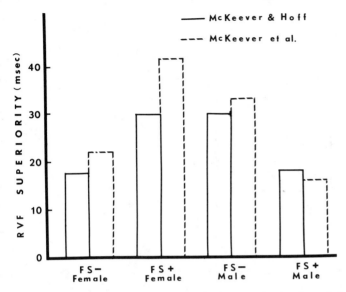

Figure 10.1. Right-visual-field-superiority magnitudes (msec) for different sex–FS groups in the McKeever and Hoff (1982) and McKeever et al. (1983) experiments.

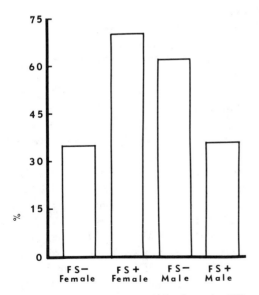

Figure 10.2. Percentages of patients in different sex–FS groups who suffered aphasia in response to left-hemisphere strokes (Hécaen et al., 1981).

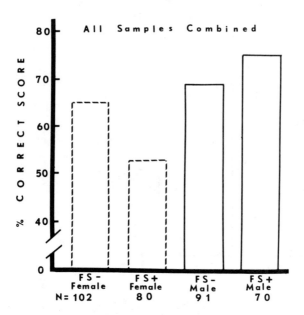

Figure 10.3. Percentage of correct scores of different sex–FS groups on the Stafford Identical Blocks Test.

Bock and Kolakowski, 1973). More important, the sex-by-FS interaction effect was also clearly significant (p < .0001). It is noteworthy that the typical male superiority on this task exists only with respect to the inferior performance of FS+ females. Although FS+ males are significantly superior to FS− females as well, the FS− females are not inferior to the FS− males.

One might speculate that the identical interactional patterns on the ONLT and SIBT could be due to differences in spatial ability lateralizations and that the apparent language laterality differences inferred from the ONLT are really reflecting spatial processing laterality differences. The ONLT, it could be argued, involves a spatial processing component and if FS− females and FS+ males were more right-hemisphere-dominant for spatial processing the result would be smaller RVF superiorities for them. This line of reasoning, however, cannot explain the language laterality differences of the Hécaen et al. (1981) patients. Furthermore, both Hoff (1981) and Marino (1981), using lateralized tachistoscopic spatial tasks, found only straightforward FS effects, not sex-by-FS effects, in spatial laterality. The data in general argue that sex–FS status does influence both language laterality and spatial visualization ability.

Concluding comments and speculations

I have presented data that I believe argue strongly against simple sex differences in cerebral organization. This conclusion offers no support for what has been a popular hypothesis. Sex nonetheless appears to be a relevant variable for understanding individual differences in cerebral organization. By means of interaction with the FS variable, sex does appear to influence both language lateralization and spatial visualization ability.

Although we have tentatively identified sex–FS status as a correlate of cerebral organizational patterns, we must admit two severe limitations to the importance of this finding. First, the magnitude of the effects, particularly with respect to spatial visualization ability, is small. Overlap among the "high spatials" and "low spatials" is considerable. Second, we have no ready conception of why the pattern exists. Thus we have effects of considerable theoretical but severely limited practical importance, and we cannot understand as yet why the effects occur.

Although it is exceedingly speculative, I would suggest that the why may ultimately be understood as a consequence of either the hormonal history or current hormonal characteristics of the various sex–FS groups. Geschwind and Behan (1982) have speculated, from interesting but indirect data, that left-handedness itself might be due to excessive fetal testosterone. If a hormonal characteristic is systematically associated with left-handedness, then it may also be associated, though perhaps to a lesser degree, with FS, and the influence could vary with the sex of the individual. Another suggestion that hormonal characteristics could be involved in the sex–FS interactions we have found comes from the studies of Broverman et al. (1968) and Petersen (1976). Basically, these studies have suggested that relative superiority of spatial over verbal ability occurs in more "androgynous" males and females, with the opposite ability pattern occurring in "non-androgynous" individuals. These data might suggest that FS − females and FS + males, who are superior in spatial ability, are more "androgynous." Finally, Waber (1976) has suggested that sexual maturation rate is associated with both lateralization differences and ability differences. This network of very loosely consonant speculations might at least be indicating a logical direction for research aiming to elucidate the why behind the sex–FS interaction effects I have reported.

11. Sex differences in the patterns of scalp-recorded electrophysiological activity in infancy: possible implications for language development

DAVID W. SHUCARD, JANET L. SHUCARD, AND DAVID G. THOMAS

Introduction

Over the past century, studies of behavioral deficits produced by unilateral cerebral lesions and cerebral disconnections, as well as anatomical, behavioral, and more recent neurophysiological studies, all indicate that certain homologous areas of the cerebral hemispheres[1] of humans are not simply duplicates of each other (as are a number of other homologous organs such as the kidneys) but differ both structurally and functionally.

The first scientific descriptions of hemispheric specialization focused on the asymmetrical cerebral representation of language. Reports by Broca (1865) and Wernicke (1874), based on different types of aphasic patients, indicated that the posterior part of the inferior frontal gyrus (Broca's area) and the posterior part of the superior temporal gyrus (Wernicke's area) of the left cerebral hemisphere play a major role in language production and comprehension, respectively. More recent evidence presented by Geschwind and Levitsky (1968), Teszner et al. (1972), Wada, Clark, and Hamm (1975), and Witelson and Pallie (1973) has shown that, indeed, Wernicke's area differs in its anatomical structure from the homologous area of the right hemisphere. Using injections of sodium amytal into the carotid artery, H. W. Gordon and Bogen (1974), Wada and Rasmussen (1960), and others have further substantiated the importance of the left hemisphere for language in most individuals.

Studies of commissurotomy ("split brain") patients by R. W. Sperry and his colleagues (Sperry, 1974) done over the last decade have produced unique evidence that when the two hemispheres are surgically disconnected they each appear conscious, that is, like "two separate

278

minds in one head" (Galin, 1974:572). Sperry and his collaborators showed further that in these "split brain" patients, the left hemisphere is capable of speech, writing, and calculation (functions that are purported to involve linear sequential processing) but is limited in its ability to solve problems involving spatial relationships and novel figures. The right hemisphere, on the other hand, seems better able to perform tasks involving complex spatial and musical patterns (functions that are purported to involve gestalt or holistic processing), although it can perform simple addition and has the use of a few words (see Galin, 1974, for review).

Many studies of cerebral function in noncommissurotomy subjects using various behavioral methods such as dichotic listening (Kimura, 1973), tachistoscopic techniques (Kimura and Durnford, 1974), and recordings of the direction of eye movements (Galin and Ornstein, 1974; Kinsbourne, 1972), as well as the previously noted studies using intracarotid amytal injections, have lent further support to the findings of differential hemispheric functioning.

More recently, investigations have attempted to relate this cerebral specialization of brain function to changes in electrophysiological measures (the electroencephalogram and evoked potential) recorded from the surface of the scalp in normal individuals. These measures are appealing because they are noninvasive, do not have to be justified in terms of an individual's medical needs, are readily quantified, and with appropriate controls should tap cortical functioning more directly than many of the other methods previously used. Consequently, normal, intact subjects can be used to study hemispheric specialization using these methods.

Electrophysiological investigations tend to support those using other techniques showing differential functioning between the two hemispheres. For example, Morrell and Salamy (1971), in studying adults, found that auditory evoked potentials produced by speech sounds (e.g., "pa," "pi") were significantly higher in amplitude in the left temporal area than the right. Molfese, Freeman, and Palermo (1975) reported similar results, as well as greater right-hemisphere evoked potential amplitudes in response to musical chords. Using the electroencephalogram (EEG) (Doyle, Ornstein, and Galin, 1974; Galin and Ornstein, 1972) and visual evoked potential (VEP) measures (Galin and Ellis, 1975), Galin and his associates also showed differences in adults between left- and right-hemisphere responses that were dependent on the tasks subjects were performing: When subjects were asked to write from memory (presumably a left-hemisphere task), the EEG and VEP measures indicated that greater activation (i.e., less EEG alpha power and lower VEP amplitude to task-irrelevant stimuli) was occurring in the left hemisphere. When these same subjects were asked to manipulate blocks (presumably a right-hemisphere task), the EEG and VEP measures, as predicted, were indicative of greater right-hemisphere activation (Galin and Ellis, 1975). McKee, Humphrey, and McAdam (1973), using EEG alpha activity, reported similar results for linguistic and musical tasks.

There have been, however, electrophysiological studies of lateralization that have not confirmed differential hemispheric functioning. Taub et al. (1976) presented musical chords and consonant–vowel sounds to adult subjects and measured differences in evoked potentials from right- and left-hemisphere scalp locations. While evidence of differentiation of function between the right and left hemispheres was obtained for musical stimuli, it was not obtained for speech sounds. Further, Tanguay et al. (1977) failed to produce "hemispheric effects" in evoked potential latency or amplitude to consonant–vowel stimuli presented to adults. Focusing on the P300 wave, Friedman et al. (1975) found inconsistent evidence for auditory evoked potentials (AEPs) to be asymmetrical over right and left hemispheres to words and human sounds. Friedman et al. concluded from a review of the literature that flaws in design and in statistical techniques, together with lack of consistency in reported findings, indicate that the relationship between the evoked potential and hemispheric functioning has yet to be demonstrated. Galambos et al. (1975) reiterated this skepticism, saying that perhaps the evoked potential is not a sensitive measure of differential hemispheric functioning. More recently, findings of cerebral asymmetries using the ongoing EEG have been questioned by Gevins et al. (1980) and by Gevins et al. (1981).

Tanguay et al. (1977) have persuasively argued that the reason for inconsistency and/or weaknesses of results in evoked response studies is that the use of "simple AER [auditory evoked response] methodology" may be incapable of reflecting complex neurophysiological events that, for instance, subserve language; in addition, factors such as set, attention, and boredom may also contribute to these discrepancies in findings. We agreed with these criticisms and believed that more robust eliciting conditions had to be developed in order to amplify right–left hemispheric differences. To this end, we have explored a novel technique that addresses many of these problems (D. W. Shucard, Shucard, and Thomas, 1977). In previous studies, evoked potentials were elicited by discrete, transient stimuli such as a single word or musical chord repeated several times. We reasoned that such a simple paradigm may not produce optimal differential hemispheric processing because the subject was not involved in active, natural verbal or musical information processing. Rather than becoming involved in the phonemic, syntactic, and semantic processing required to comprehend a narrative, subjects in previous studies typically heard single speech sounds removed from such a rich linguistic context. Similarly, we felt that the presentations of a single musical chord did not require on the part of the subject the holistic processing of the interrelationships among sequential notes and chords that is thought to involve more right-cerebral-hemisphere functions than left. Our solution was to present to subjects tasks in which they had to actively listen to ongoing narrative speech and classical music while evoked potentials were recorded to *task-irrelevant* pairs of tones superimposed on each type of ongoing stimulus.

Using this paradigm, we found that when adult subjects were processing language information (i.e., listening for content as well as attempting to detect targeted words in the verbal passages), they produced higher-amplitude bipolar AEP's from the left hemisphere to the pairs of auditory tone pips that were irrelevant to the task and were superimposed on the language stimuli being presented. Conversely, when these same subjects were processing musical information (i.e., attempting to recognize targeted musical patterns in the musical selections), they produced higher-amplitude bipolar AEPs from the right hemisphere to the task-irrelevant tone pairs (D. W. Shucard et al., 1977). The effects were most salient for the second of the paired tones. The results of this study and a replication of it (D. W. Shucard et al., 1981) showed that electrophysiological measures are indeed sensitive to differential hemispheric functioning in the normal intact human.

Cerebral functional specialization and development

Anatomical and functional lateralization

The development of hemispheric specialization of brain functions in humans has become an important topic both from a theoretical and clinical perspective. The question being frequently asked is whether specialization for language and other functions is present at birth, or whether areas of the brain come to be specialized with development. The way this question is asked invariably pits Lenneberg (1966), who believed that brain lateralization is not complete until late in childhood, against others such as Kinsbourne (1975; Kinsbourne and Hiscock, 1983), who maintains that the brain is organized in a lateralized fashion from birth or before and that fundamental aspects of brain organization do not develop postnatally. Kinsbourne concedes, however, that functions that rely on this lateralized organization, such as face recognition (for which asymmetrical responding is not found in young children but is in older children – Kinsbourne and Hiscock, 1983), may develop, but that it is the behavioral organization of the skill that changes with age, not the neural substrates.

The issues being raised about the ontogeny of cerebral specialization in the infant are undoubtedly important. We regret, however, the tendency of many investigators to treat cerebral lateralization as a unitary construct. To be specific, lateralization of brain function in development can be divided into at least two categories. We would propose, based on a developmental perspective, differentiation of the concept of lateralization into *anatomical* versus *functional* categories.

The presence of innate hemispheric differences in anatomical structure has been supported by the studies of Geschwind and Levitsky (1968), Teszner et al. (1972), Wada et al. (1975), and Witelson and Pallie (1973), who reported finding anatomical differences between homologous areas of the two hemispheres of infants. In particular, it has been found that the planum temporale of the left cerebral hemisphere (part of the classical area of Wernicke) was significantly larger than the homologous area on the right in both adults and newborns.

However, the presence of anatomical signs of lateralization at birth may not necessarily indicate that *functional lateralization* is simultaneously present. A distinction between anatomical lateralization and functional lateralization is particularly relevant when one realizes that considerable microanatomical and biochemical development takes place after birth. For example, dendritic arborization in the cortex does not reach an advanced stage of density until well after infancy, and does not approach completion until the fourth year of life (Lenneberg, 1974).

Lenneberg (1966) also alluded to the importance of the chemical composition of the brain as providing a physiological basis for the development of language. Furthermore, a number of experiments reviewed by Szentagothai (1974) indicated the importance of the interaction between environmental inputs and development of the central nervous system. Thus, even though brain structures may show anatomical asymmetry at birth, these structures may not be fully functional at birth or for some time after, owing to lack of the necessary biochemical and microanatomical development and environmental stimulation. Therefore, there may be limited functional asymmetry at a particular developmental period.

For instance, functional lateralization can occur early with regard to differences in the reception of consonant–vowel combinations. Using dichotic listening in adults, Liberman et al. (1967) demonstrated left-hemisphere superiority for reception of certain phonemes. Such lateralization, requiring only feature detectors in the cortex to be predominant over one or the other temporal area, could well be present at birth, since other complex feature detectors (see Hubel and Wiesel, 1963) are known to be prewired in infants of other species. A report by Eimas et al. (1971) suggests that acoustic feature detectors involved in speech perception may indeed be operating in early infancy. Using recovery from habituation of the sucking response, they found that infants as young as 1 month of age are able to make fine discriminations of speech sounds. Also, infants were able to perceive speech categories along the voicing continuum (voiced and voiceless stop consonants) similar to the way in which adults perceive the same sounds, even though these infants have had limited exposure to speech and very limited experience in producing these same sounds. Entus (1977) adopted the dichotic listening paradigm for use with young infants by measuring the habituation and dishabituation of high-amplitude, nonnutritive sucking to presentations of verbal (consonant–vowel syllables) or musical stimuli (single notes played by one instrument). Entus found a right-ear advantage (REA) for the verbal stimuli and a left-ear advantage (LEA) for the musical stimuli in infants approximately 50 and 100 days old, although age did not appear to influence the results significantly.

These findings suggest that infants as young as 2 months of age can distinguish certain phonetic changes better with the right ear (presumably the left hemisphere) and certain timbre changes better with the left ear (presumably the right hemisphere). Based on Entus's (1977) data, these abilities, however, do not appear to show substantial developmental differences between 2 and 5 months postnatal age. Although a replication of Entus's findings by Vargha-Khadem and Corballis (1979) failed, an attempt by Glanville, Best, and Levinson (1977) using heart-rate deceleration rather than sucking substantiated Entus's (1977) findings with a 3-month-old sample. Best, Hoffman, and Glanville (1982) again replicated both the REA for verbal stimuli and the LEA for musical stimuli using heart-rate deceleration. Best et al., however, discovered that, whereas the LEA for musical stimuli was present at 2 months, the REA for verbal stimuli was not seen until 3 months of age. Consequently, it appears that certain lateralized functions are indeed present very early in the human, but there does seem to be a period of development at least for the function or functions tapped in the dichotic listening paradigm. In addition, differentiation of the concept of lateralization into anatomical versus functional categories with respect to development may be simplistic, since within the functional category different functions may be lateralized at different developmental periods, as already indicated.

Handedness and language development

There is a fairly large literature that addresses the relationship between handedness and hemispheric dominance for language in adults. In fact, Broca, as early as 1865 (see Hécaen and Sauguet, 1971), postulated different patterns of hemispheric organization for sinistrals versus dextrals. More recently, it has been speculated that the development of language is related to the development of handedness. For example, Steffen (1974) described the developmental courses of handedness and language over the first few years of life and noted how, in general, children seem to show coincidental developments in the two domains, although he presented no data to support his contention.

This relationship between language development and the ontogenesis of handedness has been investigated by Ramsay (1980, 1984). Ramsay (1984) followed infants over several weeks and found that individual infants began to show a preference for one hand during the same week that they began to babble with duplicated syllables such as "mama." Ramsay (1980) has also found that bimanual handedness (measured as the preferred hand for the manipulation of objects that require bimanual coordination – one hand to hold the object and the other to do the manipulating) develops simultaneously with the appearance of nonrepetitive multisyllabic expression (such as "mommy" rather than "mama") at about 12 months of age. In a longitudinal sample of twelve infants, he found that eleven used their first nonrepetitive multisyllabic expression in the same month as or following the onset of bimanual handedness.

Sex-related differences in lateralization

Another developmental issue is whether there are significant sex-related differences in cerebral functional specialization. Behavioral evidence suggests that these differences may exist. For example, a number of studies have found that females show a more rapid rate of development for language-related skills in infancy and early childhood. During the first months of life girls have been found to show more spontaneous vocalizations than boys (Lewis, 1972; Lewis and Freddle, 1972; Moss, 1967) and may also have earlier maturation of speech organs (Darley and Winitz, 1961). Studies of children between 1 and 3 years of age have also shown that girls begin to speak earlier than boys (Adkins, 1971; Darley and Winitz, 1961); they express themselves more frequently (Cherry and Lewis, 1976), show earlier use of two-word sentences (Ramer, 1976), and develop a larger vocabulary at an earlier age than boys (Nelson, 1973).

Other studies have not demonstrated differences in vocalizations between the sexes in the first few months (S. J. Jones and Moss, 1972; Rheingold and Samuel, 1969; Weinraub and Fraenkel, 1977); and between the ages of 3 and 8, sex differences for certain language-related skills are contradictory (Mueller, 1972; Sause, 1976; Smith and Connolly, 1972). There does, however, appear to be enough evidence to suggest earlier and more rapid development of language-related skills in girls during the first three years of life.

Boys, on the other hand, from the age of 2 to 17 years and at high-school and college levels have been found to show slight but significant trends to score higher than females on the Stanford Binet spatial abilities measures and certain subtests of the Wechsler test (Maccoby and Jacklin, 1974; McNemar, 1942; Ralston, 1962; Trumbull, 1953). Harris (1978) has also reported that males perform better than females on a wide range of tasks involving spatial abilities, even at an early age. Further, Grossi et al. (1979) found that in 877 children between the ages of 4 and 10 years, males showed a better performance on spatial memory tests.

Behavioral studies of children that have directly addressed the issue of gender and asymmetries of cerebral function have produced mixed results. Although a majority of the studies using dichotic listening found no sex-related differences in ear advantage, several investigations using this technique showed a superior left-ear advantage (right-hemisphere specialization) in males for nonlinguistic auditory processing (see Witelson, 1977, for review). In addition, it has been hypothesized by Buffery (1970, 1971) from behavioral studies using techniques other than dichotic listening that there may be a speech perception mechanism that is more developed in the female than in the male at an earlier age and that lateralization of language may occur earlier and progress more rapidly in the female.

Electrophysiological evidence related to lateralization in infants and children

EEG and evoked potential studies

Despite the likelihood that the development of specialized functions is occurring during infancy, there have been only a few electrophysiological studies of cerebral specialization in infancy. The sparsity of these investigations is perhaps due to the difficulties in measurement that arise with applying electrophysiological techniques to awake, alert infants. Nevertheless, several studies have attempted to investigate the development of the brain in normal infants using electrophysiological methods.

Crowell et al. (1973), in studying cortical driving to light stimulation in newborns, found that there were differences in maturation between the right and left hemispheres, with the left hemisphere being slower to mature than the right. Other workers have suggested, based on studies of early lesions, that the left hemisphere matures first (Woods and Teuber, 1973). More recently, Crowell, Kapuniai, and Garbanati (1977) with 217 infants supported the findings of Crowell et al. (1973) for unilateral photic driving and reported a *decrease* in asymmetrical responding with age. At 2 days of age, 12 percent of the infants showed bilateral photic driving, whereas at 30 days, 48 percent of the infants showed bilateral driving.

Analyzing changes in the EEG power spectrum to continuous speech and music in four 6-month-old infants, Gardiner, Schulman, and Walter (1973) and Gardiner and Walter (1977) found that for all infants the power spectrum between three and five hertz decreased at left-hemisphere leads during the speech condition and at right-hemisphere leads during the music condition. Only the parietal and temporal locations yielded hemispheric differences, with the largest changes at the temporal sites.

The development of linguistic functions and their asymmetrical organization in infancy has also been studied using auditory evoked potential (AEP) techniques. Molfese and his associates (Molfese, 1977; Molfese et al., 1975, 1976; Molfese and Molfese, 1979), in a series of studies, investigated the effects of various linguistic and nonlinguistic stimuli on evoked potential amplitude asymmetry. Stimuli included musical chords and the manipulation of a number of linguistic factors such as formant structure, bandwidth, and voice onset time. Neonates, infants, children, and adults were studied. The findings from these studies in which AEPs were recorded to discrete stimuli tend to support the viewpoint that functional specialization is present at birth for grosser levels of speech processing, such as discrimination of acoustic bandwidth. More refined lateralized processing, such as the discrimination of phonetic cues like formant structure, seems to develop later.

Infant electrophysiological studies: AEP probe paradigm

In this discussion we focus on the results obtained in our laboratory with infants whose auditory evoked potentials (AEPs) were recorded while they were awake and receiving continuous auditory stimuli (e.g., speech, music). In the studies discussed we attempted to investigate cerebral specialization in infants related to complex auditory input through the presentation of pairs of tones, which acted as probes and which were superimposed on the continuous auditory stimuli. The AEPs were recorded to the probe tones, not to discrete linguistic or nonlinguistic stimuli, as has been typical of research using evoked potential methodology. This procedure, as already noted, appears to us to be sensitive to differential hemispheric involvement in information processing in adults (D. W. Shucard et al., 1977, 1981). Further, in these studies particular attention was given to methodological problems that plagued earlier electrophysiological work with infants, by carefully controlling for level of arousal, equating stimulus intensity to both ears, and studying infants within narrowly delineated age ranges (see D. W. Shucard, Shucard, and Thomas, in press; J. L. Shucard et al., 1981).

Methods. In order to examine the development of cerebral specialization of function in infants as well as possible sex-related differences, 3-month-old and 6-month-old male and female infants were studied. The 3-month-old subjects were eight male and eight female infants ranging from 10 weeks, 6 days to 13 weeks, 2 days; the 6-month-old subjects were ten male and ten female infants ranging in age from 24 weeks, 0 days to 26 weeks, 5 days. Each infant had a normal gestation time, normal birth weight, and an Apgar score of 8 or above. All of the parents were right-handed.

The AEPs to pairs of tone pips were recorded between T_4–C_z (right hemisphere) and T_3–C_z (left hemisphere) according to the International 10–20 System (Jasper, 1958), with a ground electrode located on the forehead. Two polygraph amplifier channels were used to record the EEG. The AEPs for Tone 1 and Tone 2 were averaged and printed out separately. The tone pips (600 Hz, 100 msec) were superimposed in pairs on white noise, verbal passages, and musical selections. The interval between the tones of each pair was two seconds, and a minimum of four seconds elapsed between presentations of tone pairs. All auditory stimuli were presented via lightweight headphones placed on the infant's ears. The white noise, verbal passages, and musical selections had been prerecorded on audiotape. The verbal and musical selections presented to the 3-month-old group of infants were the same as those used in a previous study with adults (D. W. Shucard et al., 1977). The 6-month-old group was presented with verbal passages taken from a standardized second-grade reader and recorded on tape by a female voice. The musical selections were from *Adventures in Music*, a collection of classical music for children. Tone pip intensity was approximately 70 db sound pressure level. The average intensity of the verbal passages and musical selections was approximately 65 db.

3-month-old group. Each infant participated in two recording sessions separated by a period of two to seven days. One experimental condition (verbal passages or musical selections) was presented during each session, and the order of conditions was counterbalanced across infants.

The infant came to the laboratory at regular feeding times and at a time when the mother felt the infant was most likely to remain alert. During each recording session the infant sat on his or her mother's lap in a sound-attenuated, electrically shielded room and was bottle or breast fed while the stimuli were presented. Occasionally, a pacifier was used if the infant finished feeding before the completion of the recording session.

A closed-circuit video system, continuous EEG recording, and the mother's observations were used to monitor the infant's level of arousal throughout each session. Only data from infants who were alert with their eyes open for approximately 95 percent of each recording session were used in the analyses.

During the *Verbal Condition*, infants were presented with verbal passages with the tone pairs superimposed on the passages. The mean length of time that the passages were presented was 11.4 min (SD = 1.2 min). The total number of tone pairs presented during the Verbal Condition ranged from 30 to 70 across all infants studied (mean = 58, SD = 12). During the *Music Condition*, the paired tone pips were superimposed on musical selections. The tones were presented in the same manner as during the Verbal Condition. The musical selections were presented for a mean of 11.3 min (SD = 2.1 min), and the number of tone pairs ranged from 40 to 80 across all infants studied (mean = 59, SD = 12). Verbal and musical stimuli were presented until enough tone pairs were delivered to produce reliable AEPs. None of the infants had a difference greater than 10 between the number of tone pairs presented between the Verbal and Music conditions. For both conditions, tone pairs were presented only when the infant was alert and quiet. Breaks were taken when needed (e.g., if the baby became fussy or had to be burped).

A separate group of 3-month-old infants, with a similar distribution for age, sex, parental handedness, gestation time, normality of birth weight, and Apgar score was studied in an identical manner, except that the tone pips were presented against a background of a "hissing" sound of 55–60 db, approximating the frequency spectrum of white noise (*Baseline Condition*). This Baseline Group was studied in order to examine the responses to the tone probes when they were not accompanied by

Table 11.1. *Auditory evoked potential mean peak latencies and standard deviations*

		P_1	N_1	P_2	N_2	P_3
3-month-olds						
Baseline	X̄	73.30	116.62	193.66	293.88	396.57
	SD	18.81	14.36	20.58	41.39	60.01
Verbal/Music	X̄	81.34	133.97	217.34	325.59	435.60
	SD	15.34	20.53	31.75	40.14	77.11
6-month-olds						
Baseline/Verbal/Music	X̄	74.30	121.50	198.50	285.47	397.97
	SD	13.97	18.03	22.01	34.34	36.64

complex auditory stimuli (verbal or musical). The infants in this condition received between 30 and 70 tone pairs (mean = 56, SD = 12), approximating the number used in the experimental conditions.

6-month-old-group. The infants in this group were tested in a similar manner to the 3-month-olds. Each 6-month-old infant, however, participated in all three conditions (Baseline, Verbal, and Music) on separate days. For the Baseline Condition, between 40 and 80 tone pairs were presented (mean = 57, SD = 10); for the Verbal Condition, between 40 and 70 pairs were presented (mean = 55, SD = 7); and for the Music Condition, between 50 and 70 pairs were presented (mean = 58, SD = 8). The Baseline Condition was always presented on the first day of testing, and the Verbal and Music conditions were counterbalanced for order across the other two testing days. All three testing sessions occurred within a twelve-day period.

Results. Four AEPs were obtained for each infant during each condition (right and left hemisphere for both Tone 1 and Tone 2); and for each AEP, four reliable peak-to-trough and trough-to-peak components were identified and designated as follows: Peak 1 (P_1–N_1), Peak 2 (N_1–P_2), Peak 3 (P_2–N_2), and Peak 4 (N_2–P_3). The mean latencies and standard deviations in milliseconds of these peaks for both the 3-month-olds and 6-month-olds are presented in Table 11.1. For the 3-month-olds, the somewhat shorter peak latencies obtained for the Baseline Condition as compared with the Verbal and Music conditions may have resulted from some perceptual masking of the tone probes that occurred during the reception of the verbal and musical stimuli. The AEPs recorded for one 3-month-old subject during the Baseline Condition and another 3-

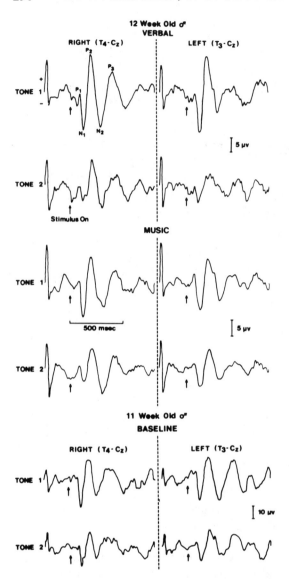

Figure 11.1. AEPs to pairs of tone pips during the Verbal, Music, and Baseline conditions. The vertical arrows indicate stimulus onset. The positive deflection at the beginning of the tracing (before the stimulus onset) is the calibration signal. Peaks 1, 2, 3, and 4 as defined in the text refer, respectively, to the negative-going peak from P_1 to N_1, the positive-going peak from N_1 to P_2, the negative-going peak from P_2 to N_2, and the positive-going peak from N_2 to P_3. Positivity at C_z with respect to T_4 or T_3 is up. (From J. L. Shucard et al., 1981. Used with permission.)

month-old subject during both the Verbal and Music Conditions are illustrated in Figure 11.1.

Although the specific paradigm used in this study has not been used by other laboratories, the peak latencies obtained here for the *earlier AEP components* compare closely with previously published reports of AEPs recorded to simple auditory stimuli for sleeping infants. For example, Ohlrich and Barnet (1972), using click stimuli, reported mean latencies for P_1, N_1, and P_2 of 63 msec, 92 msec, and 220 msec, respectively, for 1-month-olds, and 89 msec, and 193 msec, respectively, for 6-month-olds (see Table 11.1 for latency comparisons). The latencies of later AEP components in our study differed considerably from those previously reported for sleeping infants but appear to be more similar to those reported for waking adults. In the study by Ohlrich and Barnet (1972), mean latencies for N_2 and P_3 of 475 msec and 678 msec, respectively, were reported for 1-month-olds; and 425 msec and 622 msec, for 6-month-olds. D. W. Shucard et al. (1977) reported a mean latency for N_2 of 304 msec for waking adults studied under conditions similar to those of our infant investigations.

Amplitude scores for each peak were obtained by computing the peak-to-trough or trough-to-peak distance in millimeters and converting this distance to microvolts.

3-month-old group. Analyses of the data indicated that females had higher amplitude left-hemisphere AEPs as compared with the right, whereas males showed higher amplitude right-hemisphere responses compared with the left, irrespective of the experimental condition. This effect was seen for AEP components occurring later than 280 msec (Peaks 3 and 4). Thus, the pattern of AEP amplitude asymmetry for males differed significantly from that for females, irrespective of the condition (Verbal or Music) or the tone (Tone 1 or Tone 2). This relationship between males and females across conditions and tones is illustrated in Figure 11.2. The robustness of this effect is further demonstrated by the number of individual infants who showed this relationship. The mean left-hemisphere AEP amplitude collapsed across tone and condition was higher than the right in seven of eight females for Peak 3 and in eight of eight females for Peak 4, whereas the right-hemisphere response was higher than the left in seven of eight males for Peak 3 and in five of eight males for Peak 4.

The results for the Baseline Group indicated that there were no significant hemispheric AEP amplitude differences in the pattern of responding between males and females in this condition for any of the AEP components. Thus, AEP amplitude responses to tone pairs not

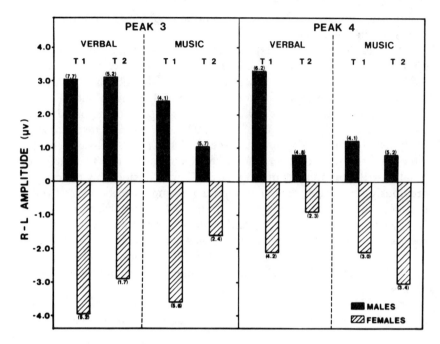

Figure 11.2. Mean amplitude right minus left (R − L) difference scores for the 3-month-old infants for AEP Peaks 3 and 4 obtained during the Verbal and Music conditions. T1 refers to Tone 1 and T2 to Tone 2. A positive value indicates that the mean right-hemisphere AEP amplitude was greater than the left, whereas a negative value indicates that the mean left-hemisphere AEP amplitude was greater than the right. Numbers on the bars in parentheses indicate standard deviations. (From J. L. Shucard et al., 1981. Used with permission.)

accompanied by auditory stimuli containing complex information (verbal and musical) did not differ significantly between males and females.

6-month-old group. Analyses of the data from 6-month-olds indicated that the males had higher amplitude right-hemisphere AEPs as compared with the left, regardless of the condition (Verbal or Music). This effect was most prevalent for Peak 2 and was comparable to the findings for 3-month-old males. The 6-month-old females, on the other hand, generally showed higher amplitude left-hemisphere AEPs for the Verbal Condition and higher amplitude right-hemisphere AEPs for the Music Condition for both Peak 2 and Peak 3. The effect differed from that for the 3-month-old females, who had greater left-hemisphere AEP ampli-

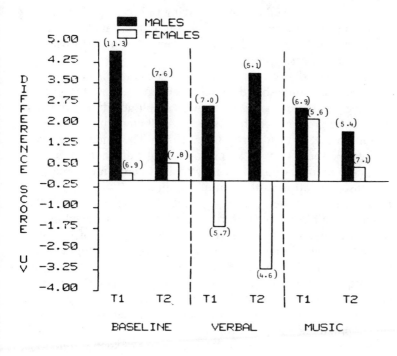

Figure 11.3. Mean amplitude right minus left (R – L) difference scores for the 6-month-old infants for AEP Peak 2 obtained during the Baseline, Verbal, and Music conditions. T1 refers to Tone 1 and T2 to Tone 2. A positive value indicates that the mean right-hemisphere AEP amplitude was greater than the left, whereas a negative value indicates that the mean left-hemisphere AEP amplitude was greater than the right. Numbers on the bars in parentheses indicate standard deviations. (From D. W. Shucard et al., in press. Used with permission.)

tudes regardless of condition. Figure 11.3 illustrates the results for the 6-month-old group.

Discussion

Using a novel electrophysiological technique, we uncovered a pattern of hemispheric development that appears to differ between male and female infants. For 3-month-old infants, speech and musical stimuli produced a pattern of evoked potential asymmetry that was more dependent on the sex of the infant than on the stimuli themselves: For females, larger left-hemisphere AEPs suggest that it is this area of the brain that was more involved in the processing of both types of stimuli, whereas the opposite pattern shown by the 3-month-old males indicates that the right hemisphere played a more active role in the processing of both speech and musical stimuli.

At 6 months, males showed essentially the same pattern of asymmetry as at 3 months. But 6-month-old females tended to show the pattern found in adults: greater left-hemisphere AEP amplitude during the Verbal Condition and greater right-hemisphere AEP amplitude during the Music Condition (D. W. Shucard et al., 1977). The findings indicate that in the female there may be a developmental shift that takes place between 3 and 6 months of age that may relate to a cognitive reorganization, at least in relation to the stimuli examined.

The results described here are consistent with the hypothesis that male and female children have differing rates of linguistic development and, more generally, perhaps differing rates or patterns of cognitive development. It may be that differences in neuronal development between males and females may cause female infants to be more receptive to complex sequential sensory input such as language than male infants, who may be more receptive to spatial types of stimuli. These speculations are consistent with those reports in the behavioral literature indicating earlier development of language-related functions in females than in males. Males are said to show earlier development of spatial functions. Along these lines, there is some evidence to suggest that early in development boys acquire language by means of object manipulation rather than by means of social interaction, with the latter variable being a very significant one for girls (Bell, Weller, and Waldrop, 1971; Clarke-Stewart, 1973; Nelson, 1973).

According to Klann-Delius (1981), the evidence from research on sex differences related to language acquisition seems to be controversial and inconclusive. Until now, there has been little biological evidence in young humans that supports the notion of differences in brain development or organization between males and females. Evidence for sex differences related to brain function has been obtained for adults and for animals, however. For example, cortical language localization, as measured by direct electrical stimulation of the human cerebral cortex, is different for males and females (Ojemann, 1983). In birds, it has been shown that the size of certain nuclei in the brain is dependent on the sex of the bird and, more specifically, on the sex hormones present (see Nottebohm, 1977). Certainly, similar processes could be acting in infants and children to produce differences in the development of cognitive processes between the two sexes.

With regard to sex differences in the development of lateralization, Buffery (1978) has suggested that girls lateralize faster and more strongly than boys. This faster and stronger lateralization is said to favor verbal functions, whereas less lateralization favors the development of spatial functions. Thus, the argument goes that because of the difference in lateralization between boys and girls, girls are better in verbal achievements, boys in spatial achievements (Buffery and Gray, 1972). Sperry et al. (in Maccoby and Jacklin, 1974) have argued that boys, not girls, lateralize earlier and more strongly, and that strong lateralization favors the development of spatial functions, whereas weak lateralization favors language or verbal functions.

None of these hypotheses has been rigorously tested in longitudinal studies beginning early in infancy. Our data, however, suggest that there are physiological differences between male and female infants as young as 3 months of age that support the notion of differences in the development of lateralization between the sexes. Further, these developmental differences in electrophysiological asymmetry may be related to the manner in which such cognitively related skills as language are acquired. Whether boys or girls are more or less lateralized and which of the sexes shows earlier lateralization do not appear to be the important issues, since from our findings both sexes show evidence of lateralization early in development. A more fruitful approach, in our view, would address the issue of developmental changes in measures that might tap into the functional organization of the brain (e.g., electrophysiological measures) and how these might relate to the acquisition of such cognitively related skills as language.

Notes

The research reported here has been supported by National Institute of Child Health and Human Development grants HD 11747 and HD15844, and by Social Behavioral Sciences Research grant 12–83 from the March of Dimes Birth Defects Foundation.

1   In this chapter we use the term "hemisphere" as it is employed here, that is, with the premise that certain areas of the cerebral hemispheres are relatively more or less involved in the performance of a given task. We wish to imply in no way that one cerebral hemisphere is exclusively involved in the performance of any task.

References

Abrahams, R. D. 1970. *Deep down in the jungle: Negro narrative folklore from the streets of Philadelphia*. Chicago: Aldine.

——— 1975. Folklore and communication in St. Vincent. In *Folklore: performance and communication*, ed. D. Ben-Amos and K. S. Goldstein, pp. 287–300. The Hague: Mouton.

——— 1976. *Talking black*. Rowley, Mass.: Newbury House.

Abrahams, R. D., and R. Bauman. 1971. Sense and nonsense in St. Vincent: speech behavior and decorum in a Caribbean community. *American Anthropologist* 73:762–772.

Adger, C. T. 1984. Communicative competence in the culturally diverse classroom: negotiating norms for linguistic interaction. Doctoral dissertation, Georgetown University.

Adkins, P. 1971. Infant sex as a factor in speech development. *Speech Teacher* 20:59–61.

Akmajian, A. 1979. Some rules of the grammar of informal style in English. In *Linguistics*, ed. A. Akmajian, R. Demers, and R. Harnish, pp. 184–205. Cambridge, Mass.: MIT Press.

Akmajian, A., S. Steele, and T. Wasow. 1979. The category AUX in universal grammar. *Linguistic Inquiry* 10:1–64.

Andersen, E. S. 1977. Learning to speak with style: a study of the socio-linguistic skills of children. Doctoral dissertation, Stanford University.

——— 1978. Will you don't snore, please? Directives in young children's role-play speech. *Papers and Reports on Child Language Development* 15:140–150.

Andrews, R. J. 1977. Aspects of language lateralization correlated with familial handedness. *Neuropsychologia* 15:769–778.

Atkinson, J. M. 1982. Review essay. Anthropology. *Signs* 8(2):236–258.

Austin, J. 1962. *How to do things with words*. Cambridge, Mass.: Harvard University Press.

Azadovskii, M. 1974. *A Siberian tale teller*. Monograph series, no. 2. Center for Intercultural Studies in Folklore and Ethnomusicology, University of Texas–Austin.

Bates, E. 1976. *Language and context: the acquisition of pragmatics*. New York: Academic Press.

Bauman, R. 1977. *Verbal art as performance*. Rowley: Newbury House.

Bauman, R., and J. Sherzer (eds.). 1974. *Explorations in the ethnography of speaking*. Cambridge: Cambridge University Press.

Bell, R. Q., G. M. Weller, and M. F. Waldrop. 1971. *Newborns and preschoolers: organization of behavior and relations between periods*. Monographs of the Society for Research in Child Development 36(42).

Bellinger, D., and J. B. Gleason. 1982. Sex differences in parental directives to young children. *Sex Roles* 8:1123–1139.

Berk-Seligson, S. 1978. Phonological variation in a synchronic/diachronic sociolinguistic context: the case of Costa Rican Spanish. Doctoral dissertation, University of Arizona, Tucson.

Best, C. T., H. Hoffman, and B. B. Glanville. 1982. Development of infant ear asymmetries for speech and music. *Perception and Psychophysics* 31:75–85.

Blank, M., and E. Franklin. 1980. Dialogue with preschoolers: a cognitively-based system of assessment. *Applied Psycholinguistics* 1:127–150.

Bloom, L., L. Roussano, and L. Hood. 1976. Adult–child discourse: developmental interaction between information processing and linguistic knowledge. *Cognitive Psychology* 8:521–552.

Bock, J. K., and N. E. Hornsby. 1981. The development of directives: how children ask and tell. *Journal of Child Language* 8:151–164.

Bock, R., and D. Kolakowski. 1973. Further evidence of sex-linked major gene influence on human spatial visualizing ability. *American Journal of Human Genetics* 25:1–14.

Bodine, A. 1975. Sex differentiation in language. In *Language and sex: difference and dominance*, ed. B. Thorne and N. Henley, pp. 130–151. Rowley, Mass.: Newbury House.

Boggs, S. T. 1978. The development of verbal disputing in part-Hawaiian children. *Language in Society* 7:325–344.

Bohannon, J. N., III, and A. L. Marquis. 1977. Children's control of adult speech. *Child Development* 48:1002–1008.

Borker, R. 1980. Anthropology: social and cultural perspectives. In *Women and language in literature and society*, ed. S. McConnell-Genet, R. Borker, and N. Furman, pp. 26–44. New York: Praeger.

Boskey, M., and K. Nelson. 1980. Answering unanswerable questions: the role of imitation. Paper presented at the Boston University conference on Child Language, October.

Bradshaw, J. L., and E. Gates. 1978. Visual field differences in verbal tasks: effects of task familiarity and sex of subject. *Brain and Language* 5:166–187.

Bradshaw, J. L., E. Gates, and N. Nettleton. 1977. Bihemispheric involvement in lexical decisions: handedness and a possible sex difference. *Neuropsychologia* 15:277–286.

Bradshaw, J. L., and M. J. Taylor. 1979. A word-naming deficit in nonfamilial sinistrals? Laterality effects of vocal response to tachistoscopically presented letter strings. *Neuropsychologia* 17:21–23.

Brenneis, D. 1980. *Straight talk and sweet talk: political discourse in a community of equals*. Working Papers in Sociolinguistics, no. 71. Southwest Educational Development Laboratory, Austin, Texas.

Brenneis, D., and L. Lein. 1977. "You fruithead": a sociolinguistic approach to children's disputes. In *Child Discourse*, ed. S. Ervin-Tripp and C. Mitchell-Kernan, pp. 49–66. New York: Academic Press.

Bright, W., and R. A. Thiel. 1965. Hispanisms in a modern Aztec dialect. *Romance Philology* 18:444–452.

Broca, P. 1865. Du siège de la faculté du language articulé. *Bulletin de la Société d'Anthropologie de Paris* 6:377–393.

Broverman, D. M., E. L. Klaiber, Y. Kobayashi, and W. Vogel. 1968. Roles of activation and inhibition in sex-differences in cognitive abilities. *Psychological Review* 5:23–50.

Brown, P. 1979. Language, interaction, and sex roles in a Mayan community: a study of politeness and the position of women. Doctoral dissertation, University of California at Berkeley.

1980. How and why are women more polite: some evidence from a Mayan community. In *Women and language and literature and society*, ed. S. McConnell-Ginet, R. Borker, and N. Furman, pp. 111–149. New York: Praeger.

Brown, P., and G. Buchbinder (eds.). 1976. *Man and woman in the New Guinea Highlands*. Washington, D.C.: American Anthropological Association.

Brown, P., and S. C. Levinson. 1978. Universals of language usage: politeness phenomena. In *Questions and politeness: strategies in social interaction*, ed. Esther N. Goody, pp. 56–311. Cambridge: Cambridge University Press.

Bruner, J. 1975. The ontogenesis of speech act. *Journal of Child Language* 2:1–20.

Bryden, M. P., and F. Allard. 1978. Dichotic listening and the development of linguistic processes. In *Asymmetrical function of the brain*, ed. M. Kinsbourne, pp. 392–404. Cambridge: Cambridge University Press.

Buffery, A. W. H. 1970. Sex-differences in the development of hand preference, cerebral dominance for speech and cognitive skill. *Bulletin of the British Psychological Society* 23:233.

1971. Sex differences in the development of hemispheric asymmetry of function in the human brain. *Brain Research* 31:364–365.

1978. Neuropsychological aspects of language development: an essay on cerebral dominance. In *The development of communication*, ed. N. Waterson and S. Snow. New York: Wiley.

Buffery, A. W. H., and J. Gray. 1972. Sex-differences in the development of spatial and linguistic skills. In *Gender differences: their ontogeny and significance*, ed. C. Ounsted and D. C. Taylor. Edinburgh: Churchill Livingstone.

Bunkachō. 1975. *Nihongo kyōiku shidō sankosho–taigū hyōgen* [Japanese education guide reference–formulaic language]. Tokyo: Okurasho Insatsukyokyu.

Caraveli Chaves, A. 1980. Bridge between worlds: the Greek woman's ritual lament as communicative event. *Journal of American Folklore* 93:129–157.

1982. The song beyond the song: aesthetics and social interaction in Greek folksong. *Journal of American Folklore* 95:129–158.

Carlson, R. 1971. Sex-differences in ego functioning: exploratory studies of agency and communion. *Journal of Consulting and Clinical Psychology* 37:267–277.

Carrell, P. 1981. Children's understanding of indirect requests: comparing child and adult comprehension. *Journal of Child Language* 8:329–346.

Cedergren, H. 1972. Interplay of social and linguistic factors in Panama. Doctoral dissertation, Cornell University.

Chaillé, C., J. Goldman, and J. Sachs. 1983. Representational object use in the symbolic play of preschool children. Paper presented at a meeting of the Society for Research in Child Development.

Chapin, N. M. 1983. Curing among the San Blas Kuna of Panama. Doctoral dissertation, University of Arizona, Tucson.

Cherry, L., and M. Lewis. 1976. Mothers and two-year-olds: a study of sex differentiated aspects of verbal interaction. *Developmental Psychology* 12:278–282.

Cheshire, J. 1978. Present tense verbs in reading English. In *Sociolinguistic patterns in British English*, ed. P. Trudgill, pp. 52–68. Baltimore: University Park Press.

Chick, G. 1980. Concept and behavior in a Tlaxcalan religious office-holding system. Doctoral dissertation, University of Pittsburgh.

Chikamatsu, M. 1979. Nihongo ni okeru danseigo to joseigo ni kansuru ikkō-satsu: wakai danjo ni mirareru shūjoshi no shiyō no soi ni tsuite [A study of male and female language in Japanese: differences in the use of sentence-final particles between young male and female]. A.B. thesis, International Christian University, Tokyo.

Chodorow, N. 1974. Family structure and feminine personality. In *Woman, culture and society*, ed. M. Rosaldo and L. Lamphere, pp. 43–66. Stanford, Calif.: Stanford University Press.

Chomsky, N. 1957. *Syntactic structures*. The Hague: Mouton.

Chung, S. 1978. *Case marking and grammatical relations in Polynesian*. Austin: University of Texas Press.

Clancy, P. 1980. Referential choice in English and Japanese narrative discourse. In *The pear stories*, ed. W. Chafe, pp. 127–202. Norwood, N.J.: Ablex.

Clarke-Stewart, K. A. 1973. Interactions between mothers and their young children: characteristics and consequences. In *Monographs of the Society for Research in Child Development* 38(153):1–109.

Clay, B. J. 1977. *Punikindu: maternal nurture, paternal substance*. Chicago: University of Chicago Press.

Comrie, B. 1978. "Ergativity." In *Syntactic typology*, ed. W. P. Lehmann, pp. 329–394. Austin: University of Texas Press.

Cook-Gumperz, J. 1981. Persuasive talk: the social organization of children's talk. In *Ethnography and language in educational settings*, ed. J. L. Green and C. Wallat, pp. 25–50. Norwood, N.J.: Ablex.

Corsaro, W. A. 1981. Entering the child's world–research strategies for field entry and data collection in a preschool setting. In *Ethnography and language in educational settings*, ed. J. L. Green and C. Wallat, pp. 117–146. Norwood, N.J.: Ablex.

Corsaro, W. A., and T. Rizzo. In press. Disputes in the peer culture of American and Italian nursery school children. In *Conflict talk: sociolinguistic investigation of arguments in conversation*, ed. A. Grimshaw. Cambridge: Cambridge University Press.

Crosby, F., and L. Nyquist. 1977. The female register: an empirical study of Lakoff's hypotheses. *Language in Society* 6(3):313–322.

Crowell, D. H., R. H. Jones, L. E. Kapuniai, and J. K. Nakagawa. 1973. Unilateral cortical activity in newborn humans: an early index of cerebral dominance? *Science* 180:205–208.

Crowell, D. H., L. E. Kapuniai, and J. A. Garbanati. 1977. Hemispheric differences in human infant rhythmic responses to photic stimulation. In *Cerebral evoked potentials in man*, ed. J. E. Desmedt. London: Oxford University Press.

Danforth, L. 1982. *The death rituals of rural Greece*. Princeton, N.J.: Princeton University Press.

Darley, F. L., and H. Winitz. 1961. Age of first word: review of research. *Journal of Speech and Hearing Disorders* 26:272–290.

Dauer, S. 1978. Language and sex roles in Buhaya. Manuscript, 19 pp. Amnesty International, New York.

Diebold, A. R. 1961. Incipient bilingualism. *Language* 37:97–112.

DiPietro, J. 1981. Rough and tumble play: a function of gender. *Developmental Psychology* 17:50–58.

Dittmann, A. 1972. Developmental factors in conversational behavior. *Journal of Communication* 22:404–423.

Dixon, R. M. W. 1979. "Ergativity." *Language* 55: 59–138.

Dorian, N. 1980. Linguistic lag as an ethnic marker. *Language in Society* 9:33–42.

Doyle, J. C., R. Ornstein, and D. Galin. 1974. Lateral specialization of cognitive mode: II EEG frequency analysis. *Psychophysiology* 11:567–578.

Dunn, L. M. 1959. *The Peabody picture vocabulary test*. Circle Pines, Minn.: American Guidance Service, Inc.

Duranti, A. 1981. *The Samoan fono: a sociolinguistic study*. Pacific Linguistics, ser. B, no. 80. The Australian University, Canberra.

Edelsky, C. 1977. Acquisition of an aspect of communicative competence: learning what it means to talk like a lady. In *Child discourse*, ed. S. Ervin-Tripp and C. Mitchell-Kernan. New York: Academic Press.

1979. Question intonation and sex roles. *Language in Society* 8:15–32.

Eimas, P. D., E. R. Siqueland, P. Jusczyk, and J. Vigorito. 1971. Perception in infants. *Science* 171:303–306.

Eisenberg, A. R., and C. Garvey. 1981. Children's use of verbal strategies in resolving conflicts. *Discourse Processes* 4:149–170.

Ellis, H. D., and A. N. Young. 1977. Age-of-acquisition and recognition of nouns presented in the left and right visual fields: a failed hypothesis. *Neuropsychologia* 15:825–828.

Entus, A. 1977. Hemispheric asymmetry in processing of dichotically presented speech and nonspeech stimuli by infants. In *Language development and neurological theory*, ed. S. J. Segalowitz and F. A. Gruber. New York: Academic Press.

Ervin-Tripp, S. 1977. Wait for me, roller skate! In *Child discourse*, ed. S. Ervin-Tripp and C. Mitchell-Kernan. New York: Academic Press.

1982. Structures of control. In *Communicating in the classroom*, ed. C. Wilkinson, pp. 27–47. New York: Academic Press.

Ervin-Tripp, S., and D. Gordon. 1984. The development of requests. In *The acquisition of communicative competence*, ed. R. Schiefelbusch and J. Pickar. Baltimore: University Park Press.

Ervin-Tripp, S., and C. Mitchell-Kernan. 1977. Introduction. In *Child discourse*, ed. S. Ervin-Tripp and C. Mitchell-Kernan, pp. 1–26. New York: Academic Press.

Ervin-Tripp, S., M. C. O'Connor, and J. Rosenberg. 1982. Language and power in the family. In *Language and power*, ed. C. Kramarae and M. Schulz. Champaign: University of Illinois Press.

Esposito, A. 1979. Sex differences in children's conversation. *Language and Society* 22:213–220.

Fairweather, H. 1976. Sex differences in cognition. *Cognition* 4:231–280.

1982. Sex differences. In *Divided visual field studies of cerebral organization*, ed. J. G. Beaumont, pp. 148–194. London: Academic Press.

Faithorn, E. D. 1975. The concept of pollution among the Kafe of the Papua New Guinea Highlands. In *Toward an anthropology of women*, ed. R. R. Reiter, pp. 127–140. New York: Monthly Review Press.

Faron, L. C. 1968. *The Mapuche Indians of Chile*. New York: Holt, Rinehart & Winston.

Farrell, S. M. 1977. Peasant farmers, masons, and maids: migration and family structure in Tlaxcala, Mexico. Doctoral dissertation, University of California at Santa Barbara.

Fasold, R. 1972. *Tense marking in black English: a linguistic and social analysis*. Washington, D.C.: Center for Applied Linguistics.

Feagin, C. 1980. Woman's place in nonstandard southern white English: not so simple. In *Language use and the uses of language*, ed. R. Shuy and A. Shnukal, pp. 88–97. Washington, D.C.: Georgetown University Press.

Fedio, P., and J. M. VanBuren. 1974. Memory deficits elicited during electrical stimulation of the speech cortex in conscious man. *Brain and Language* 1:29–42.

Fein, G., and A. R. Robertson. 1975. Cognitive and social dimensions of pretending in two-year-olds. Eric ed 119 806. Educational Resources Information Center, University of Illinois, Urbana.

Feld, S. 1982. *Sound and sentiment: birds, weeping, poetics, and song in Kaluli expression*. Philadelphia: University of Pennsylvania Press.

1984. Sound structure as social structures. *Ethnomusicology* 28, 3:383–409.

Feld, S., and B. B. Schieffelin. 1982. Hard words: a functional basis for Kaluli discourse. In *Analyzing discourse: talk and text*, ed. D. Tanner. Washington, D.C.: Georgetown University Press.

Ferguson, C. 1959. Diglossia. *Word* 15:325–340.

Fillmore, C. 1968. The case for case. In *Universals in linguistic theory*, ed. E. Bach and R. T. Harms, pp. 1–90. New York: Holt, Rinehart & Winston.

Fischer, J. L. 1958. Social influences on the choice of a linguistic variant. *Word* 14:47–56.

Flannery, R. 1946. Men's and women's speech in Gros Ventre. *International Journal of American Linguistics* 12:133–135.

Foley, W. A., and R. D. Van Valin, Jr. 1984. *Functional syntax and universal grammar*. Cambridge: Cambridge University Press.

Friedman, D., R. Simson, W. Ritter, and I. Rapin. 1975. Cortical evoked potentials elicited by real speech words and human sounds. *Electroencephalography and Clinical Neurophysiology* 38:13–19.

Gal, S. 1978. Peasant men can't get wives: language change and sex roles in a bilingual community. *Language in Society* 7:1–16.

Galambos, R., P. Benson, T. S. Smith, C. Schulman-Galambos, and H. Osier. 1975. On hemispheric differences in evoked potentials to speech stimuli. *Electroencephalography and Clinical Neurophysiology* 39:279–283.

Galin, D. 1974. Implications for psychiatry of left and right cerebral specialization–neurophysiological context for unconscious processes. *Archives of General Psychiatry* 31:572–583.

Galin, D., and R. R. Ellis. 1975. Asymmetry in evoked potentials as an index of lateralized cognitive processes: relation to EEG alpha asymmetry. *Neuropsychologia* 13:45–50.

Galin, D., and R. Ornstein. 1972. Lateral specialization of cognitive mode: an EEG study. *Psychophysiology* 9:412–418.

1974. Individual differences in cognitive style: I. Reflective eye movements. *Neuropsychologia* 12:367–376.

Gallagher, T. Contingent query sequences within adult–child discourse. *Journal of Child Language* 8:51–62.

Gardiner, M. F., C. Schulman, and D. O. Walter. 1973. Facultative EEG asymmetries in infants and adults. In *Cerebral dominance*, vol. 34, pp. 37–40. Brain Information Service Conference Report.

Gardiner, M. F., and D. O. Walter. 1977. Evidence of hemispheric specialization from infant EEG. In *Lateralization in the nervous system*, ed. S. Harnad, R. W. Doty, L. Goldstein, J. Jaynes, and G. Krauthamer. New York: Academic Press.

Garfinkel, H. 1967. Passing and the managed achievement of sex status in an intersexed person, pt. 1. In *Studies in ethnomethodology*, ed. H. Garfinkel, pp. 116–185. Englewood Cliffs, N.J.: Prentice-Hall.

Garvey, C. 1975. Requests and responses in children's speech. *Journal of Child Language* 2:41–63.

1977a. The contingent query: a dependent act in conversation. In *Interaction, conversation and the development of language*, ed. M. Lewis and L. Rosenblum. New York: Wiley.

1977b. *Play: the developing child*. London: Open Books.

Gengo Seikatsu, 1957. No. 65. Tokyo: Chikuma Shobo.

1973. No. 262. Tokyo: Chikuma Shobo.

Genishi, C., and M. DiPaolo. 1982. Learning through argument in a preschool. In *Communicating in the classroom*, ed. L. C. Wilkenson, pp. 49–68. New York: Academic Press.

Geschwind, N., and P. Behan. 1982. Left handedness: association with immune disease, migraine, and developmental learning disorder. *Proceedings of the National Academy of Science* 79:5097–5100.

Geschwind, N., and W. Levitsky. 1968. Human brain: left–right asymmetries in temporal speech region. *Science* 161: 186–187.

Gevins, A. S., J. C. Doyle, B. A. Cutillo, R. E. Schaffer, R. S. Tannehill, J. H. Ghannam, V. A. Gilcrease, and C. L. Yeager. 1981. Electrical potentials in human brain during cognition: new method reveals dynamic patterns of correlation. *Science* 213:918–922.

Gevins, A. S., J. C. Doyle, R. E. Schaffer, E. Callaway, and C. Yeager. 1980. Lateralized cognitive processes and the electroencephalogram. *Science* 207:1006–1007.

Gewertz, D. B. 1983. *Sepik River societies: a horizontal ethnography of the Chambri and their neighbors*. New Haven, Conn.: Yale University Press.

Giattino, J., and J. G. Hogan. 1975. Analysis of a father's speech to his language-learning child. *Journal of Speech and Hearing Disorders* 40:524–537.

Giles, H., D. Taylor, and R. Bourhis. 1973. Towards a theory of interpersonal accommodation through speech: some Canadian data. *Language in Society* 2:177–192.

Gilligan, C. 1982. *In a different voice: psychological theory and women's development*. Cambridge: Harvard University Press.

Gillison, G. 1980. Images of nature in Gimi thought. In *Nature, culture and gender*, ed. C. MacCormack and M. Strathern. Cambridge: Cambridge University Press.

Glanville, B. B., C. T. Best, and R. Levinson. 1977. A cardiac measure of cerebral asymmetries in infant auditory perception. *Developmental Psychology* 13:54–59.

Glasse, R. M., and M. J. Meggitt. 1969. *Pigs, pearlshells and women: marriage in the New Guinea Highlands*. Englewood Cliffs, N.J.: Prentice-Hall.

Glazer, Mark. 1976. On verbal dueling among Turkish boys. *Journal of American Folklore* 89:87–89.

Gleason, J. B. 1973. Code switching in children's language. In *Development and the acquisition of language*, ed. T. E. Moore, pp. 159–167. New York: Academic Press.

——— 1975. Fathers and other strangers: men's speech to young children. In *Georgetown University round table on language and linguistics*, ed. D. P. Dato, pp. 289–297. Washington, D.C.: Georgetown University Press, 1981.

——— 1980. The acquisition of social speech: routines and politeness formulas. In *Language: social psychological perspectives*, ed. H. Giles, W. P. Robinson, and P. N. Smith, pp. 21–27. Oxford: Pergamon Press.

Gleason, J. B., and E. B. Greif. 1983. Men's speech to young children. In *Language, gender and society*, ed. C. Kramarae and N. Henley. Rowley, Mass.: Newbury House.

Gleason, J. B., R. Y. Perlmann, and E. B. Greif. 1984. What's the magic word: learning language through politeness routines. *Discourse Processes* 7:493–502.

Gleason, J. B., and S. Weintraub. 1976. The acquisition of routines in child language. *Language in Society* 5:129–136.

Gleitman, L. R., E. L. Newport, and H. Gleitman. 1984. The current status of the motherese hypothesis. *Journal of Child Language* 1:43–79.

Goffman, E. 1963. *Stigma: notes on the management of spoiled identity*. Englewood Cliffs, N.J.: Prentice-Hall.

——— 1967. *Interaction ritual: essays on face-to-face behavior*. New York: Doubleday.

——— 1971. *Relations in public: microstudies of the public order*. New York: Basic.

——— 1974. *Frame analysis: an essay on the organization of experience*. New York: Harper & Row.

——— 1977. The arrangement between the sexes. *Theory and Society* 4: 301–331.

——— 1981. *Forms of talk*. Philadelphia: University of Pennsylvania Press.

Goldberg, S., and M. Lewis. 1969. Play behavior in the year old infant: early sex differences. *Child Development*, 40:21–32.

Goldman, L. R. 1981. Talk never dies: an analysis of disputes among the Huli. Doctoral dissertation, University College, London.

——— 1983. *Talk never dies*. London: Tavistock.

Golinkoff, R., and G. Ames. 1979. A comparison of fathers' and mothers' speech with their young children. *Child Development* 50:28–32.

Goodale, J. 1980. Gender, sexuality and marriage: a Kaulong model of nature and culture. In *Nature, culture and gender*, ed. C. McCormack and M. Strathern. Cambridge: Cambridge University Press.

Goodenough, W. H. 1981. *Culture, language and society*. 2d ed. Menlo Park, N.J.: Benjamin/Cummings.

Goodman, E. 1983. The trouble with "Tootsie." *Hartford Courant*, Jan. 4: A11.

Goodwin, C. 1981. *Conversational organization: interaction between speakers and hearers.* New York: Academic Press.

Goodwin, M. H. 1980a. Directive response speech sequences in girls' and boys' task activities. In *Women and language in literature and society*, ed. S. McConnell-Ginet, R. Borker, and N. Furman, pp. 157–173. New York: Praeger.

1980b. He-said-she-said: formal cultural procedures for the construction of a gossip dispute activity. *American Ethnologist* 7:674–695.

1980c. Processes of mutual monitoring implicated in the production of description sequences. *Sociological Inquiry* 50:303–317.

1982a. "Instigating": storytelling as social process. *American Ethnologist* 9:799–819.

1982b. Processes of dispute management among urban black children. *American Ethnologist* 9:76–96.

1983. Aggravated correction and disagreement in children's conversations. *Journal of Pragmatics* 7:657–677.

1985a. The achievement of girls' social organization across constructive play, games, and pretend play: the message "this is serious." Paper presented at the Annual Meeting of the Association for the Anthropological Study of Play, Washington, D.C.

1985b. The serious side of jump rope: conversational practices and social organization in the frame of play. *Journal of American Folklore* 98:315–330.

Gordon, D., N. Budwig, A. Strage, and P. Carrell. 1980. Children's requests to unfamiliar adults: form, social function, age variation. Paper presented at Boston University Conference on Child Language.

Gordon, H. W., and J. E. Bogen. 1974. Hemispheric lateralization of signing after intracarotid sodium amylobarbitone. *Journal of Neurology, Neurosurgery, and Psychiatry* 37:727–738.

Gossen, G. H. 1974. To speak with a heated heart: Chamula canons of style and good performance. In Bauman and Sherzer, 1974, pp. 389–413.

Gray, J. A. 1971. Sex differences in emotional behavior in mammals including man: endocrine bases. *Acta Psychologia* 35:29–46.

Gray, J. A., and A. W. H. Buffery. 1971. Sex differences in emotional and cognitive behavior in mammals including man: adaptive and neural bases. *Acta Psychologia* 35:89–111.

Greif, E. B. 1980. Sex differences in parent–child conversation. *Women's Studies International Quarterly* 3:253–258.

Greif, E. B., and J. B. Gleason. Hi, thanks and goodbye: more routine information. *Language in Society* 9:159–166.

Grossi, D., A. Orsini, C. Monetti, and G. DeMichele. 1979. Sex differences in children's spatial and verbal memory span. *Cortex* 15:667–670.

Gumperz, J. J. 1968. The speech community. *International encyclopedia of the social sciences* 9:381–386. New York: Macmillan.

1971. Social meaning in linguistic structures: code-switching in Norway. In *Language in social groups: essays by John J. Gumperz*, ed. A. S. Del, pp. 274–310. Stanford, Calif.: Stamford University Press.

Gunter, R. 1974. *Sentences in dialogue.* Columbia. S.C.: Hornbeam Press.

Gutmann, D. 1965. Women and the conception of ego strength. *Merrill-Palmer Quarterly of Behavior and Development* 2:229–40.

Guy, G. 1980. Variation in the group and the individual: the case of final stop deletion. In *Locating language in time and space*, ed. W. Labov, pp. 1–36. New York: Academic Press.

Haas, A. 1979. The acquisition of genderlect. *Annals of the New York Academy of Science* (*Language, sex and gender*) 327:101–113.

Haas, M. 1944. Men's and women's speech in Koasati. *Language* 20:142–149.

Halliday, M. A. K., and R. Hasan. 1976. *Cohesion in English*. London: Longman Group.

Halverson, C. F., and M. F. Waldrop. 1973. The relations of mechanically recorded activity level to varieties of preschool behavior. *Child Development* 44:678–681.

Hannerz, U. 1969. *Soulside: inquiries into ghetto culture and community*. New York: Columbia University Press.

Harada, S. I. 1976. Honorifics. In vol. 5: *Japanese generative grammar, Syntax and semantics*, ed. M. Shibatani, pp. 499–561. New York: Academic Press.

Haraguchi, S. 1973. Remarks on dislocation in Japanese. Unpublished paper. Cambridge, Mass.: MIT.

Harding, S. 1975. Women and words in a Spanish village. In *Toward an anthropology of women*, ed. R. R. Reiter, pp. 283–308. New York: Monthly Review Press.

Harris, L. J. 1977. Sex differences in the growth and use of language. In *Women: a psychological perspective*, ed. E. Donelson and J. Fullahorn, pp. 79–94. New York: Wiley.

1978. Sex differences in spatial ability: possible environmental, genetic, and neurological factors. In *Asymmetrical function of the brain*, ed. M. Kinsbourne, pp. 405–522. Cambridge: Cambridge University Press.

Hartup, W. W. 1978. Children and their friends. In *Issues in childhood social development*, ed. H. McGurk, pp. 130–170. London: Methuen.

Hatano, K. 1954. Otoko no bunshō, onna no bunshō [Men's style and women's style]. In *Kotoba no shinri* [The psychology of speech], ed. O. Miyagi. Tokyo: Kawade Sinsho.

Hays, T., and P. Hays. 1982. Opposition and complementarity of the sexes in Ndumba initiation. In *Rituals of manhood: male initiation in Papua New Guinea*, ed. G. H. Herdt. Berkeley and Los Angeles: University of California Press.

Heath, J. 1975. Some functional relationships in grammar. *Language* 51:89–104.

Hécaen, H., M. De Agostini, and A. Monzon-Montes. 1981. Cerebral organization in left-handedness. *Brain and Language* 12:261–284.

Hécaen, H., and J. Sauguet. 1971. Cerebral dominance in left-handed subjects. *Cortex* 7:19–48.

Hendrick, R. 1982. Reduced questions and their theoretical implications. *Language* 58(4):800–819.

Herdt, G. H. (ed.). 1982. *Rituals of manhood: male initiation in Papua New Guinea*. Berkeley and Los Angeles: University of California Press.

Heron, W. 1957. Perception as a function of retinal locus and attention. *American Journal of Psychology* 70:38–48.

Hilger, Sister M. I. 1957. *Araucanian child life and its cultural background*. Washington, D.C.: Smithsonian Institution.

Hill, J. H., and K. C. Hill, 1978. Honorific usage in modern Nahuatl: expression of social distance and respect in Nahuatl of Malinche Volcano area. *Language* 54:123–155.

1980. Mixed grammar, purist grammar, and language attitudes in modern Nahuatl. *Language in Society* 9:321–348.

1981. Variation in relative clause construction in modern Nahuatl. In *Nahuatl studies in memory of Fernando Horcasitas*, ed. F. Karttunen, pp. 89–104. Texas Linguistic Forum, vol. 18.

1986. *Speaking Mexicano*. Tucson: University of Arizona Press.

Hinds, J. 1976. Postposing in Japanese. *Eoneo* 1(2):113–125.

1978. Anaphora in Japanese conversation. In *Anaphora in discourse*, ed. J. Hinds, pp. 136–179. Edmonton: Linguistic Research, Inc.

Hiscock, M., and M. MacKay. 1985. The sex difference in dichotic listening: multiple negative findings. *Neuropsychologia* 23:441–44.

Hoff, A. L. 1981. Sex and familial left-handedness as determinants of cerebral functional asymmetry for object recognition and spatial ability. Doctoral dissertation, Bowling Green State University.

Holzman, M. 1972. The use of interrogation forms in the verbal interaction of three mothers and their children. *Journal of Psycholinguistic Research* 1:311–336.

Honko, L. 1974. Balto-Finnic lament poetry. *Studia Fennica* 17:143–202.

Howe, J. 1977. Carrying the village: Cuna political metaphors. In *The social use of metaphor: essays on the anthropology of rhetoric*, ed. J. D. Sapir and J. C. Crocker, pp. 132–163. Philadelphia: University of Pennsylvania Press.

1986. *The Kuna gathering: contemporary village politics in Panama*. Austin: University of Texas Press.

Howe, J., and L. Hirschfeld. 1981. The star girls' descent: a myth about men, women, matrilocality and singing. *Journal of American Folklore* 94:292–322.

Hubel, D., and T. Wiesel. 1963. Receptive fields of cells in striate cortex of very young, visually inexperienced kittens. *Journal of Neurophysiology* 26:994–1002.

Hudson, R. A. 1980. *Sociolinguistics*. Cambridge: Cambridge University Press.

Hughes, L. A. 1983. Beyond the rules of the game: girls' gaming at a Friends' school. Doctoral dissertation, Graduate School of Education, University of Pennsylvania.

Hymes, D. 1974. *Foundations in sociolinguistics: an ethnographic approach*. Philadelphia: University of Pennsylvania Press.

Hymes, D. H. 1962. The ethnography of speaking. In *Anthropology and human behavior*, ed. T. Gladwin and W. C. Sturtevant, pp. 13–53. Washington, D.C.: Anthropological Society of Washington.

1972. On communicative competence. In *Sociolinguistics*, ed. J. Pride and J. Holmes. Harmondsworth: Penguin Books.

1974. Studying the interaction of language and social life. In D. Hymes, *Foundations in sociolinguistics: an ethnographic approach*, pp. 29–66. Philadelphia: University of Pennsylvania Press.

1981. The "wife" who "goes out" like a man: reinterpretation of a Clackamas Chinook myth. In D. Hymes, *"In vain I tried to tell you": essays in native American ethnopoetics*, pp. 274–308. Philadelphia: University of Pennsylvania Press.

Irvine, J. 1979. Formality and informality in communicative events. *American Anthropologist* 81(4):773–790.

Jackson, J. 1974. Language identity of the Colombian Vaupés Indians. In Bauman and Sherzer, 1974, pp. 50–64.

James, S. 1978. Effect of listener age and situation on the politeness of children's directives. *Journal of Psycholinguistic Research* 7:307–317.

Jasper, H. H. 1958. The ten–twenty electrode system of the International Federation of Societies of electroencephalography: appendix to report of the committee methods of clinical examinations in electroencephalography. *Electroencephalography and Clinical Neurophysiology* 10:371–375.

1974. Error correction as an interactional resource. *Language in Society* 3:181–199.

Jespersen, O. 1925. The woman. *Language*, pp. 237–254. New York: Holt.

Jones, D. F., and A. D. Jones. 1975. Gender differences in mental function: a clue to the origin of language. *Current Anthropology* 16:626–630.

Jones, S. J., and H. A. Moss. 1972. Age, state and maternal behavior associated with infant vocalizations. *Child Development* 42:1039–1051.

Joos, M. 1961. *The five clocks.* New York: Harcourt, Brace & World.

Jorden, E. H. 1974. Female speech: persisting myth and persisting reality. In *The report of the second U.S.–Japan Joint Sociolinguistic Conference*, pp. 103–118. Tokyo: Japan Society for the Promotion of Science.

Kail, R. V., Jr., and A. W. Siegel. 1978. Sex and hemispheric differences in the recall of verbal and spatial information. *Cortex* 14:557–563.

Kaisse, E. 1983. The syntax of auxiliary reduction in English. *Language* 59(1):93–122.

Kalčik, S. 1975. " . . . Like Anne's gynecologist or the time I was almost raped": personal narratives in women's rap groups. *Journal of American Folklore* 88:3–11.

Karabenick, J., and S. Miller. 1977. The effect of age, sex and listener feedback on grade school children's referential communication. *Child Development* 48:678–683.

Karttunen, F. 1978. The development of inanimate plural marking in post-conquest Nahuatl. *Texas Linguistic Forum* 10:21–29.

Karttunen, F., and J. Lockhart. 1976. *Nahuatl in the middle years.* University of California Publications in Linguistics, no. 85.

Kaye, K., and R. Charney. 1980. How mothers maintain "dialogue" with two-year-olds. In *The social foundations of language and thought*, ed. D. Olson. New York: Norton.

Keenan (Ochs), E. 1974a. Conversation and oratory in Vakinankaratra, Madagascar. Doctoral dissertation, University of Pennsylvania.

1974b. Conversational competence in children. *Journal of Child Language* 1:163–183.

1974c. Norm-makers, norm-breakers: uses of speech by men and women in a Malagasy community. In Bauman and Sherzer, 1974, pp. 125–143.

Keenan, E. Ochs, and E. Klein. 1975. Coherency in children's discourse. *Journal of Psycholinguistic Research* 4:365–380.

Keesing, F., and M. Keesing. 1956. *Elite communication in Samoa.* Stanford, Calif.: Stanford University Press.

Keiser, R. L. 1969. *The vice lords: warriors of the streets.* New York: Holt, Rinehart & Winston.

Keller-Cohen, D., K. C. Chalmer, and J. E. Remler. 1979. The development of discourse negation in the non-native child. In *Developmental pragmatics*, ed. E. Ochs and B. B. Schieffelin, pp. 305–322. New York: Academic Press.

Kelly, R. 1977. Witchcraft and sexual relations: an exploration in the social and semantic structure of belief. In *Man and woman in the New Guinea Highlands*, ed. P. Brown and G. Buchbinder. Washington, D.C.: American Anthropological Association.

Kelly, R. R., and K. D. Orton. 1979. Dichotic perception of word pairs with mixed imagery values. *Neuropsychologia* 17:363–371.

Kimura, D. 1973. The asymmetry of the human brain. *Scientific American* 228 (March):70–78.

———. 1980. Sex differences in intrahemispheric organization of speech. *Behavior and Brain Sciences* 3:240–241.

———. 1983. Sex differences in cerebral organization for speech and praxic functions. *Canadian Journal of Psychology* 37:19–35.

Kimura, D., and M. Durnford. 1974. Normal studies on the function of the right hemisphere in vision. In *Hemisphere function in the human brain*, ed. S. J. Diamond and J. G. Beaumont. New York: Halsted.

Kindaichi, H. 1957. *Nihongo* [Japanese]. Tokyo: Iwanami Shoten.

Kinsbourne, M. 1972. Eye and head turning indicates cerebral lateralization. *Science* 176:539–541.

———. 1975. The ontogeny of cerebral dominance. *Annals of the New York Academy of Sciences* 263:244–250.

Kinsbourne, M., and M. Hiscock. 1983. Functional lateralization of the brain: implications for normal and deviant development. In *Handbook of child psychology*, vol. 2: *Infancy and developmental psychobiology*, ed. M. M. Haith and J. J. Campos. New York: Wiley.

Kitagawa, C. 1977. A source of femininity in Japanese: in defense of Robin Lakoff's "Language and Woman's Place." *Papers in Linguistics* 10(3–4):275–298.

Klann-Delius, G. 1981. Sex and language acquisition–is there any influence? *Journal of Pragmatics* 5:1–25.

Klymasz, R. 1975. Speaking at/about/with the dead: funerary rhetoric among Ukrainians in western Canada. *Canadian Ethnic Studies* 7(2):50–56.

Kochman, T. 1970. Toward an ethnography of black American speech behavior. In *Afro-American anthropology*, ed. N. E. Whitten, Jr., and J. F. Szwed, pp. 145–162. New York: Free Press.

———. 1981. *Black and white: styles in conflict*. Chicago: University of Chicago Press.

Kodish, Debora. 1981. "Never had a word between us": pattern in the verbal art of Newfoundland woman. Doctoral dissertation, University of Texas–Austin.

Koizumi, T. 1978. Nihongo no boin no tokusei [The unique character of Japanese vowels]. *Gengo* 7:10:40–49.

Kokugogakkai (ed.). 1964. *Kokugogaku jiten* [Dictionary of national language studies]. Tokyo: Tokyo-do Shuppan.

Kokuritsu Kokugo Kenkyūjo [National Language Research Institute]. 1957. *Hōkoku II: keigo to keigo ishiki* [Honorific language and honorific language consciousness]. Tokyo: Kokuritsu Kokugo Kenkyūjo.

Kramarae, C. 1981. *Women and men speaking: frameworks for analysis*. Rowley, Mass.: Newbury House.

Krauss, R., and S. Glucksberg. 1969. The development of communication competence as a function of age. *Child Development* 40:255–265.

Labov. W. 1966. *The social stratification of English in New York City.* Washington, D.C.: Center for Applied Linguistics.

1969. Contraction, deletion and inherent variability of the English copula. *Language* 45:715–762.

1970. *The study of nonstandard English.* Champaign, Ill.: National Council of Teachers.

1972a. Rules for ritual insults. In *Language in the inner city: studies in the black English vernacular,* ed. W. Labov, pp. 297–353. Philadelphia: University of Pennsylvania Press.

1972b. *Sociolinguistic patterns.* Philadelphia: University of Pennsylvania Press.

1974. The art of sounding and signifying. In *Language in its social setting,* ed. W. W. Gage, pp. 84–116. Washington, D.C.: Anthropological Society of Washington.

1978. Women's role in linguistic change. Paper presented at the Annual Meeting of the American Linguistic Society of America.

Labov, W., and D. Fanshel. 1977. *Therapeutic discourse: psychotherapy as conversation.* New York: Academic Press.

Labov, W. (ed.). 1972c. *Language in the inner city: studies in the black English vernacular.* Philadelphia: University of Pennsylvania Press.

Ladd, D. R., Jr. 1978. *The structure of intonational meaning.* Bloomington: Indiana University Press.

Lake, D., and M. P. Bryden. 1976. Handedness and sex differences in hemispheric asymmetry. *Brain and Language* 3:266–282.

Lakoff, R. 1973a. Language and women's place. *Language in Society* 2:45–80.

1973b. The logic of politeness: or minding your p's and q's. In *Proceedings of the ninth regional meeting of the Chicago Linguistic Society,* pp. 292–305. Chicago: Chicago Linguistic Society.

1975. *Language and women's place.* New York: Harper (Colophon Books).

Langness, L. L. 1967. Sexual antagonism in the New Guinea Highlands: a Bora Bora example. *Oceania* 37(3):161–177.

Leacock, E. B. 1981. *Myths of male dominance: collected articles on women cross-culturally.* New York: Monthly Review Press.

1983. Interpreting the origins of gender inequality: conceptual and historical problems. *Dialectical Anthropology* 7:263–284.

Lee, M. Y. 1976. The married woman's status and role as reflected in Japanese: an exploratory sociolinguistic study. *Signs,* 1(1):991–999.

Leehey, S. C., and A. Cahn. 1979. Lateral asymmetries in the recognition of words, familiar faces, and unfamiliar faces. *Neuropsychologia* 17:619–627.

Lein, L., and D. Brenneis. 1978. Children's disputes in three speech communities. *Language in Society* 7:299–323.

Lenneberg, E. H. 1966. Speech development: its anatomical and physiological concomitants. In *Brain function,* vol. 3: *Speech, language and communication,* ed. E. C. Carterette. Berkeley and Los Angeles: University of California Press.

1974. Maturation of the CNS and language. *Neurosciences Research Program Bulletin* 12:619–636.

Lever, J. 1976. Sex differences in the games children play. *Social Problems* 23:478–487.

Levy, J. 1969. Possible basis for the evolution of lateral specialization of the human brain. *Nature, London* 224:614–615.

Lewis, M. 1972. Culture and gender roles: there's no unisex in the nursery. *Psychology Today* 5:54–57.

Lewis, M., and R. Freddle. 1972. Mother–infant dyad: the cradle of meaning. Paper presented at symposium "Language and Thought: Communication and Affect," Erindale College, University of Toronto.

Li, C., and S. Thompson. 1976. Subject and topic: a new typology of language. In *Subject and topic*, ed. C. Li, pp. 457–490. New York: Academic Press.

Liberman, A., E. Cooper, D. Shankweiler, and M. Studdert-Kennedy. 1967. Perception of the speech code. *Psychological Review* 74:431–461.

Lishman, W. A., and E. R. L. McMeekan. 1977. Handedness in relation to direction and degree of cerebral dominance for language. *Cortex* 13:30–43.

Lopez, G. M., and L. G. Joly. 1981. Singing a lullaby in Kuna: a female verbal art. *Journal of American Folklore* 94:351–358.

McCarthy, D. 1954. Language development in children. In *Manual of child psychology*, 2d ed., ed. L. Carmichael. New York: Wiley.

Maccauley, R. 1978. The myth of female superiority in language. *Journal of Child Language* 5:353–363.

Maccoby, E., and C. Jacklin. 1974. *The psychology of sex differences*. Stanford, Calif.: Stanford University Press.

McConnell-Ginet, S. 1980. Linguistics and the feminist challenge. In *Women and language in literature and society*, ed. S. McConnell-Ginet, R. Borker, and N. Furman, pp. 3–25. New York: Praeger.

——— 1983. Review of *Language, sex, and gender: does "la différence" make a difference?* ed. J. Orasanu, M. K. Slater, and L. L. Adler; and *Sexist language: a modern philosophical analysis*, ed. M. Vetterling-Braggin. *Language* 59:373–391.

MacCormack, C., and M. Strathern (ed.). 1980. *Nature, culture and gender*. Cambridge: Cambridge University Press.

McGee, M. G. 1979. Human spatial abilities: psychometric studies and environmental, genetic, hormonal, and neurological influences. *Psychological Bulletin* 86:889–917.

McGlone, J. 1978. Sex differences in functional brain asymmetry. *Cortex* 14:122–128.

——— 1980. Sex differences in human brain asymmetry: a critical survey. *Behavioral and Brain Sciences* 3:215–263.

McKee, G., B. Humphrey, and D. W. McAdam. Scaled lateralization of alpha activity during linguistic and musical tasks. *Psychophysiology* 10:441–443.

McKeever, W. F. 1981. Sex and cerebral organization: is it really so simple? In *Sex differences in dyslexia*, ed. A. Ansara, N. Geschwind, A. Galaburda, M. Albert, and N. Gartrell. Towson, Md.: Orton Dyslexia Society.

McKeever, W. F., and A. L. Hoff. 1982. Familial sinistrality, sex, and laterality differences in naming and lexical decision latencies of righthanders. *Brain and Language* 17:225–239.

McKeever, W. F., and T. L. Jackson. 1979. Cerebral dominance assessed by object- and color-naming latencies: sex and familial sinistrality effects. *Brain and Languages* 7:175–190.

McKeever, W. F., D. R. Nolan, J. A. Diehl, and K. S. Seitz. 1984. Handedness and language laterality: discrimination of handedness groups on the dichotic consonant–vowel task. *Cortex* 20:509–523.

McKeever, W. F., K. S. Seitz, A. L. Hoff, M. F. Marino, and J. A. Diehl. 1983. Interacting sex and familial sinistrality characteristics influence both language lateralization and spatial ability in righthanders. *Neuropsychologia* 21:661–668.

McKeever, W. F., and A. D. VanDeventer. 1977. Visual and auditory language processing asymmetries: influences of handedness, familial sinistrality, and sex. *Cortex* 13:225–241.

McKellin, W. H. 1980. Kinship ideology and language pragmatics. Doctoral dissertation, University of Toronto.

McLaughlin, M. L. 1984. *Conversation: how talk is organized.* Beverly Hills, Calif.: Sage.

McNemar, Q. 1942. *The revision of the Stanford Binet Scale: an analysis of the standardization data.* Boston: Houghton Mifflin.

Madden, D. J., and R. D. Nebes. 1980. Hemispheric differences in memory search. *Neuropsychologia* 18:665–673.

Makino, S. 1970. Two proposals about Japanese polite expressions. In *Studies presented to Robert B. Lees by his students,* ed. J. M. Sadock and A. T. Vanek, pp. 163–187. Edmonton: Linguistic Research, Inc.

Malinowski, B. 1929. *The sexual life of savages in northwestern Melanesia.* New York: Harvest.

Maltz, D. N., and R. A. Borker. 1982. A cultural approach to male–female miscommunication. In *Communication, language and social identity,* ed. J. J. Gumperz, pp. 196–216. Cambridge: Cambridge University Press.

Maratsos, M. 1976. *The use of definite and indefinite reference in young children.* Cambridge: Cambridge University Press.

Marino, M. F. 1981. Determinants of cerebral dominance for clock-face reading and spatial ability: sex, familial sinisterality, or an interaction? Master's thesis, Bowling Green State University.

Martin, S. E. 1975. *A reference grammar of Japanese.* New Haven, Conn.: Yale University Press.

Mashimo, S. 1969. *Fujingo no kenkyū* [Research on women's language]. Tokyo: Tokyo-do Shuppan.

Masur, E., and J. B. Gleason. 1980. Parent–child interaction and the acquisition of lexical information during play. *Developmental Psychology* 16:404–409.

Maynard, D. W. 1985a. How children start arguments. *Language in Society* 4:1–30.

1985b. On the functions of social conflict among children. *American Sociological Review* 50:207–223.

In press. The development of argumentative skills among children. *Sociological studies of child development.*

Mead, M. 1928. *Coming of age in Samoa.* New York: Morrow Quill.

1930. *Social organization of Manu'a.* B. Bishop Museum Bulletin, no. 76. Honolulu.

1935. *Sex and temperament in three primitive societies.* New York: Morrow.

1949. *Male and female: a study of sexes in a changing world.* New York: Morrow.

Meggitt, M. 1964. Male and female relations in the Highlands of Australian New Guinea. In *American Anthropologist,* ed. J. B. Watson, 66, pt. 2(4):204–222.

Meigs, A. S. 1976. Male pregnancy and the reduction of sexual opposition in a New Guinea Highlands society. *Ethnology* 15:393–407.

Merlan, F. 1976. Noun incorporation and discourse reference in modern Nahuatl. *International Journal of American Linguistics* 42:177–191.

Miller, E. K. 1981. An ethnography of singing: the use and meaning of song within a Scottish family. Doctoral dissertation, University of Texas–Austin.

Miller, L. K., and D. Butler. 1980. The effect of set size on hemifield asymmetries in letter recognition. *Brain and Language* 9:307–314.

Miller, P., and C. Garvey. 1984. Mother–baby role play: its origins in social support. In *Symbolic play: the representation of social understanding*, ed. R. Bretherton. New York: Academic Press.

Miller, R. A. 1967. *The Japanese language*. Chicago: University of Chicago Press.

Milroy, L. 1980. *Language and social networks*. Oxford: Blackwell Publisher.

Mitchell-Kernan, C. 1972. Signifying and marking: two Afro-American speech acts. In *Directions in sociolinguistics: the ethnography of communication*, ed. J. J. Gumperz and D. Hymes, pp. 161–179. New York: Holt, Rinehart & Winston.

Mitchell-Kernan, C., and K. Kernan. 1977. Pragmatics of directive choice among children. In *Child discourse*, ed. S. Ervin-Tripp and C. Mitchell-Kernan, pp. 189–208. New York: Academic Press.

Mitscherlich, A. 1963. *Society without the father*. New York: Harcourt, Brace & World.

Moerk, E. L. 1975. Verbal interactions between children and their mothers during the preschool years. *Developmental Psychology* 11:788–794.

Molfese, D. L. 1977. Infant cerebral asymmetry. In *Language development and neurological theory*, ed. S. J. Segalowitz and F. A. Gruber. New York: Academic Press.

Molfese, D. L., R. Freeman, and D. Palermo. 1975. The ontogeny of brain lateralization for speech and nonspeech stimuli. *Brain and Language* 2:356–368.

Molfese, D. L., and V. J. Molfese. 1979. Hemisphere and stimulus differences as reflected in the cortical responses of newborn infants in speech stimuli. *Development Psychology* 15:505–511.

Molfese, D. L., V. Nunez, S. M. Seibert, and N. V. Ramanaiah. 1976. Cerebral asymmetry: changes in factors affecting its development. *Annals of the New York Academy of Sciences* 280:821–833.

Money, J., and A. A. Erhardt. 1972. *Man and woman, boy and girl*. Baltimore: Johns Hopkins University Press.

Morrell, L., and J. Salamy. 1971. Hemispheric asymmetry of electrocortical responses to speech stimuli. *Science* 174:164–166.

Moss, H. A. 1967. Sex, age, and state as determinants of mother–infant interaction. *Merrill-Palmer Quarterly* 13:19–36.

Moylan, T. 1982. System and subsystem, growth and decline, male and female: three pairs of concepts reflected in the process of language change in Oksapmin, Papua New Guinea. Paper presented at the 1982 American Anthropological Association meetings, Washington, D.C.

Mueller, E. 1972. The maintenance of verbal exchanges between young children. *Child Development* 43:19–36.

Nelson, K. 1973. Structure and strategy in learning to talk. *Monographs of the Society for Research in Child Development* 48(149):1–138.

Nomoto, K. 1978. *Nihonjin to Nihongo* [Japanese people and language]. Tokyo: Chikuma Shobo.

Nordberg, B. T. 1975. Contemporary social variation as a stage in long-term

314   *References*

phonological change. In *The Nordic languages and modern linguistics*, vol. 2, ed. K.-H. Dahlstedt, pp. 587–606. Stockholm: Almqvist & Wiksell.

Nottebohm, F. 1977. Asymmetries in neural control of vocalization in the canary. In *Lateralization in the nervous system*, ed. J. Jayne and G. Krauthamer. New York: Academic Press.

Nutini, H., and B. Bell. 1980. *Ritual kinship: the structural and historical development of the compadrango system in rural Tlaxcala*. Princeton, N.J.: Princeton University Press.

O'Barr, W. M. 1982. *Linguistic evidence: language, power and strategy in the courtroom*. New York: Academic Press.

O'Brien, D., and S. Tiffany. 1984. *Rethinking women's roles: perspective from the Pacific*. Berkeley and Los Angeles: University of California Press.

Ochs, E. 1979. Planned and unplanned discourse. In *Discourse and syntax*, ed. T. Givon, pp. 51–80. Syntax and Semantics, vol. 12. New York: Academic Press.

1982. Ergativity and word order in Samoan child language. *Language* 58:646–671.

In press. *Acquiring language in a Samoan village: a sociocultural approach to child language*. Cambridge: Cambridge University Press.

Ochs, E., and B. B. Schieffelin. 1983. *Acquiring conversational competence*. Boston: Routledge and Kegan Paul.

1984. Language acquisition and socialization: three developmental stories and their implication. In *Culture theory: essays on mind, self, and emotion*, ed. R. Shweder and R. LeVine, pp. 276–322. Cambridge: Cambridge University Press.

Ohlrich, E. S., and A. B. Barnet. Auditory evoked responses during the first year of life. *Electroencephalography and Clinical Neurophysiology* 32:161–169.

Oishi, S. 1957. Onna no kotoba wa doo kawaru ka? [How will female speech change?] *Gengo Seikatsu*, no. 65.

Ojemann, G. A. 1978. Organization of short-term verbal memory in language areas of human cortex: evidence from electrical stimulation. *Brain and Language* 5:331–340.

1983. The intrahemispheric organization of human language, derived with electrical stimulation techniques. *Trends in Neurosciences* 6:184–189.

Olivera, M. 1967. *Tlaxcalancingo*. Mexico: Instituto Nacional de Antropología e Historia.

Ortner, S. B., and H. Whitehead (eds.). 1981. *Sexual meanings: the cultural construction of gender and sexuality*. Cambridge: Cambridge University Press.

Pederson, F. A., and R. Bell. 1970. Sex differences in preschool children without histories of complication of pregnancy and delivery. *Developmental Psychology* 3:10–15.

Pellicer, D. 1982. Las migrantes indígenas en la ciudad de México y el empleo del Español como segunda lengua. Paper presented to the Tenth World Congress of Sociology, Mexico City, August.

Peng, F. C. C. 1977. Josei gengo no ch'ikisa, nendaisa to kojinsa: toshika ni yoru ikkōsatsu [Differences in women's speech by region, age, and individual: observations on urbanization]. In *Language and context*, ed. F. C. C. Peng, pp. 73–112. Tokyo: Bunka Hyoron.

Petersen, A. C. 1976. Physical androgyny and cognitive functioning in adolescence. *Developmental Psychology* 12:524–533.

Peterson, C., F. Danner, and J. Flavell. 1972. Developmental changes in children's response to three indications of communicative failure. *Child Development* 43:1463–1468.

Philips, S. 1980. Sex differences and language. In *Annual Review of Anthropology*, vol. 9, ed. B. Siegel, pp. 523–544. Palo Alto, Calif.: Annual Reviews Inc.

1984. Contextual variation in courtroom language use: noun phrases referring to crimes. *International Journal of the Sociology of Language* 49:29–50.

Piaget, J. 1926. *The language and thought of the child*. London: Kegan, Paul, Trench, Tribner.

1965. *The moral judgment of the child* (1932). New York: Free Press.

Piazza, D. 1980. The influence of sex and handedness in the hemispheric specialization of verbal and nonverbal tasks. *Neuropsychologia* 18:163–176.

Pomerantz, A. 1975. Second assessments: a study of some features of agreements. Doctoral dissertation, University of California at Irvine.

1984. Agreeing and disagreeing with assessments: some features of preferred/dispreferred turn shapes. In *Structures of social action: studies in conversation analysis*, ed. J. M. Atkinson and J. Heritage, pp. 57–101. Cambridge: Cambridge University Press.

Poole, F. J. P. 1981. Transferring "natural" woman: female ritual leaders and gender ideology among Binin-Kuskusmin. In *Sexual meanings: the cultural construction of gender and sexuality*, ed. S. B. Ortner and H. Whitehead. Cambridge: Cambridge University Press.

Power, T. G., and R. D. Parke. 1980. Play as a context of early learning: lab and home analyses. In *The family as a learning environment*, ed. I. E. Sigel and L. M. Laosa. New York: Plenum.

Prideaux, G. D. 1970. *The syntax of Japanese honorifics*. The Hague: Mouton.

Pulaski, M. A. 1973. Toys and imaginative play. In *The child's world of make-believe*, ed. J. L. Singer. New York: Academic Press.

Radcliffe-Brown, A. R. 1973. On social structure. In *High points in anthropology*. ed. P. Bohannan and M. Glazer, pp. 304–316. New York: Knopf.

Ralston, N. 1962. The advanced placement program in the Cincinnati public schools. *Personnel and Guidance Journal* 40:557–560.

Ramer, A. L. H. 1976. Syntactic styles in emerging language. *Journal of Child Language* 3:49–62.

Ramsay, D. S. 1980. Beginnings of bimanual handedness and speech in infants. *Infant Behavior and Development* 3:67–77.

1984. Onset of duplicated syllable babbling and unimanual handedness in infancy: evidence for developmental change in hemispheric specialization? *Developmental Psychology* 20:64–71.

Read, K. E. 1954. Cultures of the Central Highlands, New Guinea. *Southwestern Journal of Anthropology* 1:1–43.

Reisman, K. 1970. Cultural and linguistic ambiguity in a West Indian village. In *Afro-American anthropology: contemporary perspectives*, ed. N. E. Whitten, Jr., and J. F. Szwed, pp. 129–144. New York: Free Press.

1974. Contrapuntal conversations in an Antiguan village. In Bauman and Sherzer, 1974, pp. 110–124.

Reiter, R. R. 1975a. Men and women in the south of France: public and private domains. In *Toward an anthropology of women*, ed. R. R. Reiter, pp. 252–282. New York: Monthly Review Press.

Reiter, R. R. (ed.). 1975b. *Toward an anthropology of women*. New York: Monthly Review Press.

Remick, L. 1971. The maternal environment of linguistic development. Doctoral dissertation, University of California at Davis.

Revelle, G., J. Karabenick, and H. Wellman. 1981. Comprehensive monitoring in preschool children. Paper presented at Society for Research in Child Development, Boston.

Rheingold, H. L., and K. V. Cook. 1975. The contents of boys' and girls' rooms as an index of parents' behavior. *Child Development* 46:459–463.

Rheingold, H. L., and H. R. Samuel. 1969. Maintaining the positive behavior of infants by increased stimulation. *Developmental Psychology* 1:520–527.

Rosaldo, M. 1973. I have nothing to hide: the language of Ilongot oratory. *Language in Society* 2:193–223.

1974. Women, culture, and society: a theoretical overview. In *Women, culture, and society*, ed. M. Rosaldo and L. Lamphere, pp. 1–16. Stanford, Calif.: Stanford University Press.

1980. The use and abuse of anthropology: reflections on feminism and cross-cultural understanding. *Signs* 5(3):389–417.

Rosaldo, M., and L. Lamphere (eds.). 1974. *Women, culture, and society*. Stanford, Calif.: Stanford University Press.

Ross, J. R. 1967. Constraints on variables in syntax. Doctoral dissertation, MIT.

Rothstein, F. A. 1982. *Three different worlds: women, men, and children in an industrializing community*. Westport, Conn.: Greenwood.

Rubin, K. H., T. L. Maioni, and M. Hornung. 1976. Free play behaviors in middle- and lower-class preschoolers: Parten and Piaget revisited. *Child Development* 47:414–419.

Sachs, J. 1982. "Don't interrupt": preschoolers' entry into ongoing conversations. In *Proceedings of the Second International Congress for the Study of Child Language*, ed. C. E. Johnson and C. L. Thew. Lanham, Md.: University Press of America.

Sachs, J., and J. Devin. 1976. Young children's use of age-appropriate speech styles in social interaction and role playing. *Journal of Child Language* 3:81–98.

Sachs, J., J. Donnelly, C. Smith, and J. Dwyer. 1984. Interruption of conversation by preschool children: behavior and metalinguistic knowledge. Paper presented at the Third International Congress for the Study of Child Language.

Sachs, J., J. Goldman, and C. Chaillé. 1984. Planning in pretend play: using language to coordinate narrative development. In *The development of oral and written language in social contexts*, ed. A Pellegrini and T. Yaukey, pp. 119–128. Norwood, N.J.: Ablex.

1985. Narratives created by preschoolers in sociodramatic play. In *Play, language and story: the development of children's literate behavior*, ed. L. Galda and A. Pellegrini, pp. 45–61. Norwood, N.J.: Ablex.

Sachs, J., J. Goldman, C. Chaillé, and R. Seewald. 1980. Communication in pretend play. Paper presented at the American Educational Research Association.

Sachs, J., P. Lieberman, and D. Erickson. 1973. Anatomical and cultural determinants of male and female speech. In *Language attitudes: current trends and prospects*, ed. R. W. Shuy and R. W. Fasold. Washington, D.C.: Georgetown University Press.

Sacks, H. 1967. Unpublished lecture notes (lectures 2 and 11).

In press. On the preferences for agreement and contiguity in sequences in conversation. In *Talk and social organization*, ed. G. Button and J. R. E. Lee. Clevedon, Somerset: Multilingual Matters Ltd.

Sacks, H., E. A. Schegloff, and G. Jefferson. 1974. A simplest systematics for the organization of turn-taking in conversation. *Language* 50:696–735.

Sahlins, M. 1963. Poor man, rich man, big man, chief: political types in Melanesia and Polynesia. *Comparative Studies in History and Society* 5:285–303.

Sanday, P. R. 1981. *Female power and male dominance: on the origins of sexual inequality*. Cambridge: Cambridge University Press.

Sankoff, G. 1974. A quantitative paradigm for the study of communicative competence. In Bauman and Sherzer, 1974, pp. 18–49.

1980. *The social life of language*. Philadelphia: University of Pennsylvania Press.

Sapir, E. 1915. *Abnormal types of speech in Nootka*. Canada, Geological Survey, Memoir 62, Anthropological Series, no. 5. Ottawa: Government Printing Bureau.

1929. Male and female forms of speech in Yana. In *Donum natalicium schrignen*, ed. St. W. J. Teeuwen, pp. 79–85. Nijmegen–Utrecht: Dekker and Van de Vegt.

Sapir, J. D., and J. C. Crocker (eds.) 1977. *The social use of metaphor: essays on the anthropology of rhetoric*. Philadelphia: University of Pennsylvania Press.

Sause, E. F. 1976. Computer content analysis of sex differences in the language of children. *Journal of Psycholinguistic Research* 5:311–324.

Savin-Williams, R. C. 1976. An ethological study of dominance formation and maintenance in a group of human adolescents. *Child Development* 47:972–979.

Schachter, F., R. Shore, S. Hodapp, S. Chalfin, and C. Bundy. 1978. Do girls talk earlier? Mean length of utterance in toddlers. *Developmental Psychology* 14:388–392.

Schegloff, E. A. 1972. Notes on a conversational practice: formulating place. In *Studies in social interaction*, ed. D. Sudenow, pp. 75–119. New York: Free Press.

In press. Between macro and micro: contexts and other connections. In *The micro–macro link*, ed. J. Alexander, B. Giesen, R. Munch, and N. Smelser. Berkeley and Los Angeles: University of California Press.

Schegloff, E. A., G. Jefferson, and H. Sacks. 1977. The preference for self-correction in the organization of repair in conversation. *Language* 53:361–382.

Scheub, H. 1972. The art of Nongenile Mazithathu Zenani, a gcaleka ntsomi performer. In *African folklore*, ed. R. M. Dorson, pp. 115–142. New York: Doubleday.

Schieffelin, B. B. 1979. Getting it together: an ethnographic approach to the study of the development of communicative competence. In *Developmental pragmatics*, ed. E. Ochs and B. B. Schieffelin. New York: Academic Press.

1981a. Talking like birds: sound play in a cultural perspective. In *Paradoxes of play*, ed. J. Levy. New York: Leisure Press.

1981b. A developmental study of pragmatic appropriateness of word order and case marking in Kaluli. In *The child's construction of language*, ed. W. Deutsch. London: Academic Press.

1986. The acquisition of Kaluli. In *The cross-linguistic study of language acquisition*, ed. D. I. Slobin, pp. 529–593. Hillsdale, N.J.: Erlbaum.

In press. *How Kaluli children learn what to say, what to do and how to feel* (tentative title). Cambridge: Cambridge University Press.

Schieffelin, E. L. 1976. *The sorrow of the lonely and the burning of the dancers*. New York: St. Martin's.

1979. Mediators as metaphors: moving a man to tears in Papua New Guinea. In *Imagination of reality: essays in South East Asian coherence systems*, ed. A. L. Becker and A. Yengoyan. Norwood, N.J.: Ablex.

1980. Reciprocity and the construction of reality on the Papuan plateau. *Man* 15(3):502–517.

1981. Evangelical rhetoric and the transformation of traditional culture in Papua New Guinea. *Comparative Studies in Society and History* 23(1):150–156.

Schiffrin, D. 1984. Jewish argument as sociability. *Language in Society* 13:311–335.

Schlegel, A. 1977. *Sexual stratification: a cross-cultural view*. New York: Columbia University Press.

Schmuller, J., and R. Goodman. 1979. Bilateral tachistoscopic perception, handedness, and laterality. *Brain and Language* 8:81–91.

Schoeffel, P. 1978. Gender status and power in Samoa. *Canberra Anthropology* 1(2):69–81.

Schulman-Galambos, C. 1977. Dichotic listening performance in elementary and college students. *Neuropsychology* 15:577–584.

Scott, S., G. W. Hynd, L. Hunt, and W. Weed. 1979. Cerebral speech lateralization in the native American Navajo. *Neuropsychologia* 17:89–92.

Searle, J. 1969. *Speech acts: an essay in the philosophy of language*. Cambridge: Cambridge University Press.

Searleman, A. 1980. Subject variables and cerebral organization for language. *Cortex* 16:239–254.

Segalowitz, S. J., and C. Stewart. 1979. Left and right lateralization for letter matching: strategy and sex differences. *Neuropsychologia* 17:521–525.

Shatz, M. 1978. Children's comprehension of their mothers' question-directives. *Journal of Child Language* 5:39–46.

1983. Communication. In *Handbook of child psychology*, P. H. Mussen, general cd., vol. 11: *Cognitive development*, ed. M. J. H. Flavell and E. M. Markman, pp. 841–889. New York: Wiley.

Shatz, M., and R. Gelman. 1973. The development of communication skills: modifications in the speech of young children as function of the listener. *Monographs of the Society for Research in Child Development* 38(152):1–27.

Sherif, M., and C. W. Sherif. 1953. *Groups in harmony and tension*. New York: Harper & Row.

Sherzer, J. 1974. Namakke, summakke, kormakke: three types of Cuna speech event. In Bauman and Sherzer, 1974, pp. 263–282.

1983. A diversity of voices: men's and women's speech in ethnographic perspective. Paper presented at the Sex Differences in Language Conference, Tucson.

Shibamoto, J. S. 1980. Language use and linguistic theory: sex-related variation in Japanese syntax. Doctoral dissertation, University of California at Davis.

1981. Sex-related variation in the production of predicate types in Japanese. *Language Sciences* 3(2):257–282.

1983. Subject ellipsis and topic in Japanese. In *Studies in Japanese language use*, ed. S. Miyagawa and C. Kitagawa. Papers in Linguistics 16(1–2):233–265.

1985. *Japanese women's language.* New York: Academic Press.

Shibata, T. 1972. The honorific prefix "o-" in contemporary Japanese. *Papers in Japanese Linguistics* 1:29–69.

Shore, B. 1977. A Samoan theory of action: social control and social order in a Polynesian paradox. Doctoral dissertation, University of Chicago.

1982. *Sala'ilua: a Samoan mystery.* New York: Columbia University Press.

Shucard, D. W., K. R. Cummins, D. G. Thomas, and J. L. Shucard. 1981. Evoked potentials to auditory probes as indices of cerebral specialization of function-replication and extension. *Electroencephalography and Clinical Neurophysiology* 52:389–393.

Shucard, D. W., J. L. Shucard, and D. G. Thomas. 1977. Auditory evoked potentials as probes of hemispheric differences in cognitive processing. *Science* 197:1295–1298.

In press. The development of cerebral specialization in infancy: electrophysiologial and behavioral studies. In *Continuities and discontinuities and development*, ed. R. W. Emde and R. J. Harmon. New York: Plenum.

Shucard, J. L., D. W. Shucard, K. R. Cummins, and J. J. Campos. 1981. Auditory evoked potentials and sex related differences in brain development. *Brain and Language* 13:91–102.

Silverstein, M. 1975. Shifters, linguistic categories, and cultural description. In *Meaning in cultural anthropology*, ed. K. Basso and H. Selby. Albuquerque: University of New Mexico Press.

1981. The limits of awareness. In *Sociolinguistic working papers*, no. 84. Austin: Southwest Regional Educational Laboratory.

Singer, J. L. (ed). 1973. *The child's world of make-believe: experimental studies of imaginative play.* New York: Academic Press.

Smith, P. K., and K. Connolly. 1972. Patterns of play and social interaction in preschool children. In *Ethological studies of child behavior*, ed. N. B. Jones. Cambridge: Cambridge University Press.

Smith, P. K., and L. Daglish. 1977. Sex differences in parent and infant behavior in home. *Child Development* 48:1250–1254.

Snow, C. 1972. Mother's speech to children learning language. *Child Development* 43:549–565.

Sperry, R. W. 1974. Lateral specialization in the surgically separated hemispheres. In *The neurosciences: third study program*, ed. F. O. Schmitt and F. G. Worde. Cambridge, Mass.: MIT Press.

Stafford, R. 1961. Perception as a function of retinal locus and attention. *American Journal of Psychology* 70:38–48.

Steffen, H. 1974. Cerebral dominance: the development of handedness and speech. *Acta Paedopsychiatra* 41:223–235.

Stein, A. R. 1976. A comparison of mothers' and fathers' speech to normal and language deficient children. Doctoral dissertation, School of Education, Boston University.

Strathern, A. 1973. Kinship, descent and locality: some New Guinea examples.

In *The character of kinship*, ed. J. Goody. Cambridge: Cambridge University Press.

1979. Men's house, women's house: the efficacy of opposition, reversal and pairing in the Melpa Amb Kor cult. *Journal of the Royal Polynesian Society* 88:37–51.

Strathern, M. 1972. *Women in between: female roles in a male world, Mt. Hagen, New Guinea*. London: Seminar Press.

1980. No nature, no culture: the Hagen case. In *Nature, culture and gender*, ed. C. MacCormack and M. Strathern. Cambridge: Cambridge University Press.

Suttles, G. D. 1968. *The social order of the slum*. Chicago: University of Chicago Press.

Szentagothai, J. 1974. Plasticity in the central nervous system: its possible significance in language mechanisms. *Neurosciences Research Program Bulletin* 12:534–536.

Tanguay, P., J. Taub, C. Doubleday, and D. Clarkson. 1977. An interhemispheric comparison of auditory evoked responses to consonant–vowel stimuli. *Neuropsychologia* 15:123–131.

Taub, J., P. Tanguay, C. Doubleday, and D. Clarkson. 1976. Hemisphere- and ear-asymmetry in the auditory evoked response to musical chord stimuli. *Physiological Psychology* 4:11–17.

Tauber, M. A. 1979. Parental socialization techniques and sex differences in children's play. *Child Development* 50:225–234.

Taylor, A. R. 1982. "Male" and "female" speech in Gros Ventre. *Anthropological Linguistics* 24(3):301–307.

Taylor, D. 1969. Differential rates of cerebral maturation between sexes and between hemispheres: evidence from epilepsy. *Lancet* 7612: 140–142.

Teszner, D., A. Tzavaras, J. Gruner, and H. Hécaen. 1972. L'asymétrie droit–gauche du planum temporale. A propos de l'étude anatomique de 100 cerveaux. *Revue Neurologique* 126:444–449.

Thorne, B. 1986. Girls and boys together . . . but mostly apart: gender arrangements in elementary school. In *Relationships and development*, ed. W. W. Hartup and Z. Rubin, pp. 167–184. Hillsdale, N.J.: Erlbaum.

Thorne, B., and N. Henley (eds.). 1975. *Language and sex: difference and dominance*. Rowley, Mass.: Newbury House.

Thorne, B., C. Kramarae, and N. Henley. 1983. *Language, gender and society*. Rowley, Mass.: Newbury House.

Titiev, M. 1949. *Social singing among the Mapuche*. Anthropological Papers of the Museum of Anthropology of the University of Michigan, no. 2. Ann Arbor: University of Michigan Press.

1951. *Araucanian culture in transition*. Ann Arbor: University of Michigan Press.

Tiwary, K. M. 1975. *Tuneful weeping: a mode of communication*. Working Papers in Sociolinguistics, no. 27. Southwest Educational Development Laboratory, Austin, Texas.

Trudgill, P. 1972. Sex, covert prestige, and linguistic change in the urban British English of Norwich. *Language in Society* 1:179–195.

1974. Language and sex. In *Sociolinguistics: an introduction*, pp. 78–99. Harmondsworth: Penguin Books.

Trumbull, R. 1953. A study of relationships between factors of personality and intelligence. *Journal of Social Psychology* 38:161–173.

Vargha-Khadem, F., and M. Corballis. 1979. Cerebral asymmetry in infants. *Brain and Language* 8:1–9.

Vološinov, V. N. 1973. *Marxism and the philosophy of language* (1929–30). Trans. L. Matejka and I. R. Titunik. New York: Seminar Press.

von Glascoe, C. A. 1980. The work of playing "Redlight." In *Play and Culture: 1978 Proceedings of the Association for the Anthropological Study of Play*, ed. H. B. Schwartzman, pp. 228–231. West Point, N.Y.: Leisure Press.

Vuchinich, S. 1984. Sequencing and social structure in family conflict. *Social Psychology Quarterly* 47:217–234.

In press. The sequential organization of closing in verbal family conflict. In *Conflict talk*, ed. A. Grimshaw. Cambridge: Cambridge University Press.

Waber, D. 1976. Sex differences in cognition: a function of maturation rate. *Science* 192:572–574.

Wada, J., R. Clark, and A. Hamm. 1975. Cerebral hemispheric asymmetry in humans. *Archives of Neurology* 32:239–246.

Wada, J., and T. Rasmussen. 1960. Intracarotid injection of sodium amytal for the lateralization of cerebral speech dominance. *Journal of Neurosurgery* 17:266–282.

Wagner, R. 1967. *The curse of the Seuw: principles of Daribi Chen definition and alliance.* Chicago: Aldine.

Watanabe, T. 1963. Kazoku no yobikata [Terms of reference and address for family members]. *Gengo Seikatsu*, no. 143:42–49.

Waterhouse, V. 1949. Learning a second language first. *International Journal of American Linguistics* 15:106–109.

Weiner, A. 1976. *Women of value, men of renown: new perspectives in Trobriand exchange.* Austin: University of Texas Press.

Weinraub, M., and F. Fraenkel. 1977. Sex differences in parent–infant interaction during free play, departure, and separation. *Child Development* 48:1240–1249.

Weisner, T. S., and R. Gallimore. 1977. My brother's keeper: child and sibling caregiving. *Current Anthropology* 18(2):169–190.

Wernicke, C. 1874. *Der aphasische symptomencomplex–eine psychologisch und anatomischer basis.* Breslau: Max Cohn & Weigert.

West, C., and D. H. Zimmerman. 1985. Gender, language and discourse. In *Handbook of discourse analysis*, ed. T. A. van Dijk. London: Academic Press.

Whyte, W. F. 1943. *Street corner society.* Chicago: University of Chicago Press.

Witelson, S. F. 1977. Developmental dyslexia: two right hemispheres and none left. *Science* 195:209–211.

1985. The brain connections: the corpus callosum is larger in left-handers. *Science* 229:665–668.

Witelson, S. F., and W. Pallie. 1973. Left hemisphere specialization for language in the newborn. *Brain* 96:641–646.

Wolfram, W. 1974. The relationship of white southern speech to vernacular black English. *Language* 50:498–527.

Woods, B. T., and H. Teuber. 1973. Early onset of complementary specialization of cerebral hemispheres in man. *Transactions of the American Neurological Association* 98:113–116.

Yaeger-Dror, M. 1974. Speech styles and pitch contours on negatives. *Journal of the Acoustical Society of America* 55: supplement 543.

In press. Intonational prominence on negatives in English. *Language and Speech.*

Young, A. W., and H. D. Ellis. 1980. Ear asymmetry for the perception of monaurally presented words accompanied by binaural white noise. *Neuropsychologia* 18:107–110.

Zimmerman, D. H., and C. West. 1975. Sex roles, interruptions and silence in conversation. In *Language and sex: difference and dominance*, ed. B. Thorne and N. Henley, pp. 130–151. Rowley, Mas.: Newbury House.

Index

abandonment of Nahuatl women by husbands, 126

"Abnormal Types of Speech in Nootka" (Sapir), 15

Abrahams, R. D., 240

accusations (children's arguing analysis), 175, 230–8, 240

activities of men and women: Kaluli, 251, 253, 255, 258, 259; Samoan, 56; *see also* Kuna Indians of Panama

activity levels of girls and boys, 187

address terms, Japanese, 29

affect expression, Samoan, 59–64

age, 50; of argument-analysis children, 241; children's communicative skills and, 169; language use and, 7; Mexicano noun-number analysis and, 148; particle deletion in Japanese and, 46; Samoan gender identity and, 55, 64, 65; Samoan narratives and, 60, 61; use of first words and, 164

aggressiveness, 189, 256

aging, Nahuatl Indians and, 127

Akmajian, A. S., 76, 91

American English: contraction and deletion of subject pronouns and, 72, 75–7, 79; dialogue and, 81–5, 92; discourse context (dialogue versus monologue) and, 81–5, 91, 93; gender differences in deletions and contractions and, 91–3; gender identity and, 85–91; gender in data base and, 73–7; linguistic context and, 77–80; monologue and, 81–5, 89–90, 92; phonological and syntactic deletions and, 74; redundancy and, 91, 92; sex differences in language usage and,

16; stigmatized phonological variants and, 71–2; study overview and, 20–1; systematic contextual variation between men and women and, 71–2; verb deletions and, 74–7; voir dire procedures and, 72–3, 89–90

amytal injections, 279

Andersen, E. S., 169, 180, 186

animal people (Kuna Indian), 108

anthropologists, 177, 249

aphasia, 269, 271, 274

Araucanian Indians of Chile, 95, 99–101, 112, 113, 115, 119

arguments, 176; accusations and, 175, 230–8, 240; age of sample and, 241; black urban culture and analysis of, 171, 201, 215, 239–40; conflict and confrontation and, 200; fieldwork and, 201–2; opposition moves and, 205–15, 230; play preferences and, 203–4; pretend play mitigating utterances and boys during, 185; procedure and mode of argument interaction analysis conclusions and, 238–41; ritual insult example and, 224–5, 241–4; same-sex and opposite-sex conversations and, 171–2; same-sex disputes and, 227–38; sequence of format tying and, 215–27; subgroups (clusters) of children and, 203–4

assertiveness: of boys, 185, 187; girl's speech with lip spreading and, 187–8; in males (language socialization), 10; male speech and, 186; obliges and boys', 185; women and, 188

audiotapes: black group argument analy-

audiotapes (*cont.*)
sis and, 201, 202; input language analysis methodology and, 193–4
auditory evoked potentials (AEPs), 280, 281, 286–94
auditory evoked response (AER), 280
authority, 9, 57; language studies and, 15

Barnet, A. B., 291
basket making, Kuna Indian, 106–7
Basso, Ellen, 113
Bates, E., 165, 168–9
Beauvoir, Simone de, 115
begging, Samoan children and, 60
Behan, P., 277
Bell, B., 124, 127
Best, C. T., 283
biological processes: children's verbal styles and, 165; differences in brain organization and, 263, 266; sex differences and, 7; sex differences in language and, 1, 2–6, 92
black urban culture: analysis of argument and, 171, 201, 215, 239–40; boy's use of imperatives and girl's use of devices to mitigate obliges and, 186
Blank, M., 181
Bock, J. K., 169
Bodine, A., 16
Bogen, J. E., 278
Bohannon, J. N., III, 192
Bosavi people, *see* Kaluli of New Guinea
Bourhis, R., 90
Bradshaw, J. L., 270
brain: biological differences in organization of, 263, 266; electrical activity and linguistic competence and, 3–4; hemispheric specialization and, 3, 4; neurophysiological differences and, 263, 264, 267; research (historical overview) on sex and organization of, 263–4; testing for male–female differences (lateralization probes) and, 264; *see also* hemispheric specialization
brain damage, 4; sex differences in language and, 3
Bright, W., 122
Broca, P., 278, 284
Broverman, D. M., 277
Brown, P., 10, 17, 59, 115, 176, 205
Bruner, J., 165
Buffery, A. W. H., 285, 294–5
Bundy, C., 164

Carrell, P., 168
case markers, 92; men and ergative, 8; subject and direct-object (Japanese), 37–8; use by men and women and, 6; variations in (Samoan), 51, 52, 64–6, 68
cerebral organization, *see* hemispheric specialization
Chaillé, Christine, 178
Chalfin, S., 164
Chapin, N. M., 103
character contests, 206, 215
Cherry, L., 189
Cheshire, J., 157
childbearing, 9
Child Directed Speech (CDS); *see* parent–child interaction
children: adults and learned speech patterns of, 184–7; Araucanian, 100; arguments and black urban culture and, 171; arguments and same-sex and opposite-sex conversations and, 171–2; caretaker language input and, 170–1; clarification requests and, 166; contingent queries and, 166; directives and, 167–71, 174–5, 181, 183–6; directives and parent–child interaction and, 197–8; discourse and, 165–6; feedback of listener and, 166; gender difference and language acquisition and, 163–4; interruptions and, 167, 170, 171, 172, 186; Kaluli children's language acquisition and gender differences and, 172–3, 255–60; language competence and, 165, 167; Mexicano and, 152, 154–5; obliges and, 169–70, 181–2, 184–6; physical activity and, 187; politeness in female and assertiveness in male, 10; reformulation or revision of message and, 166–7; relative language proficiency and gender difference and, 164–5; Samoan, 54, 55, 60, 68–70; *see also* parent–child interaction; pretend play language use
Chile, *see* Araucanian Indians of Chile
Chinese, deletion of noun phrase and, 75, 76
Chodorow, N., 68, 69, 70
Chomsky, N., 190
Clancy, P., 75, 91
clarification requests and children, 166
Clark, R., 278
coding, Mexicano: peers and, 158; power code (Mexicano and inclusion of castellano), 127–31, 140, 143, 144, 145; solidarity code (Mexicano and restriction of castellano), 127–31, 143, 144, 145, 151, 154, 158, 159
cognitive aspects of language, 267
cognitive development, 294

cognitive processes, gender and language and, 2–6
communication ethnography, 17, 95, 99
communicative competence of children, 165, 167, 169, 175, 178, 200
compadrazgo relationships, Nahuatl Indian, 126
comparisons (argument analysis), 227–9
conflict, *see* arguments
confrontrations, *see* arguments
contingent queries and children, 166
conversation, Kaluli, 252–3, 257
Corballis, M., 283
Cortex, 269
Crocker, J. C., 8
cross-cultural approach to research, 26
cross-cultural commonality of some syntactic forms, 24
cross-cultural typology of speech differences, 96–9, 111–12
Crowell, D. H., 286
culture: black group and argument analysis and urban, 171, 186, 201, 215, 239–40; impact of, on children, 5; Kaluli, 250–2; status-of-women question and, 115–19; *see also* cross-cultural *entries*
curing and magic rituals, Kuna Indian: basic roles in, 101, 103; linguistic properties of, 103–4

Danner, F., 166
Dauer, S., 17
De Agostini, M., 273
deletions: in Japanese, 28, 35, 36, 45–8; Kuna Indian women and vowel, 102; phonological and syntactic (American English), 74; voir dire analysis and discourse and linguistic context, 77–85; voir dire analysis and gender identity and, 85–93; voir dire analysis and subject pronouns, 72, 75–7, 79; voir dire analysis and verb, 74–7
dialect: gender and code organization and, 6, 16–17, 71–2; Kaluli and, 250, 253, 257; social, 58
dialogue (voir dire procedure), 81–5, 92
dialogues of children (extending beyond two-turn sequences), 166
dichotic listening, 3, 4
dichotic listening tasks, 269, 279, 282
directives, 176, 181; argument analysis and, 229; children and, 167–71; father's use of, 186; obliges and, 181, 183–6; parent–child interactions and, 195, 197–8; peers and, 175; sex difference in use of, 174–5

disagreements, *see* opposition moves (children's arguing analysis)
discourse, 226; American black urban culture and, 171; argument and, 239; children's maintenance of, 165–6; and cross-cultural typology of speech differences between men and women, 98; gender differences in forms of, 25; Kuna Indians and, 102, 104, 107–10; voir dire procedure and, 81–5, 91, 93
Dittman, A., 167
division of labor: in Kaluli society, 251; Kuna Indian puberty rites and, 103; Kuna metaphoric speech and, 108; in Kuna society, 111
Dixon, R. M. W., 51
Donnelly, J., 186
Dorian, N., 133
dress: Kaluli and, 259; Nahuatl Indians and, 127; Samoan gender identity and, 55
Duranti, A., 60

Edelsky, C., 187
Eimas, P. D., 283
electroencephalograph (EEG) techniques, 269, 279–80, 285–8
embedding, argument analysis and, 218–19, 231
emotion, sex differences and, 2, 6–10
English, *see* American English
Entrus, A., 283
environment, 190
Ervin-Tripp, S., 167, 168, 187
Esposito, A., 167, 172, 186
ethnography of communication, 17, 95, 99
eye-movement analysis, 279

Falefa (Samoa), 50
family interaction: abandonment and widowhood of Nahuatl Indian women and, 126; Araucanian culture and, 100; household position of Nahuatl Indian women and, 125–6; Samoan, 64–5, 68, 69
Fanshel, D., 205, 215
feedback of listener, children and, 166, 184–5
Feld, S., 259
Fillmore, C., 51
Flannery, R., 16
Flavel, J., 166
Foley, W. A., 252
format tying sequence (children's arguing analysis), 215–27

Franklin, E., 181
Freeman, R., 279
Friedman, D., 280

Gal, S., 97, 159
Galambos, R., 280
Galin, D., 279
Gallimore, R., 69
Garbanati, J. A., 286
Gardiner, M. F., 286
Garfinkel, H., 24
Garvey, C., 166, 167
Gates, E., 270
Gelman, R., 168, 191
gender differences and language: children's use of directives and, 174–5; cross-cultural typology of cases of, 96–9; gender identity conclusions concerning American English and, 91–3; Japanese-speaking women and, 48; Kaluli children's language acquisition and, 172–3, 257–9; Kuna Indians and question of, 95–6, 107–11, 116–19; Labovian model of, 16–18; Mexicano and, 121–2, 155–9; minor nature of Samoan, 50; pretend play analysis conclusions and, 184–7; procedure and mode of argument interaction analysis conclusions and, 283–41; Sapir and, 15–16; symbolic reflections and, 27; systematic contextual variations in American English and, 71–2
gender identity: American English data base and, 73–6, 85–91; American English differences conclusions and, 91–3; American English discourse and linguistic context and, 77–85; language in children and, 198–9; Samoan, 55–6; Samoan narrative and, 59–64; Samoan speech and, 57–9; *see also names of specific languages*
Geschwind, N., 277, 278, 282
Gevins, A. S., 280
Giles, H., 90
Glanville, B. B., 283
Gleason, J. B., 170–1, 174, 175, 176, 185–6
Goffman, E., 114, 119, 206, 224
Goldman, Jane, 178
Goodenough, W. H., 201, 232
Goodman, E., 188
Goodwin, C., 171, 174–7
Goodwin, M. H., 98, 171, 174–7, 186, 188
Gordon, D., 186
Gordon, H. W., 278

grammar, 48; associated with female speech, 39; gender distinctions and, 118; lack of evidence for gender difference in ability to construct, 267; linguistic forms associated with sex of speaker and, 30; MLU and child's, 164; universality of sex differences in language question and, 26–7
Grief, E. B., 186, 197
Grossi, D., 285
Gros Ventre of Montana, 118
Gumperz, J. J., 50

Haas, M., 16, 172
Hamm, A., 278
handedness: familial sinistrality and sex and language and spatial visual ability and, 270–6; hormonal characteristics of sex–familial sinistrality and, 277; language development and, 284; right-handed subjects in lateralization studies and, 271
Hannerz, U., 239
Harris, L. J., 163, 285
Hatano, K., 31
Haya of Tanzania, 111, 114, 118, 119
Heath, J., 252
Hécaen, H., 273, 274, 276
hemispheric specialization: AEP and, 280, 281, 286–93; anatomical and functional lateralization and, 281–3; behavioral methods of studying, 279; cognitive abilities and, 3–6; differing pattern of hemispheric development between male and female infants and, 292–5; EEG and, 279–80, 285–8; handedness and language development and, 284; hemispheric language information-processing study methodology and, 279–81; hemispheric specialization studies and, 278; hormonal characteristics of sex–familiar sinistrality and, 277; infant electrophysiological studies (AEP paradigm) and, 286–92; question of existence of innate differences and, 265; question of whether males and females differ in, 265–6; review of studies of lateralization in males and females and, 268–71; sex–familial sinistrality influences on language lateralization and, 271–4; sex-related differences in lateralization and, 284–5; spatial visualization ability and sex–familial sinistrality and, 274–6; "split brain" studies and, 278–9; structure of hemispheres and, 278;

techniques for assessing language function lateralities and, 269; *see also* brain he-said-she-said confrontations (argument analysis), 231–8, 240
Hill, Jane H., 8, 22–4, 128, 172
Hill, Kenneth C., 122, 128
Hinds, J., 37
Hodapp, S., 164
Hoff, A. L., 272, 273, 274, 276
Hoffman, Dustin, 188
Hoffman, H., 283
Holzman, M., 167, 168
honorifics: in Japanese, 29, 32–3, 41, 42; in Mexicano, 131–3, 136–7, 139, 155–6
hoomu dorama (television soap-opera type serials in Japan), 18, 39, 40
hormones: lateralization and sex–familial sinistrality and, 277; sex, 2, 3, 4, 6–7
Hornsby, N. E., 169
household position of Nahuatl Indian women, 125–6
Howard, Victoria, 111
humiliatives in Japanese, 42, 43
Humphrey, B., 280
hunting, Kaluli, 255
Hymes, Dell, 17, 18, 111, 165

idobatakaigi ("well-side conference" form of spoken Japanese), 18, 40
indirect, allusive speech, 114
Indo-European languages, 16
informal speech: and deletion of subject and verb in American English, 91; Samoan, 51
input language analysis, *see* parent–child interaction
instigating sequence (argument analysis), 230–8
intelligence, gender difference and, 3
interruptions: boy–girl pairs and, 167; children's same-sex and cross-sex conversational interaction and, 172; parent–child interaction and, 197; parents and, 170, 171, 186
intracarotid amytal injections, 279
intransitive sentences, Samoan, 52–3

Jacklin, C., 2, 163
Jackson, T. L., 270, 271, 272
Jacobs, Melville, 111
James, S., 186
Japanese: biological differences and speech and, 7; case-marker use and, 6; data used to study (*idobatakaigi* and *hoomu dorama*), 40; deletion of noun phrase and, 75; honorific prefix o-usage and, 29, 41; lexicon of women's speech in, 28–30; particle deletion and, 46–7; phonology of women's speech in, 27–8; predicate politeness and, 42–3; and scoring results of analysis, 41–7; and sentence analysis of transcripts, 40–1; sentence-final particles and, 43–4; sex-related variation conclusions and, 48; stereotypical features in, 39; study overview and, 18–19, 24; subject-noun-phrase deletions and, 45; subject-noun-phrase postponing and, 45–6, 48; syntactic variations (sex-related) in, 30–9; universal aspects of gender differences in language and, 26–7
Jefferson, G., 202
Jespersen, O., 16, 22
Jones, D. F., 5
juror quesitoning, *see* voir dire procedure

Kalčik, S., 240
Kaluli of New Guinea: activities for males and females and, 253, 255, 258, 259; conversation and, 252–3, 257; culture of, 250–2; dialect and, 250, 253, 257; dress and, 259; everyday talk and, 253; gender differences in children's speech and, 172, 257–9; hunting and, 255; language analysis and, 251–2; as monolingual speakers, 252; public speaking roles and, 8; ritual and, 255; role behavior and, 258; socialization and language acquisition and, 255–60; speaker roles and, 253; speech patterning and, 8; spirit mediums and, 255; stories and, 252, 254; study overview and, 22; sung texted weeping and, 252, 254; syntax and, 254
Kango (Sino-Japanese compound words), 28, 29
Kapuniai, L. E., 286
Karabenick, J., 167
Karttunen, F., 148
Keenan (Ochs), E., *see* Ochs, E.,
Kernan, K., 168
Kimura, D., 264
Kinsbourne, M., 281
kinship system, Nahuatl Indian, 124
Kitagawa, C., 39, 44
Klann-Delius, G., 163, 294
Klymasz, R., 113
Koasati (North American Indian language), 96
Koizumi, T., 30
koyaqtun (ritualized conversation of Araucanian Indians), 100

Kuna Indians of Panama: biological differences and speech and, 7–8; curing and magic rituals and, 101, 103–4; discourse and, 102, 104, 107–10; everyday speech of, 104–5; indirect, allusive speech and, 114–15; laments (tuneful weeping) and, 8, 105–6, 109–10, 112–14; lullabies and, 8, 105–6, 109, 112; metaphoric language and, 104, 107–8; overview of speaking practices (social and cultural contexts) and, 95–6; perception of men's and women's speech and, 107; place of men and women in speaking practices of, 110–11; puberty rituals and, 101, 103; public (political gatherings) rituals and, 8, 101–3, 105, 107, 110–12; public roles and speech and, 9; speaking patterns and, 98–9, 111, 114; study overview and, 21–2; typology of cases of speech differences in cross-cultural perspective and, 96–9; universal differences in men's and women's speech and, 116–19; universality of inferior status of women (question of) and, 115–16; verbal genres and, 98–106, 109–10, 112–13; verbal virtuoso performances and, 111

Labov, W., 5–6, 16, 22, 23, 58, 71, 75, 141, 145, 176, 205, 215, 227
Ladd, D. R., Jr., 208
Lakoff, R., 10, 16, 97, 185, 205
lament (tuneful weeping), 8; Araucanian social singing (women's verbal genre) and, 100; Kaluli and, 173, 252, 254; Kuna and, 105–6, 109–10; women's verbal genres and, 112–14
Lamphere, L., 115
language acquisition: patterns of gender difference in children and, 163–4; sex differences and, 5, 294; socialization of Kaluli children and, 173, 255–60; *see also* parent–child interaction
language development: cerebral functional specialization and, 281–5; differing patterns of hemispheric development between male and female infants and, 292–5; electrophysiological evidence related to lateralization and, 285–92; hemispheric specialization studies and, 278–81
language input to children by caregiver, *see* parent–child interaction
language process bilaterality, females and, 268–9

language-use proficiency, *see* communicative competence of children
lateralization, *see* hemispheric specialization
Leacock, E. B., 116, 157
leadership roles: Araucanian Indians and speaking ability and, 100; Kuna Indians and, 101, 102
Lee, M. Y., 29
left-handedness, 266; lateralization and hormonal characteristics and, 277; lateralization review and, 270–6
Lenneberg, E. H., 281, 282
Levinson, R., 283
Levinson, S., 59, 115, 205
Levitsky, W., 278, 282
Levy, J., 268, 269
Lewis, M., 189
lexicon: language input to child and, 170; parent–child interactions and, 196; women's speech in Japanese and, 29–30, 34, 48
Li, C., 75–6, 91
Liberman, A., 282
linguistic context (voir dire analysis), 77–80
linguistic devices implying social identity (Sapir's 1915 study), 15
listener feedback, children and, 166, 184–5
lullabies, Kuna Indians and, 8, 105–6, 109, 112

McAdam, D. W., 280
McCarthy, D., 163
Maccauley, R., 163
Maccoby, E., 2, 163
McConnell-Ginet, S., 240
McGlone, J., 3, 264, 268
McKee, G., 280
McKeever, W. F., 3, 4, 189, 270, 271, 272, 274
magic rituals, *see* curing and magic rituals, Kuna Indians
Malagasey society, 57–8, 99, 104, 114, 119
Male and Female (Mead), 107, 115
"Male and Female Forms of Speech in Yana" (Sapir), 15–16
Maple Street group, 201, 204, 205, 206, 208, 227, 240–1; *see also* arguments
Marino, M. F., 276
Marquis, A. L., 192
Marxism, question of position of women and, 116
Mashimo, S., 28

mayordomías (reciprocal feasting of Nahuatl Indian men), 126
Mead, M., 7, 55, 107, 115, 118
mean length of utterance (MLU): child's grammar and, 164; differences between parents and, 194–5
Mediterranean areal pattern, 98
memorized speech, Kuna Indian, 104
message reformulation or revision among children, 166–7
metaphorical language in Kuna ritual, 104, 107–8
metapragmatic awareness, 18
Mexicano (language of Nahuatl Indians): biological differences and speech and, 7; calque on Spanish construction of relative clauses and, 138–40; children and, 152, 154–5; data-collecting interviews and, 122–3; gender differentiation and, 121–2, 155–9; honorific usages and, 131–3, 136–7, 139, 155–6; language attitude analysis (Mexicano and Spanish) and, 152–4; noun-incorporating verbs and, 134, 137–8; noun-number usage (Mexicano and Spanish) and, 148–51; paradoxical patterns of women's speech in, 121; power code (Mexicano and inclusion of castellano) and, 127–31, 140, 143, 144, 145; pressure on women to speak Spanish and, 154; public speaking roles and, 8; solidarity code (Mexicano and restricted use of castellano) and, 127–31, 143, 144, 145, 151, 158, 159; Spanish loan words and, 128–31, 133–7, 140; Spanish usage by women and, 121, 122, 133–4; stress shift and construction of possessives and, 140, 145–8; stress shift and nativizing of borrowed Spanish nouns and, 140–5; study overview and, 22–3; syncretic continuum and, 127–31; *see also* Nahuatl Indians of Mexico
Miller, S., 167
Milroy, L., 23, 157
Mitaka City (Japan), 35, 38
Mitchell-Kernan, C., 168
molas (Kuna Indian reverse appliqué work), 95, 102, 106–7, 111
Molfese, D. L., 279, 286
monologue (voir dire procedure), 73, 81–5, 89–90, 92
Monzon-Montes, A., 273
morphology: American female speech and, 92; gender-associated grammatical differences and, 16; Japanese speech and, 27, 34, 48; Mexicano and, 131, 132, 137
Morrell, L., 279
mourning, *see* lament
Moylan, T., 71
music, hemispheric-specialization analysis studies and, 280, 281, 283, 286–94
"Myth of Female Superiority in Language, The" (Maccauley), 163

Nahuatl Indians of Mexico: abandonment and widowhood of women of, 126; aging and, 127; biological differences and speech and, 7; dress and, 127; household position of women and, 125–6; interviews (data collection) among, 122–3; kinship system of, 124; personality development of women of, 127; physical and geographic aspects of community of, 123–4; social network of women and, 126–7; speech patterning and, 8; work pattern for women of, 124–6; *see also* Mexicano
narratives, Samoan, 60–4
National Language Research Institute (Japan), 32
Nelson, K., 164
neurophysiological differences between males and females, 263, 264, 267; *see also* hemispheric specialization; sex differences and language
Neuropsychologia, 269
New Guinea, 71–2; *see also* Kaluli of New Guinea
New York, 71, 145
Nomoto, K., 29
Nordberg, B. T., 158, 159
North American Indian languages, 15–16, 96, 118
noun-incorporating verbs, Mexicano, 134, 137–8
noun-number usage, Mexican and Spanish, 148–51
nouns: nativizing of borrowed Spanish (Mexicano), 140–5; possessive construction (Mexicano) and, 145–6
numbers used with nouns (Mexicano and Spanish), 148–51
Nutini, H., 124, 126

Oberwart (Austria), 159
Object Naming Latency Task (ONLT), 271–3, 276
obligatory, categorical grammatical differences between men and women, 96

obliges: defined, 169; mitigating devices and, 169, 182, 184–6; pretend-play methodology and, 181–2; prohibitions used by boys and, 170
Ochs, E., 8, 10, 17, 19–20, 24, 60, 92, 101, 114, 115, 166
O'Connor, M. C., 187
Ohlrich, E. S., 291
Okazaki (Japan), 32
opposition moves (children's arguing analysis), 205–15, 230
oratorical speech, Samoan, 50
Ortner, S. B., 18
o-usage honorific prefix in Japanese, 29, 41; *see also* honorifics

Palermo, D., 279
Pallie, W., 189, 278, 282
Panama, *see* Kuna Indians of Panama
Papua New Guinea, *see* Kaluli of New Guinea; New Guinea
parent–child interaction, 170; directives and, 197–8; home studies and, 194–5; input language analysis and, 190–2; interruptions and, 197; laboratory studies and, 196–8; lexical differences and, 196; MLU differences between parents and, 194–5; neuroanatomical and physical differences between boys and girls and, 189–90; politeness and, 196–7; research methodology and, 193–4; research setting and, 193
Parke, R. D., 187
particles: deletion of (Japanese), 46–7; emphatic (Samoan), 52; sentence-final (Japanese), 31–4, 39, 43–4; subject and direct-object (Japanese), 37–8
patterns of speech, *see* speaking-pattern differences
Peabody Picture Vocabulary Test, 272
peers: language used with, by children, 199; use of directives and, 175
Peng, F. C. C., 37
personality development of Nahuatl women, 127
personal narratives, Samoan, 60–4
personal pronouns, Japanese, 29
person implications, Sapir's concept of, 15
Petersen, A. C., 277
Peterson, C., 166
Philips, S., 16, 20–1, 70n
phonology: argument analysis and, 220–1; Mexicano and nativizing of borrowed Spanish nouns and, 140; stigmatized variants (American English) of, 71–2;

voir dire and deletion by men and, 74; women and variant use and, 16, 17; women's speech in Japanese and, 27–8
physical activity, 187
physical processes, gender and language and, 6–10
Piazza, D., 269–70
Platt, M., 60
play, language used during, *see* pretend-play language use
play preferences, argument-analysis methodology and, 203–4
politeness, 10, 16, 115, 205, 240; affect behavior (Samoan) and, 59; American English and, 92; girls and rules of, 169; girls' use of directives and, 174–5; Japanese honorifics and, 29, 32–3, 41; Japanese predicates and, 31, 32, 37, 39, 41–3; language input to children and, 170; Mexicano and, 132; parent–child interaction and, 195–7; pretend-play analysis and, 186, 187, 188
polite requests, 168–9
political gatherings of Kuna Indians, 105, 107; basic roles in, 101–3, 110–12; linguistic properties of, 103–4
Pomerantz, A., 206
possessives, Mexicano and construction of, 140, 145–8
power, 8, 57, 230; langue studies and, 15
Power, T. G. 187
predicates, Japanese, 31, 35, 37, 39, 41–3
prestige variants, social dialects and, 58
pretend-play language use: learning patterns of speech appropriate to gender from adults and, 186–7; linguistic style differences and, 185–7; listener response and, 184–5; mitigating obliges and, 169, 182, 184–6; obliges and, 181–2; playroom methodology and, 179–80; pretend category utterances and, 180–1; role assignment and, 180–1; sample and, 178–9
pronouns: affect (Samoan), 52, 59–60, 62; contraction and deletion of (American English), 72, 75–7, 79; contraction and deletion of, and discourse context (American English), 81–5, 91, 93; contraction and deletion of, and gender identity and subject (American English), 85–91; Mexicano and relative, 138–9; personal (Japanese), 29; special affect (Samoan), 52, 62
psychologists, 177, 226
puberty rituals, Kuna Indian: basic roles in, 101, 103; linguistic properties of, 103–4

public activities: Kaluli men and women and, 253, 255, 258, 259; in Samoa, 56–7; speech genres and, 8–9
public gatherings of Kuna Indians, *see* political gatherings of Kuna Indians
public speaking, 8, 9

Radcliffe-Brown, A. R., 232
Ramer, A. L. H., 164
Ramsay, D. S., 284
ranking between boys (argument analysis), 228, 229
Rasmussen, T., 278
redundancy (voir dire procedure analysis), 91, 92
reformulation or revision of message by children, 166–7
relative clauses, Mexicano and calque on Spanish construction of, 138–40
religious roles, 9; *see also* ritual roles
Reynolds, A., 20–1, 64
right-handed subjects, lateralization studies and, 271; *see also* handedness
ritual insult example (children's arguing analysis), 224–5, 241–4
ritual roles: Araucanian Indian *machi* (shaman) and, 100; Kaluli and, 255; Kuna (divided into three realms), 100–3, 105, 107, 110–11; linguistic properties of Kuna, 103–4
role assignment and pretend play, 180–1
Rosaldo, M., 8, 56, 68, 114, 115
Rosenberg, J., 187
Ross, J. R., 37

Sachs, J., 169–70, 174, 176, 186
Sacks, H., 202, 216
Salamy, J., 279
Samoan: activities of men and women and, 56; analysis of (background on), 51–7; biological differences and speech and, 7, 8; case-marker use and, 6; demeanor and social status and, 54–5; gender, age, and social factors in language use and, 50–1; gender identity and, 55–9; intransitive sentences and, 52–3; social context shift and patterns of speaking and, 66–70; socialization and gender identity and, 55–6; social organization and women's roles and, 53–7; social stratification and, 53–4; social variation in affect expression and, 59–64; social variation in ergative case marking and, 64–5; social variation in word order and, 65–6; speech behavior theory and, 57–9; speech patterning

and, 8; study overview and, 19–20, 24, 50–1; transitive sentences and, 51–2
Sankoff, G., 129
Sapir, D., 8
Sapir, E., 15–16, 24
Schachter, F., 164
Schegloff, E. A., 202
Scheub, H., 111
Schieffelin, B. B., 8, 22, 25, 172, 175–7
Schoeffel, P., 20, 54
Schulman, C., 286
semantic domains, parents and, 170
sentence analysis: Japanese study, 40–7; transitive and intransitive (Samoan), 51–3
sentence-final particles, Japanese, 43–4
separation of sexes, Samoan, 55–6
sequence of format tying (children and arguing analysis), 215–27
Sex and Temperament in Three Primitive Societies (Mead), 115
sex differences and language: biological processes and, 1–5; cognitive processes and, 2–6; emotion and, 2, 6–10; neuroanatomical and physical differences of children and, 189–90; physical processes and, 6–10; politeness and, 10, 16; relative language proficiency in children and, 164–5; research on children's language acquisition and, 163–4, 175–7; social processes and, 1, 3; universality question and, 26–7; *see also names of specific languages*
sex hormones: effects of, 6–7; male and female differences and, 2, 3, 4; *see also* hormones
sex-role identity, 198–9; *see also* gender identity
Shatz, M., 165, 168, 191
Sherzer, J., 7–9, 21–2, 24, 25, 173
Shibamoto, J. S., 18–19, 24, 34–5, 38, 39
Shibata, T., 28
Shore, B., 52, 54, 56, 57, 69
Shore, R., 164
Shucard, D. W., 3, 4, 5, 265, 266, 291, 294
Shucard, J. L., 3, 4, 5, 265, 266
Silverstein, M., 18, 24
sinistrality, 266; lateralization and hormonal characteristics and, 277; lateralization review and, 270–6; *see also* handedness
social class: hypercorrect crossover example and, 145; Japanese study and, 46; social dialects and, 58
social context: gender-differentiated as-

social context (*cont.*)
  pects of language forms and, 6; speaking and speech roles and, 7
social factors: linguistic relations and, 27,
  30; Samoan language use and, 50–1,
  59–60; Samoan langue use and wom-
  en's role and, 53–7; stereotyped features and, 39; stigmatized phonological
  variants and, 71
social identity, 15–16
socialization: Kaluli children's language
  acquisition and, 173, 255–60; Kuna lullabies and, 109; language of, 10, 192;
  Samoan and gender identity and, 55–6,
  70
social network of Nahuatl women, 126–7
social processes, sex differences in language and, 1, 3
Spanish; *see* Mexicano
spatial visualization ability, sex–familial
  sinistrality and, 274–6
speaker roles, Kaluli, 253
speaking-pattern differences: Araucanian
  culture and, 100; between men and
  women, 98–9, 117; Kuna Indians and,
  111, 114; learned by children from
  adults, 186–7; social context shift and
  Samoan, 66–70
speech-act theory, 167
speech-behavior theory, Samoan and, 57–
  9
Sperry, R. W., 278–9, 295
spirit mediums, Kaluli, 255
Stafford Identical Blocks Test (SIBT),
  274
status: language use and, 7; question of
  women's inferior, 115–16; Samoan language use and, 50, 54–5
Steffen, H., 284
stereotyping, 18; argument analysis and,
  241; features of Japanese speech and,
  39, 48; Kuna discourse analysis and,
  107–10; Mexicano and modified Spanish sound, 134, 145
stories, Kaluli, 252, 254
storytelling, 111–12, 240
storytelling procedure called instigating
  (argument analysis), 230–8
stress shift, Mexicano: construction of
  possessives and, 140, 145–8; nativizing
  of borrowed Spanish nouns and, 140–5
styles: cross-cultural typology of differences in, between men and women, 97;
  differences in children's, between boys
  and girls, 164–5; differences in male
  and female, 9–10; pretend-play analysis

and, 185–7; social context shift and
  speaking in Samoan, 66–70
subject-noun phrase, Japanese: deletions
  and, 45; postposing and, 45–6, 48
sung-texted weeping; *see* lament
suppletive forms, Japanese, 42
sympathy in Samoan, 59–63
Syntactic Structures (Chomsky), 190
syntax, 191; American female speech
  and, 92; children and communicative
  intentions and, 167; cross-cultural commonality and, 24; focus of contemporary studies and, 16, 17; input analysis
  and, 194; Kaluli and, 254; voir dire and
  deletions and, 74, 91; women's speech
  in Japanese and, 30–9, 48
Szentagothai, J., 282

tachistoscopic procedures, 269, 279
Tanguay, P., 280
task activities (argument analysis), 227,
  229–30
Taub, J., 280
Taylor, D., 90, 265
Teszner, D., 278, 282
Thiel, R. A., 122
Thomas, D. G., 3, 4, 265, 266
Thompson, S., 75–6, 91
Thorne, B., 200
titles, Samoan, 54, 56–8, 60–64
Tiwary, K. M., 112
Tokyo, 37
Tootsie (motion picture), 188
transitive sentences, Samoan, 51–2
tuneful weeping or lament, *see* lament

ulkantun (social singing of Araucanian
  women), 100
University of Connecticut, 178
Upolu (Samoan island), 50

Vakinankaratra (Madagascar), 57
Van Valin, R. D., 252
Vargha-Khadem, F., 283
Vaupés region of Amazon, 97
verbal genres: Araucanian culture and,
  100; cross-cultural survey of, 111–12,
  117; differences in, between women
  and men, 7–9, 25, 98, 99; Kuna lullabies and tuneful weeping and, 105–6,
  109–10, 112–13; Kuna ritual activities
  and, 100–4
verbs: children and discourse and, 169;
  discourse context and deletion of
  (American English), 81–5; endings in
  Japanese and, 31–2; gender identity

and deletion of (American English), 85–93; Mexicano and noun-incorporating, 134, 137–8; polite predicate form of (Japanese), 42, 43; rightward dislocations (Japanese) and, 36; Samoan language and, 51, 52; voir dire procedure and deletion of (American English), 74–7

videotaping: hemispheric studies and, 288; input language analysis methodology and, 193, 194

visual evoked potential (VEP) measures, 279–80

vocabulary, 267; language input to children and, 170

voir dire procedure (questioning of prospective jurors): comparison of speech of men and women in, 72–3; discourse context and, 81–5; gender identity and, 85–91; gender identity differences conclusions and, 91–3; gender in data base and, 73–6; judge's use of language and, 72; linguistic context and, 77–80; results of data analysis and, 76–91

Waber, D., 268, 277
Wada, J., 278, 282

Walter, D. O., 286
Watanabe, T., 29–30
Weisner, T. S., 69
Wernicke, C., 278
West, C., 98
Whitehead, H., 18
widowhood among Nahuatl women, 126
Witelson, S. F., 189, 278
Wolfram, W., 75
Women, Culture, and Society (Lamphere), 115
word order: Kaluli daily speech and, 253; Samoan and preference for verb initial, 52; Samoan and social variations and, 65–6
work: gender and differences in, 56; Nahuatl Indian women and, 124–6

Xhosa of South Africa, 111

Yaeger-Dror, M., 211–12
Yana (North American Indian language), 96

Zenani, Nongenile Mazithathu, 111
Zimmerman, D. H., 98